State and Local Government
Fifteenth Edition

EDITOR

Bruce Stinebrickner
DePauw University

Bruce Stinebrickner is Leonard E. and Mary B. Howell Professor of Political Science at DePauw University in Greencastle, Indiana, and has taught American politics at DePauw since 1987. He has also taught at Lehman College of the City University of New York (1974–1976), at the University of Queensland in Brisbane, Australia (1976–1987), and in DePauw programs in Argentina (1990) and Germany (1993). He served fourteen years as chair of his department at DePauw after heading his department at the University of Queensland for two years. He earned his BA *magna cum laude* from Georgetown University in 1968, his MPhil from Yale University in 1972, and his PhD from Yale in 1974.

Professor Stinebrickner is the co-author (with Robert A. Dahl) of *Modern Political Analysis*, sixth edition (Prentice Hall, 2003) and has published articles on the American presidential selection process, American local governments, the career patterns of Australian politicians, and freedom of the press. He has served as editor of the fourteen earlier editions of this book as well as thirty-three editions of its American Government counterpart in the McGraw-Hill Annual Editions series. His current research interests focus on government policies involving children (e.g., schooling, child custody, and foster care).

In both his teaching and his writing, Professor Stinebrickner applies insights on politics gained from living, teaching, and lecturing abroad. He currently serves on the Greencastle, Indiana, school board and on the City of Greencastle's Redevelopment Commission, both of which provide him with firsthand experiences in the workings of state and local governments.

ANNUAL EDITIONS: STATE AND LOCAL GOVERNMENT, FIFTEENTH EDITION

Published by McGraw-Hill, a business unit of The McGraw-Hill Companies, Inc., 1221 Avenue
of the Americas, New York, NY 10020. Copyright © 2012 by The McGraw-Hill Companies, Inc.
All rights reserved. Previous edition(s) © 1984–2010. Printed in the United States of America.
No part of this publication may be reproduced or distributed in any form or by any means, or stored
in a database or retrieval system, without the prior written consent of The McGraw-Hill Companies,
Inc., including, but not limited to, in any network or other electronic storage or transmission, or
broadcast for distance learning.

Some ancillaries, including electronic and print components, may not be available to customers
outside the United States.

This book is printed on acid-free paper.

Annual Editions® is a registered trademark of The McGraw-Hill Companies, Inc.

Annual Editions is published by the **Contemporary Learning Series** group within the
McGraw-Hill Higher Education division.

1 2 3 4 5 6 7 8 9 0 QDB/QDB 1 0 9 8 7 6 5 4 3 2 1

MHID: 0–07–805121–5
ISBN: 978–0–07–805121–0
ISSN: 1093-7021 (print)
ISSN: 2162-5662 (online)

Managing Editor: *Larry Loeppke*
Developmental Editor II: *Debra A. Henricks*
Permissions Coordinator: *Lenny J. Behnke*
Marketing Specialist: *Alice Link*
Project Manager: *Melissa M. Leick*
Design Coordinator: *Margarite Reynolds*
Cover Designer: *Kristine Jubeck*
Buyer: *Susan K. Culbertson*
Media Project Manager: *Sridevi Palani*

Compositor: Laserwords Private Limited
Cover Image Credits: BananaStock/Jupiterimages (inset): Joseph Sohm-Visions of
America/Stockbyte/Getty Images(background)

Editors/Academic Advisory Board

Members of the Academic Advisory Board are instrumental in the final selection of articles for each edition of ANNUAL EDITIONS. Their review of articles for content, level, and appropriateness provides critical direction to the editors and staff. We think that you will find their careful consideration well reflected in this volume.

ANNUAL EDITIONS: State and Local Government
15th Edition

EDITOR

Bruce Stinebrickner
DePauw University

ACADEMIC ADVISORY BOARD MEMBERS

Preface

In publishing ANNUAL EDITIONS we recognize the enormous role played by the magazines, newspapers, and journals of the public press in providing current, first-rate educational information in a broad spectrum of interest areas. Many of these articles are appropriate for students, researchers, and professionals seeking accurate, current material to help bridge the gap between principles and theories and the real world. These articles, however, become more useful for study when those of lasting value are carefully collected, organized, indexed, and reproduced in a low-cost format, which provides easy and permanent access when the material is needed. That is the role played by ANNUAL EDITIONS.

This book is the fifteenth edition of a reader on state and local government. Beginning with the first edition in 1984, the book has been designed for use in college courses on state and local government, and in state and local government segments of courses on American government. The educational goal is to provide a collection of up-to-date articles that are informative and interesting to students who are learning about sub-national governments in the United States.

The 50 state governments and more than 80,000 local governments in the United States have a great deal in common. They also exhibit remarkable diversity. Inevitably, the contents of the book reflect both this commonality and diversity. Some selections treat individual states or localities in considerable detail. Other articles focus on particular dimensions of more than one state or local government. Still other articles explicitly compare and contrast regions, states, or localities. Taken together, the selections provide an overview of similarities and differences among state and local governments in the United States.

When Newt Gingrich became Speaker of the House of Representatives in 1995, he and his fellow Republican members of Congress said that they would shift significant government responsibilities from the national government in Washington to the 50 states. Two prominent bills signed into law by President Clinton, one restricting unfunded mandates and the other reforming the welfare system, were aimed at making the states more important and autonomous actors in the American federal system. Taking their turn in this process of devolution, some state governments shifted selected responsibilities to their local governments.

The events of September 11, 2001, partly reversed these trends, as national, state, and local responsibilities for public safety and what came to be known as "homeland security" were reconsidered and modified. The Great Recession of 2008–2009 introduced a new chapter in national–state–local relations. Soon after President Obama assumed office in January 2009, the national government enacted an unprecedentedly large economic stimulus bill that channeled billions of dollars to state and local governments. Even though they were reeling from the Great Recession, sub-national governments were not allowed to engage in the sort of deficit spending that has consistently characterized national government financing for more than the past half-century. In turn, the stimulus funds saved many state and local governments from wholesale layoffs of teachers, police officers, firefighters,

and the like. While state and local governments certainly had to tighten their belts, the stimulus funds enabled them to avoid even more draconian measures to balance their budgets. As the two-year duration of most stimulus funding draws to a close in 2011, there are concerns about whether the sluggish recovery will produce enough revenues for state and local governments to protect against further layoffs and reductions in services.

Every selection in this book can be read in the context of the overall mosaic of national, state, and local governments in the United States. Indeed, the American political system seems to be characterized by continuing—indeed, probably never-ending—attempts to achieve an appropriate division of powers and responsibilities among national, state, and local governments.

The book is divided into seven units. Unit 1 is devoted to eighteenth- and nineteenth-century historic commentaries on American federalism and state and local governments. Unit 2 addresses relations among national, state, and local governments, and provides a mixed assessment of how much shifting of power and responsibility has actually occurred, and how well the changes that have occurred are working. Unit 3 covers elections, political parties, interest groups, referenda, news media, and related matters, and pays special attention to unusual features of state and local "linkages." Unit 4 turns to government institutions. Local politics and policy issues—in metropolitan areas, cities, and suburbs, as well as in counties and small towns—provide the subject matter for Unit 5, while Unit 6 is devoted to revenues, expenditures, and economic development. Unit 7 concludes the book with an examination of policy issues facing state and local governments.

The book generally groups articles that treat particular aspects of state and local governments in the same units and sections. For example, Unit 4 covers government institutions at both the state and local levels, with individual sections devoted to state *and* local legislatures, executives, and courts, respectively. Unit 5, which discusses metropolitan areas, is an exception to this general rule in that it focuses on issues involving local governments and mostly ignores state governments.

Deciding what articles to include when preparing this fifteenth edition of *Annual Editions: State and Local Government* was not easy. I assessed articles according to significance and relevance of the subject matter, readability for students, and usefulness for stimulating students' interest in state and local government. Potential selections were evaluated not only as they stood alone, but also as complements to other likely selections.

As always, I solicit responses to this edition as well as suggestions of articles for use in the next edition. In other words, readers are cordially invited to become advisers and collaborators in future editions by completing and mailing the postpaid article rating form at the end of this book.

Bruce Stinebrickner

Bruce Stinebrickner
Editor

Contents

UNIT 1
Early Commentaries

The concepts in bold italics are developed in the article. For further expansion, please refer to the Topic Guide.

UNIT 2
Intergovernmental Relations

UNIT 3
Linkages between Citizens and Governments

The concepts in bold italics are developed in the article. For further expansion, please refer to the Topic Guide.

The concepts in bold italics are developed in the article. For further expansion, please refer to the Topic Guide.

UNIT 4
Government Institutions and Officeholders

The concepts in bold italics are developed in the article. For further expansion, please refer to the Topic Guide.

UNIT 5
Cities and Suburbs, Counties and Towns

The concepts in bold italics are developed in the article. For further expansion, please refer to the Topic Guide.

UNIT 6
Fiscal Matters and Economic Development

UNIT 7
Policy Issues

The concepts in bold italics are developed in the article. For further expansion, please refer to the Topic Guide.

The concepts in bold italics are developed in the article. For further expansion, please refer to the Topic Guide.

Correlation Guide

The *Annual Editions* series provides students with convenient, inexpensive access to current, carefully selected articles from the public press. **Annual Editions: State and Local Government, 15/e** is an easy-to-use reader that presents articles on important topics such as *economic development, federalism, policymaking,* and many more. For more information on *Annual Editions* and other *McGraw-Hill Contemporary Learning Series* titles, visit www.mhhe.com/cls.

This convenient guide matches the units in **State and Local Government, 15/e** with the corresponding chapters in one of our best-selling McGraw-Hill Government textbooks by Saffell/Basehart.

Annual Editions: State and Local Government, 15/e	State and Local Government, 9/e by Saffell/Basehart
Unit 1: Early Commentaries	**Chapter 1:** The Setting of State and Local Government
Unit 2: Intergovernmental Relations	**Chapter 2:** Intergovernmental Relations
Unit 3: Linkages between Citizens and Governments	**Chapter 3:** Political Parties and Interest Groups **Chapter 4:** Political Participation and Elections
Unit 4: Government Institutions and Officeholders	**Chapter 5:** State and Local Legislatures **Chapter 6:** Governors, Bureaucrats, and Mayors **Chapter 7:** Courts, Police, and Corrections
Unit 5: Cities and Suburbs, Counties and Towns	**Chapter 8:** Suburbs, Metropolitan Areas, and Rural Communities
Unit 6: Fiscal Matters and Economic Development	**Chapter 9:** Financing State and Local Government
Unit 7: Policy Issues	**Chapter 10:** State and Local Policymaking: Conflict and Accommodation

Topic Guide

This topic guide suggests how the selections in this book relate to the subjects covered in your course. You may want to use the topics listed on these pages to search the Web more easily.

On the following pages a number of websites have been gathered specifically for this book. They are arranged to reflect the units of this Annual Editions reader. You can link to these sites by going to www.mhhe.com/cls

All the articles that relate to each topic are listed below the bold-faced term.

Internet References

The following Internet sites have been selected to support the articles found in this reader. These sites were available at the time of publication. However, because websites often change their structure and content, the information listed may no longer be available. We invite you to visit www.mhhe.com/cls for easy access to these sites.

Annual Editions: State and Local Government, 15/e

General Sources

Library of Congress
www.loc.gov/rr/news/stategov/stategov.html

The Library of Congress provides this page of indexes on state and local government information. Links are available to numerous national, state, and local government sites.

Open Secrets
www.opensecrets.org

While this site mostly concentrates on national political subjects like campaign contribution amounts and sources for members of Congress, it also addresses some important state and local government topics in informative ways.

U.S.A.gov
www.usa.gov

This site contains links to all state government websites and enables users to explore state agencies by subject matter, identify local government associations, and read state and local census data.

UNIT 1: Early Commentaries

Anti-Federalist Papers
www.constitution.org/afp/afp.htm

This site contains some of the most widely read anti-Federalist Papers.

The Federalist Papers Online
www.memory.loc.gov/const/fed/fedpapers.html

This site includes the full text of all 85 *Federalist Papers,* as well as the Declaration of Independence and other historic documents.

UNIT 2: Intergovernmental Relations

Advisory Commission on Intergovernmental Relations
www.library.unt.edu/gpo/acir/Default.html

Founded in 1959 and disbanded in 1996, this intergovernmental agency was aimed at strengthening the American federal system and improving the ability of national, state, and local governments to cooperate efficiently and effectively. This archived website of the ACIR provides insights into intergovernmental concerns during its 37-year existence.

U. S. Congress
www.congress.org

This site includes a congressional directory, House and Senate committee assignments, and information about laws enacted and bills being considered. Congress plays a significant role in shaping intergovernmental relations.

Council of State Governments
www.csg.org

This resource is dedicated to promoting state solutions regionally and nationally. Founded during the 1930s, the CSG enables state government officials from all three branches to share ideas and plan cooperative programs to foster the well-being of state governments and help them serve their citizens more effectively.

National Center for State Courts
www.ncsc.org

A clearinghouse for information to be shared among state courts, the National Center for State Courts and its website have the goal of improving the administration of justice in state court systems.

Oyez
www.oyez.org

This site provides information on current and historic Supreme Court cases, as well audio recordings of arguments before the Supreme Court in recent decades. Many pivotal Supreme Court rulings address intergovernmental relations.

UNIT 3: Linkages between Citizens and Governments

Democratic National Committee (DNC)
www.democrats.org

The DNC website features links to all state Democratic Party websites as well as national party policy stances and news updates.

Pew Research Center for the People and the Press
www.people-press.org

This site presents the results of public opinion polls that report citizens' views on, among other things, the press, elected officials, and public policy issues.

Project Vote Smart
www.votesmart.org

This site provides information on how national and state legislators vote on key issues and what bills they sponsor. If a candidate has filled out an issue position questionnaire, the results are displayed under the legislator's name.

Republican National Committee (RNC)
www.gop.com

The RNC site contains links to all state Republican Party websites as well as national party policy stances and news updates.

UNIT 4: Government Institutions and Officeholders

Council on Licensure, Enforcement and Regulation (CLEAR)
www.clearhq.org

CLEAR provides a forum for improving the quality and understanding of regulation.

Internet References

National Governors Association

www.nga.org

This site reports the NGA's position on legislation pending in Congress, hosts the "NGA Center for Best Practices," and addresses other matters relating to governors and state governments.

National Conference of State Legislatures

www.ncsl.org

The NCSL tracks trends on major policy issues in the states, compiles reports, and takes positions on national legislation.

National School Boards Association

www.nsba.org

The NSBA provides information to state school board associations and local school boards, advocates on their behalf, and works to strengthen school boards and improve public schooling.

The United States Conference of Mayors

www.usmayors.org

This site presents policy prescriptions, provides videos of national meetings, and includes fact sheets on issues.

UNIT 5: Cities and Suburbs, Counties and Towns

Alliance for Innovation

www.transformgov.org

The Alliance for Innovation is a network of top city and local government leaders that helps pioneer new approaches to managing cities. The site provides networking, research, and training opportunities to local governments.

International City/County Management Association (ICMA)

www.icma.org

The ICMA provides training for local government leaders and offers publications on best practices in city and county management.

National Association of Counties (NACo)

www.naco.org

The NACo site details legislative priorities, offers policy research, and links to county government sites in individual states.

National Association of Towns and Townships (NATaT)

www.natat.org

This site presents NATaT national legislative priorities and links to statewide town/township association homepages.

National League of Cities (NLC)

www.nlc.org

The NLC reports noteworthy city policy initiatives and identifies priorities for national government legislation.

UNIT 6: Fiscal Matters and Economic Development

U.S. Economic Development Administration

www.eda.gov

Located in the U.S. Department of Commerce, the EDA tries to foster economic development in communities across the United States, with a particular emphasis on regional cooperation.

Congressional Budget Office

www.cbo.gov

The CBO provides fiscal analysis of legislation and cost estimates of national government programs and proposed programs, many of which involve state and local governments.

National Association of Development Organizations (NADO)

www.nado.org

This site leads to many national, state, and local government resources, to a host of independent agencies, and to other community development resources. The NADO particularly focuses on regional development organizations that serve small metropolitan areas and rural America.

UNIT 7: Policy Issues

American Bar Association—Criminal Justice

www.americanbar.org/groups/criminal_justice.html

This site contains ABA criminal justice policy recommendations, publications, and news.

American Public Transportation Association

www.apta.com

The APTA site provides public transit news, studies, and links to national and state transportation organizations.

Community Oriented Policing Services (COPS)

www.cops.usdoj.gov

The COPS site promotes community policing strategies, grant applications, and other resources.

In the Public Interest

www.inthepublicinterest.org

This site provides criticisms of public-private partnerships and offers detailed examples of unsuccessful public-private agreements from around the nation.

U.S. Charter Schools

www.uscharterschools.org

This site contains state-by-state charter school policies, guides to creating an effective charter school, and news of charter school developments.

UNIT 1
Early Commentaries

Unit Selections

1. **Federalist, No. 17,** Alexander Hamilton
2. **Federalist, No. 45,** James Madison
3. **Nature of the American State,** James Bryce
4. **The American System of Townships . . . ,** Alexis de Tocqueville
5. **Local Government: Observations,** James Bryce

Learning Outcomes

- Compare American local governments of today with the nineteenth-century picture of American local governments provided by James Bryce and Alexis de Tocqueville.

- Building on Bryce's arguments for why American states in the late nineteenth century were more similar than one would expect, consider whether the states continue to be more similar than different in the twenty-first century.

- Students of politics frequently refer to the historic writings of Plato, Aristotle, Machiavelli, Hobbes, Locke, Rousseau, and others. Selections in this unit are examples of historic writings on American state and local governments. Explain why those who study governments look so often to the classics, even centuries after they were written.

- Construct an overall defense of the system of American state and local governments that captures the key arguments presented by the famous eighteenth- and nineteenth-century observers whose writings appear in this unit.

- Assess the arguments presented in *Federalist No. 17* and *No. 45* and how well those arguments apply to the American political system in the twenty-first century.

- Appraise the overall system of state and local governments in the contemporary United States and how well it serves Americans in the twenty-first century.

Student Website
www.mhhe.com/cls

Internet References

Anti-Federalist Papers
www.constitution.org/afp/afp.htm
The Federalist Papers Online
www.memory.loc.gov/const/fed/fedpapers.html

The American political system includes three levels of government—national, state, and local. Although not unique among nations today, this arrangement was unusual in the late eighteenth century when the United States won its independence from England. Early commentaries on the American political system paid considerable attention to each of these levels of government, as well as to interactions among the three levels. These writings suggest the important role that state and local governments have always played in the United States.

Debate about the desirability of the proposed new Constitution of 1787—the Constitution that remains in force to this day—often focused on the relationship between the national government and the states. Some people thought that the states were going to be too strong in the proposed new union, and others worried that the national government had too much power. Three prominent supporters of the new Constitution—Alexander Hamilton, James Madison, and John Jay—wrote a series of articles in 1787–1788 explaining and defending it. Many of these articles, which came to be known as *The Federalist Papers,* discussed the federal relationship between the national government and the states. So did many of the writings of other early observers. This reflects the importance that was attached to the new federal relationship right from the start.

State and local governments were also the subject of considerable attention in early commentaries by distinguished and perceptive European visitors to the American political system. Alexis de Tocqueville, a French nobleman visiting the United States early in the nineteenth century, recorded his observations in a book entitled *Democracy in America* (1835). Tocqueville remarked on the extraordinary vitality of American local government institutions, comparing what he saw in the United States with European institutions at that time. Today American local government still plays a prominent role in the country's overall governing process, probably more so than in any other nation in the world.

Later in the nineteenth century, an Englishman, James Bryce, published another influential commentary on the United States, *The American Commonwealth* (1888). Bryce discussed American federalism and American state and local governments. He described and explained differences among local government structures in three different regions of the country, the considerable similarities among the states that existed at the time of his visit, and what he saw as the lamentable performance of city governments. Like Tocqueville, Bryce was able to identify and

© Library of Congress

analyze distinctive elements of the American system of government and make a lasting contribution to the study of the American political system.

Selections in this first section of the book come from *The Federalist Papers,* Tocqueville's *Democracy in America,* and Bryce's *American Commonwealth.* These historic observations on American federalism and on state and local governments provide a baseline with which to assess contemporary state and local government in the United States.

Federalist No. 17 (Hamilton)

To the People of the State of New York:

An objection, of a nature different from that which has been stated and answered, in my last address, may perhaps be likewise urged against the principle of legislation for the individual citizens of America. It may be said that it would tend to render the government of the Union too powerful, and to enable it to absorb those residuary authorities, which it might be judged proper to leave with the States for local purposes. Allowing the utmost latitude to the love of power which any reasonable man can require, I confess I am at a loss to discover what temptation the persons intrusted with the administration of the general government could ever feel to divest the States of the authorities of that description. The regulation of the mere domestic police of a State appears to me to hold out slender allurements to ambition. Commerce, finance, negotiation, and war seem to comprehend all the objects which have charms for minds governed by that passion; and all the powers necessary to those objects ought, in the first instance, to be lodged in the national depository. The administration of private justice between the citizens of the same State, the supervision of agriculture and of other concerns of a similar nature, all those things, in short, which are proper to be provided for by local legislation, can never be desirable cares of a general jurisdiction. It is therefore improbable that there should exist a disposition in the federal councils to usurp the powers with which they are connected; because the attempt to exercise those powers would be as troublesome as it would be nugatory; and the possession of them, for that reason, would contribute nothing to the dignity, to the importance, or to the splendor of the national government.

But let it be admitted, for argument's sake, that mere wantonness and lust of domination would be sufficient to beget that disposition; still it may be safely affirmed, that the sense of the constituent body of the national representatives, or, in other words, the people of the several States, would control the indulgence of so extravagant an appetite. It will always be far more easy for the State governments to encroach upon the national authorities, than for the national government to encroach upon the State authorities. The proof of this proposition turns upon the greater degree of influence which the State governments, if they administer their affairs with uprightness and prudence, will generally possess over the people; a circumstance which at the same time teaches us that there is an inherent and intrinsic weakness in all federal constitutions; and that too much pains cannot be taken in their organization, to give them all the force which is compatible with the principles of liberty.

The superiority of influence in favor of the particular governments would result partly from the diffusive construction of the national government, but chiefly from the nature of the objects to which the attention of the State administrations would be directed.

It is a known fact in human nature, that its affections are commonly weak in proportion to the distance or diffusiveness of the object. Upon the same principle that a man is more attached to his family than to his neighborhood, to his neighborhood than to the community at large, the people of each State would be apt to feel a stronger bias towards their local governments than towards the government of the Union; unless the force of that principle should be destroyed by a much better administration of the latter.

This strong propensity of the human heart would find powerful auxiliaries in the objects of State regulation.

The variety of more minute interests, which will necessarily fall under the superintendence of the local administrations, and which will form so many rivulets of influence, running through every part of the society, cannot be particularized, without involving a detail too tedious and uninteresting to compensate for the instruction it might afford.

There is one transcendent advantage belonging to the province of the State governments, which alone suffices to place the matter in a clear and satisfactory light,—I mean the ordinary administration of criminal and civil justice. This, of all others, is the most powerful, most universal, and most attractive source of popular obedience and attachment. It is that which, being the immediate and visible guardian of life and property, having its benefits and its terrors in constant activity before the public eye, regulating all those personal interests and familiar concerns in which the sensibility of individuals is more immediately awake, contributes, more than any other circumstance, to impressing upon the minds of the people, affection, esteem, and reverence towards the government. This great cement of society, which will diffuse itself almost wholly through the channels of the particular governments, independent of all other causes of influence, would insure them so decided an empire over their respective citizens as to render them at all times a complete counterpoise, and, not unfrequently, dangerous rivals to the power of the Union.

The operations of the national government, on the other hand, falling less immediately under the observation of the mass of the citizens, the benefits derived from it will chiefly be perceived and attended to by speculative men. Relating to more general interests, they will be less apt to come home to the feelings of the people; and, in proportion, less likely to inspire an habitual sense of obligation, and an active sentiment of attachment.

The reasoning on this head has been abundantly exemplified by the experience of all federal constitutions with which we are acquainted, and of all others which have borne the least analogy to them.

Though the ancient feudal systems were not, strictly speaking, confederacies, yet they partook of the nature of that species of association. There was a common head, chieftain, or sovereign, whose authority extended over the whole nation; and a number of subordinate vassals, or feudatories, who had large portions of land allotted to them, and numerous trains of inferior vassals or retainers, who occupied and cultivated that land upon the tenure of fealty or obedience to the persons of whom they held it. Each principal vassal was a kind of sovereign within his particular demesnes. The consequences of this situation were a continual opposition to authority of the sovereign, and frequent wars between the great barons or chief feudatories themselves. The power of the head of the nation was commonly too weak, either to preserve the public peace, or to protect the people against the oppressions of their immediate lords. This period of European affairs is emphatically styled by historians, the times of feudal anarchy.

When the sovereign happened to be a man of vigorous and warlike temper and of superior abilities, he would acquire a personal weight and influence, which answered, for the time, the purposes of a more regular authority. But in general, the power of the barons triumphed over that of the prince; and in many instances his dominion was entirely thrown off, and the great fiefs were erected into independent principalities of States. In those instances in which the monarch finally prevailed over his vassals, his success was chiefly owing to the tyranny of those vassals over their dependents. The barons, or nobles, equally the enemies of the sovereign and the oppressors of the common people, were dreaded and detested by both; till mutual danger and mutual interest effected a union between them fatal to the power of the aristocracy. Had the nobles, by a conduct of clemency and justice, preserved the fidelity and devotion of their retainers and followers, the contests between them and the prince must almost always have ended in their favor, and in the abridgment or subversion of the royal authority.

This is not an assertion founded merely in speculation or conjecture. Among other illustrations of its truth which might be cited, Scotland will furnish a cogent example. The spirit of clanship which was, at an early day, introduced into that kingdom, uniting the nobles and their dependents by ties equivalent to those of kindred, rendered the aristocracy a constant overmatch for the power of the monarch, till the incorporation with England subdued its fierce and ungovernable spirit, and reduced it within those rules of subordination which a more rational and more energetic system of civil polity had previously established in the latter kingdom.

The separate governments in a confederacy may aptly be compared with the feudal baronies; with this advantage in their favor, that from the reasons already explained, they will generally possess the confidence and good-will of the people, and with so important a support, will be able effectually to oppose all encroachments of the national government. It will be well if they are not able to counteract its legitimate and necessary authority. The points of similitude consist in the rivalship of power, applicable to both, and in the concentration of large portions of the strength of the community into particular deposits, in one case at the disposal of individuals, in the other case at the disposal of political bodies.

A concise review of the events that have attended confederate governments will further illustrate this important doctrine; an inattention to which has been the great source of our political mistakes, and has given our jealousy a direction to the wrong side. This review shall form the subject of some ensuing papers.

PUBLIUS

Critical Thinking

1. What powers of state governments does Hamilton think will be fundamentally unattractive to those running the new national government, even if they do have a "love of power"?

2. Why will it always be far easier for state governments to "encroach" upon the national government than vice versa?

3. What is the one "transcendent advantage" that state governments have in any rivalry with national government authorities?

4. Are state or national governments more likely to inspire citizens' feelings of loyalty, sense of obligation, and the like? Why?

5. Given concerns that the new national government in the United States will become too powerful, what has experience in other countries with powers divided between a central authority and other smaller units shown?

From *The Federalist Papers*, 1787.

Federalist No. 45 (Madison)

To the People of the State of New York:

Having shown that no one of the powers transferred to the federal government is unnecessary or improper, the next question to be considered is, whether the whole mass of them will be dangerous to the portion of authority left in the several States.

The adversaries to the plan of the convention, instead of considering in the first place what degree of power was absolutely necessary for the purposes of the federal government, have exhausted themselves in a secondary inquiry into the possible consequences of the proposed degree of power to the governments of the particular States. But if the Union, as has been shown, be essential to the security of the people of America against foreign danger; if it be essential to their security against contentions and wars among the different States; if it be essential to guard them against those violent and oppressive factions which embitter the blessings of liberty, and against those military establishments which must gradually poison its very fountain; if, in a word, the Union be essential to the happiness of the people of America, is it not preposterous, to urge as an objection to a government, without which the objects of the Union cannot be attained, that such a government may derogate from the importance of the governments of the individual States? Was, then, the American Revolution effected, was the American Confederacy formed, was the precious blood of thousands spilt, and the hard-earned substance of millions lavished, not that the people of America should enjoy peace, liberty, and safety, but that the government of the individual States, that particular municipal establishments, might enjoy a certain extent of power, and be arrayed with certain dignities and attributes of sovereignty? We have heard of the impious doctrine in the Old World, that the people were made for kings, not kings for the people. Is the same doctrine to be revived in the New, in another shape—that the solid happiness of the people is to be sacrificed to the views of political institutions of a different form? It is too early for politicians to presume on our forgetting that the public good, the real welfare of the great body of the people, is the supreme object to be pursued; and that no form of government whatever has any other value than as it may be fitted for the attainment of this object. Were the plan of the convention adverse to the public happiness, my voice would be, Reject the plan. Were the Union itself inconsistent with the public happiness, it would be, Abolish the Union. In like manner, as far as the sovereignty of the States cannot be reconciled to the happiness of the people, the voice of every good citizen must be, Let the former be sacrificed to the latter. How far the sacrifice is necessary, has been shown. How far the unsacrificed residue will be endangered, is the question before us.

Several important considerations have been touched in the course of these papers, which discountenance the supposition that the operation of the federal government will by degrees prove fatal to the State governments. The more I revolve the subject, the more fully I am persuaded that the balance is much more likely to be disturbed by the preponderancy of the last than of the first scale.

We have seen, in all the examples of ancient and modern confederacies, the strongest tendency continually betraying itself in the members, to despoil the general government of its authorities, with a very ineffectual capacity in the latter to defend itself against the encroachments. Although, in most of these examples, the system has been so dissimilar from that under consideration as greatly to weaken any inference concerning the latter from the fate of the former, yet, as the States will retain, under the proposed Constitution, a very extensive portion of active sovereignty, the inference ought not to be wholly disregarded. In the Achæan league it is probable that the federal head had a degree and species of power, which gave it a considerable likeness to the government framed by the convention. The Lycian Confederacy, as far as its principles and form and transmitted, must have borne a still greater analogy to it. Yet history does not inform us that either of them ever degenerated, or tended to degenerate, into one consolidated government. On the contrary, we know that the ruin of one of them proceeded from the incapacity of the federal authority to prevent the dissensions, and finally the disunion, of the subordinate authorities. These cases are the more worthy of our attention, as the external causes by which the component parts were pressed together were much more numerous and powerful than in our case; and consequently less powerful ligaments within would be sufficient to bind the members to the head, and to each other.

In the feudal system, we have seen a similar propensity exemplified. Notwithstanding the want of proper sympathy in every instance between the local sovereigns and the people, and the sympathy in some instances between the general sovereign and the latter, it usually happened that the local sovereigns prevailed in the rivalship for encroachments. Had no external dangers enforced internal harmony and subordination, and particularly, had the local sovereigns possessed the affections of the people, the great kingdoms in Europe would at this time consist of as many independent princes as there were formerly feudatory barons.

The State governments will have the advantage of the Federal government, whether we compare them in respect to the immediate dependence of the one on the other; to the weight of personal influence which each side will possess; to the powers respectively vested in them; to the predilection and probable support of the people; to the disposition and faculty of resisting and frustrating the measures of each other.

The State governments may be regarded as constituent and essential parts of the federal government; whilst the latter is nowise essential to the operation or organization of the former. Without the intervention of the State legislatures, the President of the United States cannot be elected at all. They must in all cases have a great share in his appointment, and will, perhaps, in most cases, of themselves determine it. The Senate will be elected absolutely and exclusively by the State legislatures. Even the House of Representatives, though drawn immediately from the people, will be chosen very much under the influence of that class of men, whose influence over the people obtains for themselves an election into the State legislatures. Thus, each of the principal branches of the federal government will owe its existence more or less to the favor of the State governments, and must consequently feel a dependence, which is much more likely to beget a disposition too obsequious than too overbearing towards them. On the other side, the component parts of the State governments will in no instance be indebted for their appointment to the direct agency of the federal government, and very little, if at all, to the local influence of its members.

The number of individuals employed under the Constitution of the United States will be much smaller than the number employed under the particular States. There will consequently be less of personal influence on the side of the former than of the latter. The members of the legislative, executive, and judiciary departments of thirteen and more States, the justices of peace, officers of militia, ministerial officers of justice, with all the country, corporation, and town officers, for three millions and more of people, intermixed, and having particular acquaintance with every class and circle of people, must exceed, beyond all proportion, both in number and influence, those of every description who will be employed in the administration of the federal system. Compare the members of the three great departments of the thirteen States, excluding from the judiciary department the justices of peace, with the members of the corresponding departments of the single government of the Union; compare the militia officers of three millions of people with the military and marine officers of any establishment which is within the compass of probability, or, I may add, of possibility, and in this view alone, we may pronounce the advantage of the States to be decisive. If the federal government is to have collectors of revenue, the State governments will have theirs also. And as those of the former will be principally on the sea-coast, and not very numerous, whilst those of the latter will be spread over the face of the country, and will be very numerous, the advantage in this view also lies on the same side. It is true, that the Confederacy is to possess, and may exercise, the power of collecting internal as well as external taxes throughout the States; but it is probable that this power will not be resorted to, except for supplemental purposes of revenue; that an option will then be given to the States to supply their quotas by previous collections of their own; and that the eventual collection, under the immediate authority of the Union, will generally be made by the officers, and according to the rules, appointed by the several States. Indeed it is extremely

probable, that in other instances, particularly in the organization of the judicial power, the officers of the States will be clothed with the correspondent authority of the Union. Should it happen, however, that separate collectors of internal revenue should be appointed under the federal government, the influence of the whole number would not bear a comparison with that of the multitude of State officers in the opposite scale. Within every district to which a federal collector would be allotted, there would not be less than thirty or forty, or even more, officers of different descriptions, and many of them persons of character and weight, whose influence would lie on the side of the State.

The powers delegated by the proposed Constitution to the federal government are few and defined. Those which are to remain in the State governments are numerous and indefinite. The former will be exercised principally on external objects, as war, peace, negotiation, and foreign commerce; with which last the power of taxation will, for the most part, be connected. The powers reserved to the several States will extend to all the objects which, in the ordinary course of affairs, concern the lives, liberties, and properties of the people, and the internal order, improvement, and prosperity of the State.

The operations of the federal government will be most extensive and important in times of war and danger; those of the State governments in times of peace and security. As the former periods will probably bear a small proportion to the latter, the State governments will here enjoy another advantage over the federal government. The more adequate, indeed, the federal powers may be rendered to the national defence, the less frequent will be those scenes of danger which might favor their ascendancy over the governments of the particular States.

If the new Constitution be examined with accuracy and candor, it will be found that the change which it proposes consists much less in the addition of new powers to the Union, than in the invigoration of its original powers. The regulation of commerce, it is true, is a new power; but that seems to be an addition which few oppose, and from which no apprehensions are entertained. The powers relating to war and peace, armies and fleets, treaties and finance, with the other more considerable powers, are all vested in the existing Congress by the articles of Confederation. The proposed change does not enlarge these powers; it only substitutes a more effectual mode of administering them. The change relating to taxation may be regarded as the most important; and yet the present Congress have as complete authority to require of the States indefinite supplies of money for the common defense and general welfare, as the future Congress will have to require them of individual citizens; and the latter will be no more bound than the States themselves have been, to pay the quotas respectively taxed on them. Had the States complied punctually with the articles of Confederation, or could their compliance have been enforced by as peaceable means as may be used with success towards single persons, our past experience is very far from countenancing an opinion, that the State governments would have lost their constitutional powers, and have gradually undergone an entire consolidation. To maintain that such an event would have ensued, would be to say at once, that the existence of the State governments is incompatible with any system whatever that accomplishes the essential purposes of the Union.

PUBLIUS

Critical Thinking

1. According to Madison, what has experience in all past and present confederacies shown about whether the central government or the smaller units have prevailed in rivalries between them?

2. In what ways will the new central (national or federal) government be dependent on state governments?

3. Which level of government, national or state, will have more employees?

4. Which level of government, national or state, will have "few and defined" powers, and which will have "numerous and indefinite" ones?

5. What new or "invigorated" powers will the new Constitution give to the new national government?

From *The Federalist No.* 45, 1788.

Nature of the American State

JAMES BRYCE

As the dissimilarity of population and of external conditions seems to make for a diversity of constitutional and political arrangements between the States, so also does the large measure of legal independence which each of them enjoys under the Federal Constitution. No State can, as a commonwealth, politically deal with or act upon any other State. No diplomatic relations can exist nor treaties be made between States, no coercion can be exercised by one upon another. And although the government of the Union can act on a State, it rarely does act, and then only in certain strictly limited directions, which do not touch the inner political life of the commonwealth.

Let us pass on to consider the circumstances which work for uniformity among the States, and work more powerfully as time goes on.

He who looks at a map of the Union will be struck by the fact that so many of the boundary lines of the States are straight lines. Those lines tell the same tale as the geometrical plans of cities like St. Petersburg or Washington, where every street runs at the same angle to every other. The States are not natural growths. Their boundaries are for the most part not natural boundaries fixed by mountain ranges, nor even historical boundaries due to a series of events, but purely artificial boundaries, determined by an authority which carved the national territory into strips of convenient size, as a building company lays out its suburban lots. Of the States subsequent to the original thirteen, California is the only one with a genuine natural boundary, finding it in the chain of the Sierra Nevada on the east and the Pacific ocean on the west. No one of these later States can be regarded as a naturally developed political organism. They are trees planted by the forester, not self-sown with the help of the seed-scattering wind. This absence of physical lines of demarcation has tended and must tend to prevent the growth of local distinctions. Nature herself seems to have designed the Mississippi basin, as she has designed the unbroken levels of Russia, to be the dwelling-place of one people.

Each State makes its own Constitution; that is, the people agree on their form of government for themselves, with no interference from the other States or from the Union. This form is subject to one condition only: it must be republican.[1] But in each State the people who make the constitution have lately come from other States, where they have lived and worked under constitutions which are to their eyes the natural and almost necessary model for their new State to follow; and in the absence of an inventive spirit among the citizens, it was the obvious course for the newer States to copy the organizations of the older States, especially as these agreed with certain familiar features of the Federal Constitution. Hence the outlines, and even the phrases of the elder constitutions reappear in those of the more recently formed States. The precedents set by Virginia, for instance, had much influence on Tennessee, Alabama, Mississippi, and Florida, when they were engaged in making or amending their constitutions during the early part of this century.

Nowhere is population in such constant movement as in America. In some of the newer States only one-fourth or one-fifth of the inhabitants are natives of the United States. Many of the townsfolk, not a few even of the farmers, have been till lately citizens of some other State, and will, perhaps, soon move on farther west. These Western States are like a chain of lakes through which there flows a stream which mingles the waters of the higher with those of the lower. In such a constant flux of population local peculiarities are not readily developed, or if they have grown up when the district was still isolated, they disappear as the country becomes filled. Each State takes from its neighbours and gives to its neighbours, so that the process of assimilation is always going on over the whole wide area.

Still more important is the influence of railway communication, of newspapers, of the telegraph. A Greek city like Samos or Mitylene, holding her own island, preserved a distinctive character in spite of commercial intercourse and the sway of Athens. A Swiss canton like Uri or Appenzell, entrenched behind its mountain ramparts, remains, even now under the strengthened central government of the Swiss nation, unlike its neighbours of the lower country. But an American State traversed by great trunk lines of railway, and depending on the markets of the Atlantic cities and of Europe for the sale of its grain, cattle, bacon, and minerals, is attached by a hundred always tightening ties to other States, and touched by their weal or woe as nearly as by what befalls within its own limits. The leading newspapers are read over a vast area. The inhabitants of each State know every morning the events of yesterday over the whole Union.

Finally the political parties are the same in all the States. The tenets (if any) of each party are the same everywhere, their methods the same, their leaders the same, although of course a prominent man enjoys especial influence in his own State. Hence, State politics are largely swayed by forces and motives external to the particular State, and common to the whole country, or to great sections of it; and the growth of local parties, the emergence of local issues and development of local political schemes, are correspondingly restrained.

These considerations explain why the States, notwithstanding the original diversities between some of them, and the wide scope for political divergence which they all enjoy under the Federal Constitution, are so much less dissimilar and less peculiar than might have been expected. European statesmen have of late years been accustomed to think of federalism and local autonomy as convenient methods either for recognizing and giving free scope to the sentiment of nationality which may exist in any part of an empire, or for meeting the need for local institutions and distinct legislation which may arise from differences between such a part and the rest of the empire. It is one or other or both of these reasons that have moved statesmen in such cases as those of Finland in her relations to Russia, Hungary in her relations to German Austria, Iceland in her relations to Denmark, Bulgaria in her relations to the Turkish Sultan, Ireland in her relations to the United Kingdom. But the final causes, so to speak, of the recognition of the States of the American Union as autonomous commonwealths, have been different. Their self-government is not the consequence of differences which can be made harmless to the whole body politic only by being allowed free course. It has been due primarily to the historical fact that they existed as commonwealths before the Union came into being; secondarily, to the belief that localized government is the best guarantee for civic freedom, and to a sense of the difficulty of administering a vast territory and population from one centre and by one government.

I return to indicate the points in which the legal independence and right of self-government of the several States appears. Each of the forty-two has its own—

Constitution (whereof more anon).

Executive, consisting of a governor, and various other officials.

Legislature of two Houses.

System of local government in counties, cities, townships, and school districts.

System of State and local taxation.

Debts, which it may (and sometimes does) repudiate at its own pleasure.

Body of private law, including the whole law of real and personal property, of contracts, of torts, and of family relations.

Courts, from which no appeal lies (except in cases touching Federal legislation or the Federal constitution) to any Federal court.

System of procedure, civil and criminal.

Citizenship, which may admit persons (e.g. recent immigrants) to be citizens at times, or on conditions, wholly different from those prescribed by other States.

Three points deserve to be noted as illustrating what these attributes include.

I. A man gains active citizenship of the United States (*i.e.* a share in the government of the Union) only by becoming a citizen of some particular State. Being such citizen, he is forthwith entitled to the national franchise. That is to say, voting power in the State carries voting power in Federal elections, and however lax a State may be in its grant of such power, *e.g.* to foreigners just landed or to persons convicted of crime, these State voters will have the right of voting in congressional and presidential elections.[2] The only restriction on the States in this matter is that of the fourteenth and fifteenth Constitutional amendments, . . . They were intended to secure equal treatment to the negroes, and incidentally they declare the protection given to all citizens of the United States.[3] Whether they really enlarge it, that is to say, whether it did not exist by implication before, is a legal question, which I need not discuss.

II. The power of a State over all communities within its limits is absolute. It may grant or refuse local government as it pleases. The population of the city of Providence is more than one-third of that of the State of Rhode Island, the population of New York city more than one-fifth that of the State of New York. But the State might in either case extinguish the municipality, and govern the city by a single State commissioner appointed for the purpose, or leave it without any government whatever. The city would have no right of complaint to the Federal President or Congress against such a measure. Massachusetts has lately remodelled the city government of Boston just as the British Parliament might remodel that of Birmingham. Let an Englishman imagine a county council for Warwickshire suppressing the muncipality of Birmingham, or a Frenchman imagine the department of the Rhone extinguishing the municipality of Lyons, with no possibility of intervention by the central authority, and he will measure the difference between the American States and the local governments of Western Europe.

III. A State commands the allegiance of its citizens, and may punish them for treason against it. The power has rarely been exercised, but its undoubted legal existence had much to do with inducing the citizens of the Southern States to follow their governments into secession in 1861. They conceived themselves to owe allegiance to the State as well as to the Union, and when it became impossible to preserve both, because the State had declared its secession from the Union, they might hold the earlier and nearer authority to be paramount. Allegiance to the State must now, since the war, be taken to be subordinate to the Union. But allegiance to the State still exists; treason against the State is still possible. One cannot think of treason against Warwickshire or the department of the Rhone.

These are illustrations of the doctrine which Europeans often fail to grasp, that the American States were originally in a certain sense, and still for certain purposes remain, sovereign States. Each of the original thirteen became sovereign when it revolted from the mother country in 1776. By entering the Confederation of 1781–88 it parted with one or two of the attributes of sovereignty, by accepting the Federal Constitution in 1788 it subjected itself for certain specified purposes to a central government, but claimed to retain its sovereignty for all other purposes. That is to say, the authority of a State is an inherent, not a delegated, authority. It has all the powers which any independent government can have, except such as it can be affirmatively shown to have stripped itself of, while the Federal Government has only such powers as it can be affirmatively shown to have received. To use the legal expression, the presumption is always for a State, and the burden of proof lies upon any one who denies its authority in a particular matter.[4]

What State sovereignty means and includes is a question which incessantly engaged the most active legal and political minds of the nation, from 1789 down to 1870. Some thought it paramount to the rights of the Union. Some considered it as held in suspense by the Constitution, but capable of reviving as soon as a State should desire to separate from the Union. Some maintained that each State had in accepting the Constitution finally renounced its sovereignty, which thereafter existed only in the sense of such an undefined domestic legislative and administrative authority as had not been conferred upon Congress. The conflict of these views, which became acute in 1830 when South Carolina claimed the right of nullification, produced Secession and the war of 1861–65. Since the defeat of the Secessionists, the last of these views may be deemed to have been established, and the term "State sovereignty" is now but seldom heard. Even "States rights" have a different meaning from that which they had thirty years ago.[5] . . .

The Constitution, which had rendered many services to the American people, did them an inevitable disservice when it fixed their minds on the legal aspects of the question. Law was meant to be the servant of politics, and must not be suffered to become the master. A case had arisen which its formulae were unfit to deal with, a case which had to be settled on large moral and historical grounds. It was not merely the superior physical force of the North that prevailed; it was the moral forces which rule the world, forces which had long worked against slavery, and were ordained to save North America from the curse of hostile nations established side by side.

The word "sovereignty," which has in many ways clouded the domain of public law and jurisprudence, confused men's minds by making them assume that there must in every country exist, and be discoverable by legal inquiry, either one body invested legally with supreme power over all minor bodies, or several bodies which, though they had consented to form part of a larger body, were each in the last resort independent of it, and responsible to none but themselves.[6] They forgot that a Constitution may not have determined where legal supremacy shall dwell. Where the Constitution of the United States placed it was at any rate doubtful, so doubtful that it would have been better to drop technicalities, and recognize the broad fact that the legal claims of the States had become incompatible with the historical as well as legal claims of the nation. In the uncertainty as to where legal right resided, it would have been prudent to consider where physical force resided. The South however thought herself able to resist any physical force which the rest of the nation might bring against her. Thus encouraged, she took her stand on the doctrine of States Rights: and then followed a pouring out of blood and treasure such as was never spent on determining a point of law before, not even when Edward III and his successors waged war for a hundred years to establish the claim of females to inherit the crown of France.

What, then, do the rights of a State now include? Every right or power of a Government except:—

The right of secession (not abrogated in terms, but admitted since the war to be no longer claimable. It is expressly negatived in the recent Constitutions of several Southern States).

Powers which the Constitution withholds from the States (including that of intercourse with foreign governments).

Powers which the Constitution expressly confers on the Federal Government.

As respects some powers of the last class, however, the States may act concurrently with, or in default of action by, the Federal Government. It is only from contravention of its action that they must abstain. And where contravention is alleged to exist, whether legislative or executive, it is by a court of law, and, in case the decision is in the first instance favourable to the pretensions of the State, ultimately by a Federal court, that the question falls to be decided.[7]

A reference to the preceding list of what each State may create in the way of distinct institutions will show that these rights practically cover nearly all the ordinary relations of citizens to one another and to their Government.[8] An American may, through a long life, never be reminded of the Federal Government, except when he votes at presidential and congressional elections, lodges a complaint against the post-office, and opens his trunks for a custom-house officer on the pier at New York when he returns from a tour in Europe. His direct taxes are paid to officials acting under State laws. The State, or a local authority constituted by State statutes, registers his birth, appoints his guardian, pays for his schooling, gives him a share in the estate of his father deceased, licenses him when he enters a trade (if it be one needing a licence), marries him, divorces him, entertains civil actions against him, declares him a bankrupt, hangs him for murder. The police that guard his house, the local boards which look after the poor, control highways, impose water rates, manage schools—all these derive their legal powers from his State alone. Looking at this immense compass of State functions, Jefferson would seem to have been not far wrong when he said that the Federal government was nothing more than the American department of foreign affairs. But although the National government touches the direct interests of the citizen less than does the State government, it touches his sentiment more. Hence the strength of his attachment to the former and his interest in it must not be measured by the frequency of his dealings with it. In the partition of governmental functions between nation and State, the State gets the most but the nation the highest, so the balance between the two is preserved.

Thus every American citizen lives in a duality of which Europeans, always excepting the Swiss, and to some extent the Germans, have no experience. He lives under two governments and two sets of laws; he is animated by two patriotisms and owes two allegiances. That these should both be strong and rarely be in conflict is most fortunate. It is the result of skilful adjustment and long habit, of the fact that those whose votes control the two sets of governments are the same persons, but above all of that harmony of each set of institutions with the other set, a harmony due to the identity of the principles whereon both are founded, which makes each appear necessary to the stability of the other, the States to the nation as its basis, the National Government to the States as their protector.

Notes

1. The case of Kansas immediately before the War of Secession, and the cases of the rebel States, which were not readmitted after the war till they had accepted the constitutional amendments forbidding slavery and protecting the freedmen, are quite exceptional cases.

2. Congress has power to pass a uniform rule of naturalization (Const. Art. §. 8).

   Under the present naturalization laws a foreigner must have resided in the United States for five years, and for one year in the State or Territory where he seeks admission to United States citizenship, and must declare two years before he is admitted that he renounces allegiance to any foreign prince or state. Naturalization makes him a citizen not only of the United States, but of the State or Territory where he is admitted, but does not necessarily confer the electoral franchise, for that depends on State laws.

   In more than a third of the States the electoral franchise is now enjoyed by persons not naturalized as United States citizens.

3. "The line of distinction between the privileges and immunities of citizens of the United States, and those of citizens of the several States, must be traced along the boundary of their respective spheres of action, and the two classes must be as different in their nature as are the functions of their respective governments. A citizen of the United States as such has a right to participate in foreign and interstate commerce, to have the benefit of the postal laws, to make use in common with others of the navigable waters of the United States, and to pass from State to State, and into foreign countries, because over all these subjects the jurisdiction of the United States extends, and they are covered by its laws. The privileges suggest the immunities. Wherever it is the duty of the United States to give protection to a citizen against any harm, inconvenience, or deprivation, the citizen is entitled to an immunity which pertains to Federal citizenship. One very plain immunity is exemption from any tax, burden, or imposition under State laws as a condition to the enjoyment of any right or privilege under the laws of the United States. . . . Whatever one may claim as of right under the Constitution and laws of the United States by virtue of his citizenship, is a privilege of a citizen of the United States. Whatever the Constitution and laws of the United States entitle him to exemption from, he may claim an exemption in respect to. And such a right or privilege is abridged whenever the State law interferes with any legitimate operation of Federal authority which concerns his interest, whether it be an authority actively exerted, or resting only in the express or implied command or assurance of the Federal Constitution or law. But the United States can neither grant nor secure to its citizens rights or privileges which are not expressly or by reasonable implication placed under its jurisdiction, and all not so placed are left to the exclusive protection of the States."— Cooley, *Principles*, pp. 245–247.

4. It may of course be said that as the colonies associated themselves into a league, at the very time at which they revolted from the British Crown, and as their foreign relations were always managed by the authority and organs of this league, no one of them ever was for international purposes a free and independent sovereign State. This is true, and Abraham Lincoln was in this sense justified in saying that the Union was older than the States. But what are we to say of North Carolina and Rhode Island, after the acceptance of the Constitution of 1787–89 by the other eleven States? They were out of the old Confederation, for it had expired. They were not in the new Union, for they refused during many months to enter it. What else can they have been during these months except sovereign commonwealths?

5. States rights was a watchword in the South for many years. In 1851 there was a student at Harvard College from South Carolina who bore the name of States Rights Gist, baptized, so to speak, into Calhounism. He rose to be a brigadier-general in the Confederate army, and fell in the Civil War.

6. A further confusion arises from the fact that men are apt in talking of sovereignty to mix up legal supremacy with practical predominance. They ought to go together, and law seeks to make them go together. But it may happen that the person or body in whom law vests supreme authority is unable to enforce that authority: so the legal sovereign and the actual sovereign—that is to say, the force which will prevail in physical conflict—are different. There is always a strongest force; but the force recognized by law may not be really the strongest; and of several forces it may be impossible to tell, till they have come into actual physical conflict, which is the strongest.

7. See Chapter XXII. *ante.*

8. A recent American writer well observes that nearly all the great questions which have agitated England during the last sixty years would, had they arisen in America, have fallen within the sphere of State legislation. —Jameson, "Introduction to the Constitutional and Political History of the States," in *Johns Hopkins University Studies*.

Critical Thinking

1. What five circumstances, according to Bryce, contribute to making the American states more similar to one another than might be reasonably expected?

2. What does it mean to say that most state boundaries are "artificial," and not "natural growths"?

3. Which existed first, the states or the national government? How does this historical fact relate to considering why states are more similar to one another than might be expected?

4. How much power does a state have over local governments within that state?

5. What does it mean to say that every American citizen "lives in a duality"?

From *The American Commonwealth*, 1888.

The American System of Townships . . .

Why the writer begins his examination of political institutions with the township. There are townships in every nation. Difficulty of establishing and maintaining their communal freedom. Its importance. Why the writer has chosen the organization of the New England township as the main subject to examine.

ALEXIS DE TOCQUEVILLE

It is not by chance that I consider the township first.

The township is the only association so well rooted in nature that wherever men assemble it forms itself.

Communal society therefore exists among all peoples, whatever be their customs and their laws; man creates kingdoms and republics, but townships seem to spring directly from the hand of God. But though townships are coeval with humanity, local freedom is a rare and fragile thing. A nation can always establish great political assemblies, because it always contains a certain number of individuals whose understanding will, to some extent, take the place of experience in handling affairs. But the local community is composed of coarser elements, often recalcitrant to the lawgiver's activity. The difficulty of establishing a township's independence rather augments than diminishes with the increase of enlightenment of nations. A very civilized society finds it hard to tolerate attempts at freedom in a local community; it is disgusted by its numerous blunders and is apt to despair of success before the experiment is finished.

Of all forms of liberty, that of a local community, which is so hard to establish, is the most prone to the encroachments of authority. Left to themselves, the institutions of a local community can hardly struggle against a strong and enterprising government; they cannot defend themselves with success unless they have reached full development and have come to form part of national ideas and habits. Hence, until communal freedom has come to form part of mores, it can easily be destroyed, and it cannot enter into mores without a long-recognized legal existence.

So communal freedom is not, one may almost say, the fruit of human effort. It is seldom created, but rather springs up of its own accord. It grows, almost in secret, amid a semibarbarous society. The continual action of laws, mores, circumstances, and above all time may succeed in consolidating it. Among all the nations of continental Europe, one may say that there is not one that understands communal liberty.

However, the strength of free peoples resides in the local community. Local institutions are to liberty what primary schools are to science; they put it within the people's reach; they teach people to appreciate its peaceful enjoyment and accustom them to make use of it. Without local institutions a nation may give itself a free government, but it has not got the spirit of liberty. Passing passions, momentary interest, or chance circumstances may give it the external shape of independence, but the despotic tendencies which have been driven into the interior of the body social will sooner or later break out on the surface.

To help the reader understand the general principles on which the political organization of townships and counties in the United States depends, I thought it would be useful to take one particular state as an example and examine in detail what happens there, subsequently taking a quick look at the rest of the country.

I have chosen one of the states of New England.

Townships and counties are not organized in the same way in all parts of the Union; nevertheless, one can easily see that throughout the Union more or less the same principles have guided the formation of both township and county.

Now, I thought that in New England these principles had been carried further with more far-reaching results than elsewhere. Consequently they stand out there in higher relief and are easier for a foreigner to observe.

The local institutions of New England form a complete and regular whole; they are ancient; law and, even more, mores make them strong; and they exercise immense influence over the whole of society.

For all these reasons they deserve our attention.

Limits of the Township

The New England township is halfway between a *canton* and a *commune* in France. It generally has from two to three thousand inhabitants;[1] it is therefore not too large for all the inhabitants to have roughly the same interests, but is big enough to be sure of finding the elements of a good administration within itself.

Powers of the New England Township

In the township, as everywhere else, the people are the source of power, but nowhere else do they exercise their power so directly. In America the people are a master who must be indulged to the utmost possible limits.

In New England the majority works through representatives when it is dealing with the general affairs of the state. It was necessary that that should be so; but in the township, where both law and administration are closer to the governed, the representative system has not been adopted. There is no municipal council; the body of the electors, when it has chosen the officials, gives them directions in everything beyond the simple, ordinary execution of the laws of the state.[2]

Such a state of affairs is so contrary to our ideas and opposed to our habits that some examples are needed to make it understandable.

Public duties in the township are extremely numerous and minutely divided, as we shall see later on, but most of the administrative power is concentrated in the hands of a few yearly elected individuals called "selectmen."[3]

The general laws of the state impose certain duties on the selectmen. In administering these they do not require the authorization of the governed, and it is their personal responsibility if they neglect them. For example, the state law charges them to draw up the municipal voting lists, and if they fail to do so, they are guilty of an offense. But in all matters within the township's control the selectmen carry out the popular will, just as our mayors execute the decisions of the municipal council. Usually they act on their own responsibility, merely putting into practice principles already approved by the majority. But if they want to make any change in the established order to start some new undertaking, they must go back to the source of their power. Suppose they want to start a school; the selectmen summon all the voters to a meeting on a fixed day and place; they there explain the need felt; they state the means available for the purpose, how much it will cost, and the site suggested. The meeting, consulted on all these points, accepts the principle, decides the site, votes the tax, and leaves the selectmen to carry out its orders.

Only the selectmen have the right to call a town meeting, but they may be required to do so. If ten owners of property conceive some new project and wish to submit it to the approval of the township, they demand a general meeting of the inhabitants; the selectmen are bound to agree to this and preserve only the right to preside over the meeting.[4]

The people as the origin of power in the township as elsewhere. They handle their principal affairs themselves. No municipal council. The greater part of municipal authority concentrated in the hands of the "selectmen." How the selectmen function. Town meeting. List of all municipal officials. Obligatory and paid functions.

Such political mores and social customs are certainly far removed from ours. I do not, at this moment, want to pass judgment on them or to reveal the hidden reasons causing them and giving them life; it is enough to describe them.

The selectmen are elected every year in April or May. At the same time, the town meeting also elects many other municipal officials[5] to take charge of important administrative details.

There are assessors to rate the township and collectors to bring the taxes in. The constable must organize the police, take care of public places, and take a hand in the physical execution of the laws. The town clerk must record all resolutions; he keeps a record of the proceedings of the civil administration. The treasurer looks after the funds of the township. There are also overseers of the poor whose difficult task it is to execute the provisions of the Poor Laws; school commissioners in charge of public education; and surveyors of highways, who look after roads both large and small, to complete the list of the main administrative officials of the township. But the division of functions does not stop there; among municipal officials one also finds parish commissioners responsible for the expenses of public worship, fire wardens to direct the citizens' efforts in case of fire, tithing men, hog reeves, fence viewers, timber measurers, and sealers of weights and measures.[6]

Altogether there are nineteen main officials in a township. Every inhabitant is bound, on pain of fine, to accept these various duties; but most of them also carry some remuneration so that poorer citizens can devote their time to them without loss. Furthermore, it is not the American system to give any fixed salary to officials. In general, each official act has a price, and men are paid in accordance with what they have done.

Life in the Township

I have said before that the principle of the sovereignty of the people hovers over the whole political system of the Anglo-Americans. Every page of this book will point out new applications of this doctrine.

In nations where the dogma of the sovereignty of the people prevails, each individual forms an equal part of that sovereignty and shares equally the government of the state.

Each individual is assumed to be as educated, virtuous, and powerful as any of his fellows.

Why, then, should he obey society, and what are the natural limits of such obedience?

He obeys society not because he is inferior to those who direct it, nor because he is incapable of ruling himself, but because union with his fellows seems useful to him and he knows that that union is impossible without a regulating authority.

Therefore, in all matters concerning the duties of citizens toward each other he is subordinate. In all matters that concern himself alone he remains the master, he is free and owes an account of his actions to God alone. From this derives the maxim that the individual is the best and only judge of his own interest and that society has no right to direct his behavior unless it feels harmed by him or unless it needs his concurrence.

This doctrine is universally accepted in the United States. Elsewhere I will examine its general influence on the ordinary actions of life; here and now I am concerned only with townships.

The township, taken as a whole in relation to the central government, resembles any other individual to whom the theory just mentioned applies.

So in the United States municipal liberty derives straight from the dogma of the sovereignty of the people; all the American republics have recognized this independence more or less, but there were circumstances particularly favorable to its growth among the people of New England.

In that part of the Union political life was born in the very heart of the townships; one might almost say that in origin each of them was a little independent nation. Later, when the kings of England claimed their share of sovereignty, they limited themselves to taking over the central power. They left the townships as they had found them. Now the New England townships are subordinate, but in the beginning this was not so, or hardly so. Therefore they have not received their powers; on the contrary, it would seem that they have surrendered a portion of their powers for the benefit of the state; that is an important distinction which the reader should always bear in mind.

In general the townships are subordinate to the state only where some interest that I shall call *social* is concerned, that is to say, some interest shared with others.

In all that concerns themselves alone the townships remain independent bodies, and I do not think one could find a single inhabitant of New England who would recognize the right of the government of the state to control matters of purely municipal interest.

Hence one finds the New England townships buying and selling, suing and being sued, increasing or reducing their budgets, and no administrative authority whatsoever thinks of standing in their way.[7]

But there are social duties which they are bound to perform. Thus, if the state needs money, the township is not free to grant or refuse its help.[8] If the state wants to open a road, the township cannot bar its territory. If there is a police regulation, the township must carry it out. If the government wants to organize education on a uniform plan throughout the country, the township must establish the schools required by the law.[9] We shall see, when we come to speak of the administration of the United States, how and by whom, in these various cases, the townships are constrained to obedience. Here I only wish to establish the fact of the obligation. Strict as this obligation is, the government of the state imposes it in principle only, and in its performance the township resumes all its independent rights. Thus taxes are, it is true, voted by the legislature, but they are assessed and collected by the township; the establishment of a school is obligatory, but the township builds it, pays for it, and controls it.

In France the state tax collector receives the communal taxes; in America the township tax collector collects state taxes.

So, whereas with us the central government lends its agents to the commune, in America the township lends its agents to the government. That fact alone shows how far the two societies differ.

Each man the best judge of his own interest. Corollary of the principle of the sovereignty of the people. How American townships apply these doctrines. The New England township sovereign in all that concerns itself alone, subordinate in all else. Duties of the township toward the state. In France the government lends officials to the commune. In America the township lends its officials to the government.

Spirit of the Township in New England

In America not only do municipal institutions exist, but there is also a municipal spirit which sustains and gives them life.

The New England township combines two advantages which, wherever they are found, keenly excite men's interest; they are independence and power. It acts, it is true, within a sphere beyond which it cannot pass, but within that domain its movements are free. This independence alone would give a real importance not warranted by size or population.

It is important to appreciate that, in general, men's affections are drawn only in directions where power exists. Patriotism does not long prevail in a conquered country. The New Englander is attached to his township not so much because he was born there as because he sees the township as a free, strong corporation of which he is part and which is worth the trouble of trying to direct.

It often happens in Europe that governments themselves regret the absence of municipal spirit, for everyone agrees that municipal spirit is an important element in order and public tranquillity, but they do not know how to produce it. In making municipalities strong and independent, they fear sharing their social power and exposing the state to risks of anarchy. However, if you take power and independence from a municipality, you may have docile subjects but you will not have citizens.

Why the New England township wins the affection of the inhabitants. Difficulty of creating municipal spirit in Europe. In America municipal rights and duties concur in forming that spirit. The homeland has more characteristic features in America than elsewhere. How municipal spirit manifests itself in New England. What happy results it produces there.

Another important fact must be noted. The New England township is shaped to form the nucleus of strong attachments, and there is meanwhile no rival center close by to attract the hot hearts of ambitious men.

County officials are not elected and their authority is limited. Even a state is only of secondary importance, being an obscure and placid entity. Few men are willing to leave the center of their interests and take trouble to win the right to help administer it.

The federal government does confer power and renown on those who direct it, but only a few can exercise influence there. The high office of President is hardly to be reached until a man is well on in years; as for other high federal offices, there is a large element of chance about attaining to them, and they go only to those who have reached eminence in some other walk of life. No ambitious man would make them the fixed aim of his endeavors. It is in the township, the center of the ordinary business of life, that the desire for esteem, the pursuit of substantial interests, and the taste for power and self-advertisement are concentrated; these passions, so often troublesome elements in society, take on a different character when exercised so close to home and, in a sense, within the family circle.

With much care and skill power has been broken into fragments in the American township, so that the maximum possible number of people have some concern with public affairs. Apart from the voters, who from time to time are called on to act as the government, there are many and various officials who all, within their sphere, represent the powerful body in whose name they act. Thus a vast number of people make a good thing for themselves out of the power of the community and are interested in administration for selfish reasons.

The American system, which distributes local power among so many citizens, is also not afraid to multiply municipal duties. Americans rightly think that patriotism is a sort of religion strengthened by practical service.

Thus daily duties performed or rights exercised keep municipal life constantly alive. There is a continual gentle political activity which keeps society on the move without turmoil.

Americans love their towns for much the same reasons that highlanders love their mountains. In both cases the native land has emphatic and peculiar features; it has a more pronounced physiognomy than is found elsewhere.

In general, New England townships lead a happy life. Their government is to their taste as well as of their choice. With profound peace and material prosperity prevailing in America, there are few storms in municipal life. The township's interests are easy to manage. Moreover, the people's political education has been completed long ago, or rather they were already educated when they settled there. In New England there is not even a memory of distinctions in rank, so there is no part of the community tempted to oppress the rest, and injustices which affect only isolated individuals are forgotten in the general contentment. The government may have defects, and indeed they are easy to point out, but they do not catch the eye because the government really does emanate from the governed, and so long as it gets along somehow or other, a sort of parental pride protects it. Besides, there is no basis of comparison. Formerly England ruled the colonies as a group, but the people always looked after municipal affairs. So the sovereignty of the people in the township is not ancient only, but primordial.

The New Englander is attached to his township because it is strong and independent; he has an interest in it because he shares in its management; he loves it because he has no reason to complain of his lot; he invests his ambition and his future in it; in the restricted sphere within his scope, he learns to rule society; he gets to know those formalities without which freedom can advance only through revolutions, and becoming imbued with their spirit, develops a taste for order, understands the harmony of powers, and in the end accumulates clear, practical ideas about the nature of his duties and the extent of his rights.

Notes

1. In 1830 there were 305 townships in Massachusetts; the population was 610,014; that gives an average of about 2,000 for each township.

2. The same rules do not apply to the large townships. Those generally have a mayor and a municipal body divided into two branches, but a law is needed to authorize such an exception. See the law of February 23, 1822, regulating the powers of the city of Boston. *Laws of Massachusetts,* Vol. II, p. 588. [*The General Laws of Massachusetts,* Vol. II, Boston, 1823, p. 588 ff.] That applies to the large towns. Small towns also often have a particular administration. In 1832 104 such municipal administrations were counted in the state of New York. (*Williams's New York Annual Register.*) [*The New York Annual Register for the Year of Our Lord 1832,* by Edwin Williams, New York, 1832.]

3. There are three selectmen in the smallest townships and nine in the largest. See *The Town Officer,* p. 186. [Tocqueville refers here to a book by Isaac Goodwin, *Town Officer or Law of Massachusetts* (Worcester, 1829), which incidentally is to be found among the volumes of his library at the Château de Tocqueville.] See also the main laws of Massachusetts concerning selectmen:

   Law of February 20, 1786, Vol. I, p. 219; February 24, 1796, Vol. I, p. 488; March 7, 1801, Vol. II, p. 45; June 16, 1795, Vol. I, p. 475; March 12, 1808, Vol. II, p. 186; February 28, 1787, Vol. I, p. 302; June 22, 1797, Vol. I, p. 539.

4. See *Laws of Massachusetts,* Vol. I, p. 150; law of March 25, 1786.

5. *Ibid.*

6. All these officials really do exist. To find out the details of all their duties see *The Town Officer,* by Isaac Goodwin (Worcester, 1829), and the *General Laws of Massachusetts* in 3 vols. (Boston, 1823).

7. See *Laws of Massachusetts,* law of March 23, 1786, Vol. I, p. 250.

8. *Ibid.,* law of February 20, 1786, Vol. I, p. 217.

9. See the same collection, law of June 25, 1789, Vol. I, p. 367, and March 10, 1827, Vol III, p. 179.

Critical Thinking

1. According to Tocqueville, who creates kingdoms and republics? In contrast, what seems to be the origin of townships?

2. What is the connection between local government institutions and liberty?

3. What is special about the New England town(ship)?

4. What roles do town meetings and selectmen play in New England towns?

5. What is the difference between tax collection processes in France and the United States, especially as they relate to local governments?

From *Democracy in America* by Alexis de Tocqueville, 1835.

Local Government: Observations

JAMES BRYCE

This is the place for an account of local government in the United States, because it is a matter regulated not by Federal law but by the several States and Territories, each of which establishes such local authorities, rural and urban, as the people of the State or Territory desire, and invests them with the requisite powers. But this very fact indicates the immensity of the subject. Each State has its own system of local areas and authorities, created and worked under its own laws; and though these systems agree in many points, they differ in so many others, that a whole volume would be needed to give even a summary view of their peculiarities. All I can here attempt is to distinguish the leading types of local government to be found in the United States, to describe the prominent features of each type, and to explain the influence which the large scope and popular character of local administration exercise upon the general life and well-being of the American people.

Three types of rural local government are discernible in America. The first is characterized by its unit, the Town or Township, and exists in the six New England States. The second is characterized by a much larger unit, the county, and prevails in the southern States. The third combines some features of the first with some of the second, and may be called the mixed system. It is found, under a considerable variety of forms, in the middle and north-western States. The differences of these three types are interesting, not only because of the practical instruction they afford, but also because they spring from original differences in the character of the colonist who settled along the American coast, and in the conditions under which the communities there founded were developed.

The first New England settlers were Puritans in religion, and sometimes inclined to republicanism in politics. They were largely townsfolk, accustomed to municipal life and to vestry meetings. They planted their tiny communities along the seashore and the banks of rivers, enclosing them with stockades for protection against the warlike Indians. Each was obliged to be self-sufficing, because divided by rocks and woods from the others. Each had its common pasture on which the inhabitants turned out their cattle, and which officers were elected to manage. Each was a religious as well as a civil body politic, gathered round the church as its centre; and the equality which prevailed in the congregation prevailed also in civil affairs, the whole community meeting under a president or moderator to discuss affairs of common interest. Each such settlement was called a Town, or Township, and was in fact a miniature commonwealth, exercising a practical sovereignty over the property and persons of its members—for there was as yet no State, and the distant home government scarcely cared to interfere—but exercising it on thoroughly democratic principles. Its centre was a group of dwellings, often surrounded by a fence or wall, but it included a rural area of several square miles, over which farmhouses and clusters of houses began to spring up when the Indians retired. The name "town" covered the whole of this area, which was never too large for all the inhabitants to come together to a central place of meeting. This town organization remained strong and close, the colonists being men of narrow means, and held together in each settlement by the needs of defence. And though presently the towns became aggregated into counties, and the legislature and governor, first of the whole colony, and, after 1776, of the State, began to exert their superior authority, the towns (which, be it remembered, remained rural communities, making up the whole area of the State) held their ground, and are to this day the true units of political life in New England, the solid foundation of that well-compacted structure of self-government which European philosophers have admired and the new States of the West have sought to reproduce. Till 1821[1] the towns were the only political corporate bodies in Massachusetts, and till 1857 they formed, as they still form in Connecticut, the basis of representation in her Assembly, each town, however small, returning at least one member. Much of that robust, if somewhat narrow, localism which characterizes the representative system of America is due to this originally distinct and self-sufficing corporate life of the seventeenth century towns. Nor is it without interest to observe that although they owed much to the conditions which surrounded the early colonists, forcing them to develop a civic patriotism resembling that of the republics of ancient Greece and Italy, they owed something also to those Teutonic traditions of semi-independent local communities, owning common property, and governing themselves by a primary assembly of all free inhabitants, which the English had brought with them from the Elbe and the Weser, and which had been perpetuated in the practice of many parts of England down till the days of the Stuart kings.

Very different were the circumstances of the Southern colonies. The men who went to Virginia and the Carolinas were not Puritans, nor did they mostly go in families and groups of families from the same neighbourhood. Many were casual adventurers, often belonging to the upper class, Episcopalians in religion, and with no such experience of, or attachment to, local self-government as the men of Massachusetts or Connecticut. They settled in a region where the Indian tribes were comparatively peaceable, and where therefore there was little need of concentration for the purposes of defence. The climate along the coast was somewhat too hot for European labour, so slaves were imported to cultivate the land. Population was thinly scattered; estates were large; the soil was fertile and soon enriched its owners. Thus a semi-feudal society grew up, in which authority naturally fell to the land-owners, each of whom was the centre of a group of free dependants as well as the master of an increasing crowd of slaves. There were therefore comparatively few urban communities, and the life of the colony took a rural type. The houses of the planters lay miles apart from one another; and when local divisions had to be created, these were made large enough to include a considerable area of territory and number of land-owning gentlemen. They were therefore rural divisions, counties framed on the model of English counties. Smaller circumscriptions there were, such as hundreds and parishes, but the hundred died out,[2] the parish ultimately became a purely ecclesiastical division, and the parish vestry was restricted to ecclesiastical functions, while the county remained the practically important unit of local administration, the unit to which the various functions of government were aggregated, and which, itself controlling minor authorities, was controlled by the State government alone. The affairs of the county were usually managed by a board of elective commissioners, and not, like those of the New England towns, by a primary assembly; and in an aristocratic society the leading planters had of course a predominating influence. Hence this form of

local government was not only less democratic, but less stimulating and educative than that which prevailed in the New England States. Nor was the Virginian county, though so much larger than the New England town, ever as important an organism over against the State. It may almost be said, that while a New England State is a combination of towns, a Southern State is from the first an administrative as well as political whole, whose subdivisions, the counties, had never any truly independent life, but were and are mere subdivisions for the convenient dispatch of judicial and financial business.

In the middle States of the Union, Pennsylvania, New Jersey, and New York, settled or conquered by Englishmen some time later than New England, the town and town meeting did not as a rule exist, and the county was the original basis of organization. But as there grew up no planting aristocracy like that of Virginia or the Carolinas, the course of events took in the middle States a different direction. As trade and manufactures grew, population became denser than in the South. New England influenced them, and influenced still more the newer commonwealths which arose in the North-west, such as Ohio and Michigan, into which the surplus population of the East poured. And the result of this influence is seen in the growth through the middle and western States of a mixed system, which presents a sort of compromise between the County system of the South and the Town system of the North-east. There are great differences between the arrangements in one or other of these middle and western States. But it may be said, speaking generally, that in them the county is relatively less important than in the southern States, the township less important than in New England. The county is perhaps to be regarded, at least in New York, Pennsylvania, and Ohio, as the true unit, and the townships (for so they are usually called) as its subdivisions. But the townships are vigorous organisms, which largely restrict the functions of the county authority, and give to local government, especially in the North-west, a character generally similar to that which it wears in New England. . . .

It is noteworthy that the Americans, who are supposed to be especially fond of representative assemblies, have made little use of representation in their local government. The township is usually governed either by a primary assembly of all citizens or else, as in such States as Ohio and Iowa, by a very small board, not exceeding three, with, in both sets of cases, several purely executive officers.[3] In the county there is seldom or never a county board possessing legislative functions;[4] usually only three commissioners or supervisors with some few executive or judicial officers. Local legislation (except as it appears in the bye-laws of the Town meeting or selectmen) is discouraged. The people seem jealous of their county officials, electing them for short terms, and restricting each to a special range of duties. This is perhaps only another way of saying that the county, even in the South, has continued to be an artificial entity, and has drawn to itself no great part of the interest and affections of the citizens. Over five-sixths of the Union each county presents a square figure on the map, with nothing distinctive about it, nothing "natural" about it, in the sense in which such English counties as Kent or Cornwall are natural entities. It is too large for the personal interest of the citizens: that goes to the township. It is too small to have traditions which command the respect or touch the affections of its inhabitants: these belong to the State.[5]

The chief functions local government has to discharge in the United States are the following:—

Making and repairing roads and bridges. —These prime necessities of rural life are provided for by the township, county, or State, according to the class to which a road or bridge belongs. That the roads of America are proverbially ill-built and ill-kept is due partly to the climate, with its alternations of severe frost, occasional torrential rains (in the middle and southern States), and long droughts; partly to the hasty habits of the people, who are too busy with other things, and too eager to use their capital in private enterprises to be willing to spend freely on highways; partly also to the thinness of population, which is, except in a few manufacturing districts, much less dense than in western Europe. In many districts railways have come before roads, so roads have been the less used and cared for.

The administration of justice was one of the first needs which caused the formation of the county: and matters connected with it still form a large part of county business. The voters elect a judge or judges, and the local prosecuting officer, called the district attorney, and the chief executive officer, the sheriff.[6] Prisons are a matter of county concern. Police is always locally regulated, but in the northern States more usually by the township than by the county. However, this branch of government, so momentous in continental Europe, is in America comparatively unimportant outside the cities. The rural districts get on nearly everywhere with no guardians of the peace, beyond the township constable;[7] nor does the State government, except, of course, through statutes, exercise any control over local police administration.[8] In the rural parts of the eastern and middle States property is as safe as anywhere in the world. In such parts of the West as are disturbed by dacoits, or by solitary highwaymen, travellers defend themselves, and, if the sheriff is distant or slack, lynch law may usefully be invoked.

The care of the poor is thrown almost everywhere upon local and not upon State authorities,[9] and defrayed out of local funds, sometimes by the county, sometimes by the township. The poor laws of the several States differ in so many particulars that it is impossible to give even an outline of them here. Little out-door relief is given, though in most States the relieving authority may, at his or their discretion, bestow it; and pauperism is not, and has never been, a serious malady, except in some five or six great cities, where it is now vigorously combated by volunteer organizations largely composed of ladies. The total number of persons returned as paupers in the whole Union in 1880 was 88,665, of whom 67,067 were inmates of alms-houses, and 21,598 in receipt of out-door relief. This was only 1 to 565 of the whole population.[10] In England and Wales in 1881 there were 803,126 paupers, to a population of 25,974,439, or 1 to 32 of population.

Sanitation, which has become so important a department of English local administration, plays a small part in the rural districts of America, because their population is so much more thinly spread over the surface that the need for drainage and the removal of nuisances is less pressing; moreover, as the humbler classes are better off, unhealthy dwellings are far less common. Public health officers and sanitary inspectors would, over the larger part of the county, have little occupation.[11]

Education, on the other hand, has hitherto been not only a more distinctively local matter, but one relatively far more important than in England, France, or Italy. And there is usually a special administrative body, often a special administrative area, created for its purposes— the school committee and the school district.[12] The vast sum expended on public instruction has been already mentioned. Though primarily dealt with by the smallest local circumscription, there is a growing tendency for both the county and the State to interest themselves in the work of instruction by way of inspection, and to some extent of pecuniary subventions. Not only does the county often appoint a county superintendent, but there are in some States county high schools and (in most) county boards of education, besides a State Board of Commissioners.[13] I need hardly add that the schools of all grades are more numerous and efficient in the northern and western than in the southern States.[14] In old colonial days, when the English Commissioners for Foreign Plantations asked for information on the subject of education from the governors of Virginia and Connecticut, the former replied, "I thank God there are no free schools or printing presses, and I hope we shall not have any these hundred years;"[15] and the latter, "One-fourth of the annual revenue of the colony is laid out in maintaining free schools for the education of our children." The disparity was prolonged and intensified in the South by the existence of slavery. Now that slavery has gone, the South makes rapid advances; but the proportion of illiteracy, especially of course among the negroes, is still high.[16]

It will be observed that of the general functions of local government above described, three, viz. police, sanitation, and poor relief, are simpler and less costly than in England, and indeed in most parts of western and central Europe. It has therefore proved easier to vest the management of all in the same local authority, and to get on with a smaller number of special executive officers. Education is indeed almost the only matter which has been deemed to demand a special body to handle it. Nevertheless, even in America the increasing complexity of civilization, and the growing tendency to invoke governmental aid for the satisfaction of wants which were not previously felt, or if felt, were met by voluntary action, tend to enlarge the sphere and multiply the functions of local government.

How far has the spirit of political party permeated rural local government? I have myself asked this question a hundred times in travelling through America, yet I find it hard to give any general answer, because there are great diversities in this regard not only between different States, but between different parts of the same State, diversities due sometimes to the character of the population, sometimes to the varying intensity of party feeling, sometimes to the greater or less degree in which the areas of local government coincide with the election districts for the election of State senators or representatives. On the whole it would seem that county officials are apt to be chosen on political lines, not so much because any political questions come before them, or because they can exert much influence on State or Federal elections, as because these paid offices afford a means of rewarding political services and securing political adhesions. Each of the great parties usually holds its county convention and runs its "county ticket," with the unfortunate result of intruding national politics into matters with which they have nothing to do, and of making it more difficult for good citizens outside the class of professional politicians to find their way into county administration. However, the party candidates are seldom bad men, and the ordinary voter is less apt to vote blindly for the party nominee than he would be in Federal or State elections. In the township and rural school district party spirit is much less active. The offices are often unpaid, and the personal merits of the candidates are better known to the voters than are those of the politicians who seek for county office.[17] Rings and Bosses are not unknown even in rural New England. School committee elections are often influenced by party affiliations. But on the whole, the township and its government keep themselves pretty generally out of the political whirlpool: their posts are filled by honest and reasonably competent men.

Notes

1. Boston continued to be a town governed by a primary assembly of all citizens till 1822; and even then the town-meeting was not quite abolished, for a provision was introduced, intended to satisfy conservative democratic feeling, into the city charter granted by statute in that year, empowering the mayor and aldermen to call general meetings of the citizens qualified to vote in city affairs "to consult upon the common good, to give instructions to their representatives, and to take all lawful means to obtain a redress of any grievances." Such primary assemblies are, however, never now convoked.

2. In Maryland hundreds, which still exist in Delaware, were for a long time the chief administrative divisions. We hear there also of "baronies" and "townlands," as in Ireland; and Maryland is usually called a "province," while the other settlements are colonies. Among its judicial establishments there were courts of pypowdry (*piè poudré*) and "hustings." See the interesting paper on "Local Institutions in Maryland," by Dr. Wilhelm, in *Johns Hopkins University Studies,* Third Series.

   The hundred is a division of small consequence in southern England, but in Lancashire it has some important duties. It repairs the bridges; it is liable for damage done in a riot; and it had its high constable.

3. In a few Western States the Town board has (like the New England selectmen) a limited taxing power, as well as administrative duties.

4. In New York, however, there is a marked tendency in this direction.

5. In Virginia there used to be a county feeling resembling that of England, but this has vanished in the social revolution that has transformed the South.

6. The American sheriff remains something like what the English sheriff was before his wings were clipped by legislation some seventy years ago. Even then he mostly acted by deputy. The justices and the county police have since that legislation largely superseded his action.

7. Or, in States where there are no townships, some corresponding officer.

8. Michigan is now (1888) said to be instituting a sort of State police for the enforcement of her anti-liquor legislation.

9. In some States there are State poor-law superintendents, and frequently certain State institutions for the benefit of particular classes of paupers, *e.g.* pauper lunatics.

10. New York had 15,217 paupers (of whom 2810 were out-door), Colorado 47 (1 out-door), Arizona 4. Louisiana makes no return of indoor paupers, because the parishes (= counties) provide for the maintenance of their poor in private institutions. (The accuracy of these returns has been questioned.)

11. Sanitation, however, has occupied much attention in the cities. Cleveland on Lake Erie claims to have the lowest death rate of any large city in the world.

12. Though the school district frequently coincides with the township, it has generally (outside of New England) administrative officers distinct from those of the township, and when it coincides it is often subdivided into lesser districts.

13. In some States provision is made for the combination of several school districts to maintain a superior school at a central spot.

14. The differences between the school arrangements of different States are so numerous that I cannot attempt to describe them.

15. Governor Sir William Berkeley, however, was among the Virginians who in 1660 subscribed for the erection in Virginia of "a colledge of students of the liberal arts and sciences." As to elementary instruction he said that Virginia pursued "the same course that is taken in England out of towns, every man according to his ability instructing his children. We have forty-eight parishes, and our ministry are well paid, and, by consent, should be better if they would pray oftener and preach less."
—*The College of William and Mary,* by Dr. H. B. Adams.

16. The percentage of persons unable to read to the whole population of the United States was, in 1880,13.4; it was lowest in Iowa (2.4), highest in South Carolina (48.2) and Louisiana (45.8). The percentage of persons unable to write was in the whole United States 17; lowest in Nebraska (3.6), highest in South Carolina (55.4) and Alabama (50.9).

    It has recently been proposed in Congress to reduce the surplus in the U.S. treasury by distributing sums among the States in aid of education, in proportion to the need which exists for schools, *i.e.* to their illiteracy. The objections on the score of economic policy, as well as of constitutional law, are so obvious as to have stimulated a warm resistance to the bill.

17. Sometimes the party "ticket" leaves a blank space for the voter to insert the name of the candidates for whom he votes for township offices.

Critical Thinking

1. According to Bryce, what are the three different systems of rural local government in the United States?

2. What factors led to the establishment of the system of local government in New England that is anchored by towns (or townships)?

3. How did religion, differences in the European origins of the first settlers, and relations with "Indians" (now called "Native Americans") contribute to differences between the local government systems established in New England and in the South?

4. What features characterize local government in the "middle" states of New York, Pennsylvania, and New Jersey?

5. What are the chief functions of local government in the United States?

From *Local Government: Observations,* 1888.

UNIT 2

Intergovernmental Relations

Unit Selections

Learning Outcomes

- Assess the current state of intergovernmental relations in the United States.

- Identify the level of government—national, state, or local—that you think is contributing the most to the well-being of Americans and explain why.

- Identify circumstances in which the national government should impose national standards on state and local governments and in which state governments should impose state standards on their local governments.

- Determine whether states and localities should have increased responsibility for performing more tasks and providing more services to citizens and for raising money to pay for them.

- In our post-9/11 world, assess the current degree and quality of cooperation among the national, state, and local governments in the area of homeland security.

- Decide whether growth in the population of the United States in our increasingly globalized world will lead to a greater need for energetic state and local governments or a need for greater national government authority and control at the expense of state and local governments.

- Explain why intergovernmental relations in the United States change over time and do not reach a stable or permanent state.

- Distinguish between the formally federal relationship between, on the one hand, the national government and state governments and, on the other, the formally unitary relationship between state governments and local governments.

Student Website

www.mhhe.com/cls

Internet References

Advisory Commission on Intergovernmental Relations
www.library.unt.edu/gpo/acir/Default.html

U.S. Congress
www.congress.org

Council of State Governments
www.csg.org

National Center for State Courts
www.ncsc.org

Oyez
www.oyez.org

Three levels of government—national, state, and local—coexist in the American political system. They not only operate alongside one another, but they also cooperate and conflict with each other in carrying out their functions. The legal bases for relationships among governments in the American political system include the United States Constitution, 50 state constitutions, decisions by both state and federal courts, and state and national legislation. But legal guidelines do not prevent complications from arising in a three-tier system of government. These three levels of American government have been likened to a layer cake: three layers in one overarching system of government. Still using the cake analogy, political scientist Morton Grodzins has argued that a marble cake better represents the interactions of local, state, and national governments in the American political system.

According to Grodzins, these interactions are far less tidy than the model of a layer cake suggests. Governments closest to the scene seem best able to handle certain kinds of problems, but at the same time, higher, more "distant" levels of government often have access to better sources of revenue to finance government activities. Citizens give different degrees of loyalty and support to different levels of government, and the competing ambitions of politicians at different levels of government can obstruct much needed cooperation.

The formal relationship between the national government and the states is quite different from that between the states and their local governments. The national–state relationship is formally "federal" in character, which means that, in theory, the states and the national government each have autonomous spheres of responsibility. In contrast, the state–local relationship is not a federal one. Local governments are mere "creatures" of the states and are not on equal footing with their creators. In practical terms, however, the national government has generally gained the upper hand in dealings with the states, and in some circumstances, localities operate on almost equal footing with state governments.

Public school governance illustrates some of the complexities of intergovernmental relations in the American political system. Public schooling is usually viewed as primarily a local government function. But, as Grodzins pointed out, state governments play powerful roles by providing financial aid, certifying teachers, prescribing curriculum requirements, and regulating measures concerning school safety and students' health. The national government is also involved in public schooling. In the last 50 years, the United States Supreme Court and lower federal courts have made numerous decisions aimed at ending racial segregation in public schools. In addition, for several decades national government grants have helped finance various activities such as school breakfasts and lunches, and special education programs. In 2001, the No Child Left Behind Act was enacted with President Bush's strong support, and it introduced what some observers see as a historic new level of national government involvement in public schooling. Even this brief review of local, state, and national involvement in one area, schooling, should show why Grodzins believed that a marble cake better reflects

© Royalty-Free/CORBIS

the reality of the American three-tier system of government than a layer cake does.

Intergovernmental transfers of money are an important form of interaction among local, state, and national governments. "Strings" are almost always attached to money that one level of government transfers to another level. For example, when the national government provides grants to states and localities, requirements concerning the use of that money accompany the funds, although the extensiveness and specificity of the requirements vary greatly in different grant programs. Similarly, financial aid from state governments to local governments also involve strings of one kind or another.

Presidents and other government leaders often make proposals about how to structure relations and divide responsibilities among the national, state, and local governments. In the 1980s, President Reagan's "new federalism" was aimed at shifting greater responsibility back to the states and localities. The change in direction that began under Reagan continued under the first President Bush, and state and local governments had to operate in the context of what has been called "fend-for-yourself federalism."

Whatever changes the Clinton administration tried to make in intergovernmental relations faded into obscurity after Republicans took control of the House of Representatives and Senate in January 1995. Newt Gingrich, the first Republican Speaker of the House of Representatives in 40 years, made shrinking the role of the national government and giving increased responsibilities to the states an important part of his campaign promises in the November 1994 congressional elections. In turn, the House of Representatives initiated a number of bills fulfilling Gingrich's campaign promises. One bill was designed to make it very difficult for Congress to mandate that state and local governments do something without providing the necessary funding. The welfare reform bill of 1996 rewrote the welfare system that had begun in the 1930s as part of the New Deal. At the core of the reform was the devolution to state governments of more responsibilities in the provision of government assistance to the needy. While the national government remained mostly responsible for funding the welfare system, state governments were given increased responsibility for determining and implementing welfare policies. In sum, during the last two decades of the twentieth century, the United States seemed to have entered a new era of intergovernmental relations that involved substantial increases in the power and autonomy of state and local governments.

Then came the terrorist attacks of September 11, 2001. The resulting preoccupation with the war on terror produced an increase in national government power in the sphere of homeland security, with a corresponding decline in state and local responsibilities. U.S. military campaigns in Afghanistan and Iraq also distracted attention from intergovernmental relations on the domestic front. By 2011, however, the national government's long-term debt and annual deficits had become the focus of heated debate in Washington and around the country, and there were proposals to have states assume even more responsibility for administering and funding Medicaid, the program established in the 1960s to give poor Americans better access to medical care. What the future holds for the Medicaid program is anybody's guess, but it seems virtually certain that intergovernmental relations will remain an ever-changing phenomenon in the American political system.

Selections in this unit address various dimensions of the relationships among national, state, and local governments.

Demographics and Destiny

With America expected to grow by 100 million people in the next 40 years, how will states and localities run a bigger, more diverse country?

Can a country with a population that's expected to expand dramatically over the next 40 years be in decline? Visionary and author Joel Kotkin doesn't think so. In his new book, *The Next Hundred Million*, Kotkin sees a more dynamic, ethnically diverse country, brimming with technological and cultural innovation. To accommodate this expansion, America will continue to grow in urban areas, but also on the edges, in suburban and exurban towns, especially in our heartland where undeveloped land is still abundant. In this essay, Kotkin looks at how this new growth and dynamism will impact our country at the state and local level in particular. —*Governing*

JOEL KOTKIN

Over the next four decades, American governments will oversee a much larger and far more diverse population. As we gain upward of 100 million people, America will inevitably become a more complex, crowded and competitive place, but it will continue to remain highly dependent on its people's innovative and entrepreneurial spirit.

In 2050, the U.S. will look very different from the country in 2000, at the dawn of the new millennium. By mid-century, the U.S. will no longer be a "white country," but rather a staggering amalgam of racial, ethnic and religious groups—all participants in the construction of a new civilization whose roots lie not in any one country or continent, but across the entirety of human cultures and racial types. No other advanced, populous country will enjoy such ethnic diversity.

The implications of this change will be profound for governments—perhaps in ways not now commonly anticipated. Many "progressives" believe a more diverse, populous nation will need more guidance from Washington, D.C., but a more complex and varied country will increasingly not fit well into a one-size-fits-all approach.

Although the economic crisis of 2008 led to a rapid rise of federal power, there has been a stunning and largely unexpected push-back reflected, in part, by the tea party movement. Some states have passed laws that seek to restrict federal prerogatives on a host of issues. More importantly, public opinion, measured in numerous surveys, seems to be drifting away from major expansions of government power.

Of course, most Americans would accede to the federal government an important role in developing public works, national defense and regulations for health and safety. But generally speaking, they also tend to believe that local communities, neighborhoods and parents should possess the power to craft appropriate solutions on many other problems.

This also reflects our historical experience. From its origins, American democracy has been largely self-created and fostered a dispersion of power; in many European countries, and more recently in parts of Asia, democracy was forged by central authorities.

Other periods of massive government intervention, most notably after the New Deal and the Great Society, also elicited reactions against centralization. But the current push-back's speed and ferocity has been remarkable. Yet the often polarizing debate about the scope of federal power largely has ignored the longer-term trends that will promote the efficacy of an increasingly decentralized approach to governance.

Perhaps the most important factor here is the trajectory of greater growth and increasing diversity of who we are and how we live. Not only are Americans becoming more racially diverse, but they inhabit a host of different environments, ranging from dense cities to urbanized suburbs, to smaller cities and towns, that have different needs and aspirations.

Americans also are more settled than any time in our history—partially a function of an aging population—and thus more concerned with local developments. As recently as the 1970s, one in five Americans moved annually; in 2004 that number was 14 percent, the lowest rate since 1950. In 2008, barely one in 10 moved, a fraction of the rate in the 1960s. Workers are increasingly unwilling to move even for a promotion due to family and other concerns. The recession accelerated this process, but the pattern appears likely to persist even in good times.

Americans also prefer to live in decentralized environments. There are more than 65,000 general-purpose governments; the average local jurisdiction population in the United States is 6,200—small enough that non-professional politicians can have a serious impact on local issues. This contrasts with the vast preference among academic planners, policy gurus and the national media for larger government units as the best way to regulate and plan for the future.

Short of a draconian expansion of federal power, this dispersion is likely to continue. Roughly 80 to 90 percent of all metropolitan growth in the last decade took place on the periphery; at the same time, the patterns of domestic migration have seen a shift away from the biggest cities and toward smaller ones. As Joel Garreau noted in his classic *Edge City*, "planners drool" over high-density development, but most residents in suburbia "hate a lot of this stuff." They might enjoy a town center, a *paseo* or a walking district, but they usually resent the proliferation of high-rises or condo complexes. If they wanted to live in buildings like them, they would have stayed in the city.

Attempts to force major densification in these areas will be fiercely resisted, even in the most liberal communities. Some of the strongest anti-growth hotbeds in the nation are areas like Fairfax County, Va., with high concentrations of progressives—well educated people who might seem amenable to environmentally correct "smart growth"—advocating denser development along transit corridors. As one planning director in a well-to-do suburban Maryland county put it, "Smart growth is something people want. They just don't want it in their own neighborhood."

The great long-term spur to successful dispersion will come from technology, as James Martin first saw in his pioneering 1978 book, *The Wired Society*. A former software designer for IBM, Martin foresaw the emergence of mass telecommunications that would allow a massive reduction in commuting, greater deconcentration of workplaces and a "localization of physical activities . . . centered in local communities."

Technology would allow skilled people to congregate in communities of their choice or at home. Today not only knowledge workers but also those in construction trades, agriculture and other professions are home-based, conducting their operations out of trucks, vans or home offices.

Many leading-edge companies now recognize this trend. As much as 40 percent of IBM's work force operates full time at home or remotely at clients' businesses. Siemens, Hewlett-Packard, Cisco, Merrill Lynch and American Express have expanded their use of telecommuting, with noted increases in productivity.

At the same time, employment is shifting away from mega-corporations to smaller units and individuals; between 1980 and 2000, self-employed individuals expanded tenfold to include 16 percent of the work force. The smallest businesses, the microenterprises, have enjoyed the fastest rate of growth, far more than any other business category. By 2006 there were some 20 million such businesses, one for every six private-sector workers.

Hard economic times could slow this trend, but recessions have historically served as incubators of innovation and entrepreneurship. Many individuals starting new firms will have recently left or been laid off by bigger companies, particularly during a severe economic downturn. Whether they form a new bank, energy company or design firm, they will do it more efficiently—with less overhead, more efficient Internet use and less emphasis on pretentious office settings. In addition, they will do it primarily in places that can scale themselves to economic realities.

Simultaneously the Internet's rise allows every business—indeed every family—unprecedented access to information, something that militates against centralized power. Given Internet access, many lay people aren't easily intimidated into accepting the ability of "experts" to dictate solutions based on exclusive knowledge since the *hoi polloi* now possess the ability to gather and analyze information. Even the powerful media companies are rapidly losing their ability to define agendas; there are too many sources of information to mobilize mass opinion. The widespread breakdown of support for climate change is a recent example of this phenomenon.

Once the current drive for centralization falters, support for decentralization will grow, including progressive communities that now favor a heavy-handed expansion of federal power. Attempts to impose solutions from a central point will be increasingly regarded as obtrusive and oppressive to them, just as they would to many more conservative places like South Dakota. In the coming era, in many cases, only locally based solutions—agreed to at the community, municipal or state level—can possibly gather strong support.

This drive toward dispersing power will prove critical if we hope to meet the needs of an unprecedentedly diverse and complex nation of 400 million. New forms of association—from local electronic newsletters to a proliferation of local farmers markets, festivals and a host of ad hoc social service groups—are already growing. Indeed, after a generation-long decline, volunteerism has spiked among Millennials and seems likely to surge among downshifting baby boomers. In 2008, some 61 million Americans volunteered, representing more than one-quarter of the population older than 16.

It's these more intimate units—the family, the neighborhood association, the church or local farmers market—that constitute what Thomas Jefferson called our "little republics," which are most critical to helping mid-21st-century America. Here, our nation of 400 million souls will find its fundamental sustenance and its best hope for the brightest future.

Critical Thinking

1. How is the United States population projected to change by 2050, both in terms of diversity and total number of people?

2. How has Americans' mobility changed since the 1970s?

3. How has technology affected the residential concentration of Americans?

4. Do Americans prefer to live in decentralized or centralized environments?

Taking Stock

Recalling 22 years of assessing the ebb and flow of states and localities.

ALAN EHRENHALT

When the first issue of *Governing* appeared 22 years ago, the editors made clear that this was a magazine about states and localities—their strengths, weaknesses, accomplishments and challenges—not a publication focused on one level of government or the other.

At the same time, it was clear which one was the senior partner in the American federal system. States were in good fiscal shape and more innovative than they had been in years. Governors of both parties, led by Jim Blanchard in Michigan and Dick Thornburgh in Pennsylvania, were dreaming up all sorts of economic development schemes to keep their states healthy in a post-industrial world. Bill Clinton in Arkansas and Tommy Thompson in Wisconsin were experimenting with changes in welfare law that paved the way for federal welfare reform enacted a decade later.

In 1988, journalist David Osborne wrote a book detailing the many varieties of state entrepreneurship and called it *Laboratories of Democracy,* echoing the phrase coined by Justice Louis Brandeis more than 50 years earlier. President Ronald Reagan's promise to devolve power to the states may have gone largely unrealized during his two terms in office, but states treated it as a license for seeking solutions to the myriad domestic policy problems that weren't being addressed at the federal level. As anybody who was around state government in those days will recall, it was a heady time.

And it lasted quite a while. Notwithstanding a pair of moderately severe recessions, states remained the fulcrum of public policy experiment in America for the better part of two decades. When it came to health, energy policy and a wide variety of other subjects, there was far more innovation at the state level in the 1990s and 2000s than in the federal government.

The contrast between the vitality of states and cities circa 1987 couldn't have been greater. Urban America was experiencing the twin ravages of AIDS and crack cocaine. Rates of violent crime were reaching levels never before seen in the nation's history.

There were more than 2,000 homicides in New York City in 1987, nearly three times as many as a quarter-century before, and the rate was continuing to increase. Whole city sections had become bywords for physical and social degradation; Paul Newman's movie, *Fort Apache, the Bronx,* characterized one of New York's boroughs as a hellhole more reminiscent of Third World chaos than of the largest metropolis in the United States.

While crime was shooting up, urban population was plunging. Cities such as Cleveland, Detroit and St. Louis were half the size they had been a generation earlier, and their downtowns were pockmarked with empty storefronts and underused office buildings, the streets lonely and dangerous anytime after dark. New York's psyche was still damaged by the painful memory of the near-bankruptcy of the previous decade; Cleveland still had not recovered from the humiliating bond default of 1978.

This was the balance that prevailed between states and localities when *Governing* published its first issue. To call it a balance at all is to underestimate what things were like. Many states were feisty and eager to take on new challenges. Cities were struggling just to survive.

To say that the balance has shifted in 22 years would be to make an even greater understatement. In 2010, the states aren't laboratories of democracy; they aren't laboratories of anything, unless it's insolvency. The numbers are familiar enough that there's no need to spend whole paragraphs repeating them: Suffice it to say that states as a whole are facing, by reliable estimates, a combined fiscal shortfall of up to $170 billion this year and $120 billion next year; that some are looking at budget holes equal to a quarter of their general fund or even more; that they are laying off thousands of workers and furloughing many thousands more; and that this still leaves them far short of the revenue they need to meet constitutional balanced-budget requirements.

The recession may be about over, but the fiscal crisis is not. The majority of states are looking at long-term pension and retiree health-care costs that must be addressed before they can be fiscally comfortable again. So far, none of the states with the most serious long-term problems has shown much resolve in addressing them.

The bottom line is that it may be unrealistic to consider states major innovators in public policy anytime in this decade. There are creative things they can do that don't cost a lot—they can pass new laws dealing with highway safety or cable TV regulation—but since most genuine innovation requires spending, it's fair to say that the laboratories of democracy will be closed, or at least inactive, for quite a while.

If life has changed dramatically in the state capitols over the past two decades, it has changed just as much in the cities. And on the whole, it has changed for the better. To start with, there is safety. The number of homicides in New York City last year was 466, a level reached in 1987 before the end of March. Population is growing again as well, not just in New York, but also in Chicago, Washington, D.C., and numerous other cities that used to dread each decade's census for its inevitable documentation of continuing decline.

To say cities are doing better is not to minimize the perilous fiscal shape that many of them are in right now. Even as it becomes safer and more attractive to new residents, New York is having to raise taxes, lay off workers and cut back on social programs. That is a common predicament. But on the whole, urban fiscal problems are more recession-based and less structural than those of the states. Cities don't have Medicaid to worry about. Some have locked themselves into dangerous long-term pension commitments—Vallejo, Calif., went bankrupt over pension costs and San Diego nearly did a few years ago—but on the whole, cities have done better than states at avoiding this trap. And they have been more creative at finding ways to raise the revenues they need to render the services citizens demand of them. Raising taxes and fees hasn't always been the best economic development strategy, but it has helped keep budgets under control.

In any case, the renewal of cities is not primarily a fiscal matter. It is shown more clearly in the revival of residential life and street vitality all across the country; in the light rail systems taking shape in places one would never even associate with public transportation, such as Phoenix, Dallas and Charlotte, N.C.; and in the nodes of urban density that have begun to spring up along the transit lines once they are built. Most of all, urban revival is linked with changing demographics, as increasing numbers of people in their teens, 20s and early 30s, the vast majority of them singles or childless couples, express a preference for some form of urbanized life as a change from the cul-de-sac suburbia in which many of them grew up.

The urban comeback has stalled in the recession, as lending for central-city residential and commercial development has dried up. Some experts insist the comeback hasn't only stalled but ended: They believe once the economy recovers, suburban sprawl will simply resume. I think the evidence, from demographics, surveys and simple on-the-ground realities of the past few years, is clearly against them.

Whatever the future of urban revival may be, its recent past reflects a record of impressive innovation by many mayors. From the downtown development strategies of Richard M. Daley in Chicago, to the environmental activism of Greg Nickels in Seattle, the transportation planning initiatives of Michael Bloomberg in New York, and the housing reforms under Shirley Franklin in Atlanta, the past decade has seen a budding of new ideas in urban policy far more interesting than anything that preceded it for a long time.

Some may be tempted to say that the laboratories of democracy haven't closed; they simply have moved from state capitols to city halls. But I would be wary of taking the argument too far. If we have learned anything at *Governing* over the past 22 years, it is that power and creativity in the American federal system ebb and flow in cycles. The states have a huge task of restructuring ahead of them in the next decade. It will be excruciating, but once they accomplish it—and they really have no choice but to accomplish it, if they want to survive as legitimate political entities—there is reason to hope that they can eventually regain the spirit of optimism and innovation they displayed two decades ago.

If my arithmetic is right, this is the 215th Assessments column I have written as editor of *Governing*. It is also the last. I'm moving on to try my hand at some new research on the states and to finish a book I'm writing on the future of American cities. I've heard from many of you personally in the past 19 years, and have appreciated every letter and e-mail, even (or perhaps especially) the many that took issue with things I've said. I expect to pop up in print in quite a few places in the coming months and years; I hope you'll continue to let me know what you think.

Critical Thinking

1. What, according to Ehrenhalt, was the balance between the vitality of states and the vitality of cities in the late 1980s?

2. What is the balance today?

3. What are some of the changes that have occurred in cities since the late 1980s? In states?

Eminent Domain— For the Greater Good?

The U.S. Supreme Court decision in *Kelo v. New London* has prompted states to look at their own eminent domain practices.

GARRY BOULARD

When Suzette Kelo received a notice from the city of New London, Conn., to vacate her property, little did she or the city know that they were about to embark upon an historic journey that would wend its way to the U.S. Supreme Court. And little did she know that the case that ensued, *Kelo v. New London*, would prompt legislatures in several dozen states to look at their eminent domain practices.

The New London Development Corporation, a public/private effort promoting mixed-use developments, wanted Kelo's property in order to redevelop some 90 acres of her mostly working-class neighborhood. Employing the use of eminent domain, they were trying to make way for a multi-million dollar conference center and hotel complex designed to complement a new $270 million global research facility owned by Pfizer Incorporated.

The city argued that the proposed redevelopment served a "public purpose" by creating new jobs, increasing tax revenue and leading to urban revitalization that would benefit the entire community. Kelo countered that condemning private property for economic development did not qualify as a "public use" under the state and federal constitutions.

But the Supreme Court, in a 5 to 4 vote in June, decided in favor of New London. The Court determined that the comprehensive nature of the city's redevelopment plan, which was adopted pursuant to a state statute, served a public purpose that satisfied the public use requirements of the constitution. It deferred to legislative judgment in defining public use, as it had in previous court decisions. At the same time, the Court invited more state legislation by emphasizing that nothing in its decision precluded a state from restricting the use of eminent domain for economic development purposes.

Lawmakers Step In

Legislatures are following suit. At least 12 states that were in session following the Court's decision considered bills to restrict the use of eminent domain for economic development purposes. Four of them—Alabama, Delaware, Ohio and Texas—passed laws.

For critics of eminent domain, Kelo represents a practice that has become increasingly prevalent. "By our own count, over a 5-year period, we have found about 10,000 instances where a local government either used or threatened to use eminent domain in order to take a home or parcel of property from one person and give it to another," says Dana Berliner, a senior attorney with the Institute for Justice, a property rights group that represented Kelo and her fellow New London homeowners before the Supreme Court.

"It is obviously more widespread and commonly practiced than most people could ever imagine," she says. "And it is a power that essentially allows a government entity to take any person's home away from them, to ruin their business or destroy their lives, whatever the case may be."

Has a Purpose

But for city and state officials across the country, eminent domain is a vital tool, and in some cases the only tool left when it comes to improving a blighted area, transforming dangerous, abandoned and oftentimes drug-infested neighborhoods into modern mixed-use retail and residential complexes that not only create new jobs but also generate tax revenue.

"I can't even imagine how bad it would be if this tool was taken away from us," says William J. Kearns, the general counsel to the New Jersey State League of Municipalities.

"Every city has within its borders large areas of land that are sitting there unused or are in a deteriorated or dangerous condition," says Kearns.

"It would be nice if the owners of these kinds of properties would step forward and arrive at a fair market price for what they own and then sell it," Kearns says. "But all too often, owners can't be found or have no concern about the condition the property is in, and feel no responsibility to the surrounding area. To take

What's Up in Congress?

Congress didn't ignore the Kelo case. Bills were introduced that would withhold some sort of federal funding if a state or locality uses eminent domain for economic development purposes. Most of them do not define economic development.

The most important to watch:

HR 3058, the Transportation, Treasury, Housing and Urban Development, the Judiciary, the District of Columbia and Independent Agencies Appropriations Act of 2006. This bill passed both houses of Congress and is awaiting President George Bush's signature. It will prohibit transportation funds to be used to support state or local projects that seek to use eminent domain powers unless they are for public use. The bill defines public use as mass transit, rail, seaports or airports, utility projects and brownfields. It also calls for a state-by-state study on the nationwide use of eminent domain. Bill sponsors are New Jersey Representative Scott Garrett and Missouri Senator Kit Bond.

HR 4128, the Private Property Rights Protection Act of 2005. It passed the House by a margin of 376–38, and prohibits a state or locality from using eminent domain for economic development or subsequent economic development if the state or locality gets federal economic development funds. So even if the taking is completely in accordance with the state's own statutes and ordinances, the state will lose all federal economic development funds for a period of two fiscal years after a court determines there has been a violation.

HR 4128 also revokes states' constitutionally granted 11th Amendment sovereign immunity and permits private rights of action in state or federal court. Wisconsin Representative James Sensenbrenner is the sponsor.

HR 3405, the Strengthening the Ownership of Private Property Act of 2005. Approved by the House Agriculture Committee by a vote of 40–1, it withholds federal economic development funds if a state or locality uses eminent domain for private commercial development or fails to pay relocation costs to displaced property owners. An amendment limits penalties for two years and allows municipalities to "cure" the violation by returning the properties. The bill's sponsor is Texas Representative Henry Bonilla.

S 1313, the Protection of Homes, Small Businesses and Private Property Act of 2005. This bill would preempt state eminent domain authority by permitting it to be used only for a "public use." It applies to all state and local eminent domain authority that involves federal funding. The bill is in committee. Texas Senator John Cornyn is the sponsor.

There are other bills out there: HR 3083 from Montana Representative Dennis Rehberg, HR 3087 and HR 3268 sponsored by Georgia Representative Phil Gingrey, HR 2980 from Colorado Representative Tom Tancredo and HR 3315 sponsored by California Representative Maxine Waters.

—Susan Parnas Frederick, NCSL

away a city's power to change that means huge areas of blight would remain just that, and would probably only grow larger."

Eminent domain as a tool has been around since the beginning of the Republic. "It is hard to imagine how we would have grown and expanded as a country without eminent domain," says Jon Santemma, the author of "Condemnation Law and Procedures in New York," who also served on the commission that wrote the eminent domain procedure law for the state.

"The growth of the railroad industry would probably never have taken place in the 1800s had it not been for eminent domain, which gave it land to build on," Santemma says. The same can be said of the Tennessee Valley Authority and the first interstate highway network.

But these were public projects, and using eminent domain to acquire property was usually an orderly process with owners selling at a fair market price or through a process of just compensation.

"For years most people really have not paid much attention to this process," says Richard Epstein, a professor of law at the University of Chicago and the author of *Takings—Private Property and the Power of Eminent Domain.*

"Those who were subject to eminent domain accepted the reasons the government gave for wanting to acquire their land," says Epstein. "If there was a battle it had to do with how much the property was worth."

Los Angeles attorney Gary Kovacic says he's been practicing eminent domain law in relative obscurity for 29 years. "Most of that time litigation has centered around things like what is the fair market value of the property or what is the fair market value of the improvements to the property."

But in recent years, Kovacic says a growing percentage of litigation revolves around challenges to the practice of eminent domain. "That was almost unthinkable a generation ago."

Success and Failure

Along its historic waterfront, beginning in the late 1970s, the city of Baltimore launched what has been since hailed as one of the most successful uses of eminent domain. The city acquired some 150 acres of blighted and abandoned properties, including existing businesses, to make way for an urban renovation that included the Rouse company's Harborplace, which would go on to win applause from city planners around the world.

Baltimore was not only able to open up large swaths of land—some of which contained houses from the 18th century—for redevelopment, it was also able to realign city streets so that they would create an easy access to the waterfront.

"The amazing story of Baltimore's revitalization would never have taken place had it not been for the city's willingness to use eminent domain," says Rob Puentes, a fellow with the Brookings Institute's Metropolitan Policy Program.

"In fact, the challenges faced by Baltimore were typical of the challenges faced by many cities in the east and both the older suburban areas and the small towns of the Midwest that have simply run out of room to grow," says Puentes. "The only way they can get a handle on blight and limited growth is to target large sections of the city where redevelopment can only take place if what is already there is removed."

A less successful use of eminent domain, coming just as Baltimore unveiled its Harborplace, occurred in Poletown, a section of Detroit. Some 1,000 homes and 600 businesses in a predominantly Eastern European community were razed to make way for a new General Motors plant.

In 2004 the Michigan Supreme Court, reviewing the process by which eminent domain was used, agreed in a unanimous decision that the local government was "without constitutional authority to condemn the properties." Hundreds of residents said they did not want to leave Poletown and were forced out. But the court decision was too late for them. Most of Poletown's houses and businesses had long since been destroyed.

What separates Baltimore and Poletown from New London, contends New York attorney Jon Santemma, is that "the property in New London was not really blighted or debilitated at all. It was a low-income but stable neighborhood on the waterfront with families who had lived in the same house for generations."

"If eminent domain can be used in a place like New London," says Santemma, "does that mean it can be used almost anywhere else? What are the limits to its use? Is any house safe?"

Even before the *Kelo* decision, some states had been asking themselves those very questions. Arkansas, Florida, Illinois, Kentucky, Maine, Montana, South Carolina and Washington all have court decisions forbidding the use of eminent domain when the purpose is not to eliminate blight.

Since *Kelo*, Alabama, Delaware, Ohio and Texas have passed laws that restrict the use of eminent domain for private development. Alabama Senator Jack Biddle says he was inspired to propose legislation after eminent domain was used in his legislative district: "They just came in and put a bunch of individual stores out of business so that they could make way for a Wal-Mart," Biddle says. "And I didn't like that. None of these stores even had a choice and some of them had been there for 15 or 20 years."

Passed unanimously, Biddle says his bill means that "eminent domain can no longer be used for any for-profit business. It can only be applied to a genuinely declared area of blight—and it has to be that."

In Kansas, Senate Majority Leader Derek Schmidt and Senator Greta Goodwin have proposed a constitutional amendment guaranteeing that private property cannot be taken through eminent domain except for a public use.

"I think the whole issue of eminent domain has become scary to people," says Goodwin. "And this being a rural state where people greatly value their land makes the issue even more important to us."

In Maryland, Delegate David Boschert also is backing a constitutional amendment limiting the state's ability to seize private property for public use only.

"This is becoming one of the most hot-button issues I have ever seen at the state level," says Boschert. "We are hearing more and more about it from our constituents who are upset and angry. And I think they have a right to be."

But others urge caution.

In Connecticut, which generally has been supportive of the use of eminent domain for private development, Representative Michael Lawlor says lawmakers should proceed carefully when it comes to getting rid of a power that can be used for revitalizing economically depressed neighborhoods.

"You want to have the ability to take property if it is necessary to achieve a greater goal," says Lawlor. "But the process by which you accomplish that and the amount of money you have to pay in order to do it ought to be carefully thought out."

Lawlor said he is particularly concerned about public projects that may include private development. Should eminent domain be prohibited in such cases?

"A public economic development project is a lot different than a private developer trying to put in something like a mall," says Lawlor. "Should we really allow one or two property owners to hold out and demand a price so high that they could stop a project altogether? Should we risk creating opportunities for speculators to come in and buy up property and then hold out for top dollar when they sell? I think the potential for abuse exists on both sides."

Caught between trying to promote economic development, particularly in blighted areas, and protecting the rights of homeowners, some lawmakers have decided to take a second look at the process of eminent domain in their states. It is a move that is winning the support of advocates on both sides of the issue.

"It would be wrong to take away the power of eminent domain completely," says Los Angeles attorney Kovacic, who also sits on the city council of Arcadia, Calif. "But I don't think there is anything wrong with inserting as many protections into the process as you can. We can develop rules for making certain the property in question is really blighted. We can require such decisions be made by only a supermajority of the public body that votes on it."

Making certain the process is more open, thinks Puentes of Brookings' Metropolitan Policy Program, "will actually in the long run be good for both sides. It will mean that everyone will have been listened to. It will make it more likely that solutions can be found through negotiation rather than the court room."

Critical Thinking

1. What was the ruling of the U.S. Supreme Court in the *Kelo v. New London* (2005) case?

2. When did the practice of *eminent domain* begin in the United States?

3. For what sorts of projects has *eminent domain* traditionally been used?

4. What policy options relating to eminent domain were available to state legislatures after the Supreme Court's *Kelo v. New London* ruling?

GARRY BOULARD, a frequent contributor to *State Legislatures* magazine, is a freelance writer from Albuquerque, N.M.

Devolution's Double Standard

Alan Ehrenhalt

Somewhere in America, I suppose, there is a public official who believes unreservedly in devolution—believes that power, autonomy and flexibility should reside as far down in the governmental system as practically possible—and is willing to act on the basis of those beliefs, even at the expense of his own political authority.

I have a pretty clear sense of how such a politician would behave; I just never seem to come across one, no matter where in the hierarchy of government I happen to look.

An honest devolutionist would be a president who refused to impose billion-dollar burdens on the states without offering any money to pay for them. Or a governor who didn't find it clever policy to avoid a tax increase at the state level by forcing one on localities. Or a Supreme Court justice who made it a consistent practice to let legislatures enact pretty much any statute they wanted, as long as it didn't involve a blatant violation of the U.S. Constitution. We have no shortage of politicians in America who profess to believe in devolution, and invoke it regularly. What we don't have are public figures willing to follow the concept wherever it might lead.

When it's just a matter of theory, devolution commands virtually unanimous acceptance, all across the ideological spectrum. Devolution has a rich intellectual history in the Roman Catholic Church, where it goes by the name of "subsidiarity"—the principle that, as Pope John Paul II once put it, "a community of a higher order should not interfere with the life of a community of a lower order." There is language endorsing subsidiarity in virtually every document and treaty drawn up to create the current European Union.

On the American left, devolution was an article of faith in the 1960s for the radical Students for a Democratic Society, who saw it as a route to a new kind of participatory democracy through which "our monster cities . . . might now be humanized, broken into smaller communities . . . arranged according to community decision."

Much more familiarly, the Reagan administration in the 1980s, and most conservative Republicans in the years since, have taken it as a similarly self-evident truth that the best government is government close to the people, that the states are closer to the people than Washington is and the localities closer still. The 2000 Republican Party platform vows to restore the force of the 10th Amendment to the U.S. Constitution—the amendment that says any powers not specifically granted to the federal government belong to the states. The platform calls that amendment "the best protection the American people have against federal intrusion and bullying."

The Republicans made this vow just a few months after their House and Senate majorities passed a bill forbidding states to collect sales tax on Internet transactions, without a fig-leaf of an explanation why this was any of the federal government's business. It was a devolution-professing Democratic president, a former governor himself, who signed this measure into law.

One might have expected something different from George W. Bush, a conservative governor of Texas who spent six years in Austin bristling at federal intrusion into his state's affairs. But no such outburst of intellectual consistency was forthcoming.

The Bush administration's No Child Left Behind Act, passed with bipartisan support in 2001, imposes on state and local school systems the burden of administering millions of standardized tests whose cost may eventually be as high as $8 billion. A true believer in devolution might wonder what the federal government is doing in the pupil-testing business. Even an innocent reader of the Republican platform would be entitled to ask why, if the feds think such a burdensome mandate upon the states is really in the national interest, they don't at least have the courtesy to pay for it.

Those arguments didn't gain much headway when the nation's governors showed up in Washington earlier this year to plead for help with their own state deficits, caused to a significant degree by a long list of federal mandates and by the soaring expense of Medicaid, which is a joint state-federal responsibility. "We've got an issue with our own budget," the president told the governors. In other words: You're on your own. Deal with it. But keep those multiple-choice tests coming.

It's enough to make you feel genuinely sorry for the states—until you see them treating their own cities and counties the same way. Last year, North Carolina Governor Mike Easley closed a hole in the state budget by seizing more than $200 million in tax money that had been legally earmarked for local health care, education and criminal justice needs. Wisconsin Governor Jim Doyle proposed last month to cut state aid to localities by nearly $100 million, arguing that cities and counties should find a way to provide police and fire services at lower cost.

Doyle claimed credit for avoiding the humiliation of a state tax increase and warned the localities not to try any tax increases of their own. But the likelihood is that the locals will have to increase property taxes this year just to pay for the services they are required to deliver. They have no choice.

This doesn't just apply to fiscal issues. In Colorado, one of the states most fiercely protective of individual rights and state prerogatives, pro-gun legislators have been trying for the past four years to pass a law requiring local communities to legalize the carrying of concealed weapons, whether the local governments want it legalized or not. What right does the state have to preempt local gun laws? None of the proponents of this change have developed much skill at answering this question. Sam Mamet, a lobbyist for the Colorado Municipal League, has it just about right: "When Congress preempts the states," he says, "these state lawmakers squeal like stuck pigs. And in many cases they're right. And now they're doing it to us."

Nobody is innocent here. The feds stiff the states. The states stiff the cities and counties. Whenever one layer of government can push an unpleasant or costly responsibility down to the level below, it nearly always does so. The cities and counties would do it too, except they are on the bottom rung. They can't cut taxes and services and then pin the responsibility on the Salvation Army. Or at least they haven't thought of that yet.

I suppose if there is one public official in America who deserves to be taken seriously as a consistent devolutionist, it is William Rehnquist, the chief justice of the U.S. Supreme Court. Rehnquist has been a vocal advocate of states' rights since his days as a law clerk in the early 1950s, when he argued that the court's decision in *Brown v. Board of Education* went too far in imposing federal power in defiance of the 10th Amendment.

Nobody can accuse Rehnquist of forgetting about devolution once he acquired a robe of his own. In the past decade, he has ruled against a whole series of congressional statutes, in areas as diverse as gun regulation and sexual abuse of women, on the grounds that the "interstate commerce" language used to justify them provided insufficient reason to constrict state authority.

I'm willing to take Rehnquist seriously as a man who believes in devolution and wants to implement it. Still, when he steps down as chief justice, what will he be best known for: his narrow construction of federal regulatory power, or his court's vague, partisan and dubious use of the federal Equal Protection Clause to overrule the Florida Supreme Court and award the 2000 presidential election to the popular-vote loser, George W. Bush?

It is easy to portray all of these ironies as yet another example of the strong picking on the weak. But there's a dirty little secret here: In a federal system, unreasonable demands from above aren't a sign of strength. They're a sign of weakness.

When the system actually works, as it occasionally does, the leaders at the top of the pyramid do one of two things. They take up a problem, conceive a solution and figure out a way to pay for it—as the feds did with Social Security in the 1930s. Or they withdraw completely and allow lower-level governments to launch the experiments and make the rules. This is essentially what happened with welfare reform, arguably the most successful public policy initiative of the past decade.

When neither of these things happens—when one level of government simply dumps a problem on the level below, it's usually because underneath the bluster, those at the top are clueless about what to do. If the feds had any clear idea how to improve the performance of American education, they'd be promoting it. They wouldn't be telling state and local school systems to spend billions of dollars on standardized tests and then to punish the slackers.

If the U.S. Department of Homeland Security had a coherent vision of what a secure homeland actually was, it would be issuing precise directives to local responders and letting them know how much the work would cost. It wouldn't be barking out useless warnings and issuing color-coded alerts and promising that a check would be in the mail sometime in the future.

And when governors and legislatures boast about holding the line on taxes—when the truth is they are merely forcing higher taxes on those below—that's a form of weakness as well. It's a failure of the political will that democratic governments are supposed to have.

Any mandate from above, unaccompanied by the resources to help comply with it, is a scary experience for those on the receiving end. But it can also be an opportunity: to experiment, innovate and discover that there might be a way to get the job done more efficiently after all. Sometimes it turns out that the forces at the top aren't as powerful as they pretend to be.

Critical Thinking

1. What does "devolution" mean in the context of the three-tiered structure of American government?

2. How is the Roman Catholic Church's principle of "subsidiarity" related to "devolution"?

3. How common does Alan Ehrenhalt think "honest devolutionists" are in the United States? And what distinguishes an "honest devolutionist" from a politician who says that he or she believes in devolution?

4. Why, according to Ehrenhalt, are unreasonable demands that higher levels of government place on lower levels of government a sign of weakness, not of strength?

UNIT 3

Linkages between Citizens and Governments

Unit Selections

Learning Outcomes

- Assess the pros and cons of electronic voting, voting by mail, and voting by old-fashioned mechanical voting machines.

- Predict whether interest groups use different techniques when trying to influence state government policymakers than when trying to influence members of the U.S. Congress.

- Evaluate initiatives, referenda, and recalls as instruments of democratic accountability in state and local governments.

- Explain why many states have provisions for initiatives, referenda, and recalls, while the national government has no such provisions.

- Examine the pros and cons of electing state and local judges.

- Contrast how running for elective office in a small municipality differs from running for a seat in a state legislature or in the U.S. Congress.

- Determine whether local government public meetings contribute in a significant way to democratic accountability.

- Compare the vigor and health of news media reporting about state and local government affairs with national government affairs.

- Predict what sorts of viable alternatives to traditional news media might arise and assess how well they will fill the roles played by traditional news media in the past.

- Illustrate the risks of policy initiatives and referenda by describing the policy consequences of Proposition 13 in California.

Student Website

www.mhhe.com/cls

Internet References

Democratic National Committee (DNC)
www.democrats.org

Pew Research Center for the People and the Press
www.people-press.org

Project Vote Smart
www.votesmart.org

Republican National Committee (RNC)
www.gop.com

The American political system is typically classified as a representative democracy. Top government officials are elected by the people and, as a result, government is supposed to be responsive and accountable to citizens. Both the theory and the practice of representative democracy are of interest to students of American politics. Political scientists study various features that seem essential to the healthy functioning of a representative democracy: political parties, interest groups, election laws, campaign techniques, and so forth. Attention is not limited to the national government alone; state and local governments are also examined in order to assess their responsiveness and accountability.

State and local governments operate under somewhat different institutional arrangements and circumstances than the national government. In many states and some localities, voters can participate directly in the policy process through mechanisms known as initiatives and referenda. In addition, some state and local voters can participate in removing elected officials from office by a procedure known as "recall." In many localities in the New England states, an annual open meeting of all local citizens, called a town meeting, functions as the local government legislature. These mechanisms provide direct avenues for citizens to determine state and local government policies, avenues that are not available to them with respect to the national government.

Generally speaking, party organization is strongest at the local level and weakest at the national level. Party "machines" are a well-known feature of the local political landscape in the United States, and colorful and powerful "bosses" have left their mark on local political history. While the heyday of bosses and machines is past, examples of contemporary political machines still exist. National elections, especially for the presidency, are usually contested vigorously by the two major parties and, over the long haul, the two parties tend to be reasonably competitive. This is less true in states and localities, because a large majority of voters in some states and many localities are decidedly oriented toward one party or the other. Thus, in some states and localities, more significant competition can occur within the nominating process of the dominant party than between the two parties in general elections.

Party labels do not appear on the ballot in many localities, and this may or may not affect the way elections are conducted. In "nonpartisan" elections, candidates of different parties may, in fact, openly oppose one another, just as they do when party labels appear on the ballot. Another possibility is that parties

© Aaron Roeth Photography

field opposing candidates in a less than open fashion. As yet another alternative, elective offices may actually be contested without parties or political affiliations of candidates playing any role. One should not assume that formally nonpartisan elections in state and local governments bring genuine nonpartisanship, but nor should one assume the opposite.

One last feature of the political processes at the state and local level deserves mention here. While members of the Senate and the House of Representatives in Washington, DC, hold well-paid, prestigious positions, their state and local counterparts often do not. Many state legislators are only part-time politicians who earn the bulk of their livelihoods pursuing other occupations. This is also true of most general-purpose local government officials. In addition, most local school board members are unpaid, even though many devote long hours to their duties. That so many elected state and local officeholders do not get their primary incomes from their positions in government may well affect the way they respond to constituents. After all, while they and their families typically live in the community that they are representing, their livelihoods do not depend on being re-elected.

Selections in the first section of this unit address elections, referenda, initiatives, and local government public meetings. The second section treats news media and the changes that are occurring in the context of state and local governments.

On the Oregon Trail

In a backlash against new electronic calamities, vote by mail spreads far beyond its roots, one county at a time.

SAM ROSENFELD

Oregon's statewide vote-by-mail system remains unique—for now. But with little fanfare, liberalized absentee balloting laws elsewhere have prompted a steady expansion of mail voting. In the process, popular support is growing, from the ground up. States are following the gradualist pattern of expansion first set in Oregon. Laws permitting at-will absentee registration in dozens of states, and permanent absentee registration policies in California and elsewhere, are expanding the pool of voters who know and like the process.

Meanwhile, in Arizona, Colorado, and Washington, municipalities and counties have won the option to run all vote-by-mail elections for various contests. More local election administrators are opting for mail balloting to save money and simplify the process. Oregon eventually reached a tipping point of popular support that pushed the entire state to vote by mail; most observers think Washington state has now reached the same point, and other western states are close behind.

This election year may turn out to be the catalytic moment for the expansion of mail voting. Pressure from looming Help America Vote Act (HAVA) and state-level compliance requirements, combined with the continued headaches associated with implementing and securing electronic voting systems, are provoking registrars and election officials in many states to advocate switching to a system that simplifies the process, saves money, and addresses major logistical and security concerns. Meanwhile, for the first time, advocates are organizing nationally and providing cross-state support and coordination for efforts to spread mail voting. Given the ground-level trends, vote-by-mail proponents feel the wind at their backs.

Electoral Quakes

California represents the biggest and least noticed expansion of absentee balloting. The turning point for the Golden State was 2001's enactment of permanent no-excuse absentee voting. Between 2002 and 2005, use of mail voting shot up statewide by more than a million votes, with absentee ballots accounting for 27 percent of votes cast in 2002, 33 percent in 2004, and 40 percent in 2005's special election. As use has expanded

especially quickly in liberal counties, absentee voting's traditional Republican tilt has diminished. (The GOP-Democratic share of the absentee ballot vote was 47 to 41 percent in 1992; in 2005 it was 41 to 41 percent.)

While voters value the convenience, registrars actively encourage absentee voting to relieve administrative costs. "The voters are flocking to voting by mail in droves," reports Elaine Ginnold, registrar of voters for Alameda County, population 1.5 million, which includes the cities of Berkeley and Oakland. Absentee ballots accounted for 36 percent of Alameda's votes in 2004 and 47 percent in 2005's special election.

A state law passed in 2004 requires that electronic machines be equipped with paper trail printers for contemporaneous ballot verification by the voter. Counties across California had already procured machines that lacked such printers, and this year the secretary of state's office took too long to certify new machines for several counties to complete the procurement process in time for June. ("It's $12.7 million down the toilet," remarks Ginnold, referring to 4,000 noncompliant Diebold machines sitting in a warehouse in Alameda County.) Meanwhile, a lawsuit filed this year by California voters and activists seeking to block use of Diebold equipment in the June primary reflects the continued unease electronic machines inspire among significant numbers of voters.

Absentee ballots could well surpass 50 percent of the total California vote share in November. Ginnold sees 60 percent mail voting—which California might reach by the 2008 election—as a tipping point, when popular support will finally prompt either a ballot initiative to make the state all vote by mail or the reticent state legislature to give counties the option to run all-vote-by-mail elections. Either option, Ginnold says, would lead to universal vote by mail statewide. "I think what happened in Oregon is eventually going to happen here."

Going National

Oregon's neighbor to the north, meanwhile, is set to attain all vote-by-mail status imminently, having granted counties the option of choosing comprehensive vote by mail. Permanent-registration absentee balloting was first introduced in Washington state for disabled and elderly voters in the mid-1980s. It was expanded as an option for all voters, with no excuse required, early in the 1990s. "Many counties started having 75 to 85 percent of their voters choosing it," recalls Sam Reed, Washington's Republican secretary of state and a longtime proponent of vote by mail. "So last year I requested a bill to allow counties to exercise an option to go all vote by mail."

So far 34 out of 39 counties have opted for the system, and King County, encompassing Seattle and a full third of the state's registered voters, will likely do so by mid-2007. Most observers predict the remaining four counties will follow suit, and that by 2008, Washington will be the second state in the country to conduct all statewide elections by mail.

Until this year, no national advocacy outfit existed to help accelerate such absentee voting trends and leverage them to boost support for all-vote-by-mail systems. Political consultant Adam J. Smith has stepped into the organizational breach with the Portland-based Vote By Mail Project. Oregon Secretary of State Bill Bradbury serves on its board, and the outfit receives institutional and financial backing from the National Association of Letter Carriers (for obvious reasons, a major proponent of mail voting).

"We're going to support the whole continuum of vote by mail," says Smith, "from no excuse permanent absentee registration, to county option vote by mail, to statewide vote by mail. The natural progression seems to be you need to introduce the issue to people and give them the opportunity to vote this way, and inevitably the majority of people will decide they like it better." States in his sights include not only California but also Arizona, Colorado, and New Mexico—all places where liberalized absentee laws have sparked expanded use of mail balloting in recent years. Meanwhile, the recently formed Progressive Legislative Action Network is also planning to push for liberalized absentee and universal vote-by-mail laws.

Recorders in Arizona's two biggest counties estimate that 60 percent of their ballots for the 2006 midterms will be cast by mail. Phoenix and Tucson will also be holding all-vote-by-mail local elections. Meanwhile, a movement to put a statewide vote-by-mail initiative on the 2006 ballot was born when Rick Murphy, an Arizona Republican businessman, lost a congressional primary challenge in 2004 to Christian right darling Trent Franks. "It became quite obvious to Rick that the system was broken," says Fred Taylor, state director of Your Right to Vote and Murphy's partner in the vote-by-mail ballot initiative. "With a very small minority of the voters, you can win a primary election when there's such a low turnout. Rick wants to see a system that boosts engagement and dilutes the power of interest groups."

It's still early to gauge Murphy and Taylor's prospects in Arizona, but Colorado's experience in 2002 amply illustrates the pitfalls of moving too quickly for statewide change. That year, Democrat Rutt Bridges campaigned for a ballot initiative to make the entire state all vote by mail at a time when counties did not have the option to use the system and voters generally lacked experience with it. Like the majority of ballot initiatives on any issue in any election, it failed. Bridges now reflects that

states should follow a more gradualist strategy for achieving vote by mail, something Colorado has demonstrated since the 2002 loss.

Beginning in 2004, counties gained the option to run all non-partisan elections by mail in Colorado. This year, as in California, federal HAVA requirements for voting machine standards and accessibility are putting a crushing bind on county election officials and provoking requests—initiated by Denver County in February—for waivers to run vote-by-mail elections.

According to a survey of election clerks and counters, counties representing more than 80 percent of the voters in Colorado support switching to vote by mail for the midterm elections to avoid the regulatory chaos of HAVA compliance. If granted by the legislature, these would be onetime emergency waivers, but the record in other states demonstrates that further experience with mail voting invariably boosts public support for expanding the system.

Electronic Hell

Thirty states have spent more than $300 million since 2002 in federal funds to replace punch-card and lever machines with updated voting technology. Certainly there are places where the shift to direct recording electronic (DRE) systems occurred early, went smoothly, and met with general public satisfaction. And, as defenders of electronic voting technology like Ohio State's Daniel Tokaji emphasize, DRE machines do constitute a net improvement over punch-card and lever voting in terms of promoting accessibility and lowering miscount rates. But overall, the process of implementing the system in localities across the country has been marred by more difficulties than most could have imagined, contributing to a debilitating crisis of public confidence in electronic voting technology.

A 2004 North Carolina election for state agricultural commissioner, which collapsed in the wake of a major DRE programming glitch in Carteret County, served as a rallying cry for critics of electronic voting. Last December, election officials and computer experts in Florida's Leon County tested machines provided by Diebold and showed that election results could be manipulated from within the Elections Office with relative ease—and with no one knowing. Diebold responded by cutting off any communication with the county elections supervisor who'd instigated the test. Primary elections this March in Texas and Illinois, where DRE machines were used for the first time on a large scale in many localities, were the latest to be marred by major glitches in the tabulations, due to both machine errors and inadequate poll-worker training.

Also in March, Maryland made the stunning decision to dump its $90 million investment in Diebold machines due to the lack of a paper-auditing trail that could facilitate recounts. The paper-trail issue is a key fulcrum for organized resistance to electronic technology. Twenty-five states now have requirements for voter-verified paper audit trails (VVPAT) like the one in California, which are provoking major bureaucratic complications as officials attempt to graft printing technologies on to pre-existing electronic machines.

Problems with compliance provide the context for lawsuits against electronic voting machine vendors in five states beyond

California. Meanwhile, a lobbying coalition of DRE skeptics gathered on Capitol Hill the first week of April to push for Democrat Rush Holt's bill mandating VVPAT for all electronic machines, programming that allows for independent audits, and hand-counted verification for 2 percent of all ballots cast.

HAVA Heart

As Tokaji himself has demonstrated, grafting VVPAT technology on to existing electronic systems is not only proving to be cumbersome and logistically problematic, it also doesn't provide the panacea to security concerns that advocates think it does. VVPAT provisions heighten the complexity of the voting process, and handcount audits of select ballots have proven to be enormously time-consuming for election officials in places like Nevada, where it has been attempted.

Unfortunately, the response to these dilemmas by many election experts and consultants, invested as they are in the push to "make HAVA work," has been to try to reform electronic voting by plunging ever deeper into the logistical weeds of DRE compliance. Speaking at an American University conference on election reform held in late March, Tokaji listed at least four different teams of researchers and consultants, spanning various universities as well as the National Science Foundation and the National Academy of Sciences, who would be monitoring the 2006 elections and proposing further reforms.

HAVA has spawned a whole techno-academic-industrial complex. At the same conference, voting security expert Avi Rubin of ACCURATE (A Center for Correct, Usable, Reliable, Auditable, and Transparent Elections) proposed a truly daunting array of new reforms to ensure the integrity of electronic voting, from rendering all electronic systems interoperable and their coding open source, to mandating regular "threat analysis, code review, architectural analysis, and penetration testing"—so as to ensure that the system "can be trusted to the same degree as critical military, medical, and banking systems."

But this endless regress, reminiscent of *Mad Magazine's* "Spy vs. Spy," may only be leading experts and officials deeper into electronic Rube Goldberg territory and further away from the basic election reform principles HAVA was meant to address in the first place. And this reality is a big part of the context for the expansion in the ranks of officials and voters on the ground, in state after state, who are coming to prefer a simpler, lower-tech balloting method—snail mail.

Back to the Future

The local and county-level stirrings in Colorado, Arizona, and California are precisely what the Vote by Mail Project hopes to identify and catalyze nationally. But chicken-and-egg questions about process and political culture linger: Does vote by mail work in Oregon and Washington because it's a universally desirable system or because the Pacific Northwest's historic tradition of clean elections allows it to work? Is vote by mail a desirable alternative for, say, a state like Ohio or Illinois—or might it provide new opportunities for fraud and suppression in states lacking clean civic cultures?

There's no real consensus among election experts on this question, but the record of expanded mail balloting in California, Colorado, and elsewhere is virtually free of fraud or major glitches. Leading critics of mail voting, like Curtis Gans, director of the Committee for the Study of the American Electorate, cite the heightened potential for vote buying in the mail-voting process, given the lack of a truly secret ballot. (Gans can, indeed, point to a local vote-buying scandal involving absentee ballots in 2003 city elections in northern Indiana.) But Oregon, Washington, and California have not reported any vote-buying incidents during the years that vote-by-mail use has expanded there, and sustaining such fraud on a large scale without detection would likely be prohibitively difficult. Moreover, to the extent such dangers and potential unknowns remain troubling, the gradual, locality-by-locality expansion of vote by mail thus far will help observers detect problems and make proper adjustments *before* a system is implemented across the board in a given state. "We're not comparing this against 'the perfect system'—that doesn't exist," Adam Smith points out. "Possible problems that might arise can be addressed through best practices."

Proponents note the procedural safeguards built into the Oregon system—most importantly a full registry of digitized signatures that election officials cross-check against voters' signatures on ballot envelopes—that neither exist in the traditional system nor depend for their effectiveness on the honesty and civic virtue of voters. "There are a number of ways to make vote by mail more secure than polling places," says Ann Martens, Secretary of State Bradbury's communications director in Oregon. "Our county elections officials are trained by former state police forensics experts in handwriting analysis . . . [The signature cross-checking] goes through a number of levels where it's either accepted or we eventually contact the voter."

Indeed, the time and ability that vote by mail affords officials to actually contact voters about questionable ballots address a more typical progressive election concern than voter fraud—the prospect of indirect voter suppression by politicized election officials applying deliberately onerous standards to targeted demographics. What if a vote-by-mail official in, say, Ohio, was tempted to reject a significant number of ballots on spurious grounds that the envelope signature didn't match the digitized registration signature? "Checking the signatures is such a process, involving so many workers, it would be really hard to do something like that," says Smith. "Even if you could systematically weed out certain groups, all you're going to do at that point is not in fact disqualify those ballots but force people to prove that they're actually who they say they are. So there are ways to safeguard against that."

Advocates hasten to highlight the real-world polling-place scenarios that have played out in elections past, where perfectly legal neglect and shortchanging of resources on the part of election officials led to logistical bottlenecks in various localities—leading, in effect, to de facto voter suppression. The prospects of such Ohio-style scenarios recurring in future elections would be eliminated with vote by mail—as would the dangers, posed by electronic voting, of a logistical screw up or security breach without the capacity for a recount.

For More Information

Oregon Secretary of State Elections Division (www. sos.state.or.us/elections/). Also housed here: several independent evaluations of voting by mail. See: www.sos.state.or.us/executive/policy-initiatives/vbm/ execvbm.htm.

BlackBoxVoting.org provides consumer protection for elections.

VoterAction.org opposes privatized, electronic voting systems.

VoteTrustUSA.org promotes election integrity nationally.

VoteByMailProject.org provides state-by-state updates on vote-by-mail options.

Electionline.org offers news and analysis on election reform.

FairVote.org promotes inclusion, turnout, fair practices.

League of Women Voters (lwv.org) provides citizen education.

Demos.org promotes broad participation and fair elections.

Another criticism of vote-by-mail systems (also voiced in opposition to early voting provisions) is that the greatly expanded period for voting leads to "differentials in knowledge" among voters. Some might send in their ballot a week and a half prior to Election Day, and an ensuing dramatic event or development may change the dynamics of the race, leaving those early voters unable to change their decisions. But any voting date, whether it lasts one day or two weeks, is arbitrary, and may occur immediately prior to major occurrences that would have changed the electoral result in retrospect. And to the extent that a longer period for voting discourages the late-breaking artificial gimmickry and vicissitudes of political campaigns (as transmuted through media narratives and political advertising), that's more of a plus than a minus. Certainly Oregon's experience hasn't shown much voter discontent with the time differentials in voting, just as the state's experience hasn't revealed any major problems with fraud or logistics. Nor have citizens among the swelling ranks of mail voters in states outside of Oregon.

Indeed, the movement for mail voting represents a striking reversal in a nation that has always been infatuated with new technology. It is proceeding through firsthand experience, county by county, voter by voter, in a fascinating democratic rebellion against both the traditional complications of poll-site voting as well as insecurities associated with newfangled electronic technology imposed from above.

Critical Thinking

1. What is unique about Oregon's voting system?
2. What are the differences and similarities between Oregon's voting system and "liberalized absentee balloting laws" in other states?
3. What is HAVA? How has HAVA affected state governments' inclination to copy Oregon's voting system?
4. What is the Vote By Mail Project and why does the National Association of Letter Carriers support the Project?
5. How does the Pacific Northwest's tradition of clean elections relate to whether vote-by-mail systems are suitable for states with histories of greater electoral corruption?

Caperton's Coal

The Battle Over an Appalachian Mine Exposes a Nasty Vein in Bench Politics

JOHN GIBEAUT

The Harman mine in southwestern Virginia's Buchanan County was a rickety skeleton when lifelong coal man Hugh M. Caperton purchased it in 1993. But Caperton, a native of Slab Fork in neighboring West Virginia, saw gold in those Appalachian hills.

The mine yielded high-grade metallurgical coal, a hot-burning and especially pure variety that steel mills crave to fuel the blast furnaces used to make coke needed in their production process. By the end of 1993, the mine's yield had increased to 1 million tons a year, quadruple its previous output. Caperton also replaced the contract workers who used to ply the precious bituminous with 150 union miners in one of the nation's poorest states.

Then along came A.T. Massey Coal Co. and its CEO, Don L. Blankenship. Massey, which has headquarters in Richmond, Va., wanted the high-grade coal too. But Caperton at first was unwilling to sell, despite what he described as warnings from Blankenship: "He basically threatened me and said, 'Don't take me to court. We spend a million dollars a month on lawyers, and we'll tie you up for years.' "

Blankenship wasn't lying. Through a series of complex, almost Byzantine transactions, including the acquisition of Harman's prime customer and the land surrounding the competing mine, Massey both landlocked Harman with no road or rail access and left Caperton without a market for his coal even if he could ship it.

Caperton finally cried uncle in early 1998 and agreed to sell. But on the day the deal was to go down, Massey got up and walked away, sending Caperton to court instead of the bank.

"On the day of the closing, at 2 o'clock in the afternoon, they called the whole deal off," Caperton recalls. "They tanked us at the last second. It forced us into bankruptcy."

So after a stop at the federal bankruptcy court to file a Chapter 11 petition, he hauled Massey into West Virginia state court on various allegations of fraud and tortious contract interference. He won a $50 million jury verdict.

Blankenship appealed until the last cow straggled home. Besides his efforts in the courtroom, Blankenship also plunged into judicial politics—West Virginia-style—raising some $3 million in 2004 on behalf of an unknown Charleston lawyer named Brent D. Benjamin, who wanted a seat on the West Virginia Supreme Court of Appeals, the state's highest court. Both sides knew the case undoubtedly would wind up there.

Benjamin defeated a controversial Democratic incumbent in the partisan contest for the 12-year term. Sure enough, the case wound up before a court that included new Justice Benjamin.

Concerned that the seven figures in campaign backing could influence the case's outcome, Caperton's lawyers asked Benjamin to disqualify himself. He not only refused but also twice cast the third and deciding vote to reverse the judgment against Massey, the last time on April 3 after rehearing.

But Caperton wasn't quite ready to shrivel and die. The U.S. Supreme Court agreed to review his case in mid-November. In arguments scheduled for March 3, the justices will ponder whether Benjamin violated Caperton's 14th Amendment due process right by accepting the millions in campaign support from Blankenship, then deciding the case anyway.

Benjamin declined comment. Calls to Blankenship and his company's lawyers went unreturned.

Critics complain that tossing around such big bucks jeopardizes the system's integrity and independence by suggesting that justice is for sale on some clearance rack parked behind the courthouse. And a sharp rise in contributions to judicial races moved the ABA Standing Committee on Judicial Independence to attempt to clear up the often foggy rules for disqualification. The committee plans to submit its recommendations to the House of Delegates at the association's 2009 annual meeting in Chicago in August.

"Survey after survey reports that 80 percent of the public believes money influences judicial decision-making," says chair William K. Weisenberg, an assistant executive director for the Ohio State Bar Association in Columbus. "What we're dealing with here is a perception that just isn't right."

Appearances Matter

Judicial disqualification dates to Roman law, which liberally allowed parties to remove jurists deemed "under suspicion." As the English common-law tradition evolved, however, grounds for recusal tightened considerably, focusing nearly exclusively on whether the judge held a financial stake in the case.

As the American version developed, legislators, courts and model ethics codes had little trouble translating some specific conduct into black-letter grounds for recusal.

For example, judges can't hear appeals of cases they've tried. They can't sit on cases where they're material witnesses. Judges who worked as government lawyers can't hear cases in which they previously participated.

Still, there are remnants of British legal thought that create troubling practical and philosophical tensions to this day for U.S. judges facing recusal questions. For one, a duty to sit arose so cases in small jurisdictions won't go wanting for resolution in the absence of an unquestionably evenhanded jurist. The obligation to hear cases can become especially nettlesome for intermediate appeals courts and courts of last resort, where the pool of replacement judges is considerably smaller than at the trial level.

More difficult, however, are accusations of bias, because judges often equate recusal with a failure to impartially administer justice. Disqualification for bias was not an option in England.

In the United States, attempts to identify such situations through statutes and court rules have been less than successful.

Rule 2.11 of the ABA Model Code of Judicial Conduct requires disqualification "in any proceedings in which the judge's impartiality might reasonably be questioned." The ABA and the majority of court jurisdictions stress both actual impropriety and the appearance of impropriety.

While most states and the federal courts have emulated catch-all provisions like the ABA's, only two states have adopted a 1999 addition that demands recusal when a state judge receives a certain amount in campaign contributions from a party or lawyer.

West Virginia is not one of those. It is one of 39 states that picks its judges through some form of election. And while fundraising and consequent conflicts of interest can occur in any scheme—head-to-head partisan elections, nonpartisan races and retention ballots—most of the allegations of conflict seem to arise in partisan elections.

Not surprisingly, lawyers and business interests combine for anywhere from half to two-thirds of money donated to judicial candidates in a given year.

The big money breakout came in 2000, when candidates for state supreme court seats raised $45.6 million, 60 percent more than the $28.2 million raised just two years before, according to the Brennan Center for Justice at New York University School of Law.

That figure dipped to $29 million in 2002, then bounced back to $42 million in 2004. In 2008, state supreme court campaigns were projected to collect nearly $34 million, about the same as in 2006.

Although few judicial races involve fundraising with the intensity found in West Virginia, most judges have to guard against conflicts in their workaday worlds. Even federal judges, with lifetime appointments, must pay attention to what people and what documents pass through their courts. Personal, family, business and professional relationships also can sow seeds for a recusal motion alleging bias.

Still, many judges grope in the dark. No one even knows how often judges are actually asked to withdraw.

U.S. District Judge Charles N. Clevert Jr. of Milwaukee says pro se petitions almost always demand disqualification. Clevert says he relies on the reasonableness of the complaint.

"The first thing that goes through my mind is whether there is anything in the [recusal] motion relating to a prior decision or something in this case," says Clevert.

Even with regular litigators whom he knows, the more facts alleged, the more likely the recusal motion will succeed on grounds of bias in Clevert's court.

"If there are some facts in the reasonableness complaint that aren't way out in left field, then that certainly could trigger a situation that could give rise to a recusal," Clevert says.

In Missouri, state supreme court Judge Michael A. Wolff compares motions for disqualification to juror selection in high-profile cases, where prospective panelists are asked whether they can set aside outside knowledge and decide the case as it's presented in court.

"When the guy says yes, we usually go ahead and let him be seated," Wolff says. Judges especially need to apply that standard to the lawyers who appear before them, he says.

"Judges have special connections with lawyers," Wolff explains. "That's who our friends are. That's who we went to law school with. 'Can I set it aside?' If a judge says, 'Yes, I can,' then he probably can go ahead and sit. But you know what? It can look bad.

"If you can't explain it in a simple sentence, then you probably have something bad," he says. This is where the similarity to jury selection ends.

"Nobody cares who the juror is," Wolff says. "At the end of the case he goes home. He's anonymous. But the judge has a higher calling to set an example."

Weighing the Recusal

In 2003 the ABA offered up another, even stricter addition to the Model Code—since adopted in 11 states—requiring recusal when judges make statements outside court that appear to predispose them to rule a particular way in certain kinds of cases. In 2002, the Supreme Court held in *Republican Party of Minnesota v. White* that such restrictions violate the First Amendment speech rights of judicial candidates.

Indiana University law professor Charles Geyh, author of a report supporting the ABA recommendations, says the states have yet to demonstrate a full understanding of the *White* case.

"When it does come, it will be harder to disqualify judges because it puts them at odds with the electorate when you can't do what you promised," says Geyh.

The dearth of case law or other documentation also makes it tough to determine exactly why judges reject disqualification attempts. Geyh's report offers some suggestions.

Judges, he says, may refuse motions because they truly believe they can act fairly. Others may decline if they detect an attempt to gain a more sympathetic venue.

In some cases, clever court operators could try to force recusals of unsympathetic judges by seeding their campaign funds with donations. And granting a recusal motion could seem an endorsement of accusations.

Most often, however, lawyers are reluctant to ask for recusal for fear of failure.

"I always say if you're going to shoot the tiger, you'd better kill the tiger," Wolff says. "If you don't kill the tiger, then you're going to have one angry tiger."

While disqualification proceedings usually go unnoticed in the shadows, many potential conflicts, such as modest campaign giving, simply don't rise to the level of disqualification.

Caperton's lawyers could face questioning from the Supreme Court justices on what amounts may affect due process and thus open a disqualification inquiry. Though White addressed verbal comments by candidates, the justices also have long held that campaign donations are a form of First Amendment expression. But cases like the $3 million lunker from West Virginia are hard to hide.

"The magnitude and timing of the campaign contributions here gave Justice Benjamin, in appearance if not in fact, a personal interest in the outcome of this case," the ABA argued in an amicus brief supporting Caperton's cert petition. "If the facts of this case do not implicate due process concerns, then few judicial contribution cases ever will."

Caperton's lawyers call the case one of a kind. Though Massey CEO Blankenship apparently had shown little interest in donating to other political campaigns for statewide offices like governor or the legislature, he didn't mess around in channeling millions of dollars and other means of support to elect Benjamin.

In motions asking Benjamin to recuse himself, Caperton's lawyers recited Blankenship's fundraising and spending in head-throbbing detail. One version regurgitates a 26-page chunk of factual recitations and argument along with 84 appendices and exhibits.

"It's been surreal—what happened in that litigation," says Caperton lawyer David B. Fawcett of Pittsburgh. "We've never seen anything like what occurred."

Upping the Ante

As his options began to wane for getting the $50 million judgment reduced or tossed out, Blankenship moved quickly. In August 2004 he formed a section 527 organization— so named for the part of the Internal Revenue Code that allows such groups to collect money to support or oppose candidates.

Blankenship's 527, called And for the Sake of the Kids, was designed not to work for Republican challenger and political novice Benjamin, but to use televised attack ads to work for the defeat of Warren McGraw, the Democratic incumbent. McGraw was under intense public heat for joining an unsigned opinion that placed a convicted child molester on probation. Blankenship also maintained that "anti-business rulings" by McGraw poisoned the Mountain State's economic climate.

Of the $3.6 million the group raised, $2.4 million came from Blankenship, with 25 other contributors uniting to shell out the remaining $1.1 million. The organization ranked fifth nationally among other 527s in the amount raised in a state election. Blankenship also contributed $515,000 in direct support to Benjamin's campaign committee, while other donors chipped in the remaining $330,000 of the $845,000 the committee raised.

Then Benjamin went public.

"Nobody, including the people we practice law with, knew who Brent Benjamin was," says Caperton lawyer Bruce E. Stanley of Pittsburgh. "Then the billboards started popping up."

They asked a good question: "Who is Brent Benjamin?" Stanley realized a political machine had started its engine. Benjamin drove it right over McGraw in the November 2004 election, garnering 53 percent of the vote.

By November 2007, the Caperton case arrived at the state high court and was promptly ushered out on a 3-2 vote that reversed the $50 million award and included Benjamin in the majority. Benjamin supplied the decisive third vote on rehearing in April 2008 to again pitch the judgment.

Benjamin never acknowledged Caperton's disqualification motions. Caperton's lawyers never got to argue them orally or received an explanation for the decision.

Riviera Snapshot

Meanwhile, Blankenship's relations with other members of the high court began receiving notice in early 2008 when photos surfaced of Blankenship vacationing on the French Riviera with Justice Elliott "Spike" Maynard. Though he insisted he paid his own way and did nothing wrong, Maynard withdrew from the coal case in January 2008. His term as a justice ended last year with his defeat in the May primary. He did not respond to requests for comment.

Meanwhile, Justice Larry V. Starcher, an especially vociferous and public critic of Massey and its practices, had a run-in with Blankenship, who not only wanted him off the Caperton matter but also has asked the U.S. Supreme Court to use his harsh attacks to disqualify Starcher from another Massey case, *Massey Energy Co. v. Wheeling-Pittsburgh Steel Corp.*

Starcher, who retired in January, dissented in the first Caperton decision but withdrew before the rehearing. He declined comment, but in his written recusal he hinted that Blankenship had disrupted the state supreme court's business.

"The simple fact of the matter is that the pernicious effects of Mr. Blankenship's bestowal of his personal wealth, political tactics and 'friendship' have created a cancer in the affairs of this court," Starcher wrote.

Benjamin did not write an opinion when the court again held for Massey on April 3. Caperton asked the U.S. Supreme Court for cert on July 2. Three weeks later, Benjamin added a concurrence to the state court's April ruling.

Caperton had not accused Benjamin of acting improperly or actually being prejudiced by the campaign contributions. But from Benjamin's perspective, actual bias is all that counts in West Virginia.

"The fundamental question raised by the appellees and the dissenting opinion herein is whether, in a free society, we should value 'apparent or political justice' more than 'actual justice,'" Benjamin wrote in the concurrence, filed July 28.

"Actual justice is based on actualities," he asserted. "Through its written decisions, a court gives that transparency of decision-making needed from government entities. Apparent or political justice is based instead on appearances and is measured not by the quality of a court's legal analysis, but rather by the political acceptability of the case's end result as measured by dominant partisan groups such as politicians and the media, or by the litigants themselves. Apparent or political justice is based on half-truths, innuendo, conjecture, surmise, prejudice and bias."

The Fear Factor

Fawcett says it's too easy to simply blame the decision on a political atmosphere unique to West Virginia. He suggests that Massey's economic power also loomed large in the background. Massey is the nation's fourth-largest coal company and the state's major employer.

"There are certain people who will say that's just the way it is down there, including Don Blankenship," Fawcett says. "But people were afraid. He's the largest employer in the state. Who's going to call him out on that? Even the lawyers were quiet. They all were afraid."

In the short run, Fawcett, Stanley and their client are headed to Washington, D.C., where former Solicitor General Theodore B. Olson will argue their position to the justices. Long term, both lawyers are in agreement when asked how to solve the campaign contribution conundrum once and for all: "The easiest and simplest way to do it is through public financing."

Taxpayer funding may be the most viable option. Last spring, in *Duke v. Leake,* the Richmond, Va.-based 4th U.S. Circuit Court of Appeals affirmed North Carolina's state financing scheme, the nation's first for judicial elections. The Supreme Court declined to review its decision.

To be sure, disqualification issues involving bias still can arise in publicly financed systems. Nevertheless, state campaign funding appears to relieve pressure on judges and dampen the giving spirits of the usual suspects in recusal proceedings.

In an amicus brief filed with the 4th Circuit, former North Carolina judges maintained that the 2002 law works and has attracted participation by a majority of candidates. Perhaps more telling, contributions from business interests in 2004 judicial races were only a third of those in 2002. Contributions from lawyers dropped by 75 percent.

"As a result, the public is less likely to feel that wealthy parties with access to wealthy attorneys who have contributed to judicial campaigns are treated more favorably than those without such access," the former judges maintained.

Meanwhile, the ABA judicial independence panel postponed its proposals until summer in order to accommodate a decision in the Caperton case and to respond to comments on a draft report and recommendations circulated in October. As things stood in the fall, the committee planned to present a list of principles on which to base specific policies and procedures to govern disqualification.

"What we need to do is create clarity," says chair Weisenberg. "We run into a lot of gray here. We want to clear up the gray as much as possible to assist the judiciary." Highlights of the draft recommendations include:

- Disclosure by a judge, at the start of a case, of "all information known by that judicial officer that might reasonably be construed as bearing on that judicial officer's impartiality."

- Recusal decisions made by a judge other than the subject of a disqualification motion. In Illinois, for instance, disqualification motions are automatically reassigned. Judges can testify on their own behalf, but they are not required to do so.

- A more rigorous standard of appellate review, particularly in states where judges review their own recusal. While great deference is given to the decisions of a trial judge in most cases, the ABA argues that standard should change when the judge is, in effect, reviewing himself.

- Written response to a contested disqualification motion. By explaining a recusal decision, a judge reassures the parties and the public, and creates a record of his reasoning for use in any appeals.

- Peremptory challenges, which allow a lawyer to remove a judge without cause, much the same as in jury selection. Such challenges—already permitted in Arizona—would allow reassignment within 10 days and cannot be for delay.

At 53, Caperton says the case has taken its toll not only on his bank account, but also on his health.

"It's miserable," he says. "It's like living in purgatory. It's cost me everything I've got. I've spent every nickel I've ever had trying to right this wrong."

At the end of a two-hour interview, Caperton pauses to consider his daughter, born just a few months before the case was filed. The 11-year-old must figure her dad is a lawyer, Caperton says, because he regularly hangs out with them so much in court. "That's all she's ever known."

Critical Thinking

1. What steps did the A.T. Massey Coal Company take to thwart Hugh Caperton's profitable operation of the Harman coal mine in Virginia?

2. What was the outcome of the West Virginia jury trial that originally settled Caperton's suit against Massey for fraud and tortious contract interference?

3. How were campaign contributions and West Virginia's system of electing Supreme Court judges related to the outcome of Massey's appeal of the jury trial verdict?

4. What is "recusal" and what are some of the many competing ideas or rules for when recusal is appropriate or even required? In how many states are judges chosen through some sort of elections, and what "recusal" or "judicial disqualification" rules or practices apply to elected judges?

5. How long has the Caperton-Massey legal battle lasted and what effect has it had on Hugh Caperton, who filed the original lawsuit against the Massey Coal Company?

The No-Tax Pledge

In the nine states that don't levy a personal income tax, the politics of staying that course remains powerful.

JONATHAN WALTERS

I n New Hampshire, it's called "taking the pledge," a quadrennial exercise that every gubernatorial candidate must sedulously pursue: He or she must vow neither to offer up nor support establishing a state personal income tax. To do otherwise is to commit political seppuku, minus the knife.

New Hampshire is one of nine states—including Alaska, Florida, Nevada, South Dakota, Tennessee, Texas, Washington and Wyoming—that doesn't raise revenues through an income tax. But with states desperately casting about for ways to balance budgets, it would seem that such ironclad vows demanded in New Hampshire might be softening. After all, many economists praise the income tax for its progressive nature and fortuitous tendency to grow over time.

In Texas, Dick Lavine, a senior fiscal analyst at the Center for Public Policy Priorities, argues that an income tax is a critical staple of a mature and balanced state tax system. "It's inevitable if you want to operate a modern and well run state," he says. "Sales taxes just aren't as elastic. They get hit sooner in a recession, and they stay down longer. Plus, an income tax helps offset the regressivity and performs better over the long run than a sales tax."

It would seem to be empirically true that an income tax is vital to a balanced and up-to-date revenue mix—after all, 41 states have one. But arguments like Lavine's haven't been getting much traction in the states that continue to raise cash primarily through sales, property and other taxes.

"Given how bad state revenues have been during this recession, you would think it would be a time when such a tax might become attractive," says Senior Fellow Don Boyd, who closely tracks state fiscal issues for the Rockefeller Institute of Government. "But given the attitude toward taxes around the country, it's highly unlikely."

Fiscal experts confirmed Boyd's hunch in most of the nine states. In some, legislators routinely float proposals for instituting an income tax, usually with some offset that tinkers with existing taxes. And in virtually all states where the proposition seems to be a non-starter, there were efforts in the recent past that considered where an income tax might fit into a state's overall revenue raising strategy. None, however, led to a new tax.

The last time anyone talked about it in Wyoming was a decade ago. Former Republican Gov. Jim Geringer and the Legislature convened a tax commission—the Wyoming Tax Reform 2000 Committee—to look at what many viewed as the state's fiscally unhealthy overreliance on minerals taxes.

"The commission came back with a recommendation to implement an income tax and the governor said, 'Forget it,'" says Dan Neal, executive director of the Equality State Policy Center in Casper, Wyo. "Then came the energy boom in 2001, and a healthy pile of mineral tax revenues with it."

John Schiffer, the highly respected Republican chairman of the Wyoming Senate Revenue Committee, concedes that the state's heavy reliance on minerals taxes—about 50 percent of the state's revenues come from such taxes—is still a concern, but quickly adds that there has been no serious discussion of implementing an income tax since the Geringer tax commission report. At that time, Schiffer remembers, "An income tax was proposed as a third leg under the table. But when the revenue committee brought it up, it just went nowhere."

Not that Wyoming is against new taxes. Recently the Legislature voted to tax wind—from wind farms, that is. In 2012, a wind turbine tax goes into effect.

T he extent to which income taxes are a taboo subject seems to depend on the economic climate and who's in power. A decade ago, when Wyoming was seeing mineral taxes crash, it was at least acceptable to float the income-tax concept, especially when it was a Republican who was pushing the tax-mix analysis. Today, however, with the nation's economy limping along and a national debate occurring around whether taxes enhance or stifle economic growth, there's a sense that taxing income isn't politically viable in the states that don't levy it.

There's a sense that taxing income isn't politically viable in the states that don't levy it.

The last time the idea was discussed in Tennessee—in the early 2000s by former Republican Gov. Don Sundquist—the electorate's emotional response made it clear that Tennesseeans wanted no part of such a tax, says Bill Fox, director of the University of Tennessee's Center for Business and Economic Research. "The Nashville radio talk shows got hold of it," he says, "and got people riled up." Not even such well respected politicians as former Democratic Gov. Ned McWherter and former Republican Sen. Howard Baker, who teamed up to tour the state and proclaim concern over the state's tax system, could sway minds. In what might be seen as a pre-tea party outbreak, a handful of citizens even tossed rocks at the Capitol.

If anything, Fox says, the current political atmosphere around government and taxes makes the proposition even more distant. "It's absolutely off the table," he says.

Illustrating the issue's long-standing political volatility in the pertinent states is South Dakota, which came one vote away from enacting an income tax in the 1970s. With Democrats controlling the Legislature and the executive mansion for the first time in decades, the bill had passed the House, and former Gov. Richard Kneip vowed to sign it upon the Senate's approval. But the Senate was deadlocked, and so it fell to Democratic Lt. Gov. Bill Dougherty (who died in July) to cast the vote that would put the tax over the top. "He was the governor's pick," says Jim Fry, director of the South Dakota Legislative Research Council, "and so you would think he'd be in his camp. But he had real political aspirations, so he voted against the tax."

Meanwhile, some states never talk of instituting an income tax. Florida, for instance, has a prohibition written right into the state constitution. "It's not a political litmus test here," says Robert Weissert, director of communications for Florida Tax-Watch. "It's completely off the table. We have a consumption-based economy here, and so we have a consumption-based tax system."

As if a constitutional prohibition wasn't enough, a recent voter initiative now requires that any new statewide tax can only be enacted with two-thirds of the votes in an election. "So that's why I can say unequivocally that barring a constitutional convention, it's just not in the culture here," Weissert says.

Like Florida, Nevada depends heavily on tourism and taxing consumption, and it has seen its revenues crash along with the tourist trade. There has been some talk of a corporate income tax, reports Patrick Gibbons, a policy analyst with the Nevada Policy Research Institute, but nary a mumble about one on personal income—in no small part because Nevada, like Florida, has the income-tax prohibition written into its constitution.

Nevada does, however, indirectly get at personal income: It taxes a business' total payroll at 1.3 percent. It's not exactly an income tax, nor is it a corporate income tax. The latter was going to be the subject of a legislative study this year, but even the idea of studying a corporate income tax wound up dead on arrival in Carson City.

Currently one state out of the nine is seriously considering enacting an income tax. This November, Washington state will include Initiative 1098 on the ballot. It proposes to enact an income tax on individual Washingtonians making more than $200,000 a year; $400,000 for couples filing jointly. By way of politically sweetening the deal, the ballot measure reduces state property taxes by 20 percent and eliminates the state's business and occupations tax—collected on gross receipts, not profits—for 80 percent of businesses in the state. If passed, the proposal would raise $1 billion in revenues. Use of that money is also specified in the measure: It would go toward reducing class size and funding the state's Basic Health program.

Initiative 1098 is the lagged result of a tax study commission convened about eight years ago and led by Bill Gates Sr. Gary Locke, who was governor at the time, had appointed the Gates Commission to look at the state's tax mix. By the time the commission reported its recommendations—which included enacting an income tax—the political climate was already swinging hard against the notion of a new tax. (In her 2004 and 2008 campaigns, Democratic Gov. Christine Gregoire did, in fact, take Washington's version of "the pledge," but she also proposed and won a considerable increase in state gas taxes shortly after taking office.)

This year though, backed by labor unions and a strong push from the elder Gates, proponents of an income tax in Washington managed to gather enough signatures to get the tax measure on the November ballot. Currently polls have the state split at just about 50-50 on the new tax.

Even if Washington voters enact the tax, it likely won't signal the beginning of any softening when it comes to other states' inclination toward expanding revenue options. The concept will no doubt continue resurfacing in some of the other eight states, depending on who's in power and the economy's condition. But right now, the anti-tax mood seems set, and Alaska appears to exemplify that mood. "It's in the air we breathe," says Lawrence Weiss, executive director of the Alaska Center for Public Policy. "This is 'no-income-tax' air up here."

Critical Thinking

1. What does "taking the pledge" mean in New Hampshire?
2. How many states do not raise revenues through a personal income tax?
3. What are the advantages of a personal income tax in the context of a state's overall tax system?
4. What are the electoral realities faced by any candidate for governor in a state without a personal income tax?
5. What economic circumstances make establishing a state personal income tax more likely? Are Republicans or Democrats generally better positioned to make such a proposal?
6. What particulars distinguish Wyoming from most of the other states without personal income taxes? Florida?

From *Governing*, October 2010, pp. 39–40. Copyright © 2010 by e.Republic Inc. Reprinted by permission via Wright's Media. contract #77805.

California, Here We Come

Government by plebiscite, which would have horrified the Founding Fathers, threatens to replace representative government.

PETER SCHRAG

This June marks the twentieth anniversary of the passage of Proposition 13, the California voter initiative that has in many respects had a political and social impact on this era—not just in California but across much of the nation—almost as profound and lasting as that of the New Deal on the 1930s, 1940s, and 1950s.

The effect on California—which had been well above the national average in what it spent to educate its children, to provide free or nearly free higher education to every person who wanted it, for highway construction, and for a range of social services for children and the needy—was traumatic. Cutting local property taxes by more than 50 percent and capping the tax rate at one percent, Proposition 13 and the various initiatives that followed in its wake forced California to a level of spending far below the national average for such things as K–12 schooling, public-library services, the arts, and transportation. The respected journal *Education Week* said last year of California schools, "a once world-class system is now third rate." Even with a booming economy, California remains in the bottom third among the states, and far below the other major industrial states, in what it budgets per pupil.

Just as important, the march of ballot initiatives, the attack on legislative discretion, and the related acts of "direct democracy" that Proposition 13 helped to set in motion—involving taxes and spending, affirmative action, immigration, school policy, environmental protection, three-strikes criminal sentences, term limits, campaign reform, insurance rates, and virtually every other public issue—continue with unabated force, in California and beyond. In November of 1996 voters in twenty-three states were polled on a total of ninety initiatives, the most in more than eighty years (a decade ago there were forty-one), on everything from hunting rights to gambling to logging regulations to sugar production to the legalization of medical marijuana use (which was approved in Arizona and California).

This June, as if to honor the anniversary of Proposition 13, Californians will again confront a large array of sometimes nearly incomprehensible ballot measures, among them yet another one on term limits and one that would all but end bilingual education. Each proposed reform further restricts the power of the legislature and local elected officials to set priorities, respond to new situations, and write budgets accordingly. When half of the state's tax-limited general fund must, under the terms of one initiative, be spent on the schools; when a sizable chunk must, under the mandate of the state's three-strikes measure, be spent on prisons; and when lesser amounts must, under the terms of still other initiatives that have been approved in the past decade, be spent on the repayment of bonds for parkland and transportation projects, the amount left over for everything else shrinks with Malthusian inevitability—as does the state government's capacity to cope with changed circumstances. When cities and counties are prohibited from raising property-tax rates beyond Proposition 13's one percent, and when it is difficult to raise other revenues without a vote of the electorate (in many instances a two-thirds vote) or of the affected property owners, local control is drastically reduced.

Just as inevitably, public policy is increasingly distorted by the shifting of costs from the general fund to the Byzantine system of fees, assessments, and exactions that local governments have devised in their attempts to get around tax limits and other restrictions. This reinforces the larger shift from a communitarian to a fee ethic—in the support of parks and playgrounds, in the construction of new schools, and in financing a range of other services that used to be funded entirely from general taxes. As one California letter writer complained to a newspaper, why should citizens contribute to "the methodical pillaging and plundering of the taxpayer, forcing those who have no kids to pay through the nose for someone else's"?

Direct democracy is an attractive political ideal, as close to our own experience as the New England town meeting. It has never worked, however, in large, diverse political communities, and the belief that electronics, direct mail, and televised slogans can replace personal engagement has so far looked far more like fantasy than like anything derived from hard political experience. In the case of the initiative, the new populism—unlike the reform movement that wrote the initiative into the constitutions of nineteen states around the turn of the century—seems to want greater engagement in government less than it wants an auto-pilot system to check government institutions with little active involvement by the citizenry beyond occasional trips to the polls to vote on yet more initiatives.

Nothing in California's initiative process presents the downside or the implications of any issue.

California sparked the anti-government, anti-tax mood that has gripped the nation for most of the past two decades, and it remains the most extreme illustration of that mood, a cautionary tale for those enamored of plebiscitary democracy. But it is now hardly unique. Virulent anti-institutionalism, particularly with respect to government, has become a prevailing theme in our national political discourse. A decade after Ronald Reagan left office, his facile dismissal of government as "the problem," not the solution, remains a talk-show staple, a posture that serves to exonerate both civic laziness and political ignorance. And this attitude, which has become banal toward representative government, now also encompasses the related institutions of constitutional democracy: the courts, the schools, the press. Voting and serious newspaper readership are declining together. The communitarian civic ideal that they represent is giving way to "markets," a fee-for-service ethic, and the fragmented, unmediated, unedited exchange of information, gossip, and personal invective.

The media—new and old alike—may ensure against the power of Big Brother to dominate communications, but they also proliferate shared ignorance at an unprecedented rate: what used to be limited to gossip over the back fence is now spread in milliseconds to a million listeners during the evening commute, and to thousands over the Internet. And at the fringes are the militias and the "patriots," collecting weapons and supplies, training in the hills, and hunkering down against the black helicopters and the coming invasion of United Nations troops. That kind of ignorance and extremism, the new media, and the surrounding paranoia about government have all become commonplace in the past decade. Oliver Stone's *JFK* and the videos promoted by Jerry Falwell about the alleged murder of Vincent Foster work the same territory.

Tracy Westen, the president of the foundation-funded Center for Governmental Studies, in Los Angeles, has constructed a "digital scenario" for the election of 2004—a not altogether wild fantasy about thirty-five California voter initiatives on various subjects, all of which have been circulated for "signatures" online, along with a spectrum of arguments pro and con, available at the click of a voice-activated mouse, from every conceivable source. In combination with a number of new elective offices, including drug commissioner and gay-rights commissioner, those measures contribute to a total of 200 ballot decisions for each voter to make.

Among Westen's futuristic initiatives is one urging Congress to approve an amendment to Article V of the U.S. Constitution

such that the language guaranteeing every state a "Republican form of government" is modified to permit the states to replace representative democracy with direct democracy. Westen points out that most of the technology for this politopia—individually targeted campaign ads, interactive "discussions" with candidates, electronic voting—already exists. Since "state legislatures seem to be fighting more and doing less . . . and leaving the real legislation to the people," the scenario continues, "it seems the trend toward 'democracy by initiative' is inevitable." A few years ago the Canadian fringe Democratech Party wanted to submit all government decisions to the public through electronic referenda. An official Democratech statement said,

> Representative government assumes that the people need to elect someone to represent them in a faraway legislative assembly. But with modern, instantaneous communications, the people can directly make their own decisions, relegating politicians to the scrap heap of history.

Three years ago The Economist mused about the possible benefits of replacing representative democracy with Swiss-style direct democracy, in which the voters "trudge to the polls four times a year" to decide all manner of plebiscitary questions. This process would prevent lobbyists and other special interests from buying the outcome, because "when the lobbyist faces an entire electorate . . . bribery and vote-buying are virtually impossible. Nobody has enough money to bribe everybody."

California shows that the process of bedazzling voters with sound bites, slogans, and nuanced bias works as effectively in the initiative process as it does in electoral politics. Offers that sound like something for nothing (a 50 percent property-tax cut, or a guaranteed level of education funding, or a state lottery offering a payoff for schools as well as for the lucky winners) may not be bribes, but they are the nearest thing to them. And when they work at the ballot box, their effects may last far longer than those of conventional legislation.

The larger danger, of course, is precisely the nondeliberative quality of the California-style initiative, particularly in a society that doesn't have the luxury of slow alpine trudges during which to reflect on what it's about to do. Nothing is built into the process—no meaningful hearings, no formal debates, no need for bicameral concurrence, no conference committees, no professional staff, no informed voice, no executive veto—to present the downside, to outline the broader implications, to ask the cost, to speak for minorities, to engineer compromises, to urge caution, to invoke the lessons of the past, or, once an initiative is approved by the voters, to repair its flaws except by yet another ballot measure (unless the text of the initiative itself provides for legislative amendment). Indeed, if the past decade of initiatives in California demonstrates anything, it is that the majoritarianism essential to the ethos of direct democracy almost inevitably reinforces an attitude of indifference if not hostility toward minority rights. All these dangers would be exacerbated, of course, by electronic or other forms of absentee balloting, whereby voters would no longer be required to go to the local school or church or social hall and encounter their fellow citizens participating in the same civic ritual—and thus be reminded that they are, after all, part of a larger community.

To say all that, probably, is merely to say awkwardly what the Framers of the Constitution said better in Philadelphia, what Hamilton, Madison, and Jay said in *The Federalist*, and what scores of delegates said in 1787–1788 at the various state conventions leading up to ratification, even before the Terror of the French Revolution: unchecked majorities are a danger to liberty almost as great as oligarchs and absolute monarchs.

Among the most common measures, put on the ballot by the organization U.S. Term Limits in fourteen states and passed in 1996 by voters in nine, is the "Scarlet Letter" initiative, also known as the "informed voter" initiative, which instructs a state's elected officials to support a constitutional amendment limiting members of the House of Representatives to three two-year terms and members of the Senate to two six-year terms, and which requires state election officials to indicate on the ballot next to the name of each congressional incumbent and each member of the legislature whether he or she "disregarded voters' instruction on term limits." It also requires nonincumbents to indicate whether they have signed a pledge supporting the amendment; those who have not will be similarly identified on the ballot. For Paul Jacob, who heads U.S. Term Limits, no compromise is acceptable. The watchword is "No Uncertain Terms" (which also happens to be the name of the organization's newsletter).

Jacob's very inflexibility helped to derail a more moderate term-limits amendment when it came up in the House (for the second time) early last year. It would have allowed six two-year terms in the House and two six-year terms in the Senate. By denouncing it as a sellout, U.S. Term Limits helped to ensure that no term-limits amendment was approved, and thus that the organization would enjoy a long, healthy life. The large turnover in Congress in 1994 probably took enough steam out of the movement to reduce its chances of success, but not enough to end it.

Ballot initiatives reduce the power and accountability of legislatures—and thus the ability to govern.

The Scarlet Letter initiative is probably unconstitutional. (U.S. Term Limits is now asking individual candidates to pledge to serve no more than three terms in the House or two in the Senate.) In Arkansas, one of the nine states that passed it in 1996, the state supreme court struck it down, as a violation of the procedures set forth in the U.S. Constitution for amendment. Because the drafters of the Constitution, in the words of the Arkansas court, "wanted the amending process in the hands of a body with the power to deliberate upon a proposed amendment . . . all proposals of amendments . . . must come either from Congress or state legislatures—not from the people." The

U.S. Term Limits measure was "an indirect attempt to propose an amendment . . . [that would] virtually tie the hands of the individual members of the [legislature] such that they would no longer be a deliberative body acting independently in exercising their individual best judgements on the issue."

There are scattered indications that the rabid anti-government fervor of the early nineties may have peaked. (One of those indications, in the view of Nancy Rhyme, who tracks the issue for the National Conference of State Legislatures, is that only nine passed the Scarlet Letter initiative.) Certainly, term limits are not likely to be written into the Constitution any time soon.

But the issue will not go away, either in national politics or in the eighteen states that now have term limits for their legislatures written into their constitutions or otherwise written into law. On almost the same day that term limits failed (again) in the House early last year, the Scarlet Letter, funded largely by U.S. Term Limits and a handful of out-of-state term-limits organizations, qualified for the next California ballot. (U.S. Term Limits kicked in about $300,000 to the campaign to qualify the California "informed voter" measure but won't, of course, disclose where its money comes from. The organization is willing to provide a list of its National Finance Committee members, all of whom are said to have contributed more than $1,000, but will not specify which among them are its largest contributors.) A few months later the long-established California organization Field Poll reported that voter support of term limits, which stood at roughly two thirds, remained just as strong as it had been in 1990, in the months before California approved term limits for legislators and other state officials.

Nor has the initiative process lost its allure. Twenty-four states have some form of initiative in their constitutions, most of them dating from the Progressive Era. Recently there have been moves in a number of other states—including Rhode Island and Texas—to write the initiative process into their constitutions.

The pressure does not come from Hispanics or other newly active political groups, who tend to vigorously oppose these constitutional changes as openings to yet more measures like California's Proposition 187—which, until it was blocked by a federal court, sought to deny schooling and other public services to illegal immigrants. Rather, the impetus is from Ross Perot's United We Stand America and other organizations that are overwhelmingly white and middle-class. And in the states that already have the ballot initiative, there is increasing pressure to use it, sometimes generated by the dynamics of political reform itself. In California, political officeholders, from the governor down, have become initiative sponsors as a means of increasing name recognition and raising or stretching political campaign funds. And as initiatives circumscribe the power and discretion of legislatures, often the best way of responding to new circumstances—and sometimes the only way—is through yet another initiative. The result, for better or worse, is an ongoing cycle of initiative reform, frustration, and further reform.

Yet despite all the unintended consequences and the inflexibility of the initiative and other devices of direct democracy, they seem to have one thing in common, whether they are used by liberal environmentalists or by tax-cutting conservatives: they are the instruments of established voter-taxpayer groups, particularly the white middle class, against urban politicians and political organizations that represent the interests and demands of minorities, immigrants, and other marginal groups. At the turn of the century the Yankee establishment in Boston and other cities sought to create political institutions and devices to dilute the power of the upstart Irish. In its impulse and spirit the current pressure for plebiscitary solutions driven by the general electorate, in which the white middle class can still dominate, is not all that different.

The celebratory history of direct democracy centers on its inclusiveness, but in our politically more sophisticated (and no doubt more cynical) age there is a need to understand that defense of the initiative may be less disinterested than it seems. The groups that embrace and cheer it are not just "the people" fighting "the interests" or "the politicians," much less battling "Satan" and "Mammon," as the editor of the Sacramento Bee put it in the heyday of the Progressives. They are often established political interest groups trying by extraordinary means to further a cause or repulse the advances of other groups. More important, each initiative reduces the power and accountability of legislatures—and thus the general ability to govern, meaning the ability to shape predictable outcomes. And whereas the initiative may well further the Jeffersonian objective of tying government down, and thus preventing mischief, it also vastly reduces the chances that great leaders, and the visionary statecraft with which they are sometimes associated, will arise. In the battle over the initiative the Framers would be the first to recognize that our politics, rather than being too conservative, are in the Burkean sense not nearly conservative enough.

Critical Thinking

1. What is Proposition 13? When and in what state was it passed?

2. What effects did the passage of Proposition 13 have in other states that make it plausible to suggest that Proposition 13 was almost as consequential as the New Deal?

3. What is a fee-for-service ethic, and how and why has this ethic arisen in the aftermath of Proposition 13?

4. What is meant by the "non-deliberative quality" of initiatives as instruments of state government policymaking, and what are other "dangers" associated with initiatives?

5. Why is the initiative process, as it typically operates, not accurately described by the notion that "nobody has enough money to bribe everyone"?

PETER SCHRAG writes frequently on education and politics. His article in this issue appears in somewhat different form in his book *Paradise Lost: California's Experience, America's Future*, published by The New Press.

From *The Atlantic Monthly,* March 1998, pp. 20–31. Copyright © 1998 by Peter Schrag. Reprinted by permission of the author.

Taking the Initiative

A pilot project in Oregon would make the ballot a tool for civic education.

JENNIE DRAGE BOWSER

What happens to ballot initiatives when you mix a little civic education with a measure of public scrutiny and some grassroots discussion? You get something that looks a lot like Oregon's new Citizens Initiative Review. Backers think it will lead to a better-informed public with a greater appreciation of what happens when new public policies are created through the initiative process.

The idea for the pilot program was first floated in 2008 by the nonpartisan, nonprofit group Healthy Democracy Oregon. The 2008 review process brought together a randomly selected group of 23 Oregon voters, balanced to reflect the demographic diversity of the state. They spent five days together in Salem learning all they could about Measure 58, a 2008 initiative that proposed limiting bilingual education in public schools to no more than two years for any student.

Panelists heard from initiative sponsors, opponents and impartial background witnesses, policy experts and fiscal analysts. They split on the issue with nine favoring passage and 14 opposed. Each side shared its views with the public in a one-page summary. Measure 58 failed by a margin similar to the positions taken by the panel.

Based on this experience, Healthy Democracy Oregon went to the Legislative Assembly and asked lawmakers to approve including their statements in the official voters' pamphlet for 2010. The legislature agreed on two, and this year statements on Measure 73—a mandatory-minimum proposal for sex offenders and drunken drivers—and Measure 74—a proposal that would allow dispensaries to sell medical marijuana—will appear in the pamphlet.

Debate and Education

Oregon Speaker Pro Tem Arnie Roblan was an early supporter of the panel. He wants an educated electorate and believes the review panel process is an excellent model for informing people.

"The initiative process has always frustrated me because so much of the information voters get is what the two sides present," Roblan says. "That doesn't give the full picture. Unintended consequences rarely get discussed—that's just too nuanced for a 30-second radio or television ad."

The democracy group's co-director, Tyrone Reitman, echoes that concern. "An initiative campaign's job is not to inform voters, but to influence voters. The best campaigns do both, but the majority just work to influence." No one is held accountable, he says, for the quality or accuracy of the information presented once the election is over.

Oregon's idea is to give two dozen regular Oregon citizens the best education they can in five days and ask them to weigh in on the initiative. Measure 73 panelists, for example, heard from the chief proponents and opponents of the measure.

But they also received a crash course in Oregon's criminal justice system. They heard from Multnomah County Judge Eric Bloch and Lane County District Attorney Alex Gardner, along with Doug Wilson and Ken Rocco from the Oregon Legislative Fiscal Office, who gave them a briefing on corrections funding in Oregon. They also had testimony from a county judge, an administrator from the Oregon Department of Corrections and a professor of criminal justice.

The pro and con advocates got to suggest witnesses, too, and the panel heard from a crime survivor, a county sheriff and a representative of Mothers Against Drunk Driving. From the con side, they heard from two attorneys, a public defender Tom Sermack, and a representative from the group Partnership for Safety and Justice.

Roblan points to the importance of carefully vetting initiative proposals. Policy enacted by voters through initiatives dictates a large portion of Oregon's discretionary budget and is responsible for a significant share in the growth in state government.

"Voters should understand that, and hopefully this process gives them a better understanding that initiatives are going to cost resources," Roblan says.

The panel review injects a key element missing from the initiative process: public deliberation. Unlike bills in the legislature, initiatives are presented to voters as a whole, with minimal public debate and no opportunity to amend the proposal or to choose an alternative. They do not go through committees, where proposals are publicly debated and examined under the microscope of policy and fiscal analysis. Voters don't have the opportunity legislators do to say, "I like that idea, but I think there's a better way of doing it."

It's yes or no, period.

"The process exemplifies high-quality citizenship unlike any other process I've ever seen," says Elliot Shuford, co-director of the democracy group. "Panelists leave saying, 'I'm going to vote in every election from here on out, and tell everyone I know to, too.'"

Remarkable Process

The reasons people agreed to spend five long days in Salem becoming experts on an issue varied.

A few panelists cited the $150 daily stipend in addition to transportation, meals and lodging. Others agreed out of a sense of civic duty.

"My wife and I sat down and talked about how it's our chance to say something, do something, at the grassroots level," says Raul Grimes, a member of the Measure 74 panel. He saw it as his chance to reflect his belief in the American people, not just its elected representatives.

By all accounts, what happened during the review was remarkable.

"I thought I'd be able to tell who was Republican, Democrat, independent or a Tea Partier," says Rocky Krokus, an independent contractor who was a member of the Measure 73 panel. "But I didn't know anyone's affiliation and nobody knew mine. It was never brought up in the discussion. Politics never entered it. I never perceived any agendas."

Grimes, a retired teacher who also served for 22 years in the Army, says what he appreciated the most was working in the small breakout groups.

"I got to know people from the coast, the valley and the high desert areas in the east. Working with people and trying to understand their views was good for me. Parting ways at the end of the panel was difficult and emotional."

A Better Conversation

The Citizens Initiative Review could have a broader impact than merely providing better information to voters as they evaluate initiatives.

The group's co-directors hope the public develops a deeper understanding of the long-term causes and effects of various policies, and believe it is the only way the public will trust the conversation.

"People are accustomed to hyper-partisanship . . . and then they watch something totally different take place," says Shuford. "It shows a new direction for civic dialogue and public engagement."

The review is not without its critics. The chief proponents of Measure 73, the mandatory-minimum sentences initiative that under-went review in August, have been vocal in their complaints. They say panelists were not screened to assemble a group that started out with a balanced view on the topic, they were not allowed to cross-examine opponents of the measure—only panelists could ask questions—and witnesses were not questioned under oath. The democracy group directors reject these criticisms, and most review panelists do, too.

When the review panel was debated in the legislature, opponents called it "elitist." Others didn't want to see citizen panels become a part of state government, or add bureaucracy or administration to the initiative process in general.

Panelist Krokus, however, predicts citizen reviews will become so important to Oregonians that "they will be knocking down the door to participate. It's the purest form of democracy in action that all Oregonians should be proud of, and all other states should demand."

The future of the Citizens Initiative Review is far from certain, however. The legislation permitting the review panels' statements to be published in the Oregon voters' pamphlet applies only to 2010. And although there is consensus it's a good idea, questions remain about future funding and whether it should remain independent or become a state-funded program.

In addition to wanting the review to become a permanent part of Oregon's initiative process, Reitman and Shuford would like to see the idea spread to other states.

"There is no better example," Speaker Roblan says, "for educating people about the initiative than this process."

Critical Thinking

1. What is an "initiative" in the context of state government policymaking?

2. What is Oregon's Citizens Initiative Review and how will this pilot program work in an effort to better the initiative process in Oregon?

3. About how many citizens spend how many days in a typical Citizen Initiative Review educational program?

4. What was the reaction of the Oregon state legislature to a request that statements from Citizens Initiative Review participants appear in Oregon's official voters' pamphlet in 2010?

JENNIE DRAGE BOWSER is NCSL's expert on ballot measures

Public Meetings and the Democratic Process

Public meetings are frequently attacked as useless democratic rituals that lack deliberative qualities and fail to give citizens a voice in the policy process. Do public meetings have a role to play in fostering citizen participation in policy making? While many of the criticisms leveled against public meetings have merit, I argue that they do. In this article, I explore the functions that city council and school board meetings serve. While they may not be very good at accomplishing their primary goal of giving citizens the opportunity to directly influence decisions made by governing bodies, they can be used to achieve other ends, such as sending information to officials and setting the agenda. As a complement to deliberative political structures, public meetings have a role to play by offering a venue in which citizens can achieve their political goals, thereby enhancing governmental accountability and responsiveness.

BRIAN ADAMS
San Diego State University

Most local governments hold regularly scheduled meetings to discuss and decide public issues. Opportunities for citizens to voice their opinions are usually a part of these meetings. Public input may take the form of comments on specific issues before the governmental body, or it may be general comments on issues that citizens care about. In either case, citizens are given a specified period of time (frequently two to three minutes) to state their opinions and are usually prohibited from engaging other citizens or officials in dialogue.

In this article, I examine city council and school board meetings in a mid-sized city (Santa Ana, California) and ask what role public meetings have in the participatory policy process. Can they play a constructive role by allowing citizens to voice their concerns and influence policy decisions, or are they a hollow ritual that merely provides a facade of legitimacy? If we want to incorporate greater public participation into the policy process, is there a place for public meetings? I add to the literature that examines the role of public participation in policy analysis (Thomas 1990; Walters, Aydelotte, and Miller 2000) by exploring what function public meetings serve and how they fit into the larger institutional context of citizen input into the policy process.

I argue that public meetings serve an important democratic function by providing citizens with the opportunity to convey information to officials, influence public opinion, attract media attention, set future agendas, delay decisions, and communicate with other citizens. Meetings are a tool that citizens can use to achieve political objectives. This tool is ill-suited for fostering

policy deliberations or persuading officials to change a vote on a specific issue. But meetings serve another purpose: By giving citizens a venue in which they can achieve political goals, public meetings can enhance the political power of citizens and, consequently, improve governmental responsiveness to citizens.

If we keep in mind the functions that public meetings can and cannot perform, their role in the participatory policy process becomes clearer. Public meetings can complement the structures that foster citizen deliberation (such as citizen panels, forums, and roundtables) by providing citizens with the opportunity to engage in the political process before deliberations commence and after citizens have developed a set of recommendations or a consensus policy position. Even though public meetings themselves are not deliberative, they can facilitate citizen participation and the development of good policy by assisting citizens in achieving their political goals. In this article, I hope to show the purposes that public meetings serve and how they fit into a larger scheme of citizen input into policy making.

Institutional Design and Citizen Participation

In recent years, many scholars have argued for an enhancement of the extent and quality of citizen participation in policy making (Fischer 1993; deLeon 1995, 1997; King, Feltey, and Susel 1998; Roberts 1997; Schneider and Ingram 1997; Dryzek 1990). They contend that we need to develop structures and institutions to provide citizens with opportunities to participate effectively. But how do you design institutions to allow citizen input into the policy process? There are many ways that citizens can be brought into the policy process: Public hearings, citizen juries, roundtables, and electronic town meetings are examples of institutions meant to create opportunities for citizen participation.

One of the most common methods of citizen participation is the public hearing: A survey of city managers and chief administrative officers found that over 97 percent of cities use it as a strategy for dealing with citizens (Berman 1997, 107). Public hearings, which are usually required by law, allow citizens to comment on a specific issue or proposal before a governmental entity makes a decision. Despite its widespread use, public hearings are not held in high esteem. The most common critique—made by participants, academics, and governmental officials alike—is that citizen comments do not influence policy outcomes (Cole and Caputo 1984; Checkoway 1981). Citizens march up to the podium, give their two-minute speeches, the presiding official says "thank you very much," and then officials proceed with their business irrespective of the arguments made by citizens. Citizens may speak their mind, but officials do not listen and usually have their minds made up before the public hearing. Hearings, in this view, are mere democratic rituals that provide a false sense of legitimacy to legislative outcomes: Officials can say they received input from the public, and it can give their decisions the respect afforded to democratic processes, even though citizen input has no impact. Rather than a means for citizen input, hearings allow officials to deflect criticism and proceed with decisions that have already been made (Rowe and Frewer 2000; Kemp 1985; Checkoway 1981).

A second critique of public hearings is that they are a poor mechanism for deliberation (King, Feltey, and Susel 1998; Kemmis 1990, 51–53; Checkoway 1981). Citizens go to the podium, speak their peace, and then sit down. There is rarely dialogue between citizens and officials; in fact, such dialogue is usually forbidden. While citizens have a chance to state their position and support it with a reasoned argument, public hearings do not allow them to engage elected officials or other participants in a dialogue to try to persuade them to change their opinions. Public hearings do not afford citizens a venue where they can engage in public discussions about common problems and try to reach understanding with their fellow citizens and elected officials. Further, public hearings frequently degenerate into the worst sort of debate: Rather than citizens stating their opinions and offering supporting argumentation, they will employ sound bites, hyperbole, and falsehoods to criticize and demonize opponents—hardly a model of citizen deliberation.

Hearings are also criticized for attracting an unrepresentative sample of the population (McComas 2001a; Gastil and Kelshaw 2000). People who show up to meetings are more likely to be extremists on the issue being discussed because they have greater personal incentives to participate. Hearings may be dominated by those with very strong views on the subject being discussed, crowding out moderate voices that may represent large segments of the community. This dynamic has two repercussions: It undermines the legitimacy of the hearing as a venue for assessing public opinion, and it provides officials with an excuse to ignore public comments (because they believe they are not representative of what the public really thinks).

While even defenders of public hearings acknowledge they are a poor venue for deliberation, some research indicates that hearings can be an effective form of citizen participation and citizens can, at times, be representative of the public at large. In studies of the California Coastal Commission, Mazmanian and Sabatier (1980) and Rosener (1982) found that citizen participation at public hearings had an impact on the denial rate of permits under consideration by the board. Others have argued that under the right conditions (for instance, meetings held at a convenient time and advertised extensively), hearings can be effective at influencing policy and attracting a representative sample of the citizenry (McComas 2001b; Chess and Purcell 1999; Gundry and Heberlein 1984; Gormley 1986).

Dissatisfaction with public hearings as an outlet for participation has led many scholars and practitioners to develop alternative methods for involving the public in policy making. One alternative has been to modify the format of public meetings, discarding the structured and nondeliberative hearing format in favor of a roundtable or small group setting. These settings differ from traditional public hearings in that citizens have an opportunity to discuss the issue at hand and deliberate with fellow citizens and officials. Roberts (1997) argues that the public deliberation occurring at these meetings should be the foundation of an alternative way to solicit public input, and Weeks (2000) describes successful attempts to integrate meetings into a deliberative policy process.

National Issues Forums, a network committed to enhancing civic life and public involvement in politics, has experimented with alternatives to the traditional public hearing for almost 20 years. Here, citizens deliberate over public problems with the goal of developing a plan of action to address the issue (for descriptions of the type of deliberation fostered in such forums, see Mathews 1999; Doble Research Associates 2000a, 2000b, 2001). America Speaks, a nonprofit organization, promotes and organizes electronic town hall meetings that allow citizens to deliberate over policy issues. Using a mix of face-to-face deliberation and communication through technology, America Speaks attempts to empower citizens to voice their opinions and inform governmental action (America Speaks 2002).

One common obstacle to public meetings concerns size: The more people who show up at the meeting, the more difficult it is to have the type of face-to-face interaction and discussion that deliberation proponents desire. While America Speaks and other organizations have addressed some of the logistical problems caused by size, fostering deliberation in large groups is still problematic. One response has been to convene citizens panels or citizens juries to deliberate on issues (Crosby, Kelly, and Schaefer 1986; Kathlene and Martin 1991; Haight and Ginger 2000). These panels are representative samples of the public, and thus can act as a proxy for deliberation among the entire public; because it is not feasible for everyone to deliberate on an issue, selecting a representative sample to do it for them is the next best thing. Fishkin's (1991, 1995) deliberative opinion polls are a variation on this theme: Select a random sample of the public to deliberate on an issue (or an election), and their recommendations will reflect what the public at large would have decided if they had deliberated themselves.

Finally, surveys and focus groups are often considered to be a form of participation, although a qualitatively different form than those already listed. Surveys do not allow for any deliberation, nor do they allow citizens to express their individual voices, as hearings do. While focus groups allow for greater voice and deliberation, they are still limited by a structure that is meant to solicit opinions, not form them. Even though surveys and focus groups by themselves do not offer much opportunity for citizens to participate in policy making, they can be used to enhance other participation tools, such as the ones described earlier, making for a more meaningful and rich participatory structure (for examples, see Weeks 2000; Kathlene and Martin 1991).

I have described various mechanisms by which citizens can provide input into the policy process. The question I pose is this: Where, in this landscape of meetings, panels, surveys, and forums, do local city council and school board meetings fit? What role can they play?

Data and Methodology

The arguments presented in this article are based on research conducted in a mid-sized city, Santa Ana, California. Located just south of Los Angeles, Santa Ana has a population of about 320,000. At one point in its history, Santa Ana was a suburb of Los Angeles, but its links to Los Angeles (in terms of its reliance on Los Angeles for employment, shopping, and entertainment) have diminished over the past few decades, and now it can be considered a city in its own right. Fifty-five interviews with citizen participants were conducted between March and July 2001. Respondents were selected through a variety of means: Some names were gathered through newspaper reports of citizen activities, some were culled from the minutes of city council and school board meetings, and other names were given to the researcher by respondents already interviewed. Through these methods, a list was compiled of these citizens who were most active in Santa Ana politics. Most respondents were involved in civic organizations, such as neighborhood associations, PTAs, and city advisory committees. While many held formal positions (president, treasurer, etc.) within these organizations, few could draw upon extensive institutional resources to achieve political ends, and thus were relatively less powerful than many other political actors, such as union leaders and developers.[1] Generally, the respondents were citizens who were highly involved in local politics but could not be considered "political elites." There were four exceptions: three former elected officials (one city councilman and two school board trustees) and the president of the Santa Ana Chamber of Commerce.

Interviews were semistructured and asked participants about their activities in trying to influence city and school district policy (the city and school district are separate entities, but both were included in this study). After some general questions about the activities they engage in when trying to influence public policy, respondents were asked to list two or three policies they had personally been involved with, and then were asked follow-up questions on each, including questions about their strategy and effectiveness.

Attending city council and school board meetings is a very common form of participation: 98 percent of respondents reported having attended at least one meeting during the past 10 years, and most indicated they attend meetings on a regular basis.[2] Even though almost everybody stated they went to public meetings, there was some disagreement about their effectiveness. While a few respondents said that attending meetings was the most effective form of participation, most did not (the most frequent response was talking or writing to elected officials directly). Many echoed the common complaint that elected officials already have their minds made up before the meeting. Despite this widespread belief, many respondents offered other reasons why attendance at public meetings is effective. These explanations form the basis for the findings that follow. These are not meant to characterize the aggregate opinion of the respondents, as opinion varied too much to reach any firm conclusion about the attitude of respondents toward public meetings. Rather, the findings that follow describe some functions that public meetings perform and offer reasons why we should maintain this institution.

I do not present Santa Ana as a typical or representative city. Future research on other cities may find that citizens go to meetings for different reasons than they do in Santa Ana, and thus the findings that follow may not be generalizable to other cities. That said, they are valuable because they offer insight into the potential for public meetings to have a constructive role in the policy process. The findings that follow are evidence that public meetings can serve a valuable function for citizens, not that they serve those functions in all contexts or situations.

The Functions of Public Meetings

Public meetings of city councils and schools boards in California are governed by the Brown Act, which requires that all meetings of local governments be open to the public and allow for public participation. The Brown Act gives the public the right to comment on items before the legislative body, and it also stipulates that "time must be set aside for the public to comment on any other matters under the body's jurisdiction" (California DOJ 2002, vii). Thus, citizens have an opportunity to speak about agenda items, as well as any other local issues they feel are important. There are six ways that citizens can use these opportunities to accomplish their political goals.

Provide Information

Public meetings can be an effective way to convey information about public opinion to officials. One piece of information that needs to be communicated is interest in a particular issue: Letting officials know that you are out there is a necessary first step to participation. One respondent stated that attending public meetings was important because "it seems like if you don't show up at the Council meetings, the council says 'well, maybe this is a non-issue.'" Another participant made a similar point, arguing that getting a lot of people to a council meeting is critical to showing that people care about an issue (in this case, a traffic issue). There are, of course, other ways to let officials know that a particular issue is important to citizens: They may circulate petitions, write letters, or call officials directly. In some circumstances, however, attending a meeting can be the most effective way of indicating interest. Gathering a group of citizens to go to a meeting not only is relatively easy, but also clearly communicates to officials that there is interest in an issue.

Some respondents also felt that attendance at meetings was important to counterbalance opposing views and to get their message out. A common theme among respondents was that there is power in numbers, and turning out the masses at city council or school board meetings provides a political advantage by adding force to their message. This dynamic was evident on both sides of a highly contentious debate over the siting of a new school. A supporter of the school stated that "we wanted to have a lot of parents with school children there [at the public meeting] because otherwise you were going to have an imbalance." School opponents also noted their attempts to bring out large numbers to meetings, and both sides claimed they had outnumbered their opponent. Having numbers turn out for meetings is important because one common discourse in local politics concerns which side of the debate has more popular support. Absent scientific polls, actual levels of support are not known, leaving participants free to convince elected officials that they, in fact, have more support. Turnout at public meetings may be seen by officials as evidence of popular support (although frequently weak support, given the unrepresentativeness of those who attend), and thus can be used as a debating point. Lacking other information sources, elected officials may rely on turnout at public meetings, however unrepresentative, to gauge public support for or opposition to a given policy.

The comments of two former elected officials indicate they use public meetings as a source of information. One former school trustee said she kept tallies of supporters and opponents on an issue to get a feel for what the community thought. A former city councilman, talking about a proposal for a permit-parking district in a residential neighborhood, told this story:

> We were told that this was going on and the neighborhood is happy with it and the staff was happy with it, and they worked it out and it was all ready to go. Then it came before us to vote on it, all of the sudden we had a swarm of people who were against it. . . . I was prepared to go ahead and vote with it from the information I had, but then when this large constituent [sic] of business owners came out I said this is something I hadn't planned on. I can't vote on it. We need to sit down and work this through to see if we can't make both sides a little bit happier. Those groups of people got to me. . . . I would do my homework, and my colleagues—we did our homework. . . . We may have had our minds made up with the facts that we had been given, but when we would have a group come and speak against it, I wouldn't ram it on through, but make a motion to continue it. Let's hear more of what the people are trying to say and sit down and talk to them, again get that dialogue going so we can really find out what their concerns are and what we can do to alleviate it.

For this city councilman, a public hearing provided information about where his constituents stood on an issue. He did not state that public comments had persuaded him to change his thinking on an issue by offering new ideas or new interpretations. He did not say the citizens appearing at the hearing had changed his mind on an issue, or persuaded him that he was mistaken in his support for the proposal. He did, however, change his actions based on the opposition to the proposal that was evident at the public hearing. The public hearing provided new information that altered the actions he took, even if it did not persuade him that his views were mistaken. Rather than acting as a deliberative forum where ideas are exchanged and people's opinions change based on rational persuasion, the view of meetings that emerges here is of a forum in which constituents provide their elected officials with new information about their views on an issue, prompting altered behavior on the part of officials.

Officials, of course, may have other sources of information about public opinion, such as surveys, focus groups, forums, letters and phone calls from constituents, conversations with others, and media reports. Some of these, such as surveys and focus groups, reflect public opinion more accurately because the participants are more representative of the population as a whole. Despite this shortcoming, public meetings have some benefits as a vehicle for voicing public opinion. First, public meetings are useful in measuring the strength of opinion on a particular issue. Officials know that citizens who take the time to come to a meeting care about the issue under discussion, while surveys make no such indication. Further, meetings are open to anyone who wishes to speak, while surveys, focus groups, and advisory panels have restricted participation. While not having restrictions may introduce bias into the opinions presented, the open meeting has an advantage in terms of legitimacy: Citizens who feel their voices are not being represented in survey results or panel recommendations have an opportunity to express views that may be a bit off the beaten path. By providing a venue for citizens who wish to present alternative opinions, meetings can add legitimacy to the policy process. By themselves, public meetings do not provide an accurate picture of public opinion on local issues, but they can act as a valuable and important supplement to other forms of public opinion, providing both additional information and legitimacy.

A Show of Support

One recurring theme among respondents was the importance of supporting friendly elected officials who take controversial policy stands and expressing displeasure with officials who take stands they disagree with. On controversial issues, elected officials are forced to take a position that may alienate some constituents—not a desirable position for politicians who prefer to please everyone. When an elected official takes a position that is unpopular with some, his or her supporters will frequently make a point of coming to a meeting to agree with the stand taken, in a show of support for a politician in an uncomfortable situation. For example, one participant made this comment about supporting a decision on a new school: "We certainly gave Rob and Audrey [two school board members] counter high-ground to stand on. They could say, 'look. These people, our constituents, the parents of the children, they are here to support.' This gave them a public high ground to stand on to shape the argument. . . .

It didn't change anybody's mind, but it certainly helped to direct the flow of discussion."

Sometimes, officials need political cover for taking unpopular stands, which can be provided by supporters at a public meeting. If a politician is supporting the view of a small minority (for example, of one particular neighborhood) that is highly unpopular, he or she could take a major public relations hit; he or she could be characterized as out of step with the majority, catering to special interests and the like. These characterizations can be even more potent if they are out there all alone, without any support, while opponents are banging away. Citizens at public meetings, however, can provide some cover by showing public support for an unpopular position. For example, one participant explained why he had attended a meeting in support of a restaurant desiring a liquor license: "It makes it easier for them [the city council] to make a decision if they have support, rather than you making that decision on your own because you know it's right and its best for the community. It takes some of that burden, some of that responsibility, from the Council if there's public support." While the politicians supporting the liquor license might still take some political heat (there was opposition from nearby businesses), at least they can point to a group of citizens and say, "I have some support in the community for my position." From a public relations standpoint, a show of support can be critical, providing cover for a politician in a tight spot and diffusing some of the criticism. Public meetings are an excellent venue to provide this support because they are usually televised and sometimes covered by local newspapers, allowing supporters to get their message out.

Supporting sympathetic officials does not affect votes on issues, nor is it meant to. But it does have an impact. First, it strengthens the relationship between a politician and his or her supporters and creates channels of communication. Elected officials, seeing who supports them during the tough times, will be more likely to return phone calls, arrange face-to-face meetings, and listen to those constituents. Politicians appreciate support on controversial issues and, as a consequence, will be more willing to listen to their constituents on other issues. In other words, public meetings allow citizens to identify themselves as supporters, giving them an opportunity to create relationships with officials. Second, it provides an avenue by which citizens can help officials whom they want to remain in office. Popular support for a controversial vote is an important political cover: Without it, elected officials are susceptible to accusations during the next election that they are out of touch with their constituents and out of step with public opinion. Public meetings provide a means by which citizens can provide political cover for supportive politicians, thus reducing their exposure during the next election.

Shaming

Most citizens at public meetings are not there to support, but to criticize. Elected officials frequently complain about citizens who are silent until they want to vent about a decision they disagree with. At first blush, this type of behavior may seem futile. Yelling and screaming at a meeting is not likely to change the votes of elected officials, so why do citizens go to meetings to complain? One function it serves is to shame elected officials for disagreeable actions. As I have mentioned, support at a meeting can provide political cover for officials; the converse is also true. Criticizing officials in a public forum can create the perception they are out of touch with the community. This is particularly important from a media perspective: The local newspaper or television newscast is likely to report that officials were criticized by their constituents at a meeting, particularly if it is a highly controversial issue. Even if the citizens at the meeting are not representative of the community at large, the image of an official being hammered by his or her constituents is a powerful one, and one that may have important electoral implications.

One example of the shaming dynamic was seen when a group of parents went to a city council meeting to criticize a councilwoman. The issue was a proposed school that was generating a lot of controversy due to its location: The wealthy white neighborhood next to the proposed school opposed it, while many citizens in other parts of the city supported it. The decision to build or not to build was a school district decision (which is a separate entity from the city), but one councilwoman, Lisa Mills, was at the forefront of the opposition to the school. A group of school supporters went to a city council meeting to complain about Councilwoman Mills's activities on the issue and her divisive comments. One leader of the group explained why it was necessary: "[Lisa Mills] was very divisive . . . it was really a lot of lies that were coming down the pipe. A lot of people that weren't involved with the school district, that's all they were getting. So it was very important to counterbalance that. And you had to do it with numbers, you had to do that with a lot of people." Another leader of the group made this comment: "When [Mayor] Dan Young said after the meeting that he'd never ever seen anything like that before in his life, it was like 'ok, we got our message across.' To get up there and publicly censure Lisa Mills for her activities. That was something that . . . it was a distraction and a lot of energy that we didn't need to continue to fight so we went in and we hit hard and she wasn't really heard from much on that issue after that."

Since the council had no authority over the issue, school supporters were not trying to change the outcome of any policy decision: Their only purpose was to shame Councilwoman Mills. This served two purposes. First, it swayed the terms of the debate and public perceptions by indicating the amount of support the school had. Also, it gave Councilwoman Mills a political black eye, which could have been a liability during the next election (she decided not to run for a second term).

Another example illustrates the effectiveness of shaming officials at public meetings. The issue was a proposed park and community center for Delhi, a working-class Latino community. The city had been promising to build the park for years but never came forward and provided the funding. After repeated stonewalling and delays by the city, supporters decided to force the issue by going to a city council meeting. Here's how a supporter relates what happened:

> So we organized a meeting at City Council, we took about 150 people to that meeting. . . . And the questions were very simple. They were like: why haven't you kept your promises? And I think in many ways, we sort of shamed

people, we shamed them because, you know, why haven't you kept your promises? . . . And so what happened was that was aired on Comcast [the local cable company] throughout Santa Ana. . . . [S]o before you know it, I had people calling [me] . . . they were saying "they can't do this to you guys. They can't just put all the money into north Santa Ana. They have to pay attention to all these neighborhoods." People starting coming out of the woodworking, you know, they said they have to make this project for this community. So I think they [the City Council] were probably receiving those kind of calls. And the day after the meeting . . . at the meeting, the Mayor and the rest of the Council, they were kind of cool about things, very evasive, didn't act like they were disturbed in any way. But I'll tell you, the next morning, the Mayor was begging me to meet with him. He said, "please, let's sit down and let's try to work something out."

The value of this shaming strategy lies not in its capacity to persuade the council that the park was a good idea; accusing the council of lying and breaking promises is hardly the way to accomplish that goal. Rather, by embarrassing the council, it was forced to pay attention to the issue and take action (the council eventually did provide some funds for the park, although not as much as requested). A public meeting was the ideal venue for carrying out this shaming strategy. It was televised, and thus many people in the community heard the park supporters' message, placing additional pressure on the city council.[3] For council members, having to sit through a meeting at which 150 angry residents are accusing you of lying and breaking promises while other constituents watch on television is hardly an enticing prospect. We should not be surprised that this strategy bore fruit and got the city to move on the park project.

The capacity to publicly attack officials is an important aspect of democratic governance: Citizens need a venue in which they can counter what their elected officials are doing or saying. Public meetings provide that venue. They give citizens the ability to gather in one place and express opinions that run counter to what officials are saying. While citizens have other venues in which they can criticize officials—such as writing letters to the editor, staging street protests, or voting against officials in the next election—public meetings present a unique opportunity because they are public, easily accessible, and allow citizens to speak their minds. Elected officials never look good when they are being yelled at, and thus venting at public meetings can undermine and weaken the positions of elected officials. Much of the criticism that officials receive may be unjustified and unfair, and I certainly do not mean to imply that citizens are always correct or that elected officials always deserve derision. Fair or not, the ability to criticize elected officials is a cornerstone of democratic politics, and public meetings provide an excellent opportunity for citizens to do so.

Agenda Setting

The power of elites to set the agenda is well documented in the urban power literature (Bachrach and Baratz 1962; Crenson 1971; Gaventa 1980; see Polsby 1980 for a critique). Much less studied is how and under what conditions citizens can influence the agenda. We generally think of public meetings as venues where policy decisions are made, not where agendas are formulated. While in most cases this is true, meetings do provide opportunities for agenda setting by citizens. In Santa Ana, both the city council and school board allow for public comments on nonagenda items, allowing citizens to discuss issues that have not yet been formally taken up by officials. Some participants, when asked whether speaking at public meetings is effective, stated that attending a meeting the day an issue is going to be decided is useless, but going earlier in the process is very effective as an agenda-setting device. One respondent, who was both president of her neighborhood association and president of the library board (a city advisory board), has this to say about whether meetings are valuable:

You have to be smart when you do it. Like we started speaking a while ago about the library budget because they won't make their decision, they're starting to make their decisions now [March], but they'll make final decisions in June and July. I think they're thinking, too, if you speak on the agenda items, well no, its totally done before it comes to the committee. So you have to speak now about. . . . Like we spoke about CenterLine [a light rail proposal]. . . . We spoke about CenterLine before it even came up at all. And they said "why are you talking about this today?" and we said "because we know you are going to make a decision on it soon. We know you are. We've heard the buzz. So we are going to get a voice now, even though its not an agenda item or anything." I think that's where you have to be smart.

The respondent is making two interrelated points about the value of speaking at public meetings on nonagenda items. First, she is highlighting the importance of early participation. By the time a decision reaches the city council or school board, it has already been in the works for quite some time, with advisory committees, staff, and interested parties providing input. Compromises may already be built into the policy, with the key players working out agreements among themselves. Further, supporters or opponents of a policy may be able to convince elected officials of the merits of their position well before it ever gets to a formal vote. Participation, therefore, is most effective before positions harden, compromises are worked out, and advisory committees make recommendations; showing up at a city council or school board meeting on the day a policy is scheduled to be approved is, in many cases, too late in the process to make an impact. Thus, speaking on an issue to be decided that night is not the most effective way to influence decisions. Speaking at a public meeting well before a decision is made, however, can be effective: By speaking early in the process, citizens are able to get their opinions heard while officials are still deciding how they want to resolve the issue. This is why it was smart to comment on the CenterLine proposal well before it came up for a formal vote (at the time, it was unclear how the city council was going to vote).

Speaking at public meetings can also influence the agenda by making officials pay attention to issues they ordinarily would not. The respondent just quoted illustrates this with her comment about the library budget. Usually, the city does not pay much attention to the library budget and rarely provides additional funding. By speaking up early at a public meeting, citizens can establish an issue (in this case, library funding) as one that needs to be addressed. Another respondent, when asked why speaking at budget hearings is effective, said that it has some impact because "even though they've already made up their minds, it could stay up in their minds for the next budget meeting."

Agenda-setting effects tie into my first point about public meetings sending information to officials: The reason speaking at meetings may help set the agenda is that elected officials may use it as a measure of citizen interest in a topic. If citizens are coming to meetings to talk about the CenterLine proposal months before a decision is due, officials may conclude it is a highly controversial issue that deserves more attention than they are giving it. Conversely, if nobody raises the library budget as an issue, it will likely be ignored by officials (as it usually is). Not only can officials use public comments at meetings to gauge where their constituents stand on the issues of the day, but they can also use them to determine which issues are important and deserve their attention. With limited time at their disposal (elected officials in Santa Ana work part-time), they need to pick and choose the issues that get on their agenda, and citizens showing up to discuss an issue at a meeting may influence those decisions.

That said, public meetings are not the most effective way to influence governmental agendas. Motivating a group of citizens to attend a meeting to discuss an issue that will be decided far in the future is difficult. Further, elected officials may forget about public comments by the time decisions need to be made. Other forms of participation, such as writing letters, circulating petitions, or speaking directly to officials may be more effective at getting them to pay attention to certain issues. Public meetings, however, can be used in conjunction with these other methods and can further advance the agenda-setting goals of citizens. They are particularly useful in making demands on officials public. More private forms of participation, such as letter writing and speaking directly to officials, may get some attention, but they are likely to get more attention if they are coupled with a public display. One chief virtue of public meetings is that they are public, and thus can reach a larger audience than just officials and a small group of participants. They may not be a very effective method by themselves, but they can serve an important agenda-setting purpose if used along with other methods.

Many of the other participatory structures discussed previously, such as citizens' panels, forums, and roundtables, already assume an agenda that is decided by officials. Sometimes, officials use these structures to define agendas (Weeks 2000), but usually the issue to be discussed is identified and framed by officials beforehand. Citizen comments at public meetings can play a role in deciding which issues to convene panels or roundtables for and how those issues will be framed. Public meetings can provide the raw opinions and ideas that can start more deliberative (and ultimately constructive) processes to address public issues.

Delay

While it is rare for elected officials to change their votes based on citizen comments at a public meeting, it is much more common for votes to be delayed because of public outcry, especially if it is unexpected. In some cases, officials may delay to avoid making unpopular decisions with people present, hoping fewer people will be present at the next meeting. In other instances, citizens may desire a delay. One respondent told of a planning commission meeting that was discussing a development mitigation plan. A neighborhood resident, seeing the planning commission was prepared to vote against the plan, stated, "We told them we need to know what our rights are, and we asked them for a 30-day extension, and they granted it to us." This gave the neighborhood residents time to develop a strategy for accomplishing their goals. In some cases, citizens may not find out about an issue until the last minute, and thus they may not have time to take actions such as circulating petitions or organizing a letter-writing campaign which could apply pressure on officials. A delay may create time to work over officials or to gather more support in the community.

Public meetings are an excellent venue for asking for a delay: Elected officials may find it hard to ignore citizens who are merely asking for more time to study an issue, try to reach a compromise, or (as in the previous example) figure out what actions they can take. Asking for a delay is not an unreasonable request, increasing the pressure on elected officials to accommodate it. The ability of citizens to publicly ask for a delay and to provide reasons why the delay is necessary adds to the force of the request. Privately requesting a delay (in a letter or in a phone conversation) does not allow citizens to publicly state their argument in favor of a delay, and thus it is not as politically forceful. Public meetings provide the best opportunity for citizens to ask elected officials to delay a decision because they can publicly present arguments that attest to the reasonableness and wisdom of the request.

Networking

While the primary channel of communication at public meetings is from citizens to elected officials, citizens can also use meetings to communicate with each other. Communication among citizens is not easy because they usually lack the money to send out mailings and frequently lack the time to knock on doors or organize phone trees (although citizens do engage in these activities on occasion). Public meetings allow citizens to get their message out to other citizens relatively cheaply and without a significant time commitment. Usually, only citizens who are active in local politics attend or watch the meeting on television, so they are not a good venue for communication to the citizenry at large. But they are good for communicating with other citizens who are active. Public meetings can create and maintain social networks among active citizens by allowing them to let others know what they are doing. We saw one example of this with the citizen who was advocating a new park for the Delhi neighborhood. She mentioned that after the public meeting, people from other parts of the city called her about the park issue, fostering networks between her group and other neighborhoods and organizations. Of course, citizens have other ways to communicate with each other, and I do not mean to imply that public meetings are a primary, or even an effective, means of building networks. But they can help citizens get their message out and reach out to other citizens in the community.

Influencing Votes

Public meetings can serve other functions in addition to influencing the votes of officials. The six functions just listed are examples of how citizens can use meetings to achieve political goals that may indirectly influence votes by altering the political context in which the votes are taken, but they do not directly change a specific vote. Whether public meetings are effective at the latter is a point of contention in the literature. To round out my picture of the role and place of public meetings, in this section I will discuss the conditions under which meetings may be effective at directly influencing votes. Rather than claim that meetings are effective or not effective, I will explore under what conditions meetings might be influential and why.

My research uncovered one case in which a public meeting unequivocally changed the outcome of a city council decision. The issue was a citywide redevelopment project that, according to its supporters, was proposed to raise money for needed infrastructure projects such as parks and schools. Going into the meeting, most observers expected it to pass. In the weeks before the meeting, a few activists who opposed the redevelopment plan rallied citizens to go to the meeting to voice their opposition. Their efforts worked better than they had hoped: According to newspaper accounts, more than 2,000 citizens showed up to protest. After hearing a handful of irate speakers, the city council voted unanimously to table the item, and it was never brought up again. According to all sources, the redevelopment plan would have passed if it had not been for the outpouring of opposition at the meeting.

This incident illuminates some conditions in which public meetings can effectively change votes. First, elected officials were surprised at the turnout and the opposition.[4] If they had known it would generate so much opposition, they likely would have postponed the decision until they could marshal more support. Or, if they had had the resolve, they might have voted for it despite the opposition. Here we have a case in which meetings conveyed new information to officials (that is, the amount of opposition in the community) that had a direct impact on the vote. The reason it had such a profound impact was that officials did not have the luxury of a public opinion poll to gauge opposition, and thus were blindsided at the meeting. The conclusion to draw is this: If elected officials misjudge public support or opposition, meetings may change votes because they provide new information that changes officials' political calculations.

Two other conditions contributed to the public's ability to change the vote: the sheer numbers of people who appeared, and the absence of supporters. An attendance of 2,000 at a public hearing is phenomenal, particularly in a city of 320,000 people. This unusual show of force must have indicated to officials that the vote could have serious political ramifications and prompted them to change their votes on the spot. Further, the

fact that all present were opposed, made a yes vote politically dangerous. As I have mentioned, having support provides political cover. None was present here, making an affirmative vote more difficult.

One more condition may have contributed to the vote change which was not present during the redevelopment incident: the ambivalence of elected officials. Some issues may be more important to citizens than to elected officials, and the latter may be willing to change their votes based on comments at a hearing because they do not have strong feelings either way. This is not likely because elected officials are usually in tune with the wishes and demands of their constituents. But it may happen on occasion.

Whether public meetings are more effective than other forms of participation at influencing the votes of elected officials is a research question that is beyond the scope of this article. My point is not that attending meetings is the most effective strategy for changing legislative decisions, but that, under some circumstances, meetings can be used to accomplish this goal. Adding this argument to the previous section's description of other functions that meetings serve illustrates the usefulness of meetings for citizens. They may not be the best tool for accomplishing political goals, but they do add a weapon to the citizen's political arsenal which can be marshaled to enhance the effectiveness of citizen participation.

Conclusion

At the core of democracy is citizen deliberation and rational persuasion: Citizens deliberate over pressing public issues and make arguments to persuade officials (and each other) to take desired actions. Public meetings do not contribute to either of these goals: They are not deliberative, and they are not an effective vehicle for rational persuasion. Public meetings, however, have a role to play in maintaining a democratic system. Around the core of deliberation and rational persuasion is a democratic periphery of political maneuvering and pressure tactics that are essential parts of a democratic process, and this is where public meetings come into play. Meetings are a tool in the citizen's participatory toolbox that can help them accomplish political objectives—such as supporting allies, embarrassing enemies, setting the agenda, and getting their voice heard—which can add to their influence and effectiveness. The findings from Santa Ana demonstrate some ways that meetings can be used to citizens' advantage.

How do public meetings fit into the overall scheme of citizen participation and policy making? Public meetings do not directly contribute to the process of formulating effective policy solutions to public problems; other devices, such as roundtables, forums, and citizens' panels, are more effective at this task. But meetings, by helping citizens to be more effective, can enhance the responsiveness and accountability of government. Citizen deliberation and discussion on tough policy choices may lead to the formulation of better policy but, by itself, does not make government any more responsive to citizens. If citizen recommendations go unheeded, then the whole process is for naught. This is where public meetings fit in: They provide a venue for citizens to carry out a political struggle to have their voices heard and recommendations heeded. After citizens deliberate on an issue, weigh policy choices, and make recommendations, they can go to a public meeting to make their case. This is not the current role that meetings play, as most speakers at public meetings argue for their personal opinions, not collective opinions derived through deliberation. But, if additional deliberation structures are put into place, public meetings could have a valuable role by enhancing the political power of citizens and, consequently, increasing the chances that government will be responsive to their recommendations.

Public meetings can also assist citizens at the front end of the policy process by providing a venue for citizens to set the agenda and frame policy issues. In many participatory venues, the issues to be discussed are identified beforehand and a framework for discussing the issue is set. While this may be necessary to foster constructive deliberation, it limits the voice of citizens, preventing them from altering the structure of the conversation or changing how an issue is framed. At public meetings, citizens are free to identify issues that need to be discussed and offer new frameworks for understanding issues already under discussion. Before deliberation in forums, panels, or roundtables commences, citizens should have the opportunity to propose what issues need to be discussed, how the issue should be understood, and the manner in which the process should work. Public meetings could give citizens the opportunity to influence the way citizens participate, rather than having government officials decide for them.

Thus, public meetings have a role to play at the beginning and the end of participatory processes. Designing institutions that allow for citizen participation in the policy process requires us to create deliberative and constructive outlets for citizen input. But this positive political power needs to be supplemented by other forms of participation that allow citizens to flex their political muscle (see Rimmerman 1997 for a description of different forms of political participation). Both types of power are needed for a healthy democratic policy process. A process that lacks opportunities for constructive citizen deliberation will lead to disillusionment among citizens and reinforce the disconnect between citizens and their government. On the other hand, a process that allows citizens constructive input but limits their capacity to fight political battles, influence legislative votes, or criticize officials will reduce governmental responsiveness. Without the political power to back up citizen input, much of it will be duly filed, never to see the light of day again. The power to pressure, lobby, and cajole government officials is an essential complement to positive power, as constructive citizen deliberation is only valuable if officials pay attention to it. Thus, public meetings, as a venue where this can occur, cannot be replaced by more deliberative or constructive venues.

In this article, I have explored the value that public meetings have for citizens. But why would local officials want to hold them? By giving citizens an opportunity to accomplish their political goals, public meetings reduce the power and control exercised by officials. There are, however, two reasons why officials would desire to keep public meetings. First, they can provide information to officials about public opinion, particularly which issues citizens feel are important and the strength of their opinions. Second, because public meetings are an open forum in which any citizen can speak, they provide a measure of legitimacy to the policy process. As many scholars have noted, citizens are cynical about politics and government (Rimmerman 1997; Berman 1997; Harwood Group 1991), and thus likely to approach a roundtable, forum, or other project with a wary eye. By providing an open forum for citizens to express their opinions, public meetings enhance the legitimacy of the policy process, a desired commodity for public officials. While public meetings benefit citizens more than they do officials, the latter do derive some benefit and would be wise to maintain the institution.

Notes

1. Political actors commanding significant resources were intentionally excluded. The study was limited to focus on how citizens without institutional power or other resources can use public meetings as a political tool.

2. While this number is high, other forms of participation also ranked very high: 92 percent reported having circulated a petition, and 100 percent reported having spoken to an elected official. Because respondents were chosen based on the fact that they were active, we should expect such high numbers.

3. I do not know the television ratings for city council meetings, but I imagine very few people watch them. That said, those who do watch are most likely politically active, which explains the significant reaction to this meeting.

4. This observation is based on the comments of opponents who were interviewed for this study.

References

America Speaks. 2002. Taking Democracy to Scale: Reconnecting Citizens with National Policy through Public Deliberation. Paper presented at the Taking Democracy to Scale Conference, May 8–10, Warrenton, VA.

Bachrach, Peter, and Morton S. Baratz. 1962. Two Faces of Power. *American Political Science Review* 61(4): 947–52.

Berman, Evan M. 1997. Dealing with Cynical Citizens. *Public Administration Review* 57(2): 105–12.

California Department of Justice, Office of the Attorney General. 2002. *The Brown Act: Open Meetings for Local Legislative Bodies.* Informational pamphlet.

Checkoway, Barry. 1981. The Politics of Public Meetings. *Journal of Applied Behavioral Science* 17(4): 566–82.

Chess, Caron, and Kristen Purcell. 1999. Public Participation and the Environment: Do We Know What Works? *Environmental Science and Technology* 33(16): 2685–92.

Cole, Richard L., and David Caputo. 1984. The Public Hearing as an Effective Citizen Participation Mechanism: A Case Study of the General Revenue Sharing Program. *American Political Science Review* 78(2): 404–16.

Crenson, Matthew A. 1971. *The Un-Politics of Air Pollution: A Study of Non-Decisionmaking in the Cities.* Baltimore, MD: Johns Hopkins University Press.

Crosby, Ned, Janet M. Kelly, and Paul Schaefer. 1986. Citizens Panels: A New Approach to Citizen Participation. *Public Administration Review* 46(2): 170-78.

deLeon, Peter. 1995. Democratic Values and the Policy Sciences. *American Journal of Political Science* 39(4): 886–905.

———. 1997. *Democracy and the Policy Sciences*. Albany, NY: State University of New York Press.

Doble Research Associates. 2000a. Public Schools: Are They Making the Grade? Report prepared for the Kettering Foundation, Dayton, OH.

———. 2000b. Our Nation's Kids: Is Something Wrong? Report prepared for the Kettering Foundation, Dayton, OH.

———. 2001. Money and Politics: Who Owns Democracy? Report prepared for the Kettering Foundation, Dayton, OH.

Dryzek, John S. 1990. *Discursive Democracy*. Cambridge: Cambridge University Press.

Fischer, Frank. 1993. Citizen Participation and the Democratization of Policy Expertise: From Theoretical Inquiry to Practical Cases. *Policy Sciences* 26(3): 165–87.

Fishkin, James S. 1991. *Democracy and Deliberation: New Directions for Democratic Reform*. New Haven, CT: Yale University Press.

———. 1995. *The Voice of the People: Public Opinion and Democracy*. New Haven, CT: Yale University Press.

Gastil, John, and Todd Kelshaw. 2000. Public Meetings: A Sampler of Deliberative Forums that Bring Officeholders and Citizens Together. Report prepared for the Kettering Foundation, Dayton, OH.

Gaventa, John. 1980. *Power and Powerlessness: Quiescence and Rebellion in an Appalachian Valley*. Urbana: University of Illinois Press.

Gormley, William T. 1986. The Representation Revolution: Reforming State Regulation through Public Representation. *Administration and Society* 18(2): 179–96.

Gundry, Kathleen G., and Thomas A. Heberlein. 1984. Do Public Meetings Represent the Public? *Journal of the American Planning Association* 50(2): 175–82.

Haight, David, and Clare Ginger. 2000. Trust and Understanding in Participatory Policy Analysis: The Case of the Vermont Forest Resources Advisory Council. Policy Studies Journal 28(4): 739–59.

Harwood Group. 1991. Citizens and Politics: A View from Main Street America. Report prepared for the Kettering Foundation, Dayton, OH.

Kathlene, Lyn, and John A. Martin. 1991. Enhancing Citizen Participation: Panel Designs, Perspectives, and Policy Formation. *Journal of Policy Analysis and Management* 10(1): 46–63.

Kemmis, Daniel. 1990. *Community and the Politics of Place*. Norman: University of Oklahoma Press.

Kemp, Ray. 1985. Planning, Public Meetings and the Politics of Discourse. In *Critical Theory and Public Life*, edited by John Forester, 177–201. Cambridge, MA: MIT Press.

King, Cheryl Simrell, Kathryn M. Feltey, and Bridget O'Neill Susel. 1998. The Question of Participation: Towards Authentic Public Participation in Public Administration. *Public Administration Review* 58(4): 317–26.

Mathews, David. 1999. *Politics for People: Finding a Responsible Public Voice*. 2nd ed. Urbana: University of Illinois Press.

Mazmanian, Daniel A., and Paul A Sabatier. 1980. A Multivariate Model of Public Policy-Making. *American Journal of Political Science* 24(3): 439–68.

McComas, Katherine A. 2001a. Public Meetings about Local Waste Management Problems: Comparing Participants to Nonparticipants. *Environmental Management* 27(1): 135–47.

———. 2001b. Theory and Practice of Public Meetings. *Communication Theory* 11(1): 36–55.

Polsby, Nelson W. 1980. *Community Power and Political Theory: A Further Look at Problems of Evidence and Inference*. New Haven, CT: Yale University Press.

Rimmerman, Craig A. 1997. *The New Citizenship: Unconventional Politics, Activism, and Service*. Boulder, CO: Westview Press.

Roberts, Nancy. 1997. Public Deliberation: An Alternative Approach to Crafting Policy and Setting Direction. *Public Administration Review* 57(2): 124–32.

Rosener, Judy B. 1982. Making Bureaucrats Responsive: A Study of the Impact of Citizen Participation and Staff Recommendations on Regulatory Decision Making. *Public Administration Review* 42(4): 339–45.

Rowe, Gene, and Lynn J. Frewer. 2000. Public Participation Methods: A Framework for Evaluation. *Science, Technology and Human Values* 25(1): 3–29.

Schneider, Anne Larason, and Helen Ingram. 1997. *Policy Design For Democracy*. Lawrence: University Press of Kansas.

Thomas, John Clayton. 1990. Public Involvement in Public Management: Adapting and Testing a Borrowed Theory. *Public Administration Review* 50(4): 435–45.

Walters, Lawrence C., James Aydelotte, and Jessica Miller. 2000. Putting More Public in Policy Analysis. *Public Administration Review* 60(4): 349–59.

Weeks, Edward C. 2000. The Practice of Deliberative Democracy: Results From four Large-scale Trials. *Public Administration Review* 60(4): 360–72.

Critical Thinking

1. What six important democratic functions, according to Brian Adams, can local government public meetings serve?

2. What are some common criticisms that scholars have voiced about local government public meetings and public hearings?

3. What data did Brian Adams use in his research on local government public meetings in one California city?

4. What conditions, according to Brian Adams, make it most likely that public meetings can change the outcomes of local government officials' votes?

5. What does it mean to say that public meetings "have a role to play at the beginning and the end of participatory processes"?

From *Public Administration Review*, January/February 2004. Copyright © 2004 by American Society for Public Administration. Reprinted with permission.

Reloading at the Statehouse

As traditional news organizations shed state government reporters, a wide array of innovative startups is rising to fill the gap.

MARK LISHERON

L ike kids who had memorized every slight, every insult, every threat leading up to a great schoolyard brawl, the New Jersey Statehouse press corps packed Gov. Chris Christie's outer office on an evening in late May, waiting.

Through the glass doors charged Stephen Sweeney, the thick-necked ironworker organizer and state Senate president, carrying in his fist two bills passed just minutes before by the fellow Democrats flanking him. Sweeney insisted that this most theatrical hand delivery of the so-called millionaire's tax to a Republican governor sworn to veto the bills was not in any way to be construed as theater.

After keeping Sweeney waiting for a few theatrical minutes of his own, Christie emerged from his office with his own entourage. "Senator, I was wondering what took you so long," Christie said to Sweeney, smiling and breaking up the room. "I didn't want to keep you waiting," Sweeney replied to a small wave of laughter.

Christie told Sweeney he was sending the bills back without his approval. Sweeney promised he would be back after getting enough support to override the governor. "We'll see," Christie said. Sweeney and his allies turned to leave, and that was that.

The story was a big one, top of page one the next morning in Newark's Star-Ledger and almost every press outlet in the region. But it was the promise of the big political fight that had filled the room. Rarely could you count on this many reporters at the Statehouse, even for some of the big stories.

In a few significant, if depressing, ways, this was a one-act dramatization of state government coverage in America today. Coverage that people working under capitol domes, inside newsrooms, with good government groups and in universities think has been rough-sanded to the raw surface of cataclysmic clashes among politicians, parties and factions and the relentless handicapping by poll of the combatants.

The answer as to why this has happened is, on the surface, simple. As AJR has reported since 1998, there are dramatically fewer reporters covering state legislatures. A little more than a year ago, an AJR survey of newspapers found 355 full-time staff writers covering their state capitols, nearly a third fewer than the 524 in AJR's 2003 survey. (See "Statehouse Exodus," April/May 2009.)

With fewer reporters, the argument goes, the first to vanish are the stories that tell readers what elected officials do when they aren't cataclysmically clashing and why the readers should care. And with those stories goes one of the important connections between the citizen and his or her government.

Dozens of articles have been written in the past couple of years about withering statehouse coverage and the threat to our democracy. Pick your own hand-wringing headline: "As Capitol Press Corps Shrinks, Government Controls Message" from the Oklahoma Gazette; "Goodbye to the Age of Newspapers (Hello to a New Era of Corruption)" in The New Republic; or, rather bluntly, "The Capitol Press Corpse" in Texas Monthly.

Dunstan "Dusty" McNichol added his voice to the grim chorus a year ago when he complained about a New Jersey Statehouse press corps in steep decline. In a guest editorial for Alan D. Mutter's blog, Reflections of a Newsosaur (newsosaur .blogspot.com), he called the ability of the press corps in the Statehouse in Trenton to cover even basic news compromised.

"How can public debate be informed," he wrote, "or even initiated, without a sustainable press corps capable of covering and broadcasting credible information on important public policy developments?"

M cNichol's words carried weight. He was part of a team of Star-Ledger reporters who shared a Pulitzer Prize in 2005 for stories that prompted the resignation of Gov. James McGreevey. McNichol remains one of the most respected—and most unprepossessing—reporters in the New Jersey Statehouse. He was one of the familiar faces Christie called on by name after the mellow drama with Sweeney.

There were other familiar faces there that night. Tom Johnson, who had roamed the Statehouse halls for 18 years for the Star-Ledger. Kevin McArdle, a Statehouse correspondent in radio for nearly eight years. Like McNichol, who is now a star for Bloomberg News in Trenton, they were doing what they had always done in a new and different way.

Johnson and another Star-Ledger veteran, John Mooney, were putting the finishing touches on a new website, NJ Spotlight, whose slogan is "Where Issues Matter" and whose germination came from an idea of McNichol. Johnson and Mooney, with nearly 50 years of New Jersey newspaper experience between them, have received $700,000 in foundation seed money for reporting on issues like education, energy, the environment and health care.

Millennium Radio, with a dozen New Jersey stations, many of them of the talk variety, believed so strongly in the market for Statehouse news that it tapped McArdle to handle its radio reporting and help develop a news website for the flagship station, NJ101.5 FM ("Not New York. Not Philadelphia. Proud to be New Jersey"). Not long ago, Millennium launched a second site, Statehousesteps.com, an aggregator for Capitol news featuring blogs by McArdle and others.

In New Jersey and across the country, people are attempting to write a second act to the statehouse set piece. David Royse and the staff of the News Service of Florida selling pricey subscriptions for blanket coverage of the Statehouse in Tallahassee. Mark Katches and his California Watch team trying to move from a nonprofit to some other sustainable model in Sacramento. Evan Smith and Austin's Texas Tribune, whose already substantial staff is growing with an enviable sponsorship plan.

There are the watchdog websites, most of them nonprofit. There are the sites devoted to training citizens in the basics of reporting to keep an eye on their state governments. There are the bloggers, the commentators, the provocateurs and the bomb-throwers.

And in spite of having lost about 90 news department employees, the Associated Press has 75 full-time and 30 part-time bureau correspondents, and has made it a priority to keep at least one full-time staffer in every state capital, says Senior Managing Editor Michael Oreskes, himself a statehouse veteran. "We've worked very hard to protect those statehouse positions," he says. "I think the framers of our Constitution made it explicit that state governments were a crucial part of their democratic design. Being present in the statehouse is vital; it isn't an option."

The framers didn't make explicit how cluttered and fragmented and messy this vital function was going to be. The pessimists are noisier than the optimists. Tiffany Shackelford, executive director and a founder a decade ago of Capitolbeat, the Association of Capitol Reporters and Editors, says the toughest part of the role is convincing members, whether they have been put out of work or remain at a newspaper, that by reinventing themselves they can help reinvent statehouse coverage.

"I will be brutally honest: The mentality of a lot of journalists, in spite of what they can see right in front of them, is complacency," Shackelford says. "They look out there and just don't know how to make money doing what they do. I feel very strongly that for reporters to survive in this time, they are going to have to show some entrepreneurial spirit. Unfortunately, I don't see nearly enough of it. It's either change or die."

The biggest question, particularly worrisome because it is being asked by people who seem to have figured out successful alternative ways to deliver statehouse news, is the money. Foundations, donors and subscribers have contributed to significant Web launches like Texas Tribune, MinnPost, California Watch, the American Independent News Network and the News Service of Florida. There is sharp debate about sources of funding and whether ideology will poison the news well.

Many worry that with fewer trained eyes watching, those working in state government will be emboldened to make their own rules at citizen expense. And with the growing presence of the so-called citizen journalist, there is agonizing over what, exactly, are trained eyes.

For those who are changing the way Americans get their statehouse news, however, there is consensus. The alternative, to do nothing, is not acceptable.

"I think it's fair to say that this has been exhilarating and exhausting. I like feeling like I'm on the front end rather than the back end," Mooney says. "I'm surprised at how much I've learned, surprised that I would ever be in business. And I'm surprised at how much people are yearning for this kind of coverage, how much they want the spinach, maybe because there is less and less of it. It has been almost visceral with folks, asking us about getting this coverage."

If there can be optimism in New Jersey there can be optimism anywhere. Paul Starr first took up the study of what is lost when reporters go away as an alarmed reader as well as the Stuart Professor of Communications and Public Affairs at Princeton University. His scholarly and dire piece in The New Republic in March 2009, in which he contends that the very notion of journalism as the Fourth Estate or branch of government is in peril, is informed by what he has seen in New Jersey.

In a paper Starr directed and edited for New Jersey Policy Perspective in October 2009, Scott Weingart, one of his students at Princeton, makes a case that the press in the state has often been overwhelmed trying to keep track of 1,159 municipalities and school boards, each with its own push and pull on the Statehouse. The glut of government alone makes conditions ripe for corruption, Weingart writes.

That New Jersey is corrupt is taken for granted by its residents.

Its citizens have weathered the resignation of Gov. McGreevey in 2004, after he admitted that he had put his male lover on the state payroll as his homeland security chief.

An FBI investigation into a bizarre racketeering scheme involving the sale of human organs as well as money laundering, resulting in the arrest of 44 people, some of them public officials and rabbis, helped bring down Gov. Jon Corzine last year, although there was no evidence he was involved in any way. An AP account at the time pointed out that 130 New Jersey officials had been convicted or pleaded guilty of some kind of corruption since 2001.

"New Jersey's corruption problem is one of the worst, if not the worst, in the nation," Ed Kahrer, the head of the public corruption division for the FBI, told the AP. "Corruption is a cancer that is destroying the core values of this state."

Keeping tabs on all this corruption was a press that has always been decentralized and overshadowed by two big media markets, Philadelphia to the south and New York to the north. In the paper "Less News is Bad News," Weingart charts steep circulation declines at nearly every newspaper in the state at the same time those newspapers were shedding reporters.

The raw numbers in AJR's 2009 survey say that no state-house newspaper press corps was harder hit than New Jersey's, which plummeted from 35 to 15. Early that year, during a second spasm of buyouts, Newhouse's Star-Ledger announced that it would combine its Statehouse bureau with the bureau of the independently owned Record of Bergen County, keeping nine reporters and losing eight.

This spring, the Star-Ledger and Record staffs quietly moved into separate offices, and although both sides maintain the relationship remains cooperative and that Statehouse copy is shared, the animosity and territoriality is common knowledge on Press Row.

At the end of Press Row, just around the corner from the fire escape, is a plastic holder full of press releases stuck to a door. Just above the door handle is a handwritten sign, "Please do not lock door. Thank you." Below the familiar typeface reading New York Times Trenton Bureau, someone has taped another sign, "(the other) Times Trenton Bureau." Neither the New York Times nor the Times of Trenton maintains a bureau here anymore. The unlocked door hasn't been opened in months.

Gannett claims two reporters for its seven-paper New Jersey Newspaper Group. There once were six. The independent Atlantic City Press, announcing itself with a headline on the door, "Report: NJ is a Hellhole," still has one staffer here. While the Philadelphia Inquirer claims two staffers, the folks on Press Row say the paper is more likely to have a reporter parachute in for big stories.

The big news has been the steady growth of Bloomberg News, which started in Trenton with one reporter eight years ago and now has three reporters, including McNichol, and two editors stationed there. Johnson and Mooney have taken an office for NJ Spotlight across the hall from the AP, where most of the wire service's Statehouse coverage falls to two reporters.

A decade ago, the Star-Ledger had a 13-member Statehouse bureau (see "The Jersey Giant," October 2000). No one who has spent any time on Press Row pretends that the buyouts given to McNichol, Mooney, Johnson and about 40 percent of the Star-Ledger staff in 2008 and 2009 were anything other than rotten for the commonweal. Tom Martello, the bureau chief for the Star-Ledger (with or without the Record), is proud of the hard-charging, award-winning young staff he supervises. But he deeply laments the mood and the meaning of the goodbye parties he has attended.

"There are fewer people. And the fewer people with flash-lights, the more dark corners there are," Martello says, from a top-floor bureau office a few blocks from the Capitol with a panoramic view, if one is absolutely necessary, of downtown Trenton. "I can't predict the future, but you have to be worried."

Martello's star is Josh Margolin, another of the members of the Pulitzer team, and a reporter whose work ethic, access to the governor and penchant for breaking stories drive rivals crazy. Margolin considers the Statehouse the Star-Ledger's highest calling.

Margolin has not been afraid to break with editors who have said publicly they believed the Star-Ledger's coverage of the last governor's race was up to past standards. He admired the hard-nailed integrity of Jim Willse, the editor who willed the Star-Ledger to be one of the finest regional newspapers in the country.

During the buyout that would gut his creation, Willse, who retired a short time later, told his remaining staff they would not be doing more with less, they would be doing less with less.

"Clearly, there is less total coverage because there are fewer reporters," Margolin says, having invited himself into the office of Michael Drewniak, Christie's press secretary, across the hall from Press Row. "Do I think the coverage is as good as it used to be? No.

"And about what you lose when you lose all that institutional knowledge at the paper. I'll sum it up by telling you that there have been at least two or three instances where I've called the person who used to cover something I'm covering to ask for help. The clips can only tell you a certain part of the story."

Drewniak sees the loss of institutional memory from the other side of the desk and the experience of having once been a young hotshot for the Star-Ledger, like Margolin. Drewniak left newspapers in 1998, when he began to notice changes in the business that worried him. He went to work in the U.S. attorney's office in Trenton, where a comer named Christie convinced Drewniak that his run for governor was going to be about public service rather than politics.

As press secretary, Drewniak says he expected the attacks, political and editorial. What he didn't expect was the number of young reporters who clearly did not know their way around the Statehouse, or politics, or, in some cases, a complete interview.

Reporters have, on several occasions, asked Drewniak to re-create the atmosphere of a public meeting they could not attend. They sometimes ask him for help finding documents. The questions they ask betray a lack of understanding of the political process, he says.

"I know I'm going to sound like an old, crabby, crotchety reporter, but you can tell that some of these reporters never leave the newsroom," Drewniak says. "Whether this level of laziness is a function of not enough bodies, I can't say, but I think some reporters are glued to their keyboards. I have to tell them I'm not going to do their work for them."

In his experience, Drewniak says he has seen a drop in the number of stories written from the U.S. attorney's office, which is distressing because they involve the kind of lawbreaking the press has traditionally seen as surefire material. And while there were plenty of reporters around when Sweeney and the Democrats came to visit his boss over the millionaire's tax, Drewniak noted conspicuous absences.

"What happened yesterday was a historic event in gubernatorial affairs in New Jersey history," Drewniak said the following day. "And where was the New York Times, the freaking New York Times? They have pulled up stakes and left the state."

Starr saw the abandonment of the New Jersey bureau by the New York Times as a bellwether of inattention in Trenton. As he became more committed to the research, Starr found that New Jersey is just a more extreme version of almost every other state in the union.

What he did not find, even after hosting a well attended conference to discuss the crisis of journalism in the region in May 2009, was a single or satisfactory set of solutions to the problem.

Starr believes that a European model, like the British Broadcasting Co., could succeed, but only if the funding comes from a dedicated tax rather than a budget appropriation subject to political whim. If the Federal Communications Commission were to open the television broadcast spectrum to broadband, Starr says, a whole new opportunity for endowed public-service journalism could develop.

"I think we have shrinkage in the coverage that's impossible to reverse," he says. "I suspect that what we're seeing is a shift to an earlier pattern in American history, a shift to partisan sources for news. I think there is going to have to be an education process to let the public know that journalism, which was once taking care of itself, is not doing it anymore. I suspect that we are going to see a lot more experimentation."

The experimenting in New Jersey begins with but isn't restricted to NJ Spotlight. At one of the wakes for departing Star-Ledger reporters, McNichol told Mooney he had an idea for how to remain in the news business. Rather than try to re-create a smaller version of a newsroom online and hope that an audience followed, McNichol said he thought reporters needed to be entrepreneurial. Reporting expertise on particular subjects had a value. The trick was to find the customers who valued it.

Education was a natural for Mooney, who had been covering the subject for 15 years. Tom Johnson was an expert on energy and environmental issues, which were likely to remain vital. Before he could join the team he conceived, McNichol, who had won awards for his grasp of the state's budget and pension system, was hired to cover state finance for Bloomberg. He lateraled his idea to Mooney and Johnson for free with best wishes and support.

The Community Foundation of New Jersey, the John S. and James L. Knight Foundation and the William Penn Foundation agreed to underwrite NJ Spotlight. News content is free; paid subscribers receive more focused information and services such as conferences and Webinars.

"From the beginning, you have to be thinking of a sustainable way to do this," Mooney says. "Foundations aren't in the publishing business. Things have gone well so far, and we're convinced that there isn't any less demand for this kind of coverage."

In Trenton, Bloomberg believes it has figured out that its customers are willing to pay for reporting that helps readers understand the relationship between business and state government. With its success in Trenton, Bloomberg is moving ahead with plans to staff statehouses in Colorado and Texas.

Of all of the new ventures, the people on Press Row thought the website development by Millennium Radio, with its emphasis on talk radio, to be the least likely. McArdle says management is increasingly convinced that its news side can drive the talk. Early in his career, McArdle says, he was an AP rip-and-read radio man. With the press corps thinned, Millennium saw an opening for original reporting from McArdle.

On the night of the millionaire's tax bill non-confrontation, McArdle worked five hours of overtime, producing the version of the story that would run on the website, three audio versions for 9 P.M., 10 P.M. and 11 P.M. newscasts and four versions for the morning cast on the half-hour. The newscasts promoted his online coverage, and the website encouraged readers to check out the broadcasts.

McArdle's reporting and his blog are also part of Statehousesteps.com. Its presentation is not unlike that of PolitickerNJ.com, founded in 2000, in its aggregation of information and its target audience of people in state government, with an interest in it or those who cover it.

"It's a force, a multiplier, but there is still only one of me," McArdle says, heading out after a long news night to play golf. "Never in a million years did I think I'd be blogging from the Statehouse. The way I look at it, optimistically, is that I'm stepping up to the 21st century. Along the way, I've had to find ways to be more efficient."

Good government groups in New Jersey have joined the effort to refocus attention on the Statehouse. The nonprofit New Jersey Foundation for Open Government is finding greater public interest in its mission, to teach people how to secure copies of government records. President Ron Miskoff, a journalism instructor at Rutgers University and a former president of the New Jersey Society of Professional Journalists, says he thinks the public is well aware it is being shortchanged on state government coverage in local newspapers and on television.

"It's been a crazy last couple of years," Miskoff says. "I think the light has gone on that there aren't as many people in Trenton fighting the good fight. We are not seeing the stories, except for the biggest ones. It has gotten pretty bad. I don't know where America is going with all this, but I'm pretty sure New Jersey's going to get there first. New Jersey needs a better watchdog for its citizens."

Jerry Cantrell, founder of the New Jersey Taxpayers Alliance, wants to be one of those watchdogs. Cantrell is using donations to launch the nonprofit Common Sense Institute of New Jersey to do public policy research that would be available to citizens and journalists alike. Its mission statement, devoted to individual liberty, personal responsibility and economic opportunity, has the ring of conservatism to it, but Cantrell says the institute will be committed to nonpartisan research on important issues.

Heather Taylor offers a course to teach citizens the rudiments of journalism. Taylor, a journalism graduate of Rutgers, is communications director for a public service nonprofit, the Citizens' Campaign. Eventually, she would like to tailor classes specifically for state government.

Disdain for the citizen journalist movement among editorial professionals does not change the reality that, in many places in New Jersey, important government decisions are being made with no reporters in attendance, she says.

"I've heard the complaint that this is an insult to the profession," Taylor says. "I don't present this as an alternative to what the press does. I see it as offering education that will result in more robust coverage of government."

"I don't present this as an alternative to what the press does. I see it as offering education that will result in more robust coverage of government."

—Heather Taylor

Michael Delli Carpini is supportive of Taylor's work. The dean of the Annenberg School for Communication at the University of Pennsylvania and a political scientist, Delli Carpini has spent a career marking what he says is the "decline in professional journalism and the sorry state of the public's political knowledge." Nothing in his research suggests to him that the traditional press will be able to recapture its role as the central provider of public information.

The trend toward local and national coverage and away from the state in the press, although not often noted, is reflected in the boom in studies of grassroots and local politics and global and international politics in political science programs at universities and colleges, Delli Carpini says.

"There is in academia the sense that teaching or studying state politics is so 20th, even 19th, century," he says. "Grassroots and global politics are hot; state politics programs are almost nonexistent. Let's not kid ourselves. In other areas of the newspaper, there is emphasis on the sexy factor, and, outside of the conflict and the horse race, burrowing deeply into some state issue isn't sexy."

If the roster of Pulitzer Prize winners is Maxim's Hot 100 for journalism sex appeal, statehouse coverage is Marisa Tomei: highly thought of, a little older and no longer on the list. Rarely in the past 50 years has straight-on capitol coverage won journalism's top award. Prior to the Star-Ledger's McGreevey stories, you have to go back to 1994, when two Detroit News reporters shared a Pulitzer for a check-writing scandal in the Michigan House Fiscal Agency that resulted in felony convictions for the agency's executive director and a state representative, and five prison sentences.

As swashbuckling as it sounds, Jim Mitzelfeld, the News reporter who broke the story, says the way he ran down the tip was out of the old days, more Betty White than Katy Perry. (See "Missing the Story at the Statehouse," July/August 1998.)

When Mitzelfeld joined the News staff in 1988, both the News and its competitor, the Detroit Free Press, were among the nation's top 10 in circulation. The Statehouse beat was coveted and glamorous, the competition for scoops brutal. There were nearly a dozen reporters covering Lansing for the News alone.

Mitzelfeld says he stayed ahead by working Capitol offices and people every day. One of the people he cultivated told him that, somewhere in the Legislature, someone was writing checks to cash. Knowing there were five House arms with check writing privileges, he made Freedom of Information Act requests for the canceled checks for all of them. All but one agency promptly complied.

At the same time, Mitzelfeld asked for and was provided by the state Department of Treasury a printout of all state checks, which included amounts, dates and check numbers, but not payees.

When John Morberg, director of the House Fiscal Agency, finally consented to meet with Mitzelfeld, his bookkeeper provided what appeared to be a newly handwritten check register. Mitzelfeld then took out the computer printout, and when he compared it with the register, he found dozens of missing entries.

"At this point Morberg looked at his bookkeeper and said, 'Kate, get him the checks.' She said, 'You've got to be kidding.' I still remember the look on her face to this day," Mitzelfeld says.

For six hours over the next two days, Mitzelfeld created his own check registry that would later become a gold mine of Detroit News exclusives when authorities made the checks part of their criminal investigation and off limits to other reporters.

"They weren't writing checks to cash. What I found was 10 times better. They were basically writing checks to themselves, 1,800 checks, $1.8 million of petty cash over seven years. And I literally had a monopoly on the story because of my check registry."

By the time he and Eric Freedman, who had joined him on the many stories that followed, won the Pulitzer Prize for beat reporting in the spring of 1994, Mitzelfeld had left the paper to study law at the University of Michigan. The previous fall, feeling good about his work, Mitzelfeld says he asked for a pay increase that would make his salary comparable to that of top reporters on the paper. His editor made his decision to go to law school easy.

"He told me if I had wanted to make money, I shouldn't have gone into journalism," he says. "He told me he thought I might want to look into something else."

There were other reasons. Asked to give a speech in the Netherlands not long after winning his Pulitzer, Mitzelfeld spoke of a newspaper industry that wanted to be more like television. Stories from the Statehouse, he says, were becoming shorter. Some never made it into print. In one memorable exchange with an editor, Mitzelfeld said that at 12 inches his story could include a Republican and the Democratic reponse. At eight inches it could not have both. "He told me to pick one. Honestly."

Mitzelfeld, who had been a federal prosecutor on loan to the Office of Professional Responsibility for the U.S. Department of Justice in Washington, D.C., in September became investigative counsel for NASA's Office of Inspector General. Mitzelfeld says he has come to understand from the other side the value of a watchdog press. He has watched as the Statehouse bureaus for the Free Press and the News have been reduced to a total of five full-time reporters and as Ann Arbor, home of his alma mater, lost its daily newspaper, the Ann Arbor News. (The Newhouse-owned outlet still publishes local news on AnnArbor.com and publishes print editions twice a week.)

"The media plays a huge role in how an agency focuses on what it does. It's refreshing to see how much impact, in good ways, the press has on how government works," he says. "So when I think of the stories being missed in a city the size of Ann Arbor with no daily newspaper, I find that frightening."

Freedman, now an associate professor of journalism at Michigan State University, shares his Pulitzer partner's concerns. Freedman and several of his colleagues have applied for a National Science Foundation grant to begin a comprehensive look at statehouse coverage in all 50 states.

"The idea is to come up with a real sense of what is and isn't being covered," Freedman says.

Freedman, who left the News in the wake of the epic Detroit newspaper strike in 1995, says his alarm at the reduction in staffing stoked an academic curiosity about what the reporters still working in statehouses were producing. "My impression is that things are pretty skimpy beyond gubernatorial coverage," he says. "If you make the assumption the media has a vital role to play in the electoral process, then citizens should have better information with which to make their election and their policy decisions."

"If you make the assumption the media has a vital role to play in the electoral process, then citizens should have better information with which to make their election and their policy decisions."

—Eric Freedman

There is a growing sense—much of it on the Web—that stripped down state government news, the Sturm und Drang and the horse race, appealing mostly to political insiders, is undemocratic. Evan Smith, CEO and editor-in-chief of Texas Tribune, refers to it as the interruption in a great civic dialogue, a dialogue he launched the Tribune to resuscitate in Texas.

Perhaps no one in the country has made the notion of returning to issues-based state government reporting sexier than Smith, whose every move as editor of the new website has been watched for clues as to how to proceed into a very uncertain future.

(I've watched the development of Texas Tribune up close, as Austin bureau chief for Texas Watchdog, a government accountability website.)

From the start, Smith's involvement meant Texas Tribune would be paid attention to. In nine years as its top editor, Smith had put a distinctive stamp on Texas Monthly, long a National Magazine Awards darling. Although his dress and manner suggest Manhattan, Smith has a 10-gallon personality and is about as well known as anyone in a state with plenty of room for outsize personalities.

Watching the home run derby before the All-Star game with his son, Wyatt, Smith, a baseball fan of the New York Yankees sort, watched Milwaukee Brewers first baseman Prince Fielder screw himself into the ground time after time before crushing what Smith says was the hardest hit ball he'd ever seen.

"I don't think of myself as a singles hitter," he says, pointing to a framed 8-by-10 photo of his new role model on a coffee table in his office.

The $1 million in seed money from cofounder John Thornton and the promise of millions more in corporate sponsorships and memberships suggested that neither Thornton nor Smith was interested in singles. Their ambitions were confirmed—at least for their rivals in the traditional press—by a leaked memo that became known as the Manifesto. The audacious mission statement was worded in a way to suggest to some that Texas

Tribune would be making a heroic, if condescending, bid to save the moribund vestiges of journalism in Texas.

Smith says he regrets some of Thornton's hyperbolic language in what was an early iteration of a fairly simple idea: that people in Texas weren't talking about important issues because the established news outlets weren't teeing them up nearly as often as they used to.

There are considerably fewer people to do it. The AJR survey showed that every major newspaper lost statehouse staff from 2003 to 2009. The Houston Chronicle counted listings in the press books published by the state Senate and, in spite of reporters working for seven new outlets, found there were 53 reporters doing some kind of Capitol work in 2009, 30 fewer than 20 years before.

With enough cash to begin with, Thornton and Smith put together a staff of about 15 people. And with the endless newshole of the Internet, Texas Tribune promised to give its reporters plenty of time and space to deliver richly reported issue stories.

When I interviewed him in July, Smith was in the process of adding to the editorial staff and was expanding into new office space in the Tribune's downtown Austin suite. The Tribune has so far raised nearly $5 million. The site maintains more than 100 corporate sponsorships and more than 1,800 memberships. Smith dismisses no potential revenue stream out of hand.

The Tribune has so far shown a breadth that belies its promise of a more focused mission. The reporting has been strong in the expected areas: border and immigration issues, higher education and health care, politics, the lobby and ethics cases.

Through calculated hiring relying heavily on young but experienced and tech-competent reporters, the Tribune has made an impression in the creation of nearly four dozen regularly updated databases, the collection of hundreds of thousands of government documents and a sometimes dizzying number of audio, video and photo offerings.

Some veteran reporters who value their friendships in the Tribune office have sniffed privately that the Tribune has delivered a lot of solid singles and some doubles rather than Fielder-like bombs. But the site, by its mentions in rival newspaper blogs, in investigative partnerships and story publication in newspapers, is being taken as a formidable player at the Capitol in Austin. Smith predicts the Tribune will be able to show its full range of possibilities when the 82nd Texas Legislature convenes on January 11, 2011.

"If everything we are planning comes to fruition, there will never be a session as transparent, as broadly and deeply covered as this one," Smith says. "This is why we're here, and the session is no time to dick around."

As much as of his staff's success, Smith says he is proud of having offered a competitive spur to Hearst's Houston Chronicle and San Antonio Express-News, which combined their statehouse bureaus in 2007, and Belo's Dallas Morning News.

Smith is particularly impressed by Cox's Austin American-Statesman (disclosure: I used to work there), which lost bureau staff in the 2009 AJR poll, but has since held fast, committing itself to strong issues reporting around the state budget and health care. The Statesman also won admirers for its partnership with the St. Petersburg Times to create a Texas version of PolitiFact, a news and graphic package that tests the truth of statements made by government officials.

"If your only goal is for Texas to be a better place, then the more good journalism there is the better," Smith says. "We were willing to assert, arrogantly and without question, that Texans want to have a public discussion, that they want a better Texas."

Mark Katches believes that, as in Texas, the Capitol is a logical focal point for coverage in a big state. California Watch, an outcropping of the Berkeley-based Center for Investigative Reporting, exists to do state stories that no one else is doing.

When Katches was reporting a decade ago in Sacramento, he recalls competing with 85 to 90 reporters. Today there are about two dozen. The Orange County Register's bureau is run out of one reporter's home, he says. With generous foundation funding for at least the next two years, Katches has put together a staff of 11 full-time reporters, three of them working in Sacramento, along with a senior editor, giving him one of the biggest Statehouse staffs in California.

But Katches, who built Pulitzer Prize-finalist investigative teams at the Register and edited two Pulitzer winners for the Milwaukee Journal Sentinel, wasn't interested in staffing the Statehouse in Sacramento waiting to report on the debate over the latest legislation.

"From my perspective, I'd far rather do stories that nobody knows about, that somebody has to respond to and fix," Katches says. "By the time something gets to the Capitol, everybody already knows about it. It's just a matter of covering what the Legislature decides. There are other people already doing that."

California Watch works differently than the other people by marketing its stories to the news organizations it is ostensibly competing with. When California Watch broke a nursing home funding scandal in April, it created eight different versions of the story so it could be picked up and used in different ways by several of the big state newspapers as well as television and public radio stations. California Watch did the same for a story about vacation payouts for state workers, and created a payout database on its own site.

"It's a big state, and you can't assume anything by creating one homogeneous product," Katches says. "You've got to be flexible, adaptable, tailor things for your market. It certainly adds a lot of work, but there is exhilaration in the bang you get for each story, knowing that the director's cut is always on our news site."

Evan Halper, Sacramento bureau chief for the Los Angeles Times, says his paper has maintained its commitment to government accountability. For all of its corporate woes—parent Tribune Co. is in bankruptcy—management at the Times has identified Statehouse coverage as one of its core values, Halper says. Unlike every other traditional newspaper bureau in the state, the Times has added a reporter and a blogger for a total of nine staffers, including Halper, to what was already the second biggest Statehouse bureau in California, next to that of the hometown Sacramento Bee.

Because California is the eighth largest economy in the world, and so much of that economic activity moves through and around a state government that is often characterized in the press as dysfunctional, Halper says his bosses like the market for what his staff produces.

But Halper says the work of the Times, the Bee and California Watch is hardly enough. The San Francisco Chronicle, the San Jose Mercury News and the Orange County Register are conspicuous in their Statehouse staff reductions.

The problem has been so apparent that elected officials over the past few years have brought in former reporters for accountability and investigative projects in places like the Assembly Accountability Committee and the Senate Office of Oversight.

In theory, having reporters on the inside would give agencies a fresh perspective on what was expected of them, says Tom Dresslar, who left journalism after 13 years to do investigative work for the Assembly speaker. From time to time, former reporters have turned up ethics and spending problems, he says. But having government police itself is a poor substitute for an active press looking in from the outside.

"You had to go into it with your eyes wide open," says Dresslar, who is now a spokesman for the state treasurer's office. "And when you entered that building, you realized that politics was going to touch everything you do."

The threat of political taint bleeds into the question of whether the federal or state governments should use tax money to support news institutions large and small. How serious a hearing this idea will eventually get is anyone's guess.

The entrepreneurs coming out of newspapers, whose careers were shaped by the relationship between the Fourth Estate and the three others, are wary. Like David Royse, executive editor for the News Service of Florida, they are more comfortable with trusting their editorial independence to the marketplace.

The idea for News Service of Florida is so old it's new. For about a hundred years, State House News Service practiced blanket newsgathering in Boston, the kind for which political insiders and devotees would pay good money. When new ownership looked for a news market, Florida seemed to make sense.

The Miami Herald and the St. Petersburg Times had shed Statehouse reporters when they combined bureaus late in 2008. Every paper in the state rid itself of reporters in Tallahassee between the 2003 and 2009 AJR surveys. Since then, the Daytona Beach News-Journal has pulled out of the Capitol altogether and Fort Lauderdale's Sun-Sentinel reduced its staff to an administrative assistant.

Owners Russell Pergament, Stephen Cummings and Craig Sandler called on Royse, a pugnacious longtime fixture at the Capitol for the AP. Royse was impressed with the popularity of the Massachusetts service and surprised at how little of the success had to do with its Spartan website.

Imagine, Royse thought, a news service in Florida cultivating the same subscriber base—the lobby, state employee and education organizations, law firms and advocacy groups—paying more than $1,000 a year for a comprehensive Statehouse wire service e-mailed to the customer. Add to that, much of the same coverage on a modern website available to everyone.

Royse's most recent recruit is John Kennedy. After 25 years with Tribune Co., most of them covering the Statehouse for the Orlando Sentinel, Kennedy chose to take a buyout in 2008. Bob Norman reported on his decision and on the state of journalism at the time in his blog, The Daily Pulp, for the Broward Palm Beach New Times. "The Pulp has been a grim and bloody business of late," Norman wrote. "Reporting on the slaughter of the press in South Florida is like being near the front in war, hearing the bombs, knowing they aren't far away and could strike at any time. And the number of casualties just keep growing and growing."

Kennedy had spent a miserable year working for the Florida Chamber of Commerce Foundation before quitting in frustration to freelance. When Royse offered what amounted to a serious pay cut from his Chamber salary to come to work for the news service, Kennedy gratefully accepted.

"Working at the Chamber was like the theater of the absurd. It was the worst year of my life," he says. "I missed the paper badly and realized that this leopard couldn't change his spots. I love my job. I love my profession. And I was at the point of understanding I was going to have to sacrifice for it."

"I love my job. I love my profession. And I was at the point of understanding I was going to have to sacrifice for it."

—John Kennedy

Royse says Kennedy will eventually be rewarded for bringing a crucial level of authority and expertise to a bureau staffed with hungry young reporters. In less than two years, the news service, with five full-time reporters, is as big as the combined Miami/St. Pete bureau, the largest in Tallahassee.

"I don't know if it's good for democracy, but it's good for state news coverage," Royse says. "Yes, we have a target audience that we satisfy, people who know what's in the bills we write about. But you can go to our website and know what's going on over there."

Mary Ellen Klas, one of the two chiefs of the combined bureau, who draws her paycheck from the Miami Herald, welcomes the addition of new coverage at the Capitol. And not only for the competition. She is married to Kennedy. Klas was not offered a buyout, but she says she would have gladly switched roles with her husband if she had known how much he would suffer when he was out of the business. She sits in an office where Kennedy used to work as the Orlando Sentinel's bureau chief.

"It [the News Service of Florida] is our competition," Klas says. "They are becoming a place of record for the Statehouse. It has forced us to be more imaginative in our coverage."

The Herald will also be pressed by the Florida Tribune, an issues-based website. Gary Fineout, a much respected former Capitol reporter for the Miami Herald and the Tallahassee Democrat, and a small staff provide original Statehouse content under contract to LobbyTools, a legislative tracking and news aggregating site aimed at the same readership as the News Service of Florida. As part of the agreement, Fineout carries the same content on his Florida Tribune.

Fineout is the most entrepreneurial of Statehouse journalists in Florida, having supported himself for years on freelance work. He considers his blog, The Fine Print, which offers his political analysis, another platform to promote the Fineout brand.

He is, in many ways, the distillation of statehouse journalism today, deeply rooted in the traditional ways, restless, creative and excited. Fineout is pragmatic, having been part of the massive downsizing at state capitols across the country. His success is proof of a future for watching state government and a source of hope.

But like so many in the business, Fineout cannot be sure where it is all going. "I think we all recognize that this is an evolution we're part of," he says. "We're still discussing which is the better path to take. I try not to be too optimistic or totally pessimistic. I don't hold my breath for anything. The one thing I try to do is move forward."

Critical Thinking

1. What change in the amount of traditional news media's coverage of state governments has occurred in the past two decades?

2. What alternatives to traditional media coverage of state governments have arisen in the past decade or two?

3. To what is Professor Paul Starr of Princeton University referring when he notes "a shift to an earlier pattern in American history" in media news sources?

4. What are some examples of journalists being entrepreneurial in seeking financial support for their reporting work?

5. What is the "citizen journalist movement"?

6. What are "Texas Tribune" and "California Watch," what do they do, and how are they funded?

AJR Senior Contributing Writer **MARK LISHERON** is Austin bureau chief for Texas Watchdog, a government accountability news website. He covered statehouse news, among many other things, in 24 years as a reporter for the Austin American-Statesman and the Milwaukee Journal Sentinel.

Bloggers Press for Power

Whether bloggers qualify for press credentials is getting a lot of attention in state capitols.

NICOLE CASAL MOORE

A "blog swarm" began shortly after Rob Weber told a blogger why he couldn't have a press pass to cover the Kentucky Legislature.

Weber, who is director of public information at the Kentucky Legislative Research Commission, told Mark Nickolas of BluegrassReport.org that he was welcome to watch from the gallery. But he couldn't have a seat with the journalists.

This is how Nickolas headlined his post about their exchange: "A Brave New World Hits the Old World Head-On."

And this is how Weber reacted: "I'm 35 years old," he thought. "I'm the Old World?"

It got worse. A few days later, Club for Growth's blog called for a swarm. "It's time for blogging barbarians to jump the moat and tear down the gate," the blog read. Seven or eight more blogs started writing about the issue, Weber says.

This is "likely an early skirmish in what will be a lengthy nationwide struggle," read Tapscott's Copy Desk.

Even National Journal's Beltway Blogroll mentioned the situation.

Weber was more famous than he wanted to be, but he and the Kentucky Legislative Research Commission stuck by their decision at the time. But the media landscape is evolving, he says, and the precise geography of blogger country is still unknown. The question of whether bloggers qualify for press credentials is one his state will undoubtedly revisit, and others are taking up.

Bloggers aren't taking "no" for an answer. Bluegrass-Report.org's Mark Nickolas found a loophole in the Kentucky policy and qualified for credentials. He started writing a column for a local paper. Bloggers in at least Texas and Tennessee plan to apply for press passes to cover the 2007 session.

"This is an issue that's going to keep coming up," Weber says. "Blogs are gaining power. They're influencing the way stories are covered and they're revolutionizing the information distribution system. . . . There is a metamorphosis going on and nothing is the same as it was yesterday."

Into the Blogosphere

The web log was born around a decade ago. Its earliest genre, which is still its most popular, was the personal diary. Today, blog search engine Technorati.com tracks 57 million blogs, 11 percent of which discuss politics, according to the Pew Internet and American Life Project.

Although just 8 percent of American Internet users keep blogs, 39 percent of Americans read them, Pew found in a summer 2006 survey. The Blogosphere is part of the larger online media universe—a place 19 percent of Americans went for election news on a typical day in August 2006, according to another Pew study.

It's hard to count exactly how many bloggers write about legislatures, but NCSL's blog, The Thicket at State Legislatures, links to around 150 others with some connection to a statehouse. Many are part of the grassroots or citizen journalism movement like BluegrassReport.org.

State Legislatures doesn't know of any bloggers not affiliated with a print or broadcast news organizations who have credentials to cover a legislature. A majority of legislative communicators who responded to a quick survey said they would not be inclined to give a blogger the same credential status as a journalist. That's a sentiment reporters echo. But media experts say a blanket denial policy is not a good idea.

Of the 99 state legislative chambers (Nebraska is unicameral), 81 have a process to give reporters credentials. The qualifications vary, as do the perks, which range from a parking space and a beeline through security to a desk in the building and floor access.

Reaching Out to Blogs

Even without press credentials, bloggers are writing about legislatures and their members in every state. You might want to watch what they're saying, and consider reaching out to them as a new part of public relations. Here are some ideas.

1. **Peer into the blogosphere:** If you don't already know, find out which blogs write about your legislature. You can use Technorati.com to search for who has mentioned you or your legislature in a blog post. NCSL's blogroll at The Thicket at State Legislatures (ncsl.typepad.com/thethicket) can tell you who's writing blogs in each state.

2. **Don't ignore bloggers:** "The real issue is whether legislatures and the executive branch will view bloggers as a legitimate part of the public discussion," says Tennessee politics and policy blogger Bill Hobbs, of BillHobbs.com. "Will they talk to bloggers? Will they respond to their Freedom of Information Act requests?" If you don't comment, bloggers will say so. And remember: reporters read blogs.

3. **Tip off bloggers:** Bloggers can use anonymous sources. Some of them are even anonymous themselves. If you've got an important news tip you don't feel comfortable telling a reporter, tell a blogger. Eileen Smith, of InThePinkTexas.com is all ears. "People send me stories, anonymous tips and suggestions," she says. "They share things with me that they wouldn't tell reporters."

4. **Talk to bloggers directly:** Pennsylvania Representative Mark Cohen, who blogs at repmarkbcohen .blogspot.com and occasionally at national political blog DailyKos.com, sends out special e-mails to his list of bloggers. "When we reach out to bloggers, we're reaching out to the people who also read the blogs. There's a large number of people who like to get their news just from blogs," Cohen says. Sometimes he turns to the blogosphere when the mainstream media aren't interested. And that has paid off. A blogger was the first to write about his 2005 bill to increase the use of hybrid electric vehicles. The newspaper came next.

5. **Post comments on blogs:** People are turning to more informal means of communication like blogs, and PR professionals should understand and embrace that, says Robert Niles, editor of the online journalism review at the USC Annenberg School for Communication. "You're not just working with reporters now," Niles says. "You have to get in and participate in the discussion with the communities."

6. **Start your own blog:** Legislative staffer Ric Cantrell started SenateSite.com, the unofficial voice of the Utah Senate Majority, as a way to engage the public. As a bonus, says the assistant to majority leadership, he discovered a thriving community. "We comment on other blogs every day, and they offer their comments on our site as well," Cantrell says. "It's like talking to your neighbors."

Why Bloggers Want Credentials

Credibility is another big boon, bloggers say.

Eileen Smith, who blogs on InthePinkTexas.com, believes treating "qualified" bloggers as press is in the best interest of the legislature. "A known, credible blogger on the floor is better (and far less dangerous) than an unknown anonymous blogger in the gallery," Smith says. She suggests considering a blogger's education, experience and even legislative background when deciding who is "qualified." Bloggers deserve consideration, Smith says, if for no other reason than their power.

"My statewide readership consists of influential political insiders, decision makers, motivated individuals, elected officials and their staff, lobbyists and voters," Smith says. "I would contend that the reason traditional media outlets are granted press credentials is not because of their inherent objectivity, but because they have political power, influence and a direct line of communication to the public."

Smith covered the 2006 session and plans to ask for credentials in 2007. At press time, Texas officials were working on a policy that would apply to bloggers.

Martin Kennedy, an economics professor at Middle Tennessee State University, will be new to legislative blogging this session with his Legislative Report. He, too, plans to request credentials. Why? "Credibility and access," Kennedy says. "To make contacts more easily, to spread the word about the blog."

Officials in the Tennessee legislature say he'll likely get his wish. It's easy in Tennessee. He just has to rent space in the press room.

Bill Hobbs, a media relations and blogging consultant who publishes the personal political blog BillHobbs.com, believes even Tennessee's policy should be updated to be fair to "grassroots journalists" who may not be able to afford to rent space.

Letting bloggers have credentials would give the public another way to follow the legislature, Hobbs says.

"Journalists covering the state capitol can't cover every piece of legislation that's filed, but bloggers can focus on specific topics. I cover tax-type stuff, and I don't cover legislation that may affect abortion rights," he says. "Bloggers provide a second, larger set of eyes and ears and can find stories the news media missed."

Like many other web blogs that cover legislatures, Hobbs' blog contains original reporting. He digs up about 50 percent of the content himself. He has sources inside the dome, he says. He doesn't just comment on news articles.

Are Bloggers Worthy?

Based on the most common view of press credentialers, bloggers aren't worthy of press credentials. They don't subject themselves to the same ethics and accuracy standards as news reporters. They write mostly opinion. And press space is limited.

Where to Draw the Line

Based on what experts say, California has the right idea. Officials there are looking at its credentialing policy and may develop a process to let in some bloggers. All blogs shouldn't be credentialed just because they exist, experts say. But neither should all blogs be denied special access. Doing that, says Robert Niles, editor of the *Online Journalism Review* at the USC Annenberg School for Communications, is "a really good way to make your message utterly irrelevant."

"You have to decide what the new standard is going to be. If you credential everyone, you could be in a situation where you'd have to rent out the local stadium," Niles added. "You have to look at the publication."

Does the blog have a history? Niles says it's fair to say it should publish for a little while before legislatures grant it special access. Is the blog being used as ammunition for opposition research? If so, it might not qualify.

Does the blog do original research? That's the main question Mike McKean, chair of the convergence journalism faculty at the Missouri School of Journalism would ask.

"If all they do is comment upon the writings of others, maybe that's not journalism," McKean says. "If they're doing any type of original reporting, they're journalists like anyone else."

Credentialing only bloggers who are connected to mainstream media outlets is a comfortable fix, but it might be too narrow, Niles says. "They've already determined that print is inherently more legitimate than online. They need to get over that. You have to look at the publication."

Bloggers suggested looking at the number of hits a site gets. Lawyers said look at the blog's intent. If it is published to disseminate information to the public, then it just might fit under the umbrella of journalism.

And instead of renting a stadium, blogger Bill Hobbs suggests a rotating spot in the capitol press room for "citizen journalists."

Wyoming Legislative Information Officer Wendy Madsen says her office would likely provide press credentials only if the blogger was a member of a commercial media outlet. "Blogging is still the 'wild, wild west' of the journalism frontier and until there are standards for collecting, verifying, and editing information posted by bloggers, I think it is a stretch to even classify the phenomenon as journalism," she says. "That doesn't mean politicians should ignore the trend. They need to pay close attention to the blogging world to keep pace."

Allentown Morning Call reporter John L. Micek is president of the Pennsylvania Legislative Correspondents Association, which grants the long-term press passes to statehouse reporters there. He says bloggers might join the association as affiliate members, similar to membership held by journalism professors and retired reporters, but he doesn't believe they could get a full membership.

"A lot of these guys are fairly partisan, so I have concerns about opening the full membership to people who are not in a traditional sense objective reporters," says Micek, who added that this is his personal opinion; the association hasn't decided yet. "We could get into a days-long discussion of what is journalism and who is a journalist. Not to say that bloggers' work is any less credible than others but they have one point of view."

MediaNews reporter Steve Geissinger, president of the Capitol Correspondents Association of California, doesn't think it's a good idea to have partisan voices in the Capitol press corps. In California, certain press conferences aren't open to the general public, he says.

"On the officials' side, the governor and legislators don't want biased people skewing a news conference," Geissinger says. "And the media doesn't want valuable time taken up with biased questions."

The California Assembly is working with Geissinger's association to write new rules that apply to bloggers.

Scott Gant is a lawyer in Washington, D.C., whose book, *We're All Journalists Now: The Transformation of the Press and Reshaping of the Law in the Internet Age,* will be released in June. Are bloggers journalists? is a big question, but Gant takes a step further back and asks whether professional journalists should get preferential treatment at all.

Gant's argument goes back to the Bill of Rights. He says the Supreme Court has never found that the "freedom of the press" provision of the First Amendment grants any rights that "freedom of speech" doesn't apply to all citizens.

"Giving special privileges to established news organizations might violate the federal Constitution's guarantee of equal protection," Gant says. "There hasn't been enough attention to that issue."

Christine Tatum, national president of the Society of Professional Journalists, says newspapers are the "Fourth Estate"—another check and balance on our three branches of government. It would be wrong, Tatum says, not to save space for professional reporters.

"We're talking about helping advance and promote an informed citizenry, which I contend is one of the cornerstones of democracy," Tatum says. "We have to make room in these places for people who represent news organizations to be there. That's how news organizations have traditionally functioned. They're the ones who are willing to sit and listen to the blather and the grandstanding."

As for non-professional reporters, Tatum says it's hard to figure out where to draw the line. She's not alone. The Blogosphere is a murky place that can be scary, experts understand. And it's not the first time a new medium has produced confusion. In a talk to legislative communicators in October, Mark Senak, senior vice president at

Fleishman-Hillard who blogs on EyeOnFDA.com, read some quotes about the dawn of television.

This one is from a New York Times editorial in 1939. "The problem with television is that people must sit and keep their eyes glued to the screen. The average American family hasn't time for this. Therefore, the showmen are convinced that for this reason, if no other, television will never be a serious competitor of broadcasting."

Critical Thinking

1. What is the controversy about granting—or not granting—bloggers press credentials to cover a state legislature?

2. Why do bloggers want press credentials at statehouses?

3. What distinguishes most bloggers from most traditional media reporters? Why do many people think that this distinction is a good reason to deny media credentials to the former and grant them to the latter?

4. What did a 1939 *New York Times* editorial say about television as a potential competitor to radio as a source of news, and what might be the relevance of that statement to bloggers and traditional news media today?

NICOLE CASAL MOORE is an editor and writer with NCSL's Communications Division. She contributes to the magazine's blog, *The Thicket at State Legislatures.*

Cities without Newspapers

As the economic noose tightens, the notion of big cities without local dailies seems a real possibility. What would the impact be on civic life? And what might emerge to fill the gap?

RACHEL SMOLKIN

This spring, Princeton economist Sam Schulhofer-Wohl and his colleague Miguel Garrido issued a paper of vital importance to print journalists desperate for a sliver of good news: "Do Newspapers Matter? Evidence from the Closure of The Cincinnati Post."

The economists noted their findings were "statistically imprecise," yet concluded that newspapers, "even underdogs such as the Post, which had a circulation of just 27,000 when it closed—can have a substantial and measurable impact on public life."

The Cincinnati Post, a former E.W. Scripps Co. paper that expired December 31, 2007, and its Kentucky Post edition dominated circulation in the northern Kentucky suburbs, where the economists focused their inquiry. They concluded the Post's closure lowered the number of people voting in elections and the number of candidates for city council, city commission and school board in those areas. It also increased incumbent council and commission members' chances of staying in office.

"What most surprised me is I actually did find evidence that newspapers matter," says Schulhofer-Wohl, an assistant professor of economics and public affairs. At 32, he is on his second career. His first, as a journalist, included stints as a copy editor at Alabama's Birmingham Post-Herald, another now-defunct Scripps paper, and as a copy editor and reporter at the Milwaukee Journal Sentinel. "I was very worried when I went into this [research] that what I would end up proving is my whole career had been kind of pointless."

> **"I was very worried when I went into this [research] that what I would end up proving is my whole career had been kind of pointless."**
>
> —Sam Schulhofer-Wohl

Instead, Schulhofer-Wohl added to a small but growing body of economics research supporting the notion that newspapers make a difference in their communities—evidence emerging even as the industry struggles in a radically changing media environment during the worst recession since the Great Depression.

These attempts to quantify newspapers' impact on public life come as a handful of major American newspapers close and others barely cling to life. The unsettling possibility looms that some big cities could lose their sole remaining daily newspaper—and that the public won't care. If the dead-tree edition of a newspaper falls in a crowded media forest, will it matter, except to the journalists who work there? Are newer, hipper online news outlets poised to fill the void? What, if anything, will be irrevocably lost?

Journalists have long touted the indispensable role that newspapers play in a democracy, shining a bright light on the activities of elected officials. Journalism professors and political scientists have studied the way newspaper content affects readers' knowledge about local and national events.

Despite lots of legal, political and economic theory, though, "what we actually know" empirically or directly about the impact that a newspaper—or its death—has on a community "is relatively limited compared to its importance," says Matthew Gentzkow, an associate professor of economics at the University of Chicago's Booth School of Business. "What's exciting is there's been an upsurge of work on that question."

Gentzkow's own research, with colleague Jesse Shapiro, probes the impact on voter turnout in elections where U.S. newspapers have closed from the 1870s until modern times. Though they are still analyzing the data, some preliminary evidence suggests that turnout may drop significantly in communities after a newspaper closes.

At MIT, economics and political science professor Jim Snyder teamed with Stockholm University economist David Strömberg and found that members of Congress who get a lot of newspaper coverage work harder for their constituents than those who don't: They funnel more money back home and testify at more committee hearings; they also are less likely to vote along party lines.

A second project the duo is launching with a Stanford business professor explores the impact of newspaper coverage on judicial behavior. They will examine whether judges who are elected and receive lots of print coverage hand down sentences that reflect the political outlook of their area. "There is some evidence [from previous research] that judges who are elected, especially in conservative areas, are tougher in their sentencing," Snyder says. "The idea is to see whether [newspaper] scrutiny, the watchdog role, matters for judicial behavior."

Pollsters at the Pew Research Center for the People & the Press have exposed an alarming disconnect between newspapers' role in civic life and the public's appreciation of it. A Pew survey conducted in March of about 1,000 adults found that only 43 percent of Americans say losing their local newspaper would hurt civic life in their community "a lot." A mere 33 percent said they would miss reading the local paper a lot if it were no longer available.

"In our media surveys, you get the sense that many people don't recognize the source of their news, especially when it comes to online news," says Carroll Doherty, Pew's associate director. "They may be following a link, they may be forwarding a link, they may be on Facebook and click on a link. People may be getting more information from newspapers than they realize."

Notes Conrad Fink, a former journalist who teaches newspaper management and strategy at the University of Georgia: "The American public doesn't realize it, but they're going to miss us if we're gone."

The notion that newspapers actually might be gone in the foreseeable future is the subject of much anxiety on media blogs and even in major news publications, where predictions of newspaper deaths were en vogue early this year.

In a February 16 Time cover story, the magazine's former managing editor Walter Isaacson breathlessly declared: "During the past few months, the crisis in journalism has reached meltdown proportions." Isaacson, now president and CEO of the Aspen Institute, added, "It is now possible to contemplate a time when some major cities will no longer have a newspaper and when magazines and network-news operations will employ no more than a handful of reporters."

In a front-page New York Times story March 12, Mike Simonton, a senior director at Fitch Ratings who focuses on media debt, predicted: "In 2009 and 2010, all the two-newspaper markets will become one-newspaper markets, and you will start to see one-newspaper markets become no-newspaper markets."

Simonton was at it again six days later, when my own newspaper, USA Today, published a Money section cover story: "Extra! Extra! Are newspapers dying?" The article forecast that at least one city likely will soon lose its last daily newspaper and quoted Simonton as saying that newspaper deaths "could be a lot more widespread than people have been predicting."

While some of these dire prophesies seem a little overwrought, it's hard to argue with the perception that the industry is vulnerable.

Since December, six companies that publish daily newspapers have sought Chapter 11 bankruptcy protection, among them Tribune Co., which owns eight daily metro papers, including the Los Angeles Times and the Chicago Tribune; Star Tribune Holdings Corp., which owns Minneapolis' Star Tribune; the Philadelphia Newspapers LLC, owner of the Philadelphia Inquirer and Philadelphia Daily News; and the Sun-Times Media Group Inc., anchored by the Chicago Sun-Times.

Scripps' 150-year-old Rocky Mountain News in Denver published its last edition February 27. Hearst's Seattle Post-Intelligencer followed 18 days later with its last print edition. The 146-year-old paper with an editorial staff of 165 is now an online-only publication with an editorial staff of 21. Gannett's Tucson Citizen in Arizona published its final print edition May 16; the 138-year-old paper will linger as an online-only opinion site.

Hearst has threatened to close or sell its San Francisco Chronicle, the city's sole remaining paid-circulation daily, if the newspaper can't dramatically cut expenses. (Philip F. Anschutz's San Francisco Examiner is delivered free to targeted homes. See "Home Free," April/May 2007.) Hearst said February 24 that the Chronicle lost more than $50 million in 2008 and "this year's losses to date are worse."

In March, the paper's largest union agreed to drastic cuts to meet management's demands, including allowing the Chronicle to slash at least 150 union jobs. "The immediate goal is to reduce staff, and we may not know until later in the year whether other factors," such as contracting out the printing of the paper, "will help keep the Chronicle alive, says Doug Cuthbertson, executive officer of the California Media Workers Guild, which includes editorial, advertising and circulation employees.

The following month, even the nation's premier newspaper company stepped into this maelstrom of uncertainty. The New York Times Co. threatened to shutter its prestigious Boston Globe unless the Globe's unions agreed to $20 million in concessions. The paper was projected to lose $85 million this year without substantial cost reductions, according to the Times Co. After a turbulent month of negotiations, Globe Publisher P. Steven Ainsley told his newspaper in a front-page story May 8 that the threatened closure had been "extraordinarily difficult" for readers, advertisers, employees and him. He said he expected further job losses but predicted the Globe would still be publishing a year from now if union members ratify wage cuts and other concessions.

Newspaper stock prices are dismal. McClatchy, which showed great faith in the industry's future by boldly buying the Knight Ridder chain in 2006, hovered around 70 cents per share in early May. Among its 30 newspapers are the Miami Herald, Sacramento Bee and Raleigh's News & Observer. Lee Enterprises, which in 2005 acquired Pulitzer and its 14 daily newspapers, including the St. Louis Post-Dispatch, (see "Lee Who?" June/July 2005), was barely above 30 cents per share in early spring before creeping past $1 in May.

"The chairmen of McClatchy, Lee, the rest of them have a fiduciary responsibility to shareholders," Georgia's Fink says. "That is just as strong as our need to put out information to the public. They've got to respond to this. The question is: How long can a publicly owned company continue to suffer those losses?"

Fink and other analysts add that some major newspaper companies are suffering not because their papers are unprofitable but because their owners have assumed vast amounts of debt. "When operating profit drops to 10 percent or 5 percent or disappears for a couple of years, that debt burden crushes them," he says of companies such as Lee and McClatchy. Tribune Co. has a $13 billion debt, mostly incurred when real estate tycoon Sam Zell took the company private in 2007.

Fink concludes: "I think there is imminent danger of losing some of these major papers."

Some media analysts believe forecasts about newspaper closures are premature. "The trend toward one-newspaper markets has been in the works for a long, long time," says Philip Meyer, a journalism professor emeritus at the University of North Carolina at Chapel Hill and author of "The Vanishing Newspaper: Saving Journalism in the Information Age." "I don't think we're heading toward a no-newspaper trend."

John Morton, a media analyst and AJR columnist, notes that of the 1,422 daily newspapers in this country, "we never hear about, say, 1,350 of those newspapers, almost all of which are profitable . . . not as much as two or three years ago, but they're not on the edge of a cliff, either." (See The Business of Journalism, June/July 2009.)

Publicly held newspaper companies reported just over 10 percent profit last year, down from double that in 2004—and the margin was only as high as 10 percent because of dramatic cost-cutting. Still, Morton says, "Bear in mind that an awful lot of businesses don't do 10 percent in the boom years."

Yet he's concerned that newspapers' financial turnaround will be incomplete even when the economy improves. In past recoveries from recessions, newspapers recaptured almost all of the advertising revenue lost during the downturn. Now that the Internet and its free classified ad model have taken root, it's not at all clear that will happen this time. "It may mean going forward that, particularly because of a potential loss of classified generally, that newspapers will be a lot less profitable than they have in the past," Morton says.

This year's "The State of the News Media," an annual accounting of the field by the Pew Research Center's Project for Excellence in Journalism, provides a sobering assessment of the industry that should be read by all journalists, though not without large quantities of alcohol nearby. Among its array of depressing statistics, it notes that newspaper ad revenues have dropped 23 percent in the last two years, and some newspapers have lost three-quarters of their value. "By our calculations, nearly one out of every five journalists working for newspapers in 2001 is now gone, and 2009 may be the worst year yet," the report says.

Its authors add: "There is not yet a major city without a newspaper, but that, too, could be coming soon."

Partly in response to the bleak outlook for metro papers and the relentless cost reductions at those publications, an exciting rebirth is taking place in cities such as San Diego, Minneapolis, New Haven, St. Louis and Chicago. Tiny but ambitious nonprofit online ventures are springing up as supplements or alternatives to the newspapers in their cities. They focus on public affairs and watchdog journalism—the very functions that metro newspapers have long prided themselves on providing.

At voiceofsandiego.org, which has 11 total staff members, CEO Scott Lewis believes his reporters can provide the kind of accountability journalism that has long been the province of newspapers. "We have a mission here," Lewis says. "It's not to make money. It's to provide information and investigative reporting. Our reporters are not allowed to do a story unless they can answer a fundamental question: 'Why is this important?' We won't cover a celebrity who stabs his wife, which might be better for somebody who's trying to attract advertisers and readers."

Instead, the Website has helped force out the heads of two local redevelopment agencies. One faces criminal charges; the other is the subject of a grand jury investigation. It has hammered the police chief for incorrectly stating the city's crime statistics. In March, a two-part series by Kelly Thornton, a former San Diego Union-Tribune reporter, explored the impact of the Mexican drug war on San Diego. In April, a two-part series revealed a "real estate swindle, uncovered by a three-month voiceofsandiego.org investigation, involving fake buyers, duped lenders, forged documents and extravagant purchase prices, that has infected two condo projects in Escondido and one in San Marcos."

This site, which gets about 72,000 unique visitors monthly, began in February 2005 with $355,000 in startup money from Buzz Woolley, a local entrepreneur who has given a total of $1.3 million. Yet this year Woolley's annual contribution will be $200,000, roughly one-fifth of the site's budget. Lewis says the site draws revenue from 826 donors, a growing list of corporate sponsors who will contribute 15 percent of its budget this year and funders such as the John S. and James L. Knight Foundation.

At the St. Louis Beacon (stlbeacon.org), launched in April 2008 (see Drop Cap, December 2008/January 2009), Editor Margaret Wolf Freivogel has adopted a similar slogan: "News That Matters." "Instead of covering a hugely broad range of things, we try to pick what's going to be significant and have some broader impact," she says, including probing the challenges facing St. Louis public schools, the effect of the mortgage crisis on the city and the racial dimensions of the mayor's race.

Freivogel, a former reporter and editor at the St. Louis Post-Dispatch, says online journalism is a "far superior tool" for original reporting than print because it removes time and space constraints, allows links to previous work and offers opportunities for interacting with readers. "Online, it's so easy to try things, easy to experiment," she says. "That's an advantage of being a startup: You're starting with no expectations of your own or on the part of the public."

Her total staff of 17 is funded largely through donations, including a $500,000 challenge grant from Emily Pulitzer—one of the Pulitzers who owned the Post-Dispatch until 2005. Freivogel hopes to transition to a larger membership base of small donors, similar to National Public Radio's model. This year, she also began accepting ads on the Website, which attracts 28,000 unique visitors monthly.

MinnPost in Minneapolis (minnpost.com), an online public affairs site launched in November 2007, (see Drop Cap,

February/March 2008), has more than 200,000 unique monthly visitors. Joel Kramer, its founder, editor and CEO, added a full-time Washington correspondent in January—a nearly unheard of step at a time when many newspaper companies, including Copley, Newhouse and Media General, are shuttering their D.C. bureaus, (see "Endangered Species," December 2008/January 2009).

"Our mission is public affairs journalism that matters for people who care about Minnesota," says Kramer, a former editor and publisher of the Star Tribune. "A lot happens in Washington that is of unique local interest."

> ## "Our mission is public affairs journalism that matters for people who care about Minnesota. A lot happens in Washington that is of unique local interest."
>
> —Joel Kramer

Kramer hopes MinnPost will break even financially by 2011 or, if the economic slump continues, by 2012. He's using foundation money to propel MinnPost through the early years but ultimately hopes to cover expenses through advertising, sponsorship, membership and fundraising events, and tap foundation grants only for special expenses, such as investigative projects.

Lewis and Kramer say they've been flooded with calls from journalists around the country trying to start their own regional Websites and are looking into forming a consortium of nonprofit regional online news operations. The consortium also could help the startups share challenges such as creating a national advertising network or finding attorneys who could vet their investigative work.

In Denver, a group of former newspaper staffers from the deceased Rocky Mountain News tried in early spring to launch a different sort of online news outlet: the for-profit InDenverTimes.com. In mid-March, the group announced backing from three local businessmen and pledged to move forward if it got 50,000 paying subscribers by April 23 ($4.99 per month for one year), with a launch scheduled for May 4. "It's really a gamble," the site's managing editor, Steve Foster, said in mid-March. "We're not entirely sure it's going to work."

Rather than specializing in public affairs reporting, like its fledgling nonprofit brethren, the group behind InDenverTimes had hoped to provide broad coverage of the Denver metro area—albeit with a staff of about 35 instead of the Rocky's former editorial roster of 230.

For example, "sports in Denver is huge," said Foster, a former Rocky assistant sports editor for interactive. "To cover local news without covering sports, you're missing a lot of interest for the community." That's also why he sought more journalists than some other startups: "If you've got a staff of 10 people, it's not a good idea to waste them covering a Denver Broncos game, but we have to cover the Denver Broncos."

By the April 23 deadline, though, the site had attracted only about 3,000 subscribers, and Foster and his group of journalists parted with the investors. In mid-May, Foster was planning a scaled-back general interest news site, the Rocky Mountain Independent. He hoped for a mid-summer launch with a core staff of no more than a dozen, including a tech person and business manager, supported by subscription and advertising revenue. He planned to supplement the staff of former Rocky reporters and editors with paid freelance contributors and partnerships with bloggers. Foster says he and other journalists would kick in startup money for the new venture.

"For-profit is still the goal," Foster says of the revamped site, adding, "I'm willing to work for free for three months to make it a reality."

Hearst, too, tried early this spring to carve out a for-profit niche online. The Seattle Post-Intelligencer began life anew as an online-only publication with 21 editorial staffers and 14 more on the sales side as of May 18.

"My line has always been [that] I want to be the best source of breaking local news in Seattle, and I still want that to be the case," says Michelle Nicolosi, who was assistant managing editor at the old seattlepi.com and now is executive producer of the new seattlepi.com. Among the staff are some of the best-known names from the PI, including political columnist Joel Connelly and two-time Pulitzer Prize-winning cartoonist David Horsey.

"We have a . . . trusted brand in the community with the Seattle PI," says Lincoln Millstein, senior vice president of Hearst Newspapers. "We did close the paper, unfortunately, but we want to try an experiment to see if we can extend the journalism by continuing with a digital effort."

Millstein says Hearst will subsidize seattlepi.com during its first few months, but the goal is profitability. While he says "our journalism will be the heartbeat of the site," he hopes it also will offer a laboratory for community interactions—and that other Hearst papers can learn from the experiment with the "ultimate local community portal."

Borrowing from the model of The Huffington Post (huffingtonpost.com), seattlepi.com offers commentary by some prominent community figures, including Norm Stamper, a former Seattle police chief, and Rep. Jim McDermott, a Democrat whose district includes Seattle and parts of several surrounding communities.

"We have to grow beyond supporting our Websites with our newspaper content," Millstein says. Though many news sites already mix their own journalism with blogging and comments from community members, "what's missing is sort of the middle—blogging and content creation from well-known, knowledgeable sources in the community."

When decision-makers participate, he says, "They tell all their friends about it. . . . It creates a level of engagement that provides more content, drives more traffic [to the site] and attracts more advertisers."

As Millstein describes the energy and excitement he believes the revamped seattlepi.com is creating, he freely acknowledges its leaders are culling from many different sources—not only community leaders but also competing media sites and other

Hearst newspapers and magazines. When Hearst decided to close the newspaper, its executives wondered how they could replicate the PI as an online-only publication with far fewer resources, Millstein says. "We realized we can't."

The nascent online publications are promising and inspiring. At least right now, though, none is poised to replace a big-city newspaper.

That's partly a function of scale: 10, 17 or even 35 people, no matter how motivated and talented, cannot replicate the work of several hundred. It's also a reflection of newspapers' mass audience. Despite declining circulation, newspapers still reach more than 34 million people on weekdays and 42 million on Sunday in print alone, according to Audit Bureau of Circulations data for the six months ending March 31. In March, newspaper Websites' unique audience totaled 73.3 million, according to Nielsen Online. Newspapers use that mass influence to engage communities, prod policy changes and hold officials accountable.

"The power of newspapers still is their ability to aggregate audience and reach many people, particularly the opinion makers in a town or community," says Charlotte Hall, editor of the Orlando Sentinel.

The Sentinel, which has a circulation of 206,205 on weekdays and 315,298 on Sunday, has extensively documented questionable activities involving Central Florida's toll-road authority. An April 5 story revealed newly obtained Orange County grand-jury records that "detail a sophisticated political-fundraising operation" run out of the authority and "appear to place the agency's director in the middle of it–an allegation he flatly denies."

The paper's work on the topic has "raised a huge outcry in the community," Hall says, "and it's because we're the megaphone in the community." While national newspapers have larger megaphones, such local watchdog reporting is unlikely to originate in the New York Times, Wall Street Journal or USA Today. "I believe the most threatened accountability reporting is in our communities, not at the national level," Hall says.

Jim O'Shea, a former editor at the Los Angeles Times who was ousted in January 2008 over his refusal to slash the paper's battered newsroom even further, quotes the late playwright Arthur Miller's observation that a good newspaper is a "nation talking to itself." If a newspaper disappears, "What goes away is kind of an element of community leadership," O'Shea says.

O'Shea, now a Shorenstein fellow at Harvard University, says that although newspapers have scaled back their coverage of government institutions, the startups are in no position to replace their work. "For people to go in and work for next-to-nothing, with real low salaries and small staff, I applaud them, but I don't think it's a long-term solution," he says. "Who's going to cover the courthouse? That's the fundamental question."

"An investigative reporter has to be out there covering something to dig up stories," O'Shea adds. "Half the time, the best stories come from somebody who's covering a beat. . . . You don't just sit in your office and dream up investigative projects and go do them."

When those investigative projects infuriate powerful community forces, institutional strength and infrastructure are critical. For particularly large and controversial stories, such as the Boston Globe's Pulitzer Prize-winning investigation of sexual abuse by Roman Catholic priests, "you need institutional heft," says Rick Edmonds, a media business analyst at the Poynter Institute. That involves, in part, layers of critical editors, copy editors—and lawyers.

At voiceofsandiego.org, getting a media lawyer to review investigations was a need the staff didn't fully anticipate at first. "We decided to get the stories pre-vetted more often," CEO Lewis says. "We haven't been sued yet, but we realized the potential was certainly there." He has set aside $20,000 for possible legal expenses for the year.

Yet the typical libel lawsuit requires a minimum of $20,000 to $50,000 for the initial rounds of dismissal motions alone—and only about half of those succeed, according to Chuck Tobin, a media attorney at Holland & Knight and former in-house counsel for Gannett. (He also has successfully defended AJR senior contributing writer Susan Paterno against a libel suit.)

"For any journalism enterprise to have the breathing room for hard-hitting investigative reporting—and to withstand the blowback of libel litigation—it should have a nest egg of six figures available to defend its reporting," Tobin says. "That's an unfortunate reality in today's legal environment."

The exciting online work being launched right now also assumes that major metros and national papers still exist—and that the new outlets have the luxury of filling in gaps left by these publications, rather than trying to stitch together comprehensive coverage of a community.

"We will probably never be the sort of one-stop shopping as a daily newspaper," says Stephen Engelberg, managing editor of ProPublica (propublica.org), a national nonprofit investigative outlet launched last year. "This new era is going to be more reflective of people's interests, for better or worse."

> **"This new era is going to be more reflective of people's interests, for better or worse."**
>
> —Stephen Engelberg

During the presidential election, for example, ProPublica did not write about the daily political sparring or the latest campaign spending reports, but when Republican vice presidential candidate Sarah Palin began boasting about her handling of the now-infamous "Bridge to Nowhere," "we were very interested" in exploring the truth behind her statements, Engelberg says. ProPublica also evaluated claims of voter fraud.

Such coverage "does presume an existing media universe," notes Engelberg, a former managing editor at Portland's Oregonian and investigative editor at the New York Times. "If someone said to me tomorrow, 'Portland no longer has a daily newspaper. Here's 20 reporters,' what do you do? What if they're it? You go to the school board, you go to the city planning meetings. How do you get any flavor of the community into your newspaper?"

This year, leaders of the American Society of Newspaper Editors had planned to focus their annual convention on survival strategies. But in a sign of the times, on February 27—the Rocky's last day of life—ASNE canceled its convention and opted for online programming instead. The last time the group didn't meet was 1945, during the final months of World War II. "This was a very extraordinary year for the whole newspaper industry," says Hall, who was ASNE's president until the end of April. "Editors need to be in their newsrooms."

In a further sign of the times, ASNE's members voted April 6 to change the group's name to the American Society of News Editors, dropping "newspaper" from its title.

In Rob Reiner's 1987 classic, "The Princess Bride," a cynical Miracle Max provides an insightful assessment of mortality as he tries to revive the deceased hero:

"Miracle Max (Billy Crystal): *It just so happens that your friend here is only MOSTLY dead. There's a big difference between mostly dead and all dead. Mostly dead is slightly alive. With all dead, well, with all dead there's usually only one thing you can do.*

Inigo Montoya (Mandy Patinkin): *What's that?*

Miracle Max: *Go through his clothes and look for loose change."*

In the newspaper industry, where loose change is scarce these days, where is the dividing line between mostly dead and all dead? Is the Seattle P-I dead, or slightly alive? Is a newspaper dead when it folds its print edition? When it cuts delivery days? When it slashes staff?

Alan Mutter, a former top editor at the San Francisco Chronicle who now reports on the industry in his Reflections of a Newsosaur blog (newsosaur.blogspot.com), frames the issue of newspaper mortality this way: "It's increasingly unlikely that American cities are going to support two newspapers, so the next question is will they support one newspaper. That's a more complicated question. Is it a newspaper if it goes digital or publishes two days a week?"

During the last week of March, the Detroit News and the Detroit Free Press, part of a joint operating agreement between Gannett (owner of the Free Press) and MediaNews Group (owner of the News), ended home delivery except on Thursday and Friday for both papers and Sunday for the Free Press—the three heaviest advertising days. Thinner versions of the papers can still be purchased daily at convenience stores and newspaper boxes under the new system, which is intended to save money and drive subscribers to continuous coverage on the Internet.

"We're here because we're fighting for our survival," Dave Hunke, then-CEO of the Detroit Media Partnership and publisher of the Free Press, said December 16 in announcing the plan. He said the partnership has an "absolute resolve" to save both papers, "and we are not going to go away. . . . We absolutely

believe in daily newspapers and the future of newspapers." (In April, Hunke was named president and publisher of USA Today.)

The Orlando Sentinel's Hall predicts the industry is poised for a revival—but not necessarily in the form it has known before.

"As we come out of recession, we'll see an industry in which there's far more sharing of resources than we have had in the past," Hall says. She notes her paper, owned by Tribune Co., and Gannett's Florida Today, a onetime rival, share content, as do South Florida's former fierce foes, the Miami Herald, Palm Beach Post and Fort Lauderdale's Sun-Sentinel. (see "Share and Share Alike," February/March). Last year, eight of Ohio's largest newspapers also agreed to share content.

> **"As we come out of recession, we'll see an industry in which there's far more sharing of resources than we have had in the past."**
> —Charlotte Hall

The widespread sharing will not be limited to journalistic endeavors, Hall says: "Papers are going to be delivering each other; they're going to be printing each other."

She thinks more newspapers may drop some print publishing days, as Monday and Tuesday are traditionally weak advertising days. Some papers might try a super-weekend edition, combining their Friday, Saturday and Sunday offerings, à la USA Today.

Yet these models could further dilute the power and institutional heft of newspapers in major American cities, turning them into occasional visitors on subscribers' doorsteps, ones even less tailored to particular communities and their unique identities than they are right now.

"The most typical scenario is that we will continue to have newspapers in major cities, but they're going to be a good deal smaller and there will be diverse [media] players, some of them that have been around for a while and some of them brand-new," Poynter's Edmonds says. So what would happen to a town if a newspaper dies? "I think a certain amount of that is happening already," he says. "Almost all metro papers have pulled back from their coverage of the more distant suburbs."

How much is lost if a newspaper manages to survive, but dramatic cost-cutting forces it to abdicate much of its coverage of a region, as has happened in Los Angeles, Atlanta, Omaha, Dallas and many other cities? What if a newspaper eliminates nearly half of its journalists, as the Los Angeles Times, Atlanta Journal-Constitution and others have done over the past few years? The Tribune Co.-owned Baltimore Sun provided a devastating example of staff-slashing in late April, eliminating 61 people in its newsroom—about 27 percent of its news staff—including senior editors, photographers, designers and columnists.

What the newspaper industry faces is less imminent death than the specter of being mostly dead, of chopping staff and resources to the point where they sacrifice exactly what makes them so special: their coverage of courthouses and statehouses (see "State-house Exodus," April/May), their role dispensing information and facilitating community dialogue, their journalists' time to do basic beat reporting so they can write about issues intelligently.

Until the online startups expand—if they do—the onus remains on newspapers to dig up and dish out news about their cities. Newspapers are rightly trying to reinvent themselves in order to survive, experimenting with new business models, focusing on the journalistic and commercial possibilities of the Internet and working to meld print and online operations.

For newspapers' survival to matter, though, the core of the new models must remain the same as the old: the dedication to illuminating stories and rich storytelling, the commitment to serving democracy.

If those ideals continue to fray and disappear, the economists who are discovering evidence of newspapers' impact on public life could find sharply different results five years from now.

Critical Thinking

1. What did systematic research about the closing of *The Cincinnati Post* show about that closing's impact on public life?

2. What is the "exciting rebirth," in media terms, that is occurring in such cities as San Diego, Minneapolis, New Haven, and St. Louis?

3. What are some key differences, in terms of size of staff and audience, between new online news publications and traditional city newspapers?

4. What are some of the adjustments that are likely to occur in newspapers fighting for their survival?

5. Do you think that big and medium-sized city newspapers as we know them will survive? Why or why not?

RACHEL SMOLKIN is the legal affairs editor at USA Today and a former AJR managing editor.

From *American Journalism Review*, June/July 2009, pp. 18–25. Copyright © 2009 by the Philip Merrill College of Journalism at the University of Maryland, College Park, MD 20742-7111. Reprinted with permission.

Cross Examination

**Local prosecutors are the last sacred cow in journalism.
But some journalists have found the value of a more thorough.**

Steve Weinberg

Some journalistic epiphanies take a long time to form. In my case, 30 years. That is how long it took me to realize somebody needed to conduct a systematic examination of the nation's 2,341 local prosecutors' offices.

During an era when journalists tend to be skeptical about the performance of elected and appointed government officials at all levels, prosecutors qualify as the last sacred cow: assumed to be acting in the public interest, rarely scrutinized and, if covered at all, covered favorably.

In lots of newsrooms, the shorthand for the criminal justice beat is "cops and courts." That traditional label says a lot by what it fails to mention—the prosecutor. My painfully slow epiphany is that prosecutors are the linchpin of the criminal justice system. They receive information from the police about an alleged crime before any defense attorney or judge receives information, and information is power. No case can move forward without the prosecutor's assent. In most jurisdictions, about 95 percent of the crimes charged never reach trial; that means 95 percent of the time, prosecutors are acting as judge and jury combined, all behind closed doors. Furthermore, when a case does reach trial, no matter how wisely or unwisely judges, defense attorneys and juries act, it is usually won or lost because of the way the prosecutor presents the evidence.

Every day, prosecutors in district attorneys' offices throughout the United States decide if people arrested by local police should be:

- Charged with a crime.
- Placed back on the streets, or jailed.
- Allowed to sign a plea agreement, or proceed to trial.
- A candidate for the death penalty if the law permits that outcome.
- Heard after imprisonment because new evidence suggests a wrongful conviction.

Counting the elected district attorney at the top of the office pyramid and the lawyers appointed by the district attorney to serve justice, there are about 30,000 prosecutors working in the United States. Many of these prosecutors are dedicated, skilled public servants. Many others are mediocre. Some should never

have been allowed to wield power. But few people know much about their local prosecutors. Most of the time, in most of those 2,341 jurisdictions, journalists are nowhere to be seen as new prosecutors are hired, as veterans are promoted, as other veterans retire or are forced out.

The sacred cow syndrome blessedly appears to be fading in some newsrooms, however. One factor: In cases with DNA evidence, the number of documented wrongful convictions is approaching 200. They demonstrate like nothing else the fallibility of prosecutors. Everybody makes mistakes. But in a system supposedly devoted more to serving justice than to winning at all costs, in a system supposedly loaded with safeguards, how do prosecutors allow innocent people to be charged with a crime, indicted by a grand jury, incarcerated for months or years while awaiting trial, convicted and sentenced?

The Center for Public Integrity Comes Through

Hoping to find somebody to support a national examination of prosecutors, I approached Charles Lewis at the Center for Public Integrity in Washington, D.C. Lewis is a former CBS 60 Minutes producer who had his own epiphany about 15 years ago. He left his job to start an organization that would conduct investigative journalism in the public interest, in-depth, on topics normally ignored. Against gigantic odds, the Center for Public Integrity has not only survived, but thrived.

Lewis and his staff raised money from foundations and individuals to make my idea a reality. The Center hired two individuals to work with me—Neil Gordon, a Baltimore lawyer who wanted to change careers, and Brooke Williams, a recent University of Missouri Journalism School graduate.

For three years, we gathered information about the performance of every local prosecutor's office in the United States and about as many of the individual district attorneys as we could identify. In several dozen newsrooms, reporters have used our specific findings about the local prosecutor's office, posted at www.publicintegrity.org at the "Harmful Error" icon, to produce insightful follow-ups. In addition to our specific findings, our general conclusions ideally will inform future coverage of prosecutors in every newsroom.

Maurice Possley's Epiphany

To some degree, we stood on the shoulders of giants while conducting our research. Chicago Tribune reporter Maurice Possley is renowned today for his coverage of Cook County prosecutors who break the rules to convict the guilty, and sometimes the innocent. Possley, with colleagues Ken Armstrong and Steve Mills, changed the world in ways most journalists only dream about: Because of their prosecutorial misconduct exposes, first the Illinois governor and legislature, followed by officials in other states, imposed a death penalty moratorium as well as spearheading procedural reforms to the criminal justice system.

But until a few years ago, Possley was part of a widespread newsroom problem—indifferent coverage of prosecutors. Possley saw them one-dimensionally, the way so many other journalists do—as good guys trying to put bad guys behind bars.

Possley covered federal courts in Chicago, first for the Sun-Times, then for the Tribune. He might evaluate a prosecutor's courtroom performance, but gave little attention to the decision-making outside of public view leading to the trial.

In 1995, Possley started covering local courts, which tend to be grittier than the federal system. He began to see the inflexibility of prosecutors as he honed his approach to trial coverage by telling each day as "a separate story with a beginning, middle and end. I tried to always balance the day with some flavor of cross-examination, sometimes saying it was unsuccessful. Sometimes the cross-examination became the lead.... Quite a few prosecutors would make remarks about my inclusion of cross-examination. They had seen (the questioning of prosecution witnesses by defense lawyers) as meaningless or not damaging their case and questioned why I would even report it."

Possley realized that "for most prosecutors, it is a one-way street—their way. And I understood that to be a condition of the beat. Along with these realizations came the knowledge that while the prosecution does usually win, that doesn't mean the truth got found out. There were cases where you couldn't really tell where the truth was, and I could see that for many prosecutors, it was all about winning. Still, I mostly thought they got the right guy—some cases were just closer than others.... The thought that innocent people were being convicted or that justice was being undermined was really not on my radar."

The epiphany Possley needed arrived during the murder trial of Rolando Cruz in DuPage County, Ill. Police and prosecutors originally said Cruz and two other men killed a 10-year-old girl. Some police officers and prosecutors believed early on that the arrests were misguided—especially after a fourth man, a convicted murderer, confessed. The DuPage County prosecutor refused to credit the confession.

In 1995, Cruz won a directed acquittal from a judge in a trial covered by Possley. After the acquittal, a court-appointed special prosecutor recommended that seven DuPage County prosecutors and police be charged with criminal offenses for their conduct.

Possley received a question from an editor: How often does it happen that a prosecutor is indicted for misconduct? Possley had no idea, so he studied decades of reporting by the Tribune and other Chicago-area news organizations. He found himself "astounded to see how prosecutor-oriented the coverage was." During the early stages of the research, Possley continued to cover the Cook County prosecutor's office. "Many prosecutors still thought of the beat guy and the Tribune largely as their allies.... I think many of them never imagined that the result of our reporting would be critical."

Armstrong joined Possley to document 381 cases back to 1963, the date of the U.S. Supreme Court decision *Brady v. Maryland,* in which the justices said convictions could be reversed if prosecutors presented evidence they knew to be false, concealed evidence suggesting innocence, or both. The Tribune's January 1999 series put prosecutors and readers on notice that a new era of coverage had dawned.

Then, in November 1999, Armstrong and Mills published a new revelatory series, examining murder cases in which Illinois prosecutors sought the death penalty. The journalists identified 326 reversals attributed in whole or part to the conduct of prosecutors. Armstrong and Mills wrote themed articles as part of the series, examining how prosecutors use confessions extracted through police torture, perjured testimony of jailhouse informants seeking rewards and unreliable hair/fiber analysis from law enforcement forensic laboratories.

When interviewed in July, Possley was collaborating with Mills on a new project, preparing for the launch of his second book (about a Chicago murder case) and planning his fall teaching leave at the University of Montana journalism school.

Without question, Possley has become skeptical about prosecutors. Today, he says, "I try to persuade defense attorneys to provide discovery (from the prosecutor) to me. I try to actually interview witnesses before trials. I spend more time covering pretrial motions, when significant evidence often comes out and evidence that tends to contradict the prosecution often is aired. And I adhere to the belief that not everything said is the truth, even if it's under oath, and that many things are said as truth but with such semantic gymnastics as to be ridiculous."

It Takes a Village

Possley came to his epiphany alone. When he started acting on it, though, he shared it with two reporting partners, Armstrong and Mills, who helped mine the possibilities of prosecutor coverage.

Dallas Morning News reporter Holly Becka has teamed up professionally, too. In fact, she learned last year it takes a village of journalists to provide exemplary coverage of a scandal that crosses beat lines, involving prosecutors, police and judges.

Becka, a veteran cops and courts reporter, became one of those village members when a Dallas fake-drug scandal emerged: Defendants were being charged, convicted and imprisoned for possessing or selling what appeared to be narcotics, but in fact was billiards chalk planted by police informants or police themselves. Instead of asking the right questions to halt the scam, prosecutors proceeded against the hapless defendants.

"The story started on the police beat and spilled to the criminal courts beat and then to the federal beat," Becka said. "A senior general assignments reporter also pitched in during the early months of the scandal to look at policies in the district attorney's office that helped lead to the scandal. . . . Most of the stories in the early months were written by the two then-criminal courts reporters because prosecutors were dismissing drug case upon drug case, and the effects were being felt by defendants-turned-victims, their lawyers and the court system in general. More recently, our federal beat reporter has handled the story . . . because of the FBI investigation and the federal civil-rights lawsuit." Becka also credits a Morning News editorial writer, journalists at WFAA-TV and the alternative weekly Dallas Observer.

In an April 27, 2003, story that skillfully weaves together seemingly stray strands to create a new reality for readers, Becka and fellow reporter Tanya Eiserer explain how police blame prosecutors for the scandal, while prosecutors blame police. For example, prosecutors say police learned earlier than previously acknowledged that the primary drug informant lacked credibility. While corrupt informants were fooling police officers, prosecutors accepted the cases without asking the tough questions, then hammered out plea bargains with presumably guilty defendants without running the allegedly illegal seized substances through drug testing.

As stories about the scandal kept coming, Becka still had to find time to cover the routine aspects of the beat, such as profiling the Dallas assistant district attorney who was recognized as the top prosecutor in Texas. Becka used a feature lead, telling how the assistant district attorney saw prosecutors as heroes even when he was a child—heroes with the same stature as movie star tough-guy John Wayne. For 19 years, Becka explained, the child hero worshipper has been living his dream as a real-life prosecutor. Such stories inform readers of the positive and help build relationships on the beat.

Becka recently moved from the criminal courts beat to a newly created criminal justice enterprise role. "I've had so many people—members of the public, the criminal defense bar and even a few prosecutors—credit the media with forcing public officials here to do the right thing after the scandal erupted," she said. ". . . The sentiment I've heard is if the media had been asleep or uncaring, innocent people would have remained in jail."

The Value of Appellate Court Rulings

Rob Modic, a Dayton Daily News reporter since 1979, knows what the best beat reporters, including Becka, know: When keeping tabs on prosecutors, study every appellate court opinion that comments on their conduct.

The upside of studying appellate court rulings is huge: They are official records, they often contain nuggets of news amidst the normally dry prose of judges, and those rendering opinions are often former prosecutors who know first-hand what to look for when examining state conduct. An appellate ruling can be a platform for discussing a specific issue, such as whether local prosecutors regularly withhold evidence from the defense in violation of U.S. Supreme Court mandates; use jailhouse snitches as witnesses, without fully checking the snitches' accounts or fully disclosing the quid pro quo to the defense; coach state witnesses or discourage potential defense witnesses from cooperating; cross the line during trial, perhaps during opening statements, perhaps during cross-examination, perhaps during closing arguments.

Part of a three-person criminal justice team, Modic and colleagues "get together regularly to discuss filed cases at every stage," including the appellate stage. "We look at search warrants, motions to suppress (evidence), preliminary hearings. We talk to parties about overcharging and undercharging. We collect string, then put the twine together for a story."

Watch the Interactions Carefully

As a longtime St. Louis County courthouse reporter for the Post-Dispatch, Bill Lhotka knows almost all the prosecutors and defense attorneys who work opposite sides of criminal cases. Tuned-in reporters watch "for veteran prosecutors taking advantage of neophyte defense attorneys or public defenders. The reverse is also true: veteran defense attorneys running circles around new prosecutors." Neither scenario leads to the closest approximation of the truth. Winning is ingrained in prosecutors and defense counsel, but, Lhotka says, that is no excuse for cutting corners to win a case, to obsess over percentages of victory and defeat because of career advancement plans or personal vanity.

Tim Bryant covers the St. Louis City courthouse for the same newspaper. He and Lhotka sometimes compare notes, especially because the same defense attorneys often appear in both jurisdictions. The reputation of individual prosecutors among defense attorneys and judges is usually easy to learn after trust is built on the beat, Bryant says. That information can also be supplemented through close observation. "Attendance at court proceedings early in a case may be helpful," Bryant said. "For example, a prosecutor's performance in a preliminary hearing or an evidentiary hearing could likely provide clues to his effectiveness. Was he prepared? Did he show proper courtesies to the judge and the opposing lawyer, especially in a proceeding where jurors are not present? Does the prosecutor have the respect of his office's investigator and the police detectives on his case?"

Jury selection provides more evidence, but lots of reporters are absent from that stage of the trial. "Was jury selection contentious to the point that the prosecutor was accused of removing potential jurors because of their race or gender?" Bryant asked. "Then there is the trial itself. Did the defense lawyer make more than a typical number of objections? Were disputes serious enough to merit sidebar conversations with the judge, or even recesses in the trial?"

Seek Access, and You Might Find It

Access granted to journalists by district attorneys might increase understanding of the daily difficulties faced by prosecutors—and everybody wins when that occurs. But it appears that journalists rarely ask to be a fly on the wall.

Gary Delsohn of the Sacramento Bee asked. Elected district attorney Jan Scully said yes. The only restrictions: Delsohn could not write anything for his newspaper during his year inside; nobody would be quoted by name without consent; personnel matters could be ruled off-limits by Scully; Delsohn would provide periodic reports on his observations if requested. (Scully never made such a request.)

In return, Delsohn would be provided a semiprivate writing space, could wander freely, pose questions and attend meetings. "There were more than a few people in the office who thought Scully was insane," Delsohn said, " . . . but for the most part people were extremely open and accessible. Prosecutors and investigators freely discussed the most sensitive aspects of their cases in front of me. I was allowed to sit in on meetings with victims, defense attorneys, judges, police and witnesses. I was almost never told something was off limits, and after I had been showing up for a few weeks, most of the resistance that I was aware of had disappeared."

Much of what Delsohn learned appears in his book, published in August by Dutton. The book, "The Prosecutors," subtly emphasizes Delsohn's special access in the subtitle: "A Year in the Life of a District Attorney's Office." It is a primer for any outsider journalist who wants to think about how to cover prosecutors more effectively.

Prosecutors Rarely Admit Their Mistakes

Ofra Bikel is a producer of documentaries for the PBS program Frontline. After turning her attention to the criminal justice system 15 years ago, she produced the "Innocence Lost" trilogy about the mishandling of child sexual abuse cases in Edenton, N.C. In 1999, her documentary about three prison inmates exonerated by DNA testing aired as "The Case for Innocence." Last year, Frontline aired "An Ordinary Crime," Bikel's account of a North Carolina armed-robbery prosecution beset with problems.

Bikel says she is baffled by the refusal of the prosecutor to reopen the conviction of Terence Garner, given post-trial evidence that the wrong man is in prison. Baffled but not surprised, because Bikel has watched prosecutors in previous cases dig in.

"There are a few problems with prosecutors," she said. "First, because it is an adversarial system, and the defense's job is to defend their client in any way they can—within the boundaries of the law, which is quite flexible. The prosecution, as the adversary, wants to do just the opposite of the defense: Convict the defendant in any way they can. So it is a contest. The problem is that the prosecution has a double function. Besides being one side in a contest, they are supposed to represent the people and to see that justice is done. This double-headed function in a cutthroat adversarial system is very hard to maintain. Unfortunately, I have not met too many prosecutors who spend sleepless nights over the fact that they won a case but sent an innocent person to prison. The prosecutors are not villains, but they look at a case, and they see people who they think are guilty go free because of smart-ass, manipulative attorneys, and they are furious. So they, too, cut corners, and blind themselves many times to the truth, or at least to doubt."

Expect to Be Verbally Attacked by Prosecutors

Edward Humes wrote about prosecutorial error and misconduct in the office of the Kern County, Calif., district attorney. The incumbent responded with a 154-page document attacking the journalist and his findings. Both used incendiary words. Humes' book, published by Simon & Schuster, is "Mean Justice: A Town's Terror, a Prosecutor's Power, a Betrayal of Innocence." The district attorney's reply is "Junk Journalism: Correcting the Errors, False Claims and Distortions in Edward Humes' Mean Justice."

Humes, like Possley, took awhile to reach the realization that prosecutors are not always the good guys. First as a newspaper reporter, then as the author of high-end true crime books, Humes usually found defendants' claims of innocence filled with holes.

He began to change his attitude while investigating the conviction of Pat Dunn, a Bakersfield educator and businessman, for murdering his wife, Sandy. Convinced after extensive research that Dunn is innocent, and appalled at what he believed to be prosecutorial misconduct in the case, Humes examined the actions of the district attorney and his deputies over several decades. The research resulted in what appeared to be questionable patterns of behavior among specific prosecutors handling specific types of cases.

Humes possessed an advantage over Bakersfield-based journalists. He was writing a book, then would probably leave the jurisdiction to pursue a different book. Beat reporters, on the other hand, who examine prosecutor conduct sometimes see sources dry up not only in the district attorney's office, but also in other law enforcement quarters.

Investigative reporting about prosecutors' performance, Humes said, "is likely to be met with strong, even bizarre, resistance from prosecutors, who may be prone to suggesting that anyone who criticizes their actions must be a) in league with criminals; b) in league with criminal defense lawyers; c) are criminals themselves; or d) worst of all, political liberals."

The Horrible Power of Self-Delusion

Dorothy Rabinowitz has carved out a specialty in her place on the Wall Street Journal editorial board. That specialty: problematic prosecutions of alleged child molestation rings.

Her first Journal expose, published in 1995, centered on the Fells Acres Day School in Malden, Mass. Prosecutors charged Gerald Amirault, his sister Cheryl plus his mother, Violet, the founder of the day care center, with monstrous multiple molestations based on the word of preschoolers—and without a shred of physical evidence.

As Rabinowitz chronicled other fantastic-sounding child molestation cases in New Jersey, Florida, Washington State and California, an awful question occurred to her: What if the prosecutors did not believe in the guilt of those they brought to trial? What if they filed the charges to appease community outrage, to build support for a re-election campaign or a higher office? After all, the evidence of molestation seemed unbelievable when evaluated using common sense.

Rabinowitz worked up to raising her unpleasant question in her 2003 book "No Crueler Tyrannies: Accusation, False Witness, and Other Terrors of Our Times." What did the prosecutors think? she mused. "Did they actually believe in the charges they had brought, of naked children tied to trees in full public view and raped in broad daylight, as in the Amirault case; in the testimony of child witnesses who had recited obvious whoppers about robots, being stabbed with swords, and the like?"

Some prosecutors actually believe those seemingly ludicrous scenarios, and some do not, Rabinowitz concluded. Both patterns of thought are scary. One type of prosecutor cares nothing about the justice that is part of the office's sworn duty; won-lost records are paramount. The other type of prosecutor is blinded by passion, too close to the emotional residue of little children being victimized.

"The prosecutor's propensity to believe in the guilt of anyone accused of the crime of child sex abuse (is) overwhelming," Rabinowitz said. "That belief (is) fueled by investigators who share the same propensity and interrogated the children accordingly."

Critical Thinking

1. About how many local prosecutors' offices are there and what important roles do they perform in the criminal justice system?

2. What does it mean to say that prosecutors serve as judges and juries in about 95% of all criminal cases?

3. What did *Chicago Tribune* reporter Maurice Possley and his colleagues do to "change the world in ways most journalists only dream about"?

4. In what ways can appellate court opinions be helpful in studying the conduct of prosecutors?

5. What can be learned from watching prosecutors in public court proceedings?

6. What is the "double-headed function" of a prosecutor and why is it hard for him or her to maintain it?

7. What is meant by the "horrible power of self-delusion" relating to prosecutions of alleged child molestation rings?

STEVE WEINBERG is a freelance magazine writer and book author in Columbia, Mo. He served as executive director of Investigative Reporters Editors, based at the Missouri Journalism School, from 1983–1990. He teaches from time to time at the Journalism School.

A Shift of Substance

Changes in local media ownership have largely led to a decline in radio news.

BONNIE BRESSERS

When Jim Schuh was a commercial radio station manager and owner in the central Wisconsin city of Stevens Point (population: 25,000), local radio reporters covered the school board, city and county government, the surrounding towns and villages, the university, the police, local sports and two high schools. On heavy news days, a newscast scheduled to run five minutes could run nearly twice that.

There are about a dozen radio stations that serve Stevens Point today, but none offers local radio news.

"It's kind of sad, really," said Schuh who, after a 41-year-career in broadcasting, was inducted last year into the Wisconsin Broadcasters Association Hall of Fame. "I looked at it this way: It was the responsibility of the broadcast licensee to do this. You used the public airwaves and, in return, you provided your community with more than what most broadcasters are doing today. Having a contest with the local car dealer isn't local broadcasting."

Chris Allen, now an associate professor of communication at the University of Nebraska in Omaha, remembers his days as one of six local journalists at KRNT in Des Moines in the late 1970s and early 1980s. A competing station had seven local news people; even the rock-and-roll station had three.

But there is only one station making a serious attempt at local news in Des Moines today. In Omaha, which at one time had three or four radio stations providing local news, there are none.

Local news on commercial radio, once a competitive information lifeline for millions of Americans, has been on a steady path of decline caused by what more than one expert calls the "Perfect Storm" of trends and events that started some 20 years ago and peaked with the Telecommunications Act of 1996.

"I'm really depressed about what's happened," said John Vivian, a journalism professor at Winona (Minn.) State University and author of the popular textbook, "The Media of Mass Communication." "Years ago radio had immediacy, it was exciting, it was a priority. There were reports from the scenes where things were happening. You got a news update every hour—or more when something was breaking."

But commercial radio is no longer a reliable source of local information, even during times of breaking news and major emergency, says David Rubin, dean of the Newhouse School of Public Communications at Syracuse University in New York. Rubin said he turned to the longtime local AM radio news leader for its emergency broadcasting when the series of electrical failures

that crippled parts of the Northeast, Midwest and Canada last August left his home in Fayetteville, N.Y., without power.

"If you don't have electric power, and you need to know what's happening, television, the Internet, the local newspaper—none of them are of any use to you," he said.

Rubin knew what a radio station dedicated to local news would do: The news crew would report to work en masse regardless of prearranged shifts and schedules. The station's disaster coverage plan would be implemented and reporters would he dispatched to gather information at key sites. Local officials would be in the studio taking questions from anxious callers. Commercials would be suspended. A community that was literally in the dark would get information and, thus, the assurance that it had the information it needed to respond.

But the longtime local news leader is now owned by broadcasting conglomerate Clear Channel which, Rubin said, did a "particularly poor job of covering the impact of the outage on the community" despite its assertions that by consolidating local broadcast stations it could pool resources to provide better local coverage than before.

To its credit, Rubin said Clear Channel made some changes as a result of Aug. 24, including replacing the news director, adding newsroom staff and developing a coverage plan for disasters.

"It's been healthy from that perspective," Rubin said. "There's been a little progress. But it will take continued vigilance and a national effort."

Bob Betcher, who has covered radio and television for 15 years for the Scripps Treasure Coast Newspapers in Florida, shares Rubin's concerns. For example, he says some local radio stations have an agreement with the CBS network television station in West Palm Beach to simulcast its audio coverage in the event of an emergency. But the television station is 40 to 70 miles from the coverage areas of the radio stations. In addition, many stations are automated overnight, they operate with skeletal staffs on weekends, and AM stations—typically the "talk" band—are required to reduce their signals at night.

"God forbid that anything should happen at 10 A.M. on a Sunday or after 7 P.M. on weeknights," Betcher said. "I wonder where and how I would learn that information."

It is no small issue: What does the public-interest standard, long the guiding principle under which broadcasters operated, mean in an era when broadcast consolidation and monopoly ownership make it unlikely that local radio can adequately cover the community—from city councils, school boards and local controversies to emergencies, disasters and threats to national security?

Indeed, the decline of local radio news most greatly affects its historic stronghold: small-town and rural America, where television coverage was not universal and people depended on the ubiquitous radio for everything from tornado warnings to agricultural alerts, says Ed Staats, whose 41-year career in 10 offices of The Associated Press included overseeing broadcast services. And as small-town newspapers cut staff—or closed their doors altogether—the civic life of entire communities has been left unexamined.

"Radio news was bubbling all over America," Staats said. "Now there's nobody out in the 3,000-plus counties in the United States covering local news the way they were. That's a major loss. That's at the heart of what the impact has been."

But there are some bright spots on the local news landscape, Staats and others agree. The University of Nebraska's Allen sees annual broadcast contest entries as a member of the Board of Directors of the Northwest Broadcast News Association, a six-state regional news organization. He says some small-market stations in rural communities still do excellent reporting on city government, school boards, the environment, local controversies and human-interest stories.

"But almost all of the stations we're talking about are operations with one and two people who work 20 hours a day," Allen said. "They're invisible. York, Nebraska, has 4,000 people. They have a great radio station there, but it's not a huge market."

Another of those bright spots may be KORN Radio, a station with a long-held commitment to local news that serves a 70-mile radius of Mitchell, S.D. News director J.P. Skelly covers government bodies such as city council, school board and county commission and generates local talk programming that examines community issues and often features local newsmakers.

"If there's news to be found, I'll find it," Skelly said. "But I also have to be very selective."

Still, many media observers say, the overall role of local radio news has been seriously eroding for decades and the future is unclear. Deregulation, consolidation, economics, technology, demographics and declining audience interest are among the trends that coalesced to move local commercial radio news away from its historical position as pivotal in meeting the information needs of the local citizenry.

Deregulation

Many media observers lay blame for the current state of local radio news with the Telecommunications Act of 1996, which increased the number of stations a broadcast group can own in a market to up to eight, depending on the market size, and eliminated the rule that capped the number of stations one company can own at 40. But the 1996 Act, passed in the Clinton administration, was the outcome of a steady erosion of broadcast regulations that actually began a quarter of a century earlier under the Carter administration.

"The genie had been out of the bottle;" said Man G. Stavitsky, associate dean and professor at the University of Oregon School of Journalism and Communication in Eugene, Ore., and a reviewer for The State of the News Media 2004 report released in March by the Project for Excellence in Journalism. "If you trace the deregulation flow, it began with Carter FCC when we first chipped away at ownership and content rules. It kept gaining momentum and, in 1996, the dam burst."

The Carter administration likely did not foresee the outcome when it launched its government-wide initiative against bureaucratic red tape and burdensome paperwork. But in its attempt to "pare away the regulatory underbrush," as Stavitsky puts is, the Federal Communications Commission began reviewing regulations that had been enacted decades earlier when radio was in its infancy. The broadcast industry, which chaffed under the regulations, saw an opening with the Carter FCC and began a massive and ongoing lobbying effort. The Reagan FCC followed with its philosophy that TV was more akin to an appliance—nothing more than a "toaster with pictures." One regulation after another that had defined "public interest" was eliminated and, by the late 1980s, the requirement that broadcasters applying for license renewals report how many hours they would devote to public affairs programming was gone.

"But you don't leave the public-interest standard out until you have something to replace it with" said Syracuse University's Rubin. "The last time I looked, the public still owned the airwaves."

Public ownership notwithstanding, radio stations throughout the country cut their local news operations in favor of far less costly fare, including entertainment programming and often "lowbrow" talk shows.

In addition to eliminating public affairs content requirements, the Telecommunications Act of 1996 allowed multiple-station ownership, which exacerbated the problem and contributed to the decline of local commercial radio news.

Consolidation and Economics

According to the Project for Excellence in Journalism's State of the News Media 2004 report, broadcast groups Clear Channel, Cumulus Broadcasting and Citadel Communication Corp. owned fewer than 1,000 stations in 1999. They now own about 1,600 stations, with Clear Channel owning 1,207. The 1996 Act, the report says, allowed Clear Channel, which had owned only 43 stations, to buy the 460-station AMFM Inc. The five largest broadcast groups now own more than 14 percent of the total number of stations in the United States.

But the debt involved with consolidation encourages broadcast owners to cut jobs and costs to pay the debt service and make the networks profitable. Most of the companies are publicly owned, which experts suggest encourages their allegiance to Wall Street and corporate stockholders rather than a public that owns the airwaves. General managers who historically have become rooted in the community as they worked their way up the station ladder increasingly are being replaced with corporate managers who have little loyalty and commitment to the locality.

"It's all designed to produce as cheap a product as possible and to appeal to as many people as possible in your demographic niche and to squeeze out all competition so the public doesn't have a place to go except to, maybe, the satellite networks which, of course, are not local," Rubin said.

Wisconsin broadcaster Schuh, who was general manager of one station and owner of another, acknowledges that "wall-to-wall music" has a greater profit margin than news, but he doesn't agree the stations that provide good local news coverage can't make handsome profits. And it's important, he says, to look at the psychographics of the listenership rather than the demographics.

"The listeners are the 40-plus or 50-plus people, but they're community leaders and business owners," he said. "They are the ones who are generally your sponsors, and that ties in with good community involvement. The decision-makers listen to your product to keep up with things in the community."

Even with groups that retain a barebones commitment to local news, the University of Oregon's Stavitsky says reduced staffs now produce news for multiple stations.

"Before you had six news people, with six takes on local news, working at six different stations," he said. "Now you may have one or two people providing the same news product across all six stations. You ask if they're doing local news and they say 'Yes, absolutely, we're doing six newscasts during morning drive-time.' But there's less diversity of voices."

And those six people are stretched so thin, experts say, they must rely on press releases, telephone interviews and stories lifted from the local newspaper rather than attending city council meetings, going to news conferences and covering local events.

Commercial stations committed to cost reductions turned to another source of programming in the 1980s and 1990s that was cheaper than local news: the so-called news/talk format. At one end of the spectrum, news/talk shows include programs such as National Public Radio's "Talk of the Nation," which provides serious—albeit not local—programming. But while some stations point to news/talk programming as evidence they have not abandoned the local news market, media observers are quick to point out that taking stories from the local newspaper and inviting often vitriolic local listeners to voice their opinions is a far cry from doing serious, in-depth reporting on the local issues of the day.

Regardless of the level of quality, news/talk was the most common format on AM radio in the 1990s, and Rush Limbaugh is still the most-listened to talk show in the nation with an audience of more than 14 million people a week.

Radio, sandwiched in the evolutionary media timeline between newspapers and television, is experiencing what newspapers experienced before and what local television news has started experiencing since, says Bob Priddy, chairman-elect of the national Radio Television News Directors Association and news director of MissouriNet, a statewide commercial network that provides primarily state government reporting and political news to 65 Missouri radio stations.

"What we have seen in radio in the last 20 years we will see in television: the consolidation of more and more newsrooms, doing news for more than one station without many additional resources, reduced commitment to news, fewer people being spread thinner," Priddy said. "What we have seen in radio in the last 20 years we will see in television. We have been seeing it already in the last 10 years."

Technology

Technological advances also have contributed to the homogenization of local news, media observers say. Satellite and broadband delivery now enables broadcast companies to generate programming from a central hub for distribution throughout the network of radio stations. Pieces of local information can be transparently spliced into generic news broadcasts, giving listeners the erroneous impression that local newscasters within their local communities generate the newscasts.

Finally, the University of Oregon's Stavitsky says, the latest technological phenomenon—satellite networks such as Sirius Satellite Radio and XM Satellite Radio—offers "anti-local" radio programming that allows listeners to access the same radio station from New York City to San Francisco.

But, like a pendulum that has swung too far, anti-local programming may offer a solution to the current state of local radio news.

"Some people in the industry are saying the only way we can compete against satellite and the Internet is to rediscover our local roots," Stavitsky said. "That will be what differentiates us. The problem is news is expensive. But if they continue to get their lunch eaten by satellite and the Web and young people abandoning radio, that may be the only way to survive."

Demographics and Audience Interest

Local commercial radio news is following a pattern first seen in the local newspaper industry as circulations started declining 30 years ago, largely because of the industry's failure to attract younger readers for whom local news is not a top priority.

Local radio, both local news and music, is less a part of the "media diet" of young people, says Stavitsky. For one thing, he says, young people today have portable music players that contain their complete CD libraries. For another, commercial talk radio, which requires less fidelity, is on the AM band, "which young people ignore."

Indeed, Winona University's Vivian and other academicians point to a gradual disengagement of young people in the civic affairs of the community.

"Civic affairs," Vivian said simply, "is a gigantic tune-out."

But, media observers say, the problem extends well beyond the younger generation and involves a society that seems to place less value on news and information.

"Look at some of the political issues," said RTNDA's Priddy. "People clamor for better roads but they reject fuel tax increases when fuel taxes are the only way to pay for better roads. They don't have to watch politicians because, with term limits, the politicians will be gone. You have a certain amount of public irresponsibility. Lethargy and irresponsibility are combined to bring a slump in the service they get. They don't demand better. And federal deregulation has played a role in this."

The Case for Public Radio

Kevin Klose, president and chief executive officer of National Public Radio, sees a far different confluence of coincidental phenomena that he says have contributed to huge increases in audiences for NPR and its member stations: As commercial radio stations consolidated and gutted their local news offerings in the 1980s and 1990s, public radio's evolving capacity to produce national news programming was followed by its extension into local news. The second- and third-most-listened-to programs on both commercial and noncommercial radio— "Morning Edition" and "All Things Considered," respectively—were both formatted to encourage local member stations to generate local news programming that can be added to the national mix.

Of the 275 mother ship stations, about 150 produce local news, a total that Klose says is increasing. And the signals from those 275 stations are "repeated" to 475 other stations throughout the country.

Twenty years of evolution in the production of news and information programming were capped by two events early in the 21st Century that caused a dramatic surge in NPR's already growing audience. The 37-day end to the 2000 presidential election between George W. Bush and Al Gore became riveting news of continuous interest for more than a month. And less than a year later, the terrorist attacks on Sept. 11, 2001, produced an audience desperate for in-depth and high-quality, credible news.

"NPR and the local stations mixed up a marvelous tapestry of authentic local news, local hosts, local perspectives, interwoven with superb national and foreign coverage from us," Klose said. "And NPR audiences don't spike—once they start listening, they keep listening."

Indeed, Klose says, Abitron statistics bear that out. In 1999, 13 million of the 20 million people who listened to NPR stations each week listened to NPR-generated programming. That 13 million had increased to 16 million on Sept. 10. 2001, and to 20 on Sept. 12. Today, 30 million people listen to NPR stations, with 22 million listening to NPR-generated programming.

Steve Chiotakis, who is the local "Morning Edition" host and a producer with NPR's member station WBHM in Birmingham, Ala., has split his 16-year career equally between public and commercial radio.

Like Klose, he sees public radio as the last bastion for people serious about local radio news.

"I love my medium," he said. "I love radio. People want news and they want it now. Who better than radio? We've been doing it for 80 years."

But commercial radio news, Chiotakis says, "is dying a really fast death."

The Future

Without doubt, NPR is attracting larger and larger audiences as commercial radio moves away from news, says the University of Oregon's Stavitsky, but the bottom line remains: Local news is expensive. Two-thirds of the NPR member stations are licensed to universities, many of which are questioning where to put increasingly scarce resources in the face of colossal state budget deficits. Declining local economies may affect the level of underwriting available to the member stations.

"A lot of them are struggling to keep the local news there," Stavitsky said. "But overall, public radio is still a much more hospitable place for local journalism than commercial radio is."

So if a windstorm of trends and events contributed to the current state of local commercial radio news, what is the possibility that forces can be reversed or, at the least, moderated? Many media observers are not optimistic.

Stavitsky and the University of Nebraska's Allen agree that there are pockets of good local news programming in both small and large markets, but both question a future for local radio news in the face of public indifference to news in general.

And while RTNDA's Priddy argues that radio has reinvented itself many times in many ways—and will do so again—others suggest a more systemic problem that will require significant public will to reverse. Syracuse University's Rubin, for example, says change needs to come from a federal government willing to confront the broadcast industry's powerful lobby.

Inroads could be made, he says, under scenarios such as these:

- Broadcast groups that didn't meet revenue targets decided to sell stations, and the FCC, in an effort to prevent station-trading among big chains, enacted rules to encourage local ownership.
- Congress and the FCC recognized the results of their actions and rolled back the number of stations an owner could own, although that's admittedly unlikely.
- The FCC enacted regulations that made chain ownership more expensive and more accountable to the public in hopes of encouraging chains to divest. For example, if the FCC re-enacted the Fairness Doctrine, which had required that broadcast stations air all sides of public issues, so talk show programming such as Rush Limbaugh and Michael Savage could be challenged station-by-station, market-by-market.
- The FCC returned to license renewal every three years and, as part of the renewal process, required that stations ascertain whether they were meeting the public interest and report their findings in an open forum as they did in the past.
- The FCC again required public affairs programming.
- Commercial broadcasters were taxed, and the tax revenues were used to support robust noncommercial local news operations.

"If I can think of this sitting here in Syracuse, why can't the people in Washington? This will take a national effort, a new administration, a new FCC and a new FCC chairman" Rubin said. "Am I optimistic? No, I'm not."

Critical Thinking

1. What "shift of substance" has occurred in radio broadcasting in the United States?

2. Why is commercial radio no longer a good source of information about local affairs, including what local governments are doing?

3. How have the Telecommunications Act of 1996, technological advances, and audience demographics contributed to the decline in radio broadcasting of local news?

4. How do public radio and its broadcasting habits relate to shifts in what commercial radio stations broadcast?

BONNIE BRESSERS is an assistant professor of journalism at the A.Q. Miller School of Journalism and Mass Communications at Kansas State University.

UNIT 4
Government Institutions and Officeholders

Unit Selections

Learning Outcomes

- Compare and contrast the powers and responsibilities of a president of a school board, an elected chief executive of a small municipality, a city manager, a school superintendent, the mayor of a large city, a state governor, and the president of the United States.

- Compare and contrast your state constitution with the United States Constitution—in length, the subjects covered, ease of reading, and your familiarity with it.

- Assess whether it is preferable to have well-paid and prestigious, elected government positions, as in the national government, or low-paid, part-time elected posts, as are common in local governments and many state legislatures. Assess which makes for more representative government.

- Evaluate whether citizens should be empowered to participate directly in a government's policy process by means of initiatives, referenda, or town meetings or, alternatively, legislating should be left to elected representatives.

- Compare and contrast the responsibilities and autonomy of three different representative bodies in state and local government: state legislatures, city councils, and school boards.

- Categorize and assess the leadership styles of Governor Chris Christie of New Jersey, Governor Scott Walker of Wisconsin, and Deputy Mayor Steven Goldsmith of New York City.

- Assess the pros and cons of imposing term limits on state legislators, governors, and city mayors.

- Recommend a metaphor to replace sausage-making as a means of illustrating and explaining how the state legislative process works.

- Assess the wisdom of mandatory sentencing laws in criminal cases and allowing children to appear in court when their custodial arrangements are being addressed.

- Identify key attributes that make for a good state legislature and a good appointee to serve in the executive branch of a state government.

Student Website
www.mhhe.com/cls

Government institutions are to state and local political systems what skeletons are to people. They shape the general outlines of government policymaking processes in the same way that bones shape the outlines of the human body. For state and local governments, as well as for the national government, institutions are critical elements in the governing process.

There are important state-by-state variations in executive, legislative, and judicial structures and in the degree to which citizens have access to the policymaking process. In strong governor states, chief executives hold substantially greater appointive, budgetary, and veto powers than those in weak governor states. The roles of parties, committees, and leaders differ among state legislatures, as does the degree of professionalism among legislators. The roles of state courts vary according to the contents of state constitutions, as well as a state's political and judicial traditions. In some states, the state's highest court plays a role that is roughly comparable to that of the United States Supreme Court at the national level. The highest courts in most states, however, are generally less prominent. States also differ in whether judges are elected or appointed. With respect to policymaking and government as a whole, some states allow for direct citizen involvement through the devices of initiative, referendum, and recall, while others do not. Many of these structural details of state governments are spelled out in each state's written constitution, although state constitutions generally do not play as prominent or symbolically important a role in state government as the United States Constitution does in national government.

Local governments do not incorporate the traditional three-branch structure of government to the extent that state and national governments do. Legislative and executive powers are often given to a single governing body, with the members choosing one of themselves to be the nominal chief executive or presiding official when the body meets. For example, school boards typically elect their own board president to preside over meetings, but they hire a professional educational administrator, called a superintendent, to manage day-to-day

© PhotoLink/Getty Images

affairs of the district and provide educational leadership. What is true of school districts is roughly paralleled in many other local governments.

In contrast, the structures of strong-mayor cities resemble executive–legislative arrangements in national and state governments. The traditional notion of an independent local judiciary as a third branch does not apply in a straightforward way at the local government level. Local courts, to the extent that they exist, do not restrain the other branches of local government in the way that state and national courts are empowered to restrain their respective legislative and executive branches. As with state judges, some local judges are appointed and some are elected.

This unit on institutions is organized along traditional legislative, executive, and judicial lines. The first section treats state and local legislatures, with the latter category including city and town councils, school boards, town meetings, and the like. The second section turns to governors and local government executives, while the third and last section treats state and local courts.

Internet References

Council on Licensure, Enforcement and Regulation (CLEAR)
www.clearhq.org

National Governors Association
www.nga.org

National Conference of State Legislatures
www.ncsl.org

National School Boards Association
www.nsba.org

The United States Conference of Mayors
www.usmayors.org

The Legislature as Sausage Factory

It's about Time We Examine This Metaphor

When you get right down to it, making sausage is a lot different than making laws, no matter what the old saw says.

ALAN ROSENTHAL

If you spend any time hanging around legislatures or around Congress for that matter, you will inevitably hear the expression, "There are two things you don't want to see being made—sausage and legislation." Attributed to Otto von Bismark (1815–1898), Germany's chancellor, the metaphor of sausage making and lawmaking has had a remarkably long run. But, I wonder, does it still apply or are today's sausages and legislation on separate tracks, unlike in the 19th century?

In connection with a book I am writing, I have been closely observing lawmaking in four states. So when I had the opportunity to observe sausage making at the Ohio Packing Company, I took it.

Established as a neighborhood butcher shop in 1907, Ohio Packing has two processing facilities in Columbus, one of which turns out 40,000 pounds of sausage a day. As sausage factories go, this is a medium-sized plant. Larger plants are more automated and have more bells and whistles, but the process is nearly the same. Rick Carter, the quality control manager in the facility, served as my guide.

The Guts of Sausage Making

Sausage making occurs in distinct stages, each of which takes place in a specified room or area. First comes the raw materials cooler, where sausage ingredients are mixed according to computer formulations. A vat will hold 2,000 pounds of one-quarter fat trimmings and three-quarters lean trimmings. At the second stage, the raw materials proceed to the sausage kitchen. A grinder processes up to 40,000 pounds per hour, a blender allows water and seasoning to be added, an emulsifier reshapes the content into a new form, and natural hog casings are stuffed with ingredients.

The Cooking Process Is The Third Stage. Huge Processing Ovens Dry, Smoke, Cook Or Steam The Sausage. A Gas Fire, Using Hickory Chips, Provides Natural Smoking. The Chilling Or Holding Area Is The Fourth Stage. Here, The Sausage Sits Around Waiting To Be Packaged, Which Comes Fifth And Is Accomplished By Three Large Machines. With The Assistance Of 10 To 15 Packagers, The Machines Wrap Multiple Sausages In Plastic Film. Sixth Is Storage In A Huge Freezer With A Capacity Of About A Million Pounds. Finally, Seventh Is The Shipping Area Where Wrapped, Packaged Sausage Waits To Be Loaded On Trailer Trucks.

The Sausage Link

At first glance, sausage making and lawmaking would appear to be a lot alike.

Just as pork, beef and chicken make their way stage by stage to the shipping docks, so a bill is introduced, reviewed by a committee, considered on the floor of one house and then further reviewed by committee and on the floor of the other house. The two houses have to concur before the bill proceeds to the governor for his or her decision to sign, not sign or veto. In sausage making what you see is what you get. However, the "How a Bill Becomes a Law" formulation that is supposed to describe the process in Congress and state legislatures is way off the mark. So, let's compare the processes of sausage making and lawmaking in some of their significant dimensions.

Accessibility. It is not easy to get into a sausage factory, unless you work there or are a raw ingredient. Because of the possibilities of liability and contamination, the public is barred. I could not get in on my own recognizance, but had to secure a letter of introduction from the president of the Ohio Senate. Such a letter is not needed to get into the legislative process. The statehouse is most accessible. Public tours are offered. More important, people can observe the legislature indirectly through the media and more directly through C-Span coverage, which is aired in almost half the states. Constituents can visit with their legislators at home or in the capital. Furthermore, members of the public not only are observers, but, mainly through interest groups and their lobbyists, are also participants. They can make

In Search of the Perfect Metaphor

The legislature has been compared in other metaphors as well as Bismark's—among others, to a circus, marketplace and zoo.

Two interesting metaphors are offered by John A. Straayer in his book, *The Colorado General Assembly*. First is the legislature as an arena in which "a score of basketball games are progressing, all at one time, on the same floor, with games at different stages, with participants playing on several teams at once, switching at will, opposing each other in some instances and acting as teammates in others."

Second is the legislature as a casino, where there are lots of tables, lots of games, the stakes are high, there are winners and losers, but the outcome is never final, for there is always a new game ahead.

Just because the legislature as sausage factory does not stand the test of empirical examination doesn't mean there isn't a metaphor that can do the job. State Legislatures invites legislators, legislature staff and other readers to offer metaphorical candidates, even ones that only apply to part of the process or apply only in part, but not entirely.

Mail your submissions to Sharon Randall, NCSL, 1560 Broadway, Suite 700, Denver, CO 80202 or fax to 303–863–8003 or e-mail to Sharon.Randall@ncsl.org.

demands and help shape what comes out. Contamination is welcome in the legislature; it is a major element of democracy.

Coherence. The 60 people of Ohio Packing who make sausage work in different areas and engage in different operations. But they are all part of one team, making a variety of products according to specification. No one tries to introduce a substitute sausage or attach a bratwurst amendment to a frankfurter. No one wants to prevent a sausage from coming out. In the legislative process, there may be as many teams as there are individual members of the particular legislature. There is a Republican team, a Democratic team, a House team, a Senate team, a liberal team, a conservative team, an urban team, a suburban team and so on. Often, as in Congress and many states today, these teams are quite evenly matched. These teams are not in the business of producing the same product, but often are competing with one another over legislation and over the state budget.

Regularity. Sausage making strives for uniformity. Constant testing takes place to ensure the proper measurement of ingredients—fat content, moisture, seasoning and so forth. The process is strictly regulated by the U.S. Department of Agriculture, whose applicable regulations currently run into thousands of pages (there were only 86 pages of federal regulations in 1914) and whose inspector makes at least one visit a day to check on the operations of the Ohio Packing Company. In addition, the process is monitored diligently in-house by quality control personnel.

Not so with the legislative process, where uniformity is virtually unheard of, measurement of content is illusory, and just about every bill—and certainly every important bill—gets

individualized treatment. At the outset, one can predict what will come out of the sausage factory. It is impossible to predict what will come out of the legislature. We are pretty sure that every year or two we will have a budget, but that is as far as certainty goes.

Efficiency. Sausage making has to be efficient if Ohio Packing is to survive and prosper. Only a few weeks elapse from the time the raw materials are unloaded at the shipping dock to the time when the finished products are loaded onto trucks bound for distributors and retailers. And most of that time is spent on a shelf, waiting for orders to arrive. Not so with the legislative process. Noncontroversial bills may be enacted within a month or so, but significant legislation may take years before enactment. Not infrequently, the legislature fails to meet its budget deadline, as New York has failed for 17 consecutive years, or fails to finish its budget before constitutional adjournment, as is the case of Minnesota this year. Legislatures are hardly efficient if any economic sense. Nor should we expect them to be.

Comprehensibility. The process of making sausage ought not be minimized; it is complex. But it is also comprehensible. In an hour-and-a-half tour, I could figure it out. I have been a student of the legislative process for more than 30 years, but I still can't figure it out. The legislature is too human, too democratic and too messy to be totally comprehensible.

Product. There is no denying that sausage comes in many varieties. Ohio Packing produces 250 different items, although most are variations on the same theme: breakfast and Italian sausage, bratwurst, frankfurters, bologna and salami are the major items under the sausage umbrella. The brand names that Ohio Packing supplies also vary. Harvest Brand is the company's own label. Through a license agreement with Ohio State University, it also manufactures and sells Buckeye Hot Dogs and Brutus Brats; and it is the coast-to-coast distributor of Schmidt's Bahama Mama (a spicy, smoked sausage).

Whatever the brand, however, the labeling required by USDA provides consumers with more information than they could possibly absorb: the brand name; product name; ingredients by proportion, including seasoning; nutrition facts; inspection legend; net weight statement; signature line (that is, who manufactured the sausage); and a handling statement.

New Metaphor Needed

Legislation is much more diverse than sausage, law is much greater in scope. And it is much more indeterminate. Consumers can read the enactment and the bill analyses leading up to it, but they can never be sure of how a law or program will be funded and implemented and how it will actually work. No accurate labeling system has ever been devised.

The products as well as the processes of sausage making and lawmaking are almost entirely different. Bismark has been at rest for more than a century; his metaphor ought to be laid to rest also. We can search for another metaphor, although I doubt that we will find one. The legislative process in Congress and the state is *sui generis,* incomparable, not like anything else in our experience—and pretty much the way it ought to be.

Critical Thinking

1. What is the well-known statement by Otto von Bismark that linked legislation and sausage?

2. What are differences and similarities between sausage-making and legislating with respect to accessibility, coherence, regularity, efficiency, comprehensibility, and product?

3. Why, according to Alan Rosenthal, is a new metaphor needed to illuminate important elements in the legislative process?

ALAN ROSENTHAL is a professor of political science at the Eagleton Institute of Politics at Rutgers University.

Termed Out

States with term-limited legislators are seeking ways to counteract the drawbacks of high turnover.

RUSSELL NICHOLS

There's an expansive view from the 10th floor corner office of state Sen. Dennis Olshove. From his suite in Lansing, Mich., you can see the main entrance of the state's Capitol, the impressive courtyard that leads up to it and the off-white Capitol dome that reaches into a canvas of clouds.

On a recent early winter afternoon, the view inside that corner office, however, is bleak: Boxes and folders clutter the floor. Files, mementos and thank-you letters litter a wooden desk. In the adjacent room, a paper shredder groans.

"Come back in three weeks," Olshove says, "and this room will be completely empty. The walls will be painted, and the history will be gone."

For the past eight years, Olshove walked from this legislative office building to the Capitol, where he pushed pieces of legislation on various matters like fire safety and renewable energy, medical issues and emergency unemployment benefits. Some bills passed, others never saw the light of day. But Olshove's days in the Michigan Legislature now are finished forever.

It's not by choice, however.

Olshove was elected to the state House of Representatives in 1991, took a break and then migrated to the Senate in 2002. Now he's been kicked out due to the state's term limits, which put a cap of three two-year terms for the state House and two four-year terms for the state Senate. Never again can Olshove run for the Legislature, and he and his fellow Michigan legislators aren't the only ones prohibited from being state legislators again.

Across the country, term limits are throwing lawmakers out of office and forcing extreme makeovers in several state legislatures. In the United States, 378 legislators in 14 states were term-limited this past year, according to an analysis by the National Conference of State Legislatures. But the facelift in the Michigan Legislature has been the most extreme: Due to term limits, 29 of the 38 senators will be replaced along with 34 of 110 House members. In addition, the state will have a new governor, attorney general and secretary of state.

All of this is taking place at a difficult time in state governance: Financial turbulence clouds the future and raises questions about the need for experienced legislators—ones who

know the ins and outs of passing laws in a timely manner and finding solutions to problems through the legislative process. A steep learning curve may be a luxury in times such as these. That's why, whatever state leaders believe about the merits of term limits, they are in agreement on one point: If term limits are in place, action should be taken to counteract the negative effects of high turnover and an inexperienced legislative body. That is, new legislators must be equipped quickly and effectively with the tools and tactics to handle the tasks they face. Nobody wins if lawmakers are forced to sit idly through their terms because they never learned the ropes.

Formal limits for state officials date back to Colonial days, but it wasn't until the early 1990s that legislative term limits became a target of government reformers. Spurred by voter mandates, 15 states put legal restrictions on the number of terms a member may serve in a particular office. The underlying idea was that term limits could bring new faces to the legislature—thus a constant flow of fresh ideas to state government. Moreover, term limits, its proponents suggested, would keep legislators from hogging valuable seats as "career politicians."

When Michigan voters enacted term limits in 1992, it wasn't just the fresh ideas and new faces that voters were concerned with. They hoped term restrictions would sever ties between legislators and lobbyists, and open the door to a new world of policymaking possibilities.

Some hopes have been realized. Term limits have reportedly pumped life into the Michigan Legislature by improving diversity and helping local residents connect to a government that has a more everyday-citizen look to it. "I hear stories of the old days and the legislators were treated literally like royalty," says state Rep. Tom McMillin, a certified public accountant who just finished his first term. "Everybody bowed to these people. Term limits guarantee that we get away from the whole idea of kings and princes. We gain much more in having a citizen legislature."

The legislative ticking clock, supporters say, also keeps the governing body from falling into a stale political routine, and it forces legislators to focus on the task at hand. There isn't time for new legislators to buy into conventional wisdom and inside-the-box thinking, suggests Jack McHugh, senior legislative analyst for the Mackinac Center for Public Policy, a free-market think tank based in Midland, Mich. "That's a good thing," he says. "If you don't have term limits, you're guaranteed to get a whole bunch of guys and gals whose thinking never veers outside the box, and they remain there for decades."

But there has also been an outcry over the counterproductivity of term limits. Term-limit opponents say experience matters, and when veterans term out, rookie lawmakers lose the vets' institutional knowledge. That, in turn, promotes short-term thinking. In rocky times, seasoned legislators may be best suited to pushing through the difficult solutions that lie ahead.

There are questions about how effective term limits have been in states that have a long track record with them. A 2004 study by the Public Policy Institute of California, for instance, found that instead of revolutionizing the state Legislature with innovation, new members often emulated their precursors, and the policymaking process suffered. "Legislative committees screen out fewer bills, the legislative process does not encourage fiscal discipline nor link requests to spending limits," the report noted, "and committee membership and leadership continuity impacts experience and expertise crucial to effective policymaking."

In Michigan, a 12-year study by Wayne State University found that term limits have dissolved important checks and balances, and increased lobbyists' influence. Marjorie Sarbaugh-Thompson, a political science professor at the university and the study's lead author, says there is no question that the problem stems from the limited time new legislators have to understand their jobs and a lack of veteran leadership to guide them. "It's very difficult to bring new legislators up to speed," she says. "They're just barely getting a grasp of what the job consists of when they're on their way out the door."

As disenchantment with term limits echoed through several state legislative chambers, some states decided to backtrack. In 2002, the Idaho Legislature became the first state to repeal its own term limits. Whereas many other efforts to repeal have fallen short at the polls, legislatures or the courts in five other states—Massachusetts, Oregon, Utah, Washington and Wyoming—followed in Idaho's footsteps.

For states that are keeping term limits in place, the trend is toward working against the negative factors by providing new legislators with better support, communication and advanced planning. "The more time that the clerk and secretary can spend with incoming legislators," says Craig Ruff, a senior policy fellow at Public Sector Consultants, a Lansing-based policy research firm, "the faster and easier it will be for legislators to adapt to new roles." Not surprisingly, that is why Olshove, whose seat was won by state Rep. Steve Bieda, met several times with his successor to tell him what to expect.

Perhaps a perfect model of an effective orientation is the boot camp for new lawmakers based in Sacramento, Calif. For the past 12 years, the Robert M. Hertzberg

Capitol Institute has provided training to new members and their employees on topics ranging from state ethics rules and computer systems to committees. Open year-round in a legislative office building, lawmakers go through an in-depth overview of processes, dissect statutes to digestible levels and receive large binders loaded with information and resources.

The program was initiated by Hertzberg, who as a freshman legislator went to a half-day of training that, he says, "didn't teach me anything about becoming a legislator." Years later, the former speaker of the Assembly decided to do something about it. He spent some time thinking about the issue and asking himself, "What do legislators need, and how do legislators learn?"

The comprehensive, intensive program that Hertzberg and former Republican Assembly Leader Bill Leonard designed helps new members understand the need-to-know details of the job. "At the superficial level, it's about term limits, but it's more about a cultural shift," Hertzberg says. "All institutions have to modernize to deal with rapid change. We're trying to create a long-term resource."

This past November, Hertzberg headed up an initial tour for the newest class of legislators—something he tries to do every year. He herded 25 of the 28 new members who showed up to the chamber floors, the travel office, the nurse's office and other need-to-know spots. He talked about his days in state government and shared details of the Capitol's past to impart history and context.

In other states, mentor programs match freshmen with senior members, and chamber seat assignments are arranged to prevent cliques. Some states even select key legislative leaders in advance so they'll have a jump-start on critical issues. "A few states now choose the speaker designate a year ahead, and they're brought in on the budget meetings," says Thomas Little, director of curriculum development and research for the State Legislative Leaders Foundation. "They know they only have two years, so they can't afford to spend the first year trying to find out what's going on."

With the timer running, veteran lawmakers might feel inclined to keep the governing group as small as possible to maximize efficiency. But legislators can learn faster through participation, says Eric Herzik, chair of the political science department at the University of Nevada, Reno. New members, he suggests, should be identified and mentored more directly than in the pre-term limit days when they could observe from the sidelines. "The idea of a good-old boy group is harder to maintain in a time-shortened career," Herzik says. "The way around it is to bring other members into the decision-making process earlier."

There's also a movement toward providing training throughout the term. Last year, for instance, Michigan's McMillin took freshmen legislators to meet with the clerk to discuss amendments, strategies and parliamentary procedures, and he plans to hold ongoing orientations in the future. "A freshman coming in under our leadership will feel like they're part of the process and won't be overwhelmed," he says. "I want to make sure they understand the nuances."

There are other problems spawned by term limits. One is partisanship. Term-limited lawmakers have less interest in bridging the divide between parties than pushing a partisan agenda, which hampers political progress, says Sarbaugh-Thompson. "The friendships are missing," she says. "People don't know each other. The country at large has very little respect for political experience. I think they think of it as campaigning instead of governing."

There are also issues revolving around a lack of institutional memory, which some say boosts power for lobbyists: Their knowledge on certain issues gives them leverage. But in many ways, term limits also force lobbyists to start from scratch and reintroduce themselves whenever a new member enters the political arena. In that sense, veteran staffers may have more of an inside track when it comes to legislative influence. But in the chamber, *who* lawmakers know matters as much as—if not more than—*what* lawmakers know. And many will admit that they have a hard time keeping track of who's who.

"I was here before term limits, so I got to see the transition," Olshove says. "Now if I'm in a room for any event, some people may be legislators, but I don't know who they are."

In the late 1990s, a group of Michigan lawmakers set out to forge relationships through field trips called "legislative exchanges." On nonformal session days, they caravanned to various districts for excursions. Sometimes they stayed overnight in a hotel or motel, and they would meet for dinner.

"We went to each other's districts to better understand the whole state so we could work together across the aisle," says Sen. Patty Birkholz, who just termed out of the state Legislature. "When you're traveling together, it helps force relationship-building."

Since then, the legislative exchanges have been all but forgotten. In the past few years, hopes of making solid connections cracked under the weight of party pressure—and the fact that legislators come and go in a flash.

During one of his final days in the Legislature, Olshove looks at a picture in his office of Senate members circa 2004. "Gone, gone, gone, gone, gone," he says, moving his finger from member to member in the picture. "This is ridiculous. All these folks are gone. That's term limits for you."

One of his staff members notifies him that a class is waiting for him in the Capitol. Students from Siersma Elementary School, located in his district, visit the Capitol every November as part of the curriculum. For the past five years, Olshove has volunteered to give a tour of the Senate Chamber to the kids, "his constituents," he calls them.

Once in the building, Olshove leads a few dozen fifth-graders into the south wing of the second floor, his stomping grounds. There he breaks down the lawmaking process, using a pretend proposal: No school on Fridays. The kids cheer, and then groan when he admits that the governor probably wouldn't sign off on that bill.

Then he opens the floor for questions. The students fire away with random questions about his favorite color (he doesn't have one), what he does for fun (spends time with his children), and whether he'll ever run for governor (no). Olshove then points to one student raising her hand in the middle of the crowd.

"Do you like your job?" she asks.

The kids haven't learned about term limits in class. They have no idea that next November, a brand new senator will be here giving the tour of the Senate Chamber. But they wait with wide eyes to hear his answer.

"I do," he says. "You get to meet all sorts of people every day, and you never know what to expect. And remember, any one of you can get elected one day."

With that, the kids gather around him for a group picture. Olshove smiles for the camera and for the kids, his constituents for only a few more weeks.

Critical Thinking

1. How many states have legal restrictions on the number of terms that a state legislator may serve in a legislative chamber?

2. What was the underlying idea that led to the imposition of term limits during the 1990s?

3. What are some advantages of term limits that seem to have been realized in many state legislatures?

4. What are some negative consequences of term limits?

5. What are some steps that state legislatures with term limits have taken to negate some of their negative consequences?

6. What effects on partisanship and institutional memory have term limits had in state legislatures?

From *Governing*, January 2011, pp. 20–25. Copyright © 2011 by e.Republic Inc. Reprinted by permission via Wright's Media. contract #77805.

What Legislatures Need Now

The prescription for change offered 40 years ago in "The Sometime Governments" has run its course, but legislatures still face plenty of institutional challenges.

KARL KURTZ AND BRIAN WEBERG

The challenges of today's legislatures are complex. They involve questions of integrity, will, commitment and trust, and the solutions are not at all clear. The realities of today's government and politics require a new approach to strengthen legislatures. What's needed is a process that clarifies the current problems, what changes are needed and how to put those remedies into place.

In the 1970s, the Citizens Conference on State Legislatures launched a remarkable movement to strengthen our nation's legislatures by publishing "The Sometime Governments: An Evaluation of the 50 American Legislatures."

The book included sweeping recommendations for change. The guidelines were designed to give legislatures more resources of time, compensation, staff and facilities. Forty years later, that agenda for reform has been largely accomplished or is no longer as relevant.

In large measure, "The Sometime Governments" succeeded in igniting two decades of effort by legislatures in every state to build capacity—the amount of session time, the number of members, committee organization, facilities and staffing.

It provided state-specific marching orders and a battle plan to reform-minded political troops ready and able to carry out its agenda. At the time of its publication, American politics were in transition. The one-person, one-vote court decisions of the 1960s and subsequent redistricting after the 1970 census opened state legislatures to a surge of new members in the 1974 elections.

They were a generation inspired by Kennedy, but also battered by the Vietnam War and the Watergate scandal. Armed with ideas set out in "The Sometimes Governments" and fueled by private foundation support, they transformed state legislatures.

For the next two decades, legislative leaders in almost every state engaged their members, the public and others concerned about legislatures in efforts to redesign and rebuild their institutions. These efforts were historic in scope and accomplishment. Legislatures became more muscular, agile, intelligent and independent than at any other time in American history.

The reform agenda of "The Sometime Governments" fell on hard times in the 1990s. There was a backlash, fueled by growing public cynicism about government, that developed against what political scientists call the "professionalization" of state

'The Sometime Governments'

The Citizens Conference on State Legislatures was a private nonprofit organization formed in 1964 to improve state legislatures. With a major grant from the Ford Foundation, it launched a 50-state study of legislatures in 1969 and published "The Sometime Governments: An Evaluation of the 50 American Legislatures" in 1971.

Based on criteria for "functional, accountable, informed, independent and representative" legislatures, the book evaluated state legislatures and ranked them from one to 50. The rankings caused a considerable stir among state lawmakers, and were an effective call to action: No state wanted to remain ranked in the bottom half of the list or to be below its neighbors or rivals.

The book contained both general recommendations for all states and specific recommendations for each legislature. The recommendations focused on such things as the length of the session, number of members, committee organization, facilities and staffing. They were highly prescriptive and specific.

During the study, the Citizens Conference was directed by Larry Margolis, former chief of staff to California Speaker Jesse Unruh, who led the transformation of the California Legislature into a full-time, professional body in the late 1960s. The implicit standard of "The Sometime Governments" was that all legislatures should look like California's, which, not surprisingly, came out No. 1 in the rankings.

legislatures. In almost all of the 24 states that allow voter initiatives, measures were placed on the ballot to limit the terms of state lawmakers. Virtually all of them passed, though some were later invalidated by courts or repealed, leaving 15 states today with term limits.

An NCSL study in 2007 showed term limits had significantly weakened state legislatures, especially in relation to the governor. Other initiatives placed limits on the tax and spending powers of legislatures in many states.

In this atmosphere of public distrust and cynicism toward government, it became difficult for legislatures to strengthen and grow in the fashion advocated by "The Sometime Governments." In the last 20 years—outside of the area of technology, which has its own momentum and societal drive—legislatures mostly have stopped taking steps such as adding staff, building more facilities or increasing the amount of time spent on the job. By the 1990s, the Citizens Conference's recommendations had run their course. They had done their job of stimulating positive change.

In the last 20 years legislatures mostly have stopped taking steps such as adding staff, building more facilities or increasing the amount of time spent on the job.

Problems Persist

While some of the issues raised in "The Sometime Governments" have been resolved, new ones have emerged.

The process of legislative improvement is never-ending, requiring constant tinkering and adjustment, state by state. Partly as a result of the previous success of strengthening legislatures, they face new problems today. In his book, "Engines of Democracy: Politics and Policy in State Legislatures," Rutgers University political scientist Alan Rosenthal identifies ailments confronting contemporary representative democracy.

- **Partisanship.** Strong party allegiance can organize conflict and disagreement, but in excess can lead to incivility and a lack of willingness to negotiate and compromise. Hyper-partisanship, as some have called it, undermines political trust and support for democratic institutions. Some state legislatures today, but by no means all, suffer from excessive partisanship.
- **Integrity.** The overwhelming number of state lawmakers behave ethically. The misdeeds of a few members, however, tar the entire institution. The public believes the majority of legislators are out to serve themselves, and they are for sale to the highest bidder.
- **Deliberation.** The work of standing committees, which was a major focus of the earlier legislative strengthening movement, has been undermined in many states in recent years. Partisan considerations have been a detriment to substantive study, analysis of and deliberation on all sides of an issue. Top legislative leaders and party caucuses too often bypass or downplay the committee process. Term limits have also weakened committees as they have been deprived of experience and expertise.
- **Responsibility.** Rosenthal is concerned about the unwillingness of some legislators to make difficult fiscal decisions because of constituent opposition, the growing tendency for committees to fail to screen out bills that lack support or merit and the practice of lawmakers not

voting against someone else's bill for fear that he or she will vote against their own.
- **Public cynicism.** Today's excessive public mistrust of democratic institutions is harmful. Cynicism discourages qualified people from running for office, promotes a reluctance by members to address unpopular but necessary issues, encourages simplistic institutional reforms such as term limits, and increases the public's unwillingness to comply with legislative decisions.
- **Institutional commitment.** Rosenthal writes that lawmakers often pay little attention to the institution and distance themselves from it. "If they do not devote themselves to their institution's well-being, who can they expect to do the job for them? The responsibility is primarily theirs—and it is not being adequately shouldered."

New Set of Questions

Rosenthal's list of ailments ring true and it's vital they be addressed and remedied. But it's important to emphasize that not all states have experienced all of these problems. The need for legislative improvement differs from state to state. The only problem on the Rosenthal list that is common to all the states is public cynicism, and even then there are a few states—Alaska, Idaho, North Dakota and Wyoming are examples—in which the legislature has relatively high public opinion ratings. As the Citizens Conference recognized 40 years ago, an agenda for legislative strengthening needs to be state specific.

But how can we create a state-specific agenda?

We suggest a basic set of questions that legislators, legislative staff, political scientists and interested citizens should ask and answer about the performance of their legislature. These questions are standards of a sort, expectations of what a good legislature should be.

1. Does the legislature effectively share power with the governor? Does the legislature initiate and enact its own legislation and make independent decisions about the state budget? Does the legislature provide effective oversight of executive actions?
2. Does the redistricting process for the legislature result in reasonably compact, contiguous and competitive legislative districts that do not provide an undue advantage to one party and incumbent legislators?
3. Do the members provide effective constituent service including answering requests for information, casework, local projects and public expenditures? Is the proportion of women and racial and ethnic minorities in the legislature reasonably reflective of the population of the state?
4. Does the legislature take into account interests of the state as a whole instead of the cumulative interests of districts and constituencies?
5. Is there a reasonable balance in the legislature between the need to have strong, effective leaders who guide members on procedural and policy choices and the need

for internal democracy that disperses power and protects the rights of individual members?

6. Does the majority party have enough clout to get things done? Are the rights of the minority party protected?

7. Is the degree of partisanship in the legislature reasonable? Does the legislature engage in consensus-building? Are opposing sides willing to negotiate differences and find compromises to difficult problems?

8. Does the legislature have integrity? Do the members of the legislature and the capitol community behave in ethical ways?

9. Do individual citizens and organized groups with an interest in an issue have the opportunity to participate in the lawmaking process? Are all viewpoints heard and treated fairly by the legislature? Is the influence of moneyed interests that contribute to political campaigns appropriate relative to their role in the state's economy and well-being?

10. Does the legislature study and deliberate on issues effectively? Does it allow give-and-take and the open exchange of ideas at all stages of the formal and informal legislative process, especially the committee stage? Are legislative committees strong, attentive and involved in critical decision making?

11. Do the members of the legislature care about and protect the well-being of the institution? Is there adequate continuity in the membership of the legislature to promote institutional values, build up expertise, and pass on knowledge and skills? Are the leaders and members committed to educating the public about the legislative institution and defending its values?

12. Does the legislature have adequate resources—staff, time, facilities, technology—to do its job, and are those resources managed effectively? Is there an appropriate balance between partisan staff who provide strategic advice and guidance to members and nonpartisan staff who provide unbiased analysis and manage the institution?

Solutions Are the Challenge

Each state—depending on its history, traditions and culture—will have different answers to these questions, and people within the same state will disagree. But if the answer is "no" on any set of questions, this is an area to strengthen.

Once those areas are defined, finding solutions becomes the challenge. Most 21st century problems in legislatures will not be solved by throwing more resources at them or even by structural and procedural changes. The remedies for these ailments are more likely to come through education, training and cultural changes in the institution—all of which may be difficult to bring about.

Most 21st century problems in legislatures will not be solved by throwing more resources at them or even by structural and procedural changes.

Legislators, staff, academics and committed citizens need to come together to draw up a new agenda to strengthen legislatures.

The reformers of the 1970s had a difficult task of transforming state legislatures into something more than "sometime governments." But, in retrospect, their task seems easy compared to today's work of building integrity, will, commitment and trust.

The challenges facing today's more robust legislatures are even more daunting. But that shouldn't stop them. They need to find the mechanisms and a spirit similar to those of a previous generation of dedicated people who improved America's state legislatures.

Critical Thinking

1. What were the main points of the 1971 publication entitled *The Sometime Governments: An Evaluation of the 50 American Legislatures*?

2. How did state legislatures, in general, respond to prescriptions in the *The Sometime Governments*?

3. What new set of problems did political scientist Alan Rosenthal identify in his *Engines of Democracy* book that appeared several decades after *The Sometimes Governments*?

4. What basic set of questions do the authors of this article present for legislators, legislative staff, and others to use in evaluating state legislatures today?

KARL KURTZ runs NCSL's Trust for Representative Democracy. **BRIAN WEBERG** directs NCSL's Legislative Management program.

From *State Legislatures*, July/August 2010, pp. 47–50. Copyright © 2010 by National Conference of State Legislatures. Reprinted by permission.

Are City Councils a Relic of the Pas

One of America's oldest political institutions isn't adapting very well to 21st-century urban life.

ROB GURWITT

You notice two things right off about the 19th Ward in St. Louis. The first is that pretty much everywhere there's construction, there's also a large sign reading, "Assistance for the project provided by Michael McMillan, Alderman." The second is just how limited Alderman McMillan's domain happens to be. Walk a few minutes in any direction, and you're out of his ward. You don't see the signs anymore. You also don't see as much construction.

Within the friendly confines of the 19th, St. Louis looks like a city busily reviving. There are new high schools being built, scattered apartments and loft projects underway, efforts to rejuvenate the historic arts and entertainment district, and a HOPE VI retrofit of an enormous public housing facility. While all this activity has some powerful people behind it, just one person has had a hand in all of it, and that is McMillan himself. Only 31, he has been on the St. Louis Board of Aldermen for six years, and in that time has made it clear that his ambitions for his ward—and by extension, himself—are high. "I don't have other obligations," he says. "I'm not married, I have no kids, I have no other job. It's one of my competitive edges."

Cross the ward boundary, and you find out what "competitive edge" means in St. Louis politics. North of the 19th, and for some distance to the east, stretch a series of neglected, depopulated neighborhoods that do not in any way suggest urban revival. This is, in part, a consequence of private market decisions: These neighborhoods don't have much clout within the corporate suites where such decisions are made. But equally important, they don't have much clout in local government, either—at least not when it comes to large-scale development projects.

That's because in St. Louis, each of the 28 ward aldermen is the gatekeeper of development in his or her little slice of the city. If they're shrewd and well connected, like Michael McMillan, the ward does fine. If they're inattentive, or maladroit at cutting deals, or on the outs with local developers, or just plain picky, which is the case in more than a few wards, hardly anything gets done. "You don't see a Mike McMillan coming out of some of these devastated wards," says one City Hall insider. "They have a voice, but if it's weak, what do they really get?"

To be sure, even the weak aldermen in St. Lou uses. They get potholes filled and streetlights fixed, on how to handle code violations or deal with hou and see that garbage gets picked up in alleyways w tractors dump it illegally. This hands-on attention is bad thing. In the words of Jim Shrewsbury, who as pre the Board of Aldermen runs at large and is its 29th men city's deeply entrenched system of political micro-mana "protects neighborhoods and gives people a sense of influ As members of a democratic institution, that's what city cilmen are supposed to do. But when that's about all ma them do, in a city that is struggling to emerge from yea economic debility, even Shrewsbury agrees that somethin wrong. The system, he says, "creates a sense of parochial and feudalism. We become the Balkans."

Feuding and Hot Air

The concept of balkanization could be applied these days to councils and boards of aldermen in many of America's biggest cities—perhaps most of them. Look around the country and you can quickly compile a dossier of dysfunction.

Sometimes it is a case of pursuing tangents, as the Baltimore City Council likes to do. In a recent commentary about what it called "the hot-air council," the Baltimore Sun suggested that frequent resolutions on foreign affairs, hearings on the differences between telephone exchanges, and debate about counteracting "the negative images of Baltimore, as portrayed in 'real-crime' fiction, TV dramas and movies" suggested that the members didn't have enough real work to do.

Other councils become so embroiled in internal maneuvering that they lose their relevance. In Philadelphia, where a former mayor once referred to the city council as "the worst legislative body in the free world," there was a brief period of council influence in the mid-1990s, when John Street was council president and worked closely with Mayor Ed Rendell. Now, however, Street is mayor and finds himself in regular tangles with various council factions. "It's like an opera where

dy has a different libretto," says Mark Alan Hughes, an
affairs professor at the University of Pennsylvania and col-
for the *Philadelphia Daily News*. "The melodrama is
's just the meaning that's completely obscure."

re are councils where bickering and infighting are so
e that the entire body acquires an image of irresponsible
ess. In Detroit recently, one member charged that support-
the city's mayor had sabotaged the electric massager in
esk chair to give her a jolt when she used it. Not surpris-
, the public's response was disdainful—what most people
was a group of elected officials engaged in sabotaging its
reputation.

here are places where, if you want to find the future of the
being pondered, the council chamber is the last place you'd
k. "What you have," says a close watcher of civic affairs in
tsburgh, "is a group of people who primarily deal with very
undane, housekeeping things in their districts. That's what
ey do, it's what they're interested in, and it's the way they see
eir power." The real power lies in the mayor's office and with
e city's still-strong civic and corporate leadership.

Finally, there are councils whose problem has not been an
absence of energy but a hyperactive compulsion to argue over
everyday management decisions and prevent important decisions from being made. In Hartford, Connecticut, the city charter for years gave most of the political power to the council,
but the council had a long history of intervening in the day-to-
day administration of city services and tying itself up in petty
squabbles corrosive to the morale of residents, as well as city
employees. In the 1990s, the council essentially torpedoed the
program of Mayor Mike Peters, who appeared to have broad
voter support for his economic reform and revival ideas. Small
surprise that when they were finally given a straightforward
chance last November to change things, the city's voters opted
to create a new form of government that strengthened the mayor
at the council's expense.

None of this is to say that councils in large cities never tackle
important issues or play a key role in crafting policy. Council
members in Los Angeles, for instance, have a great deal to say
about basic infrastructure issues, in their districts and across the
city. And for all its infighting, the Philadelphia City Council did
help to re-shape Street's ambitious urban renewal program, the
Neighborhood Transformation Initiative, to be more responsive
to neighborhood concerns.

But in all too many large cities these days, the power of councils is, at most, the power to stop things. The wellsprings of
citywide innovation and progress lie elsewhere. It is telling that
until this past year, neither of the two major national organizations speaking for cities addressed the specific concerns of big-
city councils. The National League of Cities is dominated by
small- and medium-sized jurisdictions; the U.S. Conference of
Mayors, which focuses on larger cities, doesn't address council
members at all. "We're literally locked out of the one national
group that deals with big cities," observes Nick Licata, a Seattle
council member.

Licata, who was struck by the dearth of representation from
places like his when he first attended a League of Cities meeting,
has put together a new "Central Cities Council" at the League,
for council members in the 100 or so largest cities to share information and strategies on common issues. "We're not communicating on a regular basis, we're not exchanging information
on local programs we can learn from, and on the national level,
when we should be lobbying, we don't have our act together,"
he says. "This should help us link up."

Still, the sense of floundering one often gets watching big-
city councils isn't really a surprise. Over the years, as mayors
have moved to get a handle on crime, economic development
and even school management, and as semi-private institutions—redevelopment authorities, stadium authorities, transit authorities, convention center authorities, tax increment
finance districts—have proliferated, the role of councils in
the most critical issues of urban governance has atrophied.
Individual council members, the Michael McMillans of the
country, may still have a share of power and influence, but
the bodies on which many of them serve have lost their identity. "I think city councils have been neutered in most cases,"
says Dennis Judd, an urban affairs specialist at the University
of Illinois-Chicago. "They are engaging in the most trivial
aspects of urban government, rather than the most important
aspects."

Under these circumstances, it is hard not to wonder whether
city councils are becoming relics of the political past, poorly
adapted to making the decisions of 21st-century urban life. In
all too many cases, they seem in danger of becoming the dino-
saurs of American local government.

Out of the Loop

There was a moment not long ago when the St. Louis Board
of Aldermen managed to command national attention, but it's
one local politicians would rather forget. In the midst of a
tense and racially charged ward redistricting debate in 2001,
Alderman Irene Smith was conducting a filibuster when she
asked whether she could go to the bathroom. Told by Board
President Shrewsbury that the rules required her to yield the
floor to do so, she summoned her supporters, who brought in
a trash can and surrounded her with improvised drapes while
she appeared to urinate into the can. "I was mortified," says
a St. Louis politician who happened to be watching on cable
television at the time. "If you've been in the aldermanic chambers, they call to mind a time when the city was a powerful
city, a grand place. To think of her staging that in there! The
stock of the entire board of aldermen went down." Smith was
later indicted on charges of public indecency but was acquit-
ted in January on the reasoning that no one could know for
sure whether she was actually urinating or simply pretending
to do so.

To those who spend their time in City Hall, the incident was
puzzling, because Smith, a lawyer and former judge, is generally seen as one of the more careful and thoughtful members
of the board. "She's bright, she knows how to read the law, she
asks tough questions in committee hearings," says one aldermanic insider. But to many in the city at large, there was little

question about how to interpret her outburst: Not even its own members accord the board much respect any longer.

The fact is, for all the opportunities that ambitious aldermen have to promote development within their own neighborhoods, it's been a while since the board has played a significant role in shaping matters of vital interest to St. Louis as a whole. One of the biggest issues on the plate of Mayor Francis Slay—himself a former board president—is a new stadium for the St. Louis Cardinals baseball team, and while pieces of the complex deal he has put together will require aldermanic approval, the board itself has had very little role in constructing it.

"When I was in City Hall," says a former aide to one of Slay's recent predecessors, "I only went to the board if I absolutely had to. The truth is, I never felt the need to involve people there on the front end in order to get something passed on the back end. In the 1970s or '80s, if a mayor had a stadium project, he'd have had to line up five or six people on the board before he even went public with it." Because that didn't happen in the current situation, the aide argues, this stadium deal is just a stadium deal—it is not part of any broader city commitment to, say, refurbishing public sports facilities or community centers in the neighborhoods.

There are any number of theories about what has led the board of aldermen to its diminished citywide import, and many of them focus on its size. The 28 wards were created in 1914, when St. Louis had 680,000 people. They remained in place when the city reached its peak of 850,000 in 1950. And they're still there, half a century later, when it's down to 340,000. This means that each alderman represents about 12,500 people. Chicago's 50-member city council, which is one of the largest in the country, would have to grow to 200 members if its wards were the same size as those in St. Louis.

If all you expect of an alderman is close attention to garbage pickup and street repairs, of course, small wards are just fine. But they have a cost, as well. For one thing, they form a low barrier to political entry. In some wards, a politician needs as few as 800 votes to get elected. When the city was larger, says former Mayor Freeman Bosley Jr., "you had to be a real leader to get on the board, someone who could put together thousands and thousands of votes. That plays into your ability to put people together and pull them in a direction. So as the years have gone by, the number of go-to people has diminished."

To be sure, it's possible to overstate the case. "Just because we were once a city of 800,000 people doesn't mean we had rocket scientists serving on the board of aldermen," notes Jim Shrewsbury. "I don't think someone makes a decision between running a corporation and being an alderman." But it's equally true that city councils are, in essence, a political proving ground—former U.S. House Minority Leader Richard Gephardt, for instance, got his start on the St. Louis Board of Aldermen. The less skill and vision they demand of their members, the poorer a city's civic life is likely to be.

"If you can make the council a place where young people who are interested in public policy think they ought to be, then it serves as a farm system to create people who understand how local government works and who have sympathy

for it," says Mike Jones, a former alderman who now runs the regional Empowerment Zone. "Because the real question is, Where do you get local leadership from? On a city council where you've got to work hard to get elected, it takes good political instincts and hones them into political and policy-making skills."

Ironclad Privilege

Over time, the small size of the constituencies and the rules of the institution itself have combined to make the lure of parochialism more and more irresistible. In the 1950s, following passage of the federal Urban Renewal Act of 1949, aldermen in St. Louis suddenly found themselves with real power in their neighborhoods as the arbiters of development. That law, says Lana Stein, a University of Missouri-St. Louis historian, "brought a huge pot of money, and the aldermen had to pass bills authorizing urban renewal projects and highway projects. They were courted by Civic Progress [the group of corporate movers and shakers at the time] and by the mayor. Even though there were working-class people and saloon keepers elected to the board, they became a much bigger deal because of what they were voting on."

But if the urban renewal money brought the board instant influence, it also led inexorably to parochialism. As requests grew for new housing or redevelopment in the wards, they ran into the ironclad principle of aldermanic privilege—the notion that no member of the board would interfere in matters affecting another member's ward.

Fifty years later, developers still need help from the city, and that usually means a vote from the aldermen, supporting a "blighting" provision or providing a tax abatement or creating a tax-increment financing district. If you happen to live in a ward with an active, responsive alderman who knows how to put together development deals, you're fortunate. But there's scarcely anyone left on the board looking at what makes sense for the city as a whole. Aldermen rarely feel any right or responsibility to look closely at deals being made in others' wards.

When a group of downtown residents recently challenged plans backed by their alderman to demolish a historic, marble-fronted building to make way for a parking garage, the board deferred to the alderman's wishes by essentially ignoring the protest. The demolition plans were backed by the mayor and by his allies, and the developers insisted that the garage was vital to their plans, even though there are underused garages within a block's walk.

The local residents, part of a small but growing group of loft dwellers who form one of the few tangible signs of hope for St. Louis' downtown, attended the one aldermanic hearing on the matter and found no one to talk to. "It was a farce," says Margie Newman, one of their leaders. "There was no opportunity to make our case. Literally, there was an alderman with the Sunday comics held up in front of his face, and of the six on the committee, three were wandering in and out. Remember, this was at our one opportunity to bring our case."

Indeed, confirms Matt Villa, a young alderman who represents the city's far southeast, there is little incentive on the board

Bodies Large and Small

Size of selected city councils

City	Number of Districts	Average Size of District
Los Angeles	15	246,000
Phoenix	8	165,000
New York	51	157,000
Kansas City	6	74,000
Memphis*	9	72,000
San Francisco**	11	71,000
Milwaukee	17	35,000
Minneapolis	13	29,000
Richmond	9	22,000
St. Louis	28	12,000

*Two districts have three members each, the others each have one, for a total of 13 members

** City/county supervisors

Source: Governing research

to pay attention to what others are doing when you don't have to. "In our neighborhood," he says, "there's a neighborhood association and a housing corporation, and we sit down to plan the next five years and never take into consideration what other wards are doing. I don't even know how a citywide plan would be embraced by 28 aldermen."

And because the board itself doesn't have an independent capacity to look carefully at measures that come before it—it has very few staff members, and those who want help, such as Michael McMillan, raise funds on the side to pay for an assistant—it often approves important decisions with scarcely any scrutiny at all. "We give pay raises and pension raises and things like that," Villa says, "without really knowing the fiscal impact. The alderman who's sponsored it explains, we pass it, and years later it turns out it wasn't a $5 million impact, it was a $50 million impact."

Charter Changes

If there's anyone unhappy with this state of affairs, it's Jim Shrewsbury, who as president would like the board to become more independent and active. "The truth is, most legislation and ideas originate with the administration," he says. "The vast majority of bills are administration-sponsored bills; they have the resources and the interest and the concentration. Sometimes, I wish we were more careful and would scrutinize them more carefully. And I wish there were more innovation, that more legislation originated here." But he is also quick to point out that in the calculus of the 28 politicians who serve alongside him, that may be more of a risk than they want to take. "I know that on Election Day, the one thousand people who hate me will be there," he explains. "I don't know how many of the

thousands who like me will be. I'm prepared to lose my office for something that was in *Profiles in Courage*. If it's not, you start to wonder whether it's worth getting involved."

Yet it's possible that change will come to the St. Louis Board of Aldermen anyway. Although St. Louis is technically a "strong mayor" city, the political reality is that the mayor is constitutionally among the weakest in the country for a city this size. Power has to be shared with a half-dozen other elected officials; the state controls the police through a board on which the mayor has only his own seat; budget decisions and city contracts have to be approved by two of the three members of the Board of Estimate and Apportionment, which is made up of the mayor, comptroller and aldermanic president. "St. Louis is probably the nation's best case of an unreformed government," says the University of Illinois' Dennis Judd, referring to the nationwide movement early in the last century to give mayors enhanced authority. "It's as if it never was touched by the reformers."

Like the board's awkward size, all of this is a result of the 1914 city charter, which is still in effect. But last November, voters statewide approved a home-rule provision for St. Louis that will allow it to take up charter change. Although most of the attention is likely to go to placing more power in the hands of the mayor, there is plenty of sentiment among civic leaders for shrinking the size of the board of aldermen.

This is happening in other big cities with similar problems. Contraction is on the docket in Milwaukee, where some aldermen themselves have proposed shrinking the Common Council from 17 to 15 members, and in Baltimore, where voters last November approved trimming the city council from 19 to 15. Baltimore's initiative, backed by a coalition of labor unions and community organizations, was opposed by most of the city's elected leadership, but it passed overwhelmingly.

It's unclear how much impact tinkering with council size will really have, in St. Louis or anywhere else. But it's clear that some fundamental changes will have to take place for city councils such as these to maintain any real relevance at all in coming years.

By any standard, there is still important work for these bodies to do. Cities need robust political institutions, and by all rights, city councils ought to be among them—they are, after all, the one institution designed to serve as the collective voice of residents and communities, whether their members are elected in districts or at large. But when little is expected of them, because a city's most important decisions are made elsewhere, it's no surprise that over time the ambitions of their members shrink to take in smaller and smaller patches of turf.

There are undeniable benefits to this. Two decades ago, voters in St. Louis overwhelmingly turned down an initiative to cut the number of wards. They felt, says Shrewsbury, "that government had gotten so complicated and big, the only way their voice could be heard was having an alderman who paid close attention." It may be that all most people really want from their city council is the kind of personal stroking that is often hard to come by elsewhere in a big city. But it's also hard to escape the feeling that, as Judd puts it, "when citizens are consulted these days, it's about things that are less and less consequential. What we're seeing is the slow strangulation of local democracy."

Critical Thinking

1. In what sense is every St. Louis ward alderman the "gate-keeper of development" in his or her ward?

2. What are some pros and cons of St. Louis's "deeply entrenched system of micro-management"?

3. What sorts of "tangents" do some city councils pursue?

4. What does it mean to suggest that small wards in a city result in a "low barrier to political entry"?

5. What is meant by the "principle of aldermanic privilege" and how is it connected to parochialism in the functioning of the St. Louis city council?

First, Kill All the School Boards

A modest proposal to fix the schools.

MATT MILLER

It wasn't just the slate and pencil on every desk, or the absence of daily beatings. As Horace Mann sat in a Leipzig classroom in the summer of 1843, it was the entire Prussian system of schools that impressed him. Mann was six years into the work as Massachusetts secretary of education that would earn him lasting fame as the "father of public education." He had sailed from Boston to England several weeks earlier with his new wife, combining a European honeymoon with educational fact-finding. In England, the couple had been startled by the luxury and refinement of the upper classes, which exceeded anything they had seen in America and stood in stark contrast to the poverty and ignorance of the masses. If the United States was to avoid this awful chasm and the social upheaval it seemed sure to create, he thought, education was the answer. Now he was seeing firsthand the Prussian schools that were the talk of reformers on both sides of the Atlantic.

In Massachusetts, Mann's vision of "common schools," publicly funded and attended by all, represented an inspiring democratic advance over the state's hodgepodge of privately funded and charity schools. But beyond using the bully pulpit, Mann had little power to make his vision a reality. Prussia, by contrast, had a system designed from the center. School attendance was compulsory. Teachers were trained at national institutes with the same care that went into training military officers. Their enthusiasm for their subjects was contagious, and their devotion to students evoked reciprocal affection and respect, making Boston's routine resort to classroom whippings seem barbaric.

Mann also admired Prussia's rigorous national curriculum and tests. The results spoke for themselves: illiteracy had been vanquished. To be sure, Prussian schools sought to create obedient subjects of the kaiser—hardly Mann's aim. Yet the lessons were undeniable, and Mann returned home determined to share what he had seen. In the seventh of his legendary "Annual Reports" on education to the Commonwealth of Massachusetts, he touted the benefits of a national system and cautioned against the "calamities which result . . . from leaving this most important of all the functions of a government to chance."

Mann's epiphany that summer put him on the wrong side of America's tradition of radical localism when it came to schools. And although his efforts in the years that followed made Massachusetts a model for taxpayer-funded schools and state-sponsored teacher training, the obsession with local control—

not incidentally, an almost uniquely American obsession—still dominates U.S. education to this day. For much of the 150 or so years between Mann's era and now, the system served us adequately: during that time, we extended more schooling to more people than any nation had before and rose to superpower status. But let's look at what local control gives us today, in the "flat" world in which our students will have to compete.

The United States spends more than nearly every other nation on schools, but out of 29 developed countries in a 2003 assessment, we ranked 24th in math and in problem-solving, 18th in science, and 15th in reading. Half of all black and Latino students in the U.S. don't graduate on time (or ever) from high school. As of 2005, about 70 percent of eighth-graders were not proficient in reading. By the end of eighth grade, what passes for a math curriculum in America is two years behind that of other countries.

Dismal fact after dismal fact; by now, they are hardly news. But in the 25 years since the landmark report *A Nation at Risk* sounded the alarm about our educational mediocrity, America's response has been scattershot and ineffective, orchestrated mainly by some 15,000 school districts acting alone, with help more recently from the states. It's as if after Pearl Harbor, FDR had suggested we prepare for war through the uncoordinated efforts of thousands of small factories; they'd know what kinds of planes and tanks were needed, right?

When you look at what local control of education has wrought, the conclusion is inescapable: we must carry Mann's insights to their logical end and nationalize our schools, to some degree. But before delving into the details of why and how, let's back up for a moment and consider what brought us to this pass.

130,000 Little Red Schoolhouses

Our system is, more than anything, an artifact of our Colonial past. For the religious dissenters who came to the New World, literacy was essential to religious freedom, enabling them to teach their own beliefs. Religion and schooling moved in tandem across the Colonies. Many people who didn't like what the local minister was preaching would move on and found their own church, and generally their own school.

This preference for local control of education dovetailed with the broader ethos of the American Revolution and the

Founders' distrust of distant, centralized authority. Education was left out of the Constitution; in the 10th Amendment, it is one of the unnamed powers reserved for the states, which in turn passed it on to local communities. Eventually the United States would have 130,000 school districts, most of them served by a one-room school. These little red schoolhouses, funded primarily through local property taxes, became the iconic symbols of democratic American learning.

Throughout the late 19th and early 20th centuries, nothing really challenged this basic structure. Eventually many rural districts were consolidated, and the states assumed a greater role in school funding; since the 1960s, the federal government has offered modest financial aid to poorer districts as well. But neither these steps, nor the standards-based reform movement inspired by *A Nation at Risk,* brought significant change.

Many reformers across the political spectrum agree that local control has become a disaster for our schools. But the case against it is almost never articulated. Public officials are loath to take on powerful school-board associations and teachers' unions; foundations and advocacy groups, who must work with the boards and unions, also pull their punches. For these reasons, as well as our natural preference for having things done nearby, support for local control still lingers, largely unexamined, among the public.

No Problem Left Behind

Why is local control such a failure when applied to our schools? After all, political decentralization has often served America well, allowing decisions to be made close to where their impact would be felt. But in education, it has spawned several crippling problems:

No way to know how children are doing. "We're two decades into the standards movement in this country, and standards are still different by classroom, by school, by district, and by state," says Tom Vander Ark, who headed the education program at the Bill and Melinda Gates Foundation from 1999 through 2006. "Most teachers in America still pretty much teach whatever they want."

If you thought President Bush's 2001 No Child Left Behind legislation was fixing these problems, think again. True, NCLB requires states to establish standards in core subjects and to test children in grades 3–8 annually, with the aim of making all students "proficient" by 2014. But by leaving standards and definitions of "proficiency" to state discretion, it has actually made matters worse. *The Proficiency Illusion*, a report released in October by the conservative Thomas B. Fordham Foundation, details how. "'Proficiency' varies wildly from state to state, with 'passing scores' ranging from the 6th percentile to the 77th," the researchers found:

> Congress erred big-time when NCLB assigned each state to set its own standards and devise and score its own tests . . . this study underscores the folly of a big modern nation, worried about its global competitiveness, nodding with approval as Wisconsin sets its eighth-grade reading passing level at the 14th percentile while South Carolina sets its at the 71st percentile.

The lack of uniform evaluation creates a "tremendous risk of delusion about how well children are actually doing," says Chris Cerf, the deputy chancellor of schools in New York City. That delusion makes it far more difficult to enact reforms—and even to know where reforms are needed. "Schools may get an award from their state for high performance, and under federal guidelines they may be targeted for closure for low performance," Vander Ark says. This happens in California, he told me, all the time.

Stunted R&D. Local control has kept education from attracting the research and development that drives progress, because benefits of scale are absent. There are some 15,000 curriculum departments in this country—one for every district. None of them can afford to invest in deeply understanding what works best when it comes to teaching reading to English-language learners, or using computers to develop customized strategies for students with different learning styles. Local-control advocates would damn the federal government if it tried to take on such things. Perhaps more important, the private sector generally won't pursue them, either. Purchasing decisions are made by a complex mix of classroom, school, and school board officials. The more complicated and fragmented the sale that a company has to make, the less willing it is to invest in product research and development.

Incompetent school boards and union dominance. "In the first place, God made idiots," Mark Twain once wrote. "This was for practice. Then He made School Boards." Things don't appear to have improved much since Twain's time. "The job has become more difficult, more complicated, and more political, and as a result, it's driven out many of the good candidates," Vander Ark says. "So while teachers' unions have become more sophisticated and have smarter people who are better-equipped and -prepared at the table, the quality of school-board members, particularly in urban areas, has decreased." Board members routinely spend their time on minor matters, from mid-level personnel decisions to bus routes. "The tradition goes back to the rural era, where the school board hired the schoolmarm and oversaw the repair of the roof, looked into the stove in the room, and deliberated on every detail of operating the schools," says Michael Kirst, an emeritus professor of education at Stanford University. "A lot of big-city school boards still do these kinds of things." Because of Progressive-era reforms meant to get school boards out of "politics," most urban school districts are independent, beyond the reach of mayors and city councils. Usually elected in off-year races that few people vote in or even notice, school boards are, in effect, accountable to no one.

Local control essentially surrenders power over the schools to the teachers' unions. Union money and mobilization are often decisive in board elections. And local unions have hefty intellectual and political backing from their state and national affiliates. Even when they're not in the unions' pockets, in other words, school boards are outmatched.

The unions are adept at negotiating new advantages for their members, spreading their negotiating strategies to other districts in the state, and getting these advantages embodied in state and sometimes federal law as well. This makes it extraordinarily difficult for superintendents to change staffing, compensation, curriculum, and other policies. Principals, for their part, are compliance machines, spending their days making sure that federal, state, and district programs are implemented. Meanwhile, common-sense reforms, like offering higher pay to attract teachers to underserved specialties such as math, science, and special education, can't get traction, because the unions say no.

Financial inequity. The dirty little secret of local control is the enormous tax advantage it confers on better-off Americans: communities with high property wealth can tax themselves at low rates and still generate far more dollars per pupil than poor communities taxing themselves heavily. This wasn't always the case: in the 19th century, property taxes were rightly seen as the fairest way to pay for education, since property was the main form of wealth, and the rich and poor tended to live near one another. But the rise of commuter suburbs since World War II led to economically segregated communities; today, the spending gap between districts can be thousands of dollars per pupil.

But local taxes represent only 44 percent of overall school funding; the spending gaps between states, which contribute 47 percent of total spending, account for most of the financial inequity. Perversely, Title I, the federal aid program enacted in the 1960s to boost poor schools, has widened the gaps, because it distributes money largely according to how much states are already spending.

What Would Horace Do?

I asked Marc Tucker, the head of the New Commission on the Skills of the American Workforce (a 2006 bipartisan panel that called for an overhaul of the education system), how he convinces people that local control is hobbling our schools. He said he asks a simple question: If we have the second-most-expensive K–12 system of all those measured by the Organization for Economic Cooperation and Development, but consistently perform between the middle and the bottom of the pack, shouldn't we examine the systems of countries that spend less and get better results? "I then point out that the system of local control that we have is almost unique," Tucker says. "One then has to defend a practice that is uncharacteristic of the countries with the best performance.

"It's an industrial-benchmarking argument," he adds.

Horace Mann wouldn't have used this jargon, but his thinking was much the same. In his time, the challenge was to embrace a bigger role for the state; today, the challenge is to embrace a bigger role for the federal government in standards, funding, and other arenas.

The usual explanation for why national standards won't fly is that the right hates "national" and the left hates "standards." But that's changing. Two Republican former secretaries of education, Rod Paige and William Bennett, now support national standards and tests, writing in *The Washington Post*: "In a world of fierce economic competition, we can't afford to pretend that the current system is getting us where we need to go." On the Democratic side, John Podesta, a former chief of staff to President Clinton and the current president of the Center for American Progress (where I'm a senior fellow), told me that he believes the public is far ahead of the established

political wisdom, which holds that the only safe way to discuss national standards is to stipulate that they are "optional" or "voluntary"— in other words, not "national" at all.

Recent polling suggests he's right. Two surveys conducted for the education campaign Strong American Schools, which I advised in 2006, found that a majority of Americans think there should be uniform national standards. Most proponents suggest we start by establishing standards and tests in grades 3–12 in the core subjects—reading, math, and science—and leave more-controversial subjects, such as history, until we have gotten our feet wet.

According to U.S. Department of Education statistics, the federal government accounts for 9 percent, or $42 billion, of our K–12 spending. If we're serious about improving our schools, and especially about raising up the lowest, Uncle Sam's contribution must rise to 25 or 30 percent of the total (a shift President Nixon considered). Goodwin Liu, a University of California at Berkeley law professor who has studied school financing, suggests that a higher federal contribution could be used in part to bring all states up to a certain minimum per-pupil funding. It could also, in my view, fund conditional grants to boost school performance. For example, federal aid could be offered to raise teachers' salaries in poor schools, provided that states or districts take measures such as linking pay to performance and deferring or eliminating tenure. Big grants might be given to states that adopt new national standards, making those standards "voluntary" but hard to refuse. The government also needs to invest much more heavily in research. It now spends $28 billion annually on research at the National Institutes of Health, but only $260 million—not even 1 percent of that amount—on R&D for education.

What of school boards? In an ideal world, we would scrap them—especially in big cities, where most poor children live. That's the impulse behind a growing drive for mayoral control of schools. New York and Boston have used mayoral authority to sustain what are among the most far-reaching reform agendas in the country, including more-rigorous curricula and a focus on better teaching and school leadership. Of course, the chances of eliminating school boards anytime soon are nil. But we can at least recast and limit their role.

In all of these efforts, we must understand one paradox: only by transcending local control can we create genuine autonomy for our schools. "If you visit schools in many other parts of the world," Marc Tucker says, "you're struck almost immediately . . . by a sense of autonomy on the part of the school staff and principal that you don't find in the United States." Research in 46 countries by Ludger Woessmann of the University of Munich has shown that setting clear external standards while granting real discretion to schools in how to meet them is the most effective way to run a system. We need to give schools one set of national expectations, free educators and parents to collaborate locally in whatever ways work, and get everything else out of the way.

Nationalizing our schools even a little goes against every cultural tradition we have, save the one that matters most: our capacity to renew ourselves to meet new challenges. Once upon a time a national role in retirement funding was anathema; then suddenly, after the Depression, we had Social Security. Once, a federal role in health care would have been rejected as socialism; now, federal money accounts for half of what we spend on health care. We started down this road on schooling a long time ago. Time now to finish the journey.

Critical Thinking

1. Who was Horace Mann and what impressed him about the Prussian system of schools in the mid-19th century?

2. What are the key elements of the "radical localism" that plays an important role in the governance of American public schools?

3. What are the arguments in favor of "nationalizing" our system of public education?

4. What are the historical origins of the U.S. system of "radical localism" in governing public education?

5. How has local control contributed to lack of uniform evaluation of students, stunted research and development, teacher union dominance, and financial inequity?

6. What change in public school governance structures has occurred in Boston and New York?

7. How might minimizing or eliminating local control of schools as currently exists lead to more genuine autonomy for individual schools?

From *The Atlantic*, January/February 2008. Copyright © 2008 by The Atlantic Media Co. www.theatlantic.com Reprinted by permission of Tribune Media Services.

The Private Life of E-Mail

The digital age has complicated the definition of what's a public document.

PAM GREENBERG

What's public some of the time, private some of the time, and potentially confusing almost all of the time?

If you're a state legislator, it's probably your e-mail.

Consider this scenario. You're at your desk on the House floor, thumbing through e-mail messages on your personal BlackBerry. One message is from your wife, asking if you will be at parent teacher conferences. Another message is a Black-Berry "PIN" message from a lobbyist, explaining her position on a bill coming up for a vote. On the desk in front of you is your state-owned laptop, which displays messages from constituents in your state e-mail account. Another window on the laptop is opened to your private Yahoo e-mail account. In yet another browser window, your Facebook page is open, showing the messages you've sent to your friends, constituents and legislative colleagues.

Which of these communications is a public record? Which messages will you save, and which will you delete? The answer can depend on the state you live in, the content of the messages, court rulings and how your state's constitution is written.

Openness and transparency in government are essential democratic principles that foster accountability, promote the public trust and prevent abuses by those in power. But there are important privacy interests and fundamental constitutional doctrines that require a careful balancing act when considering public records laws. E-mail and new technologies create added complexities and challenges to the debate.

What's Private?

In six states—Colorado, Delaware, Montana, New Jersey, Rhode Island, Texas—statutes specifically address whether legislators' e-mails are considered public records. In most of these states, the laws are the result of a balancing act between the public's right to know and an individual's right to privacy.

In Delaware, the balancing act surfaced earlier this year when the General Assembly considered amending the state's Freedom of Information Act. The bill brought the legislature under the same public records and open meetings provisions that applied to other government officials and agencies. The bill

was at risk of failing because some lawmakers felt legislators' e-mails should be kept private.

"One of their biggest concerns was that we have so many e-mails from constituents talking about sensitive problems, problems with health care, and some are very descriptive," says Delaware House Majority Leader Peter C. Schwartzkopf. "We support open government and the public's right to know, but quite frankly, constituents bare their souls to us sometimes. When it comes to private conversations, there's a difference between need to know and want to know."

> **"When it comes to private conversations, there's a difference between need to know and want to know."**
>
> —Delaware House Majority Leader Peter C. Schwartzkopf

That does not mean, however, that the e-mails are protected in criminal proceedings or investigations of wrongdoing, he says.

In a blog posting about the Legislature's public records law, former Utah Senator David L. Thomas described another reason why some legislators want to keep their e-mail correspondence private. "Citizens have a right of privacy in personal and confidential correspondence, without which their constitutional right to petition their government would be negatively affected," he says. "No right to privacy means no whistle-blowers. Citizens want to feel secure in contacting their elected representatives without the fear that someone is spying on them."

But open government groups don't see it that way.

"It's not very often I talk to citizens who want their e-mail private," says Lucy Dalglish, executive director of the Reporters Committee for Freedom of the Press. "Citizens generally want help, and unless their message falls into the category of sensitive medical or financial information, it should be public. If the message is that sensitive, you should be able to make some of the exemptions in your regular state public records law apply to that communication."

"If the message is that sensitive, you should be able to make some of the exemptions in your regular state public records law apply to that communication."

—Lucy Dalglish, executive director of the Reporters Committee for Freedom of the Press

Constitutional Question

Legislators are often criticized for exempting themselves from public records laws that apply to other public officials. In some states, however, the exemptions are the result of long-standing state constitutional provisions similar to the U.S. Constitution's Speech or Debate Clause. Speech and debate provisions grant legislators a "legislative privilege" in connection with legislative work, freeing them to deliberate candidly without intimidation from the judicial or executive branch.

Steven Huefner, a law professor at the Michael E. Moritz College of Law at Ohio State University, says without these protections, the legislative process could be harmed, "diminishing legislators' willingness to think creatively, solicit diverse opinions and advice, or explore what in hindsight turn out to be blind alleys."

This legislative privilege has been cited in a variety of court rulings, attorney general opinions and other disputes that have resulted in conflicting decisions about the privacy of legislative records and communications.

Other kinds of state constitutional provisions also come into play.

Are IMs a Meeting?

Courts have consistently found e-mails are more like a memo than a conversation. But what about instant messages, text messages and chat rooms?

In Virginia, the state Supreme Court ruled e-mails among three or more members of a public body are not subject to open meeting requirements because they do not constitute "immediate comment and response." The court noted, however, that "some electronic communication may constitute a 'meeting,' and some may not."

It specifically noted that in Internet chat rooms or instant messaging, the communication is virtually simultaneous and could be considered a public meeting.

The Missouri General Assembly confirmed this view in legislation passed in 2006. Meetings conducted through conference call, videoconference, Internet chat or Internet message board can be public meetings if any public business is discussed or decided, or if public policy is formulated. The law also requires a notice of these types of meetings to be posted in advance on a public website.

Managing "Smoking" E-Mail

Advances in technology and the growth of electronic communications have elevated the importance of electronic evidence. In fact, information stored in computers and on electronic devices frequently is the "smoking gun" in litigation.

In 2006, the Federal Rules of Civil Procedures were amended to require federal courts to treat electronic documents the same as paper documents in litigation discovery requests. Almost half the states have adopted specific rules to manage electronic discovery, often referred to as e-discovery.

"Most states require that, when there is 'reasonable anticipation of litigation,' records—paper and electronic—must be preserved in case they must eventually be disclosed," says Robert Joyce, a professor of public law and government at the University of North Carolina.

The changes in discovery requirements have created significant challenges for government.

More than 95 percent of a typical state agency's documents are in electronic form, according to Gary Robinson, the former chief information officer in Washington state who chaired an e-discovery working group for the National Association of State Chief Information Officers.

E-discovery requests can include extremely volatile information such as e-mail, voice mail, instant messages, wikis and blogs, and other communications delivered through or stored via the Internet. Because of the difficulty of identifying where information is located and how it can be retrieved, e-discovery obligations can be very expensive. If a party in litigation is unable to locate and retrieve discoverable information, he may be penalized for his failure, and that could hurt his chances of winning the lawsuit.

E-discovery is proving to be a strong motivator for states to strengthen records management and digital preservation efforts.

—Jo Anne Bourquard, NCSL

In Delaware, for example, legislators heard conflicting legal opinions about whether their proposed legislation was constitutional.

"The state's constitution says one General Assembly cannot bind the hands of the next," says Schwartzkopf, "so there was discussion about putting the FOIA provisions in legislative rules instead of statute. But the bottom line is that we expect other political divisions to operate under FOIA, so there's no reason we shouldn't hold ourselves to that standard."

Content Is Key

In some states, including Alaska and Florida, the content of a message—regardless of format or physical characteristics—determines if it's a public record.

"The mere fact that an e-mail message is received on a government computer issued to a public official for the conduct of the public's business does not of itself make the e-mail message a public record," says Robert Joyce, a professor of public law and government at the University of North Carolina. "The invitation to go bowling does not become a public record just because it was received on a government computer."

> **"The invitation to go bowling does not become a public record just because it was received on a government computer."**
>
> —Robert Joyce, University of North Carolina

And just because an e-mail message is received on a personal home computer or BlackBerry does not, in itself, mean the e-mail is not a public record.

In Alaska, former Governor Sarah Palin regularly used her private Yahoo e-mail account instead of the state e-mail system to communicate with aides and to conduct state business. An Alaska Superior Court judge in August ruled just because the records related in some way to state business didn't mean they were necessarily public record.

A 2003 Florida Supreme Court decision also illustrates the content versus format question. A Florida newspaper had requested all the e-mails of two city employees, arguing that it was entitled to them since they were made on publicly owned computers. The employees sorted the e-mails, and supplied only those that related to official business. Deciding in favor of the employees, the court held that the determining factor of whether a document is a public record lies in the nature of the record, not its physical location. Personal e-mails, the court said, do not fall within the scope of the transaction of official business and therefore are not public records.

Technology Outstrips the Law

BlackBerries, iPhones and other devices are becoming essential tools for many state lawmakers, but their text messaging capabilities in particular are raising new questions.

"They might make it easier to communicate with constituents and other legislators, but there's really no functional difference in writing a message and a letter," says Dalglish. "Many public officials think that using a BlackBerry is like a telephone conversation, but it's not a phone call, it's a memo. If you don't want something to be part of the permanent record, pick up the phone. Courts have consistently found that e-mails are more like a memo than a conversation."

Handheld devices also come with new features that can create more questions. In Florida, staff and commissioners of the Public Service Commission used PIN numbers to exchange messages BlackBerry-to-BlackBerry with Florida Power & Light lobbyists. PIN messages usually do not pass through an e-mail server and are easily deleted, raising suspicion that the PINs were being used to circumvent public records laws. The local controversy also prompted some media outlets to question similar types of exchanges between lawmakers and lobbyists during legislative hearings.

New Sites, New Concerns

Social networking sites also are raising questions for public officials who use them. The city of Coral Springs, Fla., sought an attorney general opinion about whether a city Facebook page, and any communications and other information about the city's Facebook "friends" (including the friends' respective Facebook pages), would be subject to the state's public records laws. The attorney general said a determination would depend on whether the information was made or received as part of official business by or on behalf of a public agency. Commissioners' communications on the city's Facebook page could also be subject to Florida's Sunshine Law and its retention schedules. Some social media users might not be aware that even on sites that allow them to keep postings private, the information could be made available to anyone if required by public records laws, by the site's terms of use contract, or even by other "friends" or users.

Discussions about the open records implications of public officials' use of social media are also coming up in other states. A recent online article by Megan Crowley of the Utah Center for Public Policy and Administration suggests that public officials should analyze the content of their social media postings to determine if they fall under the state's Government Records Management Act. Questions Crowley suggests considering include: "Does the information exist in another or original format? Is the information meaningful in conducting government business and for how long? Is the social media page being presented by a person in an official government role, or is it presented as their own personal page?"

In Washington, the State Archives website offers similar guidance to state and local government about the retention of posts on blogs, wikis and social networking sites such as Facebook and Twitter.

Save or Delete?

The proprietary nature of social media sites and the sheer volume of e-mail and text messaging may tend to discourage elected officials from saving messages that might otherwise be retained as part of the public record.

"The nature of e-mail works in some ways to make retention harder and in other ways to make it," says the University of North Carolina's Joyce.

"Retention is harder, on the one hand, because deleting is so easy and so tempting. It's easier, on the other hand, because long-term storage of data is technically quite possible."

Dalglish of the reporters group says the drive for open records has been underway for a long time and is a factor in this debate.

Few States Deal Directly with E-Mail

Six states specifically address in statute whether legislators' e-mail communications are public record.

- Colorado law classifies e-mail messages sent or received by legislators as public records, but exempts communications that a constituent "would have reason to expect to remain confidential."
- New Jersey law treats e-mail as a public record, but excludes information legislators receive from a constituent or concerning a constituent.
- In Rhode Island, e-mail messages between legislators and constituents or other elected officials are exempt from the public records law.
- Delaware excludes from public disclosure any e-mails received or sent by members of the Delaware General Assembly.
- Texas law prohibits public disclosure of electronic communications between citizens and members of the Legislature and the lieutenant governor unless the citizen authorizes disclosure.
- In Montana, all electronic messages used for transaction of official business are deemed public records, including constituent communications, "unless constitutionally protected by individual privacy interests."

"We started passing public records laws decades ago. For citizens to be actively engaged in their communities, they need information," she says. "They need to know how decisions are being made and how their tax dollars are being spent, and they should have a presumptive access to that information. New technologies are a blessing and a curse."

Critical Thinking

1. What values are fostered by the openness and transparency supported by public records laws?
2. What are key arguments for allowing legislators' e-mail to be exempt from public records laws?
3. What is "legislative privilege" and how is it justified?
4. According to the Virginia Supreme Court, what distinction between e-mails and instant messaging among members of a public body might justify a difference in applicability of open meeting requirements?
5. How many states specifically address whether legislators' e-mail communications are public records? And what are the rules in the different states?

PAM GREENBERG follows public records and technology issues for NCSL.

From *State Legislatures*, January 2010, pp. 20–23. Copyright © 2010 by National Conference of State Legislatures. Reprinted by permission.

When I Run Out of Fights to Have, I'll Stop Fighting

Chris Christie, governor of New Jersey, became the most celebrated Republican in America by tagging public-sector workers like cops and firefighters—and especially teachers—as 21st-century welfare queens.

MATT BAI

Like a stand-up comedian working out-of-the-way clubs, Chris Christie travels the townships and boroughs of New Jersey, places like Hackettstown and Raritan and Scotch Plains, sharpening his riffs about the state's public employees, whom he largely blames for plunging New Jersey into a fiscal death spiral. In one well-worn routine, for instance, the governor reminds his audiences that, until he passed a recent law that changed the system, most teachers in the state didn't pay a dime for their health care coverage, the cost of which was borne by taxpayers.

And so, Christie goes on, forced to cut more than $1 billion in local aid in order to balance the budget, he asked the teachers not only to accept a pay freeze for a year but also to begin contributing 1.5 percent of their salaries toward health care. The dominant teachers' union in the state responded by spending millions of dollars in television and radio ads to attack him.

"The argument you heard most vociferously from the teachers' union," Christie says, "was that this was the greatest assault on public education in the history of New Jersey." Here the fleshy governor lumbers a few steps toward the audience and lowers his voice for effect. "Now, do you really think that your child is now stressed out and unable to learn because they know that their poor teacher has to pay $1^{1/2}$ percent of their salary for their health care benefits? Have any of your children come home—*any* of them—and said, 'Mom.'" Pause. "'Dad.'" Another pause. "'Please. Stop the madness.'"

By this point the audience is starting to titter, but Christie remains stead-fastly somber in his role as the beseeching student. "'Just pay for my teacher's health benefits,'" he pleads, "'and I'll get A's, I swear. But I just cannot take the stress that's being presented by a $1^{1/2}$ percent contribution to health benefits.'" As the crowd breaks into appreciative guffaws, Christie waits a theatrical moment, then slams his point home. "Now, you're all laughing, right?" he says. "But this is the crap I have to hear."

Acid monologues like this have made Christie, only a little more than a year into his governorship, one of the most intriguing political figures in America. Hundreds of thousands of YouTube viewers linger on scenes from Christie's town-hall meetings, like the one in which he takes apart a teacher for her histrionics. ("If what you want to do is put on a show and giggle every time I talk, then I have no interest in answering your question.") Newly elected governors—not just Republicans, Christie says, but also Democrats—call to seek his counsel on how to confront their own staggering budget deficits and intractable unions. At a recent gathering of Republican governors, Christie attracted a throng of supporters and journalists as he strode through the halls of the Hilton San Diego Bayfront Hotel like Bono at Davos.

While Christie has flatly ruled out a presidential run in 2012, there is enough conjecture about the possibility that I felt moved to ask him a few weeks ago if he found it exhausting to have to constantly answer the same question. "Listen, if you're going to say you're exhausted by that, you're really taking yourself too seriously," Christie told me, then broke into his imitation of a politician who is taking himself too seriously. "'Oh, Matt, please, stop asking me about whether I should be president of the United States! The leader of the free world! Please stop! I'm exhausted by the question!' I mean, come on. If I get to that point, just slap me around, because that's really presumptuous. What it is to me is astonishing, not exhausting."

There is, in fact, something astonishing about the ascent of Chris Christie, who is about as slick as sandpaper and who now admits that even he didn't think he would beat Jon Corzine, the Democrat he unseated in 2009. Some critics have posited that Christie's success in office represents merely the triumph of self-certainty over complexity, the yearning among voters for leaders who talk bluntly and with conviction. Yet it's hard to see Christie getting so much traction if he were out there castigating, say, immigrants or Wall Street bankers. What makes Christie compelling to so many people isn't simply plain talk or swagger, but also the fact that he has found the ideal adversary for this moment of economic vertigo. Ronald Reagan had his "welfare queens," Rudy Giuliani had his criminals and "squeegee men," and now Chris Christie has his sprawling and powerful public-sector unions—teachers, cops and firefighters who Christie says are driving up local taxes beyond what the citizenry can afford, while also demanding the kind of lifetime security that most private-sector workers have already lost.

It may just be that Christie has stumbled onto the public-policy issue of our time, which is how to bring the exploding costs of the public workforce in line with reality. (According to a report issued last year by the Pew Center on the States, as of 2008 there was a $1 trillion gap, conservatively speaking, between what the states have promised in pensions and benefits for their retirees and what they have on hand to pay for them.) Then again, he may simply be the latest in a long line of politicians to give an uneasy public the scapegoat it demands. Depending on your vantage point, Chris Christie is a truth-teller or a demagogue, or maybe even a little of both.

To say that New Jersey has a budget problem wouldn't really be accurate. The state has at least three major budget problems related to the costs of the public workforce, all of which contribute to a shortfall that the state's legislative accounting office projects to be almost $11 billion this year—an amount that's more than a third of the state's total budget. And in order to understand what's happening in statehouses all over the country, and what Christie is trying to do about it in New Jersey, it helps to have some sense of how these problems tie together.

1. First, there's the local aid. New Jersey sends 40 percent of its annual budget to an overlapping tangle of 566 municipalities and 600-plus school districts; in order to help them slow the mutantlike growth of local property taxes, which are among the highest in the country. Each of these little hamlets and districts negotiates its own labor contract with the police and firefighters, sanitation workers and, most consequentially, teachers, which means the contracts established by the most affluent communities end up setting a statewide standard—a process that drives up everyone else's costs to a level that the local governments simply can't sustain by themselves.

2. Second, in the long term, New Jersey doesn't have nearly enough money on hand to cover its pension obligations to teachers and other state workers. At no time in the last 17 years has New Jersey fully met its annual obligation to the pension fund, and in many of those years, the state paid nothing at all. (That didn't stop one governor, Donald DiFrancesco, a Republican, from increasing payouts by 9 percent and lowering the retirement age before he left office, which would be kind of like Bernie Madoff writing you a $1 million check before heading off to jail.) Even had the state been contributing faithfully to the fund as it was supposed to, however, there would still be trouble ahead. That's because New Jerseyans, who are glass-half-full kind of people, have assumed an improbably healthy return of 8.25 percent annually on the state pension fund. The actual return over the last 10 years averaged only 2.6 percent.

3. Finally, the state will pay close to $3 billion this year in health care premiums for public employees (including retired teachers), and that number is rising fast. New Jersey has set aside exactly zero dollars to cover it. All told, in pensions and health care benefits, New Jersey's "unfunded liability"—that is, the amount the actuaries say it would need to find in order to meet its obligations for the next 30 years—has now passed the $100 billion mark.

There was little in Christie's uninspiring campaign to make anyone think he would address these issues with more tenacity than the governors who preceded him. A U.S. attorney whose only overtly political experience entailed serving on the Morris County Board of Chosen Freeholders (seriously, they still call it that), Christie had only a fraction of Corzine's public exposure or personal fortune. About the only thing he had going for him was that Corzine was pervasively unpopular. And so rather than come up with a lot of actual ideas, which Corzine would then be free to oversimplify and distort in a barrage of television ads, Christie simply offered up a bunch of conservative platitudes and tried to make the campaign a referendum on the Democratic governor. (When we talked during the campaign, Christie could articulate little by way of an agenda, except to say that he would "get in there and make it work.") Even a lot of Republicans thought Christie was underwhelming as a campaigner.

In the end, Christie won by about four points on Election Night in 2009, with little notion of what he was going to do next. When I asked him if there was any one moment of clarity that put him on the path from cautious candidate to union-bashing conservative hero, Christie pointed to a meeting about a month into the transition, when his aides came to him brandishing an analysis of the state's cash flow produced by Goldman Sachs. They advised the governor-elect that, without some serious action, the state could fail to meet payroll by the end of March. After scrutinizing the budget, Christie told me, his team came to the conclusion that the only way to get control of local taxes and state spending was to go after the pension and health care benefits that the public-sector unions held sacrosanct. From that point on, it seems, Christie has conducted his governorhip as if he were still a grandstanding prosecutor, taking powerful unions on perp walks with evident enthusiasm.

The centerpiece of Christie's frenzied agenda, which passed the Democratic-controlled Legislature last July, is a strict cap on local property taxes, which will be allowed to rise no more than 2 percent every year. When combined with a reduction in state aid, what this means, practically speaking, is that New Jersey's townships and cities will have to hold the line when negotiating municipal labor contracts if they want to remain solvent, because they can't rely on either their residents or the state for more money.

To help them do that, Christie has put forward 33 measures that are part of what he calls his "toolkit" for reform. These include, for instance, a proposal that would allow localities to opt out of the civil-service system altogether, giving them more control over hiring and firing local officials, and another that would limit the cash payouts that retiring workers can take for their unused sick days. On the pension front, if Christie has his way with the Legislature, most union members would contribute more to their plans than they have up to now, and all of them would retire later and receive lower benefit payments.

The crux of Christie's argument is that public-sector contracts have to reflect what has happened in the private sector, where guaranteed pensions and free health care are becoming relics. It's not surprising that this stand has ingratiated Christie to conservatives in Washington; advocacy groups and activists on the right have carried out a long campaign to discredit the ever-shrinking labor movement in the private sector, and what Christie has done, essentially, is to blast his way into the final frontier, taking on the public-sector unions that have come to wield enormous political power. More surprising is how the governor's proposals are finding sympathy from less-partisan budget experts, if only because they don't see obvious alternatives. "I've tried to look at this objectively, and I just don't know of any other option," says Richard Keevey, who served as budget director for a Democratic governor, Jim Florio, and a Republican governor, Tom Kean. "You couldn't tax your way out of this."

Union leaders, on the other hand, are howling. The heads of the police and firefighters' unions say that Christie's cuts to local aid have already cost the state several hundred firemen and police officers, and they warn that his 2 percent cap on property taxes will have dire effects on public safety, as more towns and cities try to shave their payrolls to conform with the cap. "I don't think they're going to get it until the body bags pile up," Anthony Wieners, president of the police union, warns darkly.

Leaders of the teachers' union, meanwhile, are apoplectic about Christie's proposed changes to their pension plan, which they say will penalize educators for the irresponsibility of politicians. After all, they point out, it wasn't the unions who chose not to fund the pension year in and year out, and yet it's their members who will have to recalibrate their retirements if the benefits are cut.

When I made this same point to Christie, he simply shook his head. What's done is done, he told me, and it's time for someone to tell these workers the truth, which is that the state is simply never goint to have the money to make good on its commitments. "Listen, if they want to travel in the Michael J. Fox time machine and change time, I guess we could try that," he said. "We could get the DeLorean out and try to go back there. But I think realistically that that was just a movie and make-believe. So we've got to live with what we've got."

> "Listen, if they want to travel in the Michael J. Fox time machine and change time, I guess we could try that," Christie says of the teachers' unions. 'We could get the DeLorean out and try to go back there.

Chris Christie is fat. You can use nicer words if you want—rotund, portly, big-boned—but it is what it is, and the governor will be the first to tell you so. And because he's fat, a lot of people, consciously or not, tend to assume certain things about Christie—that he's undisciplined and impulsive, graceless and bullying. (Corzine's most brutal campaign ad accused Christie of 'throwing his weight around.") At times, Christie seems to exploit this persona. He likes to present himself as the proverbial bull in the china shop, the ungainly, somewhat boorish guy who lacks the artifice to keep from saying whatever obvious truth pops into his head. "I don't think you elected me because of my charm and good looks," Christie likes to say, just to show he's in on the joke.

And yet, to portray Christie in this cartoonish way, as so many critics do is to vastly underestimate his skill as a politician. The most sophisticated communicators of the modern era hammer at a consistent argument about their moment and the response it demands, and they choose carefully constructed metaphors to make the choices ahead seem obvious—think of Ronald Reagan's morning in America, or Bill Clinton's bridge to the 21st century. And Christie's communications strategy is about as sophisticated as any you will find in American politics right now.

Take Christie's choice of a somewhat mundane image, the "toolkit," as a unifying frame for his proposals. As a metaphor, the toolkit works on two levels, depending on the audience. You can visualize it either in the sense of screwdrivers and hammers or, if you work in an office all day, you might envision it more as a software suite. Either way, the toolkit symbolizes flexibility and local control. It's a way of saying that Christie isn't putting unwieldy restrictions on towns and cities, as the cops and firefighters charge—he's just empowering those towns and cities with a variety of implements and gadgets with which to attack their budget problems themselves.

In sustaining his assault on the public-employee unions, Christie knows he has to make his subject comprehensible. One reason that leaders in a state like New Jersey haven't been able to get a handle on pension and benefit costs, despite years of dire warnings from good-government advocates, is that the subject is agonizingly dull and all but impossible to explain. There are myriad plans for all the different public-employee unions, various contribution formulas for each one and actuarial projections that require an advanced degree to unravel.

Christie, it turns out, has a preternatural gift for making the complex seem deceptively simple. Last month I saw him hold forth at a town-hall meeting in Chesilhurst, a South Jersey borough of about 1,600. Chesilhurst is about half African-American, and I sensed more curiosity than enthusiasm among the racially mixed crowd as it flowed into the little community-center gymnasium. An unusually large number of folding chairs were empty. About 20 minutes after the program was supposed to start, there came over the loud-speakers the kind of melodramatic instrumental that might introduce a local newscast, or maybe an Atlantic City magic show, and in came Christie, taking his position in the center of the crowd. The theme of the week was pension-and-benefits reform, and in his introductory remarks, Christie explained the inefficiency in the state's health care costs not by wielding a stack of damning statistics, as some politicians might, but by relating a story.

When he was a federal prosecutor, Christie told the audience, he got to choose from about 100 health-insurance plans, ranging from cheap to quite expensive. But as soon as he became governor, the "benefits lady" told him he had only three state plans from which to choose, Goldilocks-style; one was great, one was modestly generous and one was rather miserly. And any of the three would cost him exactly 1.5 percent of his salary.

"'You're telling me,'" Christie said he told the woman, feigning befuddlement, "'that no matter which one I pick, the good one or the O.K. one or the bad one, I'm going to pay $1^{1/2}$ percent of my salary?' And she said, 'Yes.'

"And I said, 'Then everyone picks the really good one, right?' And she said, 'Ninety-six percent of state employees pick the really good one.'

"Which led me to have two reactions," Christie told the crowd. "First, bring those other 4 percent to me! Because when I have to start laying people off, they're the first ones!" His audience burst into near hysterics. "And the second reaction was, of course I would choose the best plan," Christie said, "and so would you.

"Now listen, I don't think this is groundbreaking stuff," Christie added. 'I don't think this means that instead of being governor, you know, "I should be at NASA, working on the space shuttle. I'm no genius. Just seems to me that if you give people an option to get something for nothing, they'll take it." Scanning the nodding faces around me, it seemed there wasn't a person in the gymnasium, at that point, who wouldn't have voted to make state workers and teachers pay more for the better plan.

Another thing Christie understands about political messaging, especially when your adversaries are out there portraying you as callous, is that it has to be grounded in the personal. "If you're asking people to do some really difficult things, which I am asking them to do," Christie told me, "then I think they feel more comfortable doing those things if they know you."

And so the 48-year-old Christie makes a point of sharing intimate details of his life and times—that he uses an asthma inhaler, that he has struggled with dieting and exercise since his days as a high-school catcher came to an end, that his mother told him on her deathbed that he should go back to work because nothing between them had been left unsaid. That last one, which elicited audible gasps of sympathy from the audience in Chesilhurst, is his way of saying that he wants to leave nothing unsaid between him and the voters, either, even if they both occasionally get hurt.

"My mother said to me all the time, 'Christopher, you're going to have choices in your life between being loved and being respected,'" Christie told his rapt audience, strains of emotion creeping into his voice. "'And you should choose respected. Because if you're respected, love can come.' She said, 'But seeking love without also being respected—well that love doesn't last.'" It was as if some weird brain-switching

experiment had taken place, and somewhere, at that very moment, Oprah was giving a talk about state budgets and tax policy.

There's one more piece of political narrative that Christie seems to grasp, which is that every story has both a protagonist and an antagonist, someone who stands for change and someone who plays the foil. Christie never had to look far to cast his ideal antagonists. They sit just across the street and one block down from the State House, in the building occupied by New Jersey's major teachers' union.

With 200,000 members and more than $100 million in dues, the New Jersey Education Association is easily the most powerful union in New Jersey and one of the more powerful local unions in the country. In Trenton, the union's organizing might—and its willingness to use that might to intimidate candidates and lawmakers—has sunk a small shipyard of promising careers. So it's not hard to see why the twilight struggle between Chris Christie and "the bully of State Street," as he likes to refer to the teachers' union, has transfixed New Jersey's political observers for the last year. It's as mesmerizing as an episode of "The Real Housewives of New Jersey," only harder to watch, mostly because Christie can be so unrelentingly brutal.

"We have similar personalities," Stephen Sweeney, the Democratic president of the state Senate, told me recently, when ruminating on Christie's style. "The difference between he and I is, I have an off switch and he doesn't. You know, if I knock you down, I'll pick you up, brush the dirt off your back, try to build a relationship and go forward. He knocks you down, like with the teachers, and he'll stomp on you, kick on you until he can kill you."

The war between Christie and the union has two fronts, so closely interrelated that it's hard to separate them.

1. First there's the fight over budgeting issues like pensions and benefits.
2. And then there's the "year of education reform," as Christie has proclaimed 2011, in which he intends to push his case for merit pay, charter schools and the abolition of teacher tenure—all of which are, of course, anathema to the union.

At times in this epic clash, it can be hard to know where personal animus leaves off and political gamesmanship kicks in. All that's clear is that Christie seems to be winning every turn. Last April, for instance, Christie claimed to be infuriated by a joke memo circulated by the president of the Bergen County chapter of the union. "Dear Lord," it read in part, "this year you have taken away my favorite actor, Patrick Swayze, my favorite actress, Farrah Fawcett, my favorite singer, Michael Jackson, and my favorite salesman, Billy Mays. I just wanted to let you know that Chris Christie is my favorite governor."

In a 15-minute meeting, the union's president, Barbara Keshishian, apologized to Christie for the memo, but she refused to fire the Bergen County president, which further infuriated the governor. If his chief of staff had sent out such an e-mail, Christie told her, he would have been fired immediately. "That conversation embodies the elitism and the double standard that the teachers' union thinks applies to them," Christie told me last month, recounting the confrontation. We were sitting in the restaurant of the Hay-Adams Hotel in Washington, where state troopers and aides with cellphones buzzed around the empty dining room. Christie was in town to headline a dinner for the New Jersey Chamber of Commerce. "And you know what? I can't entirely blame them for it, because politicians have treated them differently than everybody else, because they've been scared of them. And so part of the blame goes on the political culture of New Jersey that has helped to enable this elitist, double-standard attitude."

The death-wish incident instantly became lore in Trenton and proved politically advantageous to the governor. It gave him a pretense to break off all communication with the union; he has refused to meet personally with Keshishian or her deputies since. And he has repeatedly used the ill-advised memo to portray himself as the courageous victim of unhinged union activists. At least once a week, it seems, he reminds some audience that the union once "wished for my death," as if he were Robert Kennedy staring down the Teamsters.

Perhaps the most consequential episode between Christie and the union, at least as far as public perception was concerned, had to do with the pay freeze. Almost as soon as the scope of the budget problem became clear, the governor called on teachers, who received scheduled raises during the recession, to accept a one-year freeze. He reminded the teachers that a lot of private-sector workers felt lucky if they could keep their current salaries, and he said a voluntary freeze would enable the union to avoid widespread teacher layoffs in cash-poor school districts. Most local chapters of the union ignored him. Ultimately some 10,000 union members—teachers and support staff—saw their jobs eliminated. Christie hasn't stopped talking about it since.

The union maintains that Christie's plea was mere gimmickry, because the layoffs would have happened even if its local chapters acceded to the demand for a freeze. But even if this is true, it would seem to reflect a staggering lack of political calculation. Had the teachers agreed to take the short-term hit by acquiescing to a temporary freeze, it would have been worlds harder for Christie to then run around the state demanding longer-term concessions on pensions and benefits. And when the layoffs did materialize, the governor would most likely have shouldered most of the blame. Instead, the whole affair seemed to prove Christie's point about the union's self-involvement, and it enabled him to blame the teachers themselves for the layoffs.

During our conversation at the Hay-Adams, I suggested to Christie that the teachers had given him a valuable political gift by refusing to compromise. "I don't look at it as a gift to me," he replied. "I look at it as a huge mistake by them, and also a window into who they are.

"Let's assume that they're smart, because I think they are," he went on. "So then, why don't you do it? Because they believe they are entitled to it. They believe they are special and different and that they shouldn't have to share the sacrifice. And that's, I think, what's ultimately driving public opinion against them."

One afternoon last month, at the modern, airy headquarters of the N.J.E.A., I sat with Barbara Keshishian, the union's president, and Vincent Giordano, its executive director, and listened as they tried to puzzle out why it was that Christie seemed so determined to humiliate them.

"Frankly, I for one don't say we're always 100 percent right on every single issue, and certainly neither is the administration across the street," said Giordano, a bald and goateed organizer who has been at the union for 40 years. "The difference is the tone and the mean-spiritedness of the way he talks about us. He has made us basically the whipping boy for anything that goes wrong in New Jersey and the country and in Bangladesh if there's an earthquake. It seems that we're just the cause of all the problems in our society today.

"I don't know what he's got buried down there inside of him that causes him to be this totally driven," Giordano said. "I don't think he's really supportive of a public-education system. If he was, he might send his kids to public school, which he doesn't." (Christie and his wife, Mary Pat, a bond trader, have four children, ages 7 to 17, and all attend Catholic schools.) "I think he's not very enamored with public services in general. Public employees, public education, public pension systems—somehow he's allergic to the word 'public.' Somebody ought to get him some kind of medication that gets him off of that allergy he has to anything that's public."

The two union leaders made several points in defense of their stances against pension reform and the pay freeze. They pointed out that despite all Christie's talk of shared sacrifice, he refused to renew a tax on millionaires in New Jersey that would have raised about $800 million this year—not enough to solve the state's fiscal problems, certainly but enough to restore most of the school aid that was slashed from the budget. They noted that they already made concessions on teachers' pensions in 2007 and 2008, when they agreed to increase contributions by 10 percent and to raise the retirement age from 60 to 62. They mentioned that the average salary of a New Jersey teacher is about $67,000, and the average pension is between $35,000 and $40,000. "Try living on that in the state of New Jersey," Giordano said. "I don't see why we've suddenly been identified as fat cats."

In the union's view, Christie is simply trying to exploit the downward spiral of the American labor movement. First, greedy companies, claiming pressures from the new global market, began rolling back the pensions and benefits that private-sector unions negotiated over a period of decades. And now, instead of trying to find a way to restore those hard-earned benefits for all workers, politicians like Christie are using corporate America's bad behavior as an excuse to take benefits away from the last set of union members who managed to cling to them—those in the public sector. Christie is pitting one set of middle-class workers against the other, perhaps in the hope that private-sector unions will ultimately turn on their brethren in the public workforce, or that the public unions will turn on one another. And the end result will be that everyone loses.

All of this seems to add up to a reasonable counterargument to Christie's main indictments against the teachers' union, and so I asked Keshishian and Giordano why they thought they were having such a problem making their case to the public. After all, according to a Quinnipiac University poll conducted this month, most voters in New Jersey still admire teachers themselves, but only 27 percent have a favorable view of the union, while 44 percent say their view is unfavorable. By contrast, Christie's job approval has been consistently hovering above the 50 percent mark.

"He is the governor!" Keshishian said, her voice rising. "People listen to him! You know, he could be in a crowd of people, and they're going to interview the governor! And people, I guess, believe that what the governor says is the truth." Keshishian taught high-school math for 29 years, but her grasp on civics sounded a bit shaky. It doesn't seem especially likely that Christie is breaking through because he is a politician and therefore people take to heart his every word.

What the union's leadership seems not to have considered is that public sentiment around budgets and public employees has shifted in a fundamental way. For decades, as Keshishian and Giordano were rising up through the union, it probably made sense to adopt a strategy of "no surrender," to dig in and outlast the occasional politician who might dare to threaten the union's hard-earned gains. But over the last 10 years or so, most American workers have come to expect less by way of benefits and security from their employers. And with political consensus building toward some kind of public-school reform, teachers' unions in particular have lost credibility with the public. Forty-six percent of voters in a poll conducted by Stanford and the Associated Press last September said teachers' unions deserved either "a great deal" or "a lot" of blame for the problems of public schools.

And so, when the union draws a hard line against changes to its pay and benefit structure, you can see why it might strike some sizable segment of voters as being a little anachronistic, like mimeographing homework assignments or sharpening a pencil by hand. In a Pew Research Center poll this month, 47 percent of respondents said their states should cut pension plans for government employees, which made it the most popular option on the table.

Some unions are more attuned than others to this gradual changing of the climate. The American Federation of Teachers, for example, which is by far the smaller of the two major teachers' unions nationally, has consciously tried to position itself as a more pragmatic union and has proposed a lot of its own classroom reforms in a campaign to get out in front of public opinion. In Newark, New Jersey's largest city, A.F.T. organizers have signaled that they will work with Christie on changes to the pension and health care system, in addition to negotiating on issues like merit pay. "Better to be seated at the table than to be on the menu" is how Joseph Del Grosso, the union's leader in Newark, explained the strategy to me.

But the larger and mightier N.J.E.A. has made the decision to hunker down and fight all comers. And because of that, its leaders run the risk of confirming the public's darkest suspicions about them, whether they have salient points to make or not. "They may have dug themselves a hole that will be very difficult to dig themselves out of," Del Grosso says of his competitor. "They *are* on the menu."

And so this is why Christie has gone out of his way to anoint the teachers' union as the most sinister force in the galaxy—not because he has some long-buried torment with a teacher to work through, but because the union does a very capable job of representing for him everything about the public sector that voters don't like. He knows there is a risk in using this strategy: he has to make sure his war on the union doesn't ultimately come to seem like a war on individual teachers, which is why he tries constantly to draw a distinction between the union and its members. ("I love teachers—I just can't stand your union," is one of Christie's signature lines.) For now, though, even some of labor's strongest advocates will tell you that Christie has the teachers and other public-sector unions backed up against a hard wall of political reality.

"My politics are union politics," Sweeney, the Senate president, assured me when I visited him in his State House office. He reminded me that he is not only the state's top elected Democrat, but also a union ironworker. And yet, he said, "what I think that public-sector employees have to do is look at what's going on around them, look at all the pain around them, and understand that no one hates them, but they want them to sacrifice like everyone else. It's that simple."

The political dynamic in New Jersey tells you a lot about what's driving similar conversations all over the country. Last year alone, 18 states either raised the pension-contribution levels for public employees or reduced benefits for their retirees, according to Susan Urahn, the managing director of the Pew Center for the States. Three states—South Dakota, Colorado and Minnesota—decided to eliminate cost-of-living raises for state workers who have already retired. (As a result, all three states are now ensnared in court challenges over whether they can alter benefits for current retirees—cases that could have a huge impact on state budgets, depending on how far states are ultimately allowed to go in rolling back already-promised benefits.) Illinois raised its retirement age to 67, and Vermont, Michigan and Utah introduced "hybrid" retirement plans that are a step away from the defined-benefit pension plans that were the standard for much of the 20th century.

Now a new class of governors from both parties is promising to revisit union contracts in order to put their states on firmer fiscal ground. In Wisconsin, Scott Walker, an aggressive new Republican governor, just proposed legislation that would limit the rights of public workers to collectively bargain. "You can't have one group who are the haves," Walker told me recently, meaning government workers, "and one group, the private-sector workers, who are the have-nots." Walker's move led to protests in Madison, drawing President Obama into the debate and raising the prospect of French-style labor uprisings among public workers across America.

In part, the viral movement against public-sector unions is a result of political necessity. In states all over the country, balancing the budget has become an annual exercise in Copperfield-like illusion. Over the past decade, governors have exhausted all the easy options for eradicating, or at least hiding, deficits—building casinos and adding new fees, issuing bonds and securitizing tobacco revenue. Now, facing a painfully slow recovery and the end of stimulus spending from Washington, governors from both parties are finding that there are simply no more gimmicks left to exploit. They have to deal with what has long been an unspoken reality—that state governments have made a mountain of promises they can't keep.

It's also true, though, that what used to be unspeakable, politically, simply isn't anymore. It's not as if the problem of public pensions suddenly got so much worse than it was before (the shortfalls have been building steadily for years, after all), nor is this new crop of governors somehow genetically bolder than their predecessors. If politicians of both parties are suddenly willing to go after the pensions and health care plans of teachers and cops and firefighters, it's probably not only because they're out of budgeting options, but also because suddenly they see it as politically advantageous. In other words, not only are public employees' contracts no longer untouchable for any politician who wants to stay in office, but it turns out that the opposite is true; taking the fight to the unions is a good way to bolster your credentials as a gutsy reformer with voters who have been losing faith for years in public schools and government bureaucracies.

This, more than anything else, is the lesson that Chris Christie has impressed on his contemporaries. The question now, and what a lot of these other governors are watching to see, is whether Christie can convert his anti-union riffs into a revised social contract for public servants. While he has enacted several pivotal pieces of his agenda, Christie has yet to pass more than a handful of the measures in his toolkit. This year will mark a major test of his staying power. The question a lot of political observers are asking, in New Jersey and nationally, is whether Christie's argument will begin to lose its resonance as voters inevitably grow weary of the hostility and the rhetorical smack downs. Sooner or later, most people tend to tire of the boorish guy at the party, even if he's entertaining, and even if he has a point.

Christie waves away such concerns. "When I run out of fights to have, I'll stop fighting," he told me. Until then, you will find him out on the town-hall circuit, play-acting, berating and emoting his way toward some kind of public reckoning, leaving nothing unsaid.

Critical Thinking

1. What government office does Chris Christie hold and how long has he held it?

2. With what "public issue of our time" has Christie become publicly identified?

3. What three major problems stemming from the costs of the New Jersey public workforce are facing the state?

4. What, according to Christie, are the two key elements in his "toolkit" for addressing New Jersey's fiscal problems?

5. How many states in 2010 either raised pension-contribution levels for public employees or reduced benefits for retirees?

The Badgered State

Wisconsin Governor Scott Walker Is the Left's Public Enemy No. 1

Robert Costa

Madison, Wis.

Snow is falling here. The coffee shops have closed. The college bars are shuttered. A lone police car inches along State Street, icy slush glazing its wheels. The heavyset patrolman eyes me warily: Trench coats and suit jackets are rare in these parts. We nod, and he continues on, spotlights floating through the Lake Monona fog.

Up on the knoll, a white dome gleams. In the midnight quiet, I trudge toward it, past a graybeard professor and hulking Teamsters. Near the door, a skinny girl decked out in a ruby University of Wisconsin sweatshirt smokes a cigarette. Her friend is hooked into her iPhone, texting her classmates, urging them to visit. I move inside, out of the cold. The marble hall is dark, dimly lit by sunflower-yellow lamps. There is a faint hum.

Ambling down the corridor, sidestepping grungy pillows, acoustic guitars, and empty pizza boxes, I near the center of this stately building. The humid, sweat-scented air flares the nostrils. The hum becomes a roar: Thousands are packed into all four wings of the building. They wear bright purple SEIU T-shirts, lime green AFSCME ponchos, and fraying flannel. Gently elbowing my way through the dreadlocks and past the stacked hand drums, I find myself under the rotunda, at the center of a bizarre, union-sponsored slumber party.

A couple of feet away, a high-school teacher grabs a bullhorn and, much as the shaman calls the rain, begins to lead those assembled in a sing-along of "Union Maid," a Woody Guthrie ditty. The scene is like a Grateful Dead concert without the plugged-in licks, a raucous temple for aging activists and impressionable youth. "Welcome to paradise," chuckles a capitol guard.

For much of February, the Wisconsin state capitol was occupied by labor leaders, undergraduates, and a potpourri of lefty radicals. They were loud and they were angry. On cardboard signs and sprawling banners, they railed against Gov. Scott Walker, the Badger State's rookie executive, who earlier in the month had proposed a budget-repair bill that would break the grip of public-sector unions in a state that has long been dominated by them.

Walker, a 43-year-old Republican, was skewered by liberal pundits. Protesters compared him to Adolf Hitler, Hosni Mubarak, and Darth Vader. But he ignored their cries and made a compelling, unflinching argument for fiscal prudence. For conservatives, it was an awe-inspiring sight. George Will observed that Walker's steely determination called up the ghosts of Ronald Reagan and Margaret Thatcher, who so famously tangled with union bosses three decades ago.

But Walker's fight was more than an echo of glory past: It emerged, with speed and fervor, as the definitive state-level budget battle in the Age of Obama. Since Walker rolled out his plan, a half-dozen states have seen similar union-fueled uprisings as they grapple with budget gaps and benefit-addicted government workers. Walker, an unassuming man who speaks with a nasal midwestern accent, is suddenly a nationally recognized fiscal hawk and, to many Republicans, a hero.

On Friday, February 11, days after the Green Bay Packers topped the Pittsburgh Steelers in the Super Bowl, Madison was a picture of placidity. Walker, still settling in, had few enemies. He did not need a Google alert for his name. Few national reporters were paying attention to him. Wisconsin's GOP stars—Rep. Paul Ryan, a leader in the U.S. House, and Sen. Ron Johnson, a Tea Party–inspired freshman—owned the spotlight.

One press conference changed that. Facing an immediate budget deficit of $137 million and a $3.6 billion shortfall over the next two years, Walker took to the podium behind his first-floor office at the capitol and told a handful of scribes that bold action was needed. "The path to long-term financial solvency for our state requires shared sacrifices from everyone," he said. Walker's plan asked state workers to contribute 5.8 percent of their salaries toward their pensions and to pay 12.6 percent of their health-insurance premiums. Most controversially, he aimed to limit collective bargaining for nearly all state employees by restricting future government-union haggles to wages and excluding pensions and other benefits. He unveiled this all softly, with none of the frank combativeness of Gov. Chris Christie of New Jersey, who gained headlines last year for his tussle with the public sector. Walker's aides say their boss saw the fiscal mess as spectacle enough—no need to wag a finger.

But he might as well have thrown acid at the Left. The eye-rubbing reactions poured in. Here was a greenhorn Republican governor taking on the unions in a state that in 1959 became the first to grant public workers collective-bargaining rights. A GOP nobody was going to throttle the political culture in a capitol where a statue of "Fighting" Bob La Follette, a progressive legend, stands vigil between the legislative chambers. For Democrats and their allies, it was almost unbelievable. Republican governors had come and gone, to be sure, but none had so fiercely and so quickly attempted to tear at the fabric of the state government's cozy, union-friendly culture.

Jill Bakken, a spokeswoman for the American Federation of Teachers in Wisconsin, spoke for many with her initial response. "State employees are shocked and bewildered about how 50 years of labor peace can be unraveled by a governor who has been in office for six weeks," she said. Fellow Democrats, sensing trouble, began to mobilize. Organizing outfits such as MoveOn.org stirred online buzz. By Sunday evening, hundreds were gathered outside the state capitol and the governor's mansion, demanding that Walker back down.

The crowds began to swell on Tuesday and Wednesday, when Madison-area teachers abandoned their classrooms in protest. Although teacher strikes are illegal in Wisconsin, teachers danced around the law and organized "sickouts." Supportive physicians scribbled phony doctor's notes for those in need. The Madison epidemic spread from Kenosha to Superior—schools were shut down across the state, and teachers reinforced their ranks at the capitol. "We teach the children!" one legion cried as they marched below Walker's office. "We are the mighty teachers!" bellowed another.

According to the *Wisconsin State Journal,* anti-Walker forces hit the 10,000 mark by Tuesday afternoon and 20,000 by Wednesday. Sleeping bags started to appear by committee rooms. Inflatable mattresses popped up near state senate offices. Police officers, themselves members of a union allied with the protesters, abstained from confronting the squatters. There were no metal detectors or other security measures, and the capitol doors remained wide open, day and night. Zero arrests were made.

Walker plowed ahead. He knew that he had the votes to pass his plan, regardless of the kicking and screaming. Republicans hold a 19–14 edge in the state senate and a 57–38–1 majority in the state assembly. But to have a vote, elected representatives have to show up: Specifically, the Wisconsin senate requires the presence of a 20-senator quorum before considering any fiscal measure. Knowing this, the 14 Democratic state senators promptly went on the lam.

By the evening of February 18, the entire Democratic caucus from the upper chamber was in hiding, holed up at hotels in northern Illinois and Chicago. They giggled with bloggers over the phone that, in Dick Cheney style,

they were calling from "undisclosed locations." As the senators evaded state troopers dispatched by the state senate to haul them back to work, busloads of labor supporters began to arrive in Madison. The Left was digging in—and man, did they love it. MSNBC's Ed Schultz set up shop. Teaching assistants from the University of Wisconsin began to organize a commune of sorts, operating out of a hearing room on the capitol's third floor. Even President Obama jumped into the mix, calling Walker's maneuver an "assault on unions."

A week after Walker's initial presser, with a circus rollicking outside his office and the national press pouring into Dane County airport, the unions approached and dangled an offer: They would accept Walker's terms on pensions and health benefits but would not give up collective-bargaining power. "We will not—I repeat, we will not—be denied our rights to collectively bargain," said Marty Beil, the leader of the state employees' union. The chants around Capitol Square quickly picked up this spin. Public-school teachers wearing varsity jackets belted out: "It's not about the money!"

Walker responded coolly to the deal. He later told me that he immediately figured it to be a red herring. He argued that his budget fix was designed to help school districts and municipalities tighten their belts in coming years. Labor wanted to make the kerfuffle about his alleged thirst for "union busting," but the governor would not bite. If collective bargaining remained, he reasoned, then few local leaders would be able to balance their budgets—not with the unions holding all of the cards.

Astounded that Walker would not buckle, labor brass called in reinforcements. Richard Trumka, the national president of the AFL-CIO, convened a rally Friday evening. Jesse Jackson and others flocked to the scene. On Saturday, approximately 70,000 people showed up at the capitol, circling the building for hours. Firefighters marched hand in hand with teachers, corrections officers raised their fists in front of a nearby Starbucks, students scurried over from UW-Madison's campus. Out-of-state supporters flooded in.

So did the Tea Party. Thousands of Walker supporters appeared with Gadsden flags and Old Glory, cutting right through the labor masses toward the capitol. They set up a makeshift stage, their pro-Walker posters waving under the clear blue sky. Conservative favorites such as publisher Andrew Breitbart, presidential candidate Herman Cain, and Samuel "Joe the Plumber" Wurzelbacher cheered on the crowd and chastised the absent state senators. "Recall them all!" was a common chant. Walker loved it.

The day after the Saturday showdown, the governor and I met in his capitol office. He implored the on-the-run legislators to "come home." For the first time, I saw a flash of disdain from Walker, whose calm usually reminds me of a placid public-radio newsreader. This battle was dragging on with no conclusion in sight. But Walker would not budge and insisted that he could outlast the Democrats, even if protests swamped the capitol for months.

"They have no endgame," he said with a hint of exasperation. "They don't know what they are doing. They got caught up in the hysteria and decided to run, but that's not how this works. You have got to be in the arena."

Walker had seen this movie before. From 2002 to 2010, he served as chief executive of Milwaukee County, a blue community of nearly a million. He was elected to the post after county executives had lavished extensive pension perks upon themselves, inspiring an outbreak of flinty fiscal conservatism even in liberal voters—at least for a time. After nearly a decade as a state legislator, during which time he was a popular guest on Wisconsin's talk-radio circuit and was viewed as a rising Republican star, he found himself managing an out-of-control budget in a major Midwestern city. It was an abrupt change of pace.

From the outset, Walker led as an unapologetic conservative and began to make immediate, deep cuts. Budgets were slashed and public workers laid off. The local unions were apoplectic. Walker soldiered on and never once raised property taxes. The county's bond rating improved, and its debt was reduced. Walker, a low-key speaker but a pol with solid gut instincts, even donated thousands in salary back to the taxpayers. For a middle-class father of two teenage sons, that was more than a gimmick.

"We were dealing with many of the same fights I'm fighting right now: pension reform and health-care benefits," Walker recalled. "We were challenging the status quo. We reined in spending, reined in the size of government, and reduced the size of the work force."

Year after year, he roiled big-government Democrats with his streamlined county budgets. "People would sit in the chambers when I presented my budgets. I'd have whole sections of the gallery filled with AFSCME leaders in green shirts holding up signs that read 'Negotiate, don't dictate.' So I have great credibility when I talk about the need to change collective bargaining. I saw firsthand how the unions thumbed their noses at local elected officials."

"'We are not budging'—that is the unions' mindset," Walker sighed as the protesters rumbled beyond his door. "Even if you wanted modest changes in health-care and pension contributions, you could not get it. One year, I even tried a 35-hour workweek for a couple weeks, and they told me to forget it. 'Go lay people off,' they said, 'you'll be gone soon enough. We may not get our people back, but our benefits won't be reduced.' They had no interest in doing anything reasonable with local officials."

By late February, with Democratic state senators still roosting in Illinois, assembly Republicans hustled to pass the governor's budget bill. It was a slow, arduous process: Lower-chamber Democrats did not flee, but they did filibuster, via amendments and long-winded floor speeches, for 61 hours straight. On February 24, there were rumors that the Democrats would finally stop the theatrics. But they kept riffing well into the night.

At 1 A.M. on Friday, February 25, Rep. Bill Kramer, the GOP speaker pro tempore, decided he had seen enough. He grabbed his gavel, halted the debate, and called for a vote. It was over in seconds. Walker's bill passed 51 to 17, with nearly one-third of the sleepy chamber, including 25 Democrats, not voting—some were absent, others confused by the sudden end to the filibuster.

Bedlam ensued. Democratic legislators, clad in orange shirts like their union backers, took to the floor. They raised their arms and pointed their fingers at their GOP colleagues, echoing the chants of those huddled throughout the capitol. There were yelps and groans; some screamed "Shame!" at Republicans, others called the process undemocratic. The shout-fest was akin to the British House of Commons at its absolute worst. But Walker had won a crucial victory in the war to pass his bill. If that meant that the absentee Democratic senators stayed in Illinois and started rooting for the Chicago Bears, never to return home again, he could live with that.

At the end of my conversation with Walker, the throbbing drums of the protesters began to bleed through the granite. Walker shrugged off the noise. "These tens of thousands of protesters have every right to be heard," he told me. "But there are 5.5 million people in this state, and those taxpayers also have a right to be heard. I, for one, am not going to let the protesters overshadow, or shout out, the interest of the state's taxpayers. And I believe that they are with us in trying to balance this budget."

Indeed, Walker sees his brawl with union bosses as an important testing ground for other governors dealing with in-the-red budgets. "I was talking to former governor Tommy Thompson about this the other day," he said, his hands clasped. "Wisconsin set the table back in the Nineties on welfare reform. We were a leader there, and we were a leader on education reform. Now we are talking about budgetary and fiscal reform. Wisconsin, in many cases, sets the pace."

Scott Walker sees his brawl with union bosses as an important testing ground for other governors dealing with in-the-red budgets.

And Scott Walker intends to set the pace for Wisconsin.

Critical Thinking

1. What government office does Scott Walker hold and what did he do early in 2011 that produced fierce controversy and protests in his state?

2. Why did the entire Democratic caucus of the Wisconsin state senate go to Illinois in response to Governor Walker's proposal?

3. What government offices had Walker held before becoming governor?

4. In what two policy areas, according to Governor Walker, had the state of Wisconsin been a leader before the 2011 controversy over budgetary and fiscal reform?

From *The National Review*, March 21, 2011, pp. 26–28. Copyright © 2011 by National Review, Inc, 215 Lexington Avenue, New York, NY 10016. Reprinted by permission.

If He Can Make It There . . .

As New York's new deputy mayor for operations, Steve Goldsmith faces a daunting set of challenges—running the country's largest police department, keeping the city safe from terrorists, and erasing a $3 billion deficit. Good thing he was once mayor of Indianapolis.

DANIEL S. COMISKEY

In a black SUV headed east across the Brooklyn Bridge, Steve Goldsmith powers up his iPad for a few minutes of Twitter between meetings. His driver-bodyguard weaves in and out of the congested traffic, trying to get the deputy mayor to the headquarters of the New York City Fire Department in time for a tour. Scanning tweets from multiple city heads, Goldsmith smirks as he receives one from Mayor Michael Bloomberg. "The boss is tweeting me about the latest tourism numbers," he says, then reads the message aloud: "Twenty-four million visitors and counting have come to New York so far in 2010 . . . what took *you* so long?"

Several months have passed since Bloomberg named him deputy mayor for operations, putting him in charge of more than 200,000 employees and effectively tasking him with running the largest city in the country, but Goldsimth remains an outsider here. The 63-year-old Republican can't yet point you to a good restaurant. He hasn't seen a Broadway show. When the mayor offered him the position as part of a third-term shakeup, Goldsmith had never even lived in the region. The infamously earnest former Indianapolis mayor struggles to recall a single night out since he landed in New York in April.

But in his own methodical way, Goldsmith has been learning this place. As he explains on the ride to the fire department, his 18-hour, 20-meeting days take him across the metropolis. On walks along Morningside Park on the Upper West Side, he sometimes calls the transportation department about cracks in the street. He refers to his meetings with the Solid Waste Management Board as "really exciting." And always, everywhere, he looks for places to trim. Of all the overwhelming responsibilities of the job—heading the police, fire, transportation, and emergency-management departments to name just a few—wrangling New York's $3 billion deficit unsettles him the most. "I got a call from another mayor the other day, and he was worrying about his $70 million hole," he says in his distracted, fast-talking style. "I just laughed."

Anyone familiar with Goldsmith's record knows that this position fits him as neatly as his traditional blue suits. While he was never known for his people skills, the national press celebrated his transformation of downtown Indy in the 1990s as "the Indianapolis miracle." The wiry conservative downsized government here with almost religious zeal. For the past decade, he has been teaching new mayors at Harvard. Few people in the country offer more expertise on how to run a city than Goldsmith.

Running Gotham, though, presents some unique challenges even for the veteran politician. For one thing, the deputy mayor position comes with all of the responsibility of being an executive and none of the celebrity. When his vehicle pulls up to the Fire Department building, the guard at the gate delays it because the man has never heard of him. Ten minutes go by with the SUV idling at the booth. "It appears that I'm going to have to use my senior city status to get into a city building," Goldsmith says with deadpan wit. "Will someone tell this guy that he works for me?"

At the Age of 12, Steve Goldsmith became the youngest Eagle Scout in the country. He served as president of the student council at Broad Ripple High School. At Wabash College, he edited the student newspaper. After graduating from the University of Michigan Law School, one of the best in the U.S., he ran for Marion County prosecutor—although his opponent, the respected elder judge Andrew Jacobs Sr., made it a long shot.

"All signs were that Steve was going to get beat," says George Geib, a professor of history at Butler University who served on Goldsmith's 1978 campaign committee. "But he did something not a lot of politicians had thought of in those days—he appointed a research committee. They looked into Jacobs' record and discovered he wasn't a particularly good administrator. Steve saw the wedge, and he acted on it."

Engineering a colossal upset, Goldsmith edged Jacobs by a few thousand votes. And in a telling sign of things to come, one of his first acts as prosecutor was to downsize his own office. He cut nearly a third of his staff and moved himself out of a big, cushy office into a smaller one. The era of Goldsmith efficiency had begun.

Over the course of the next decade, the brilliant young prosecutor made it increasingly clear in interviews that he wanted to run for mayor. But the beloved Republican Bill Hudnut, who served for four terms from 1976 to 1992, refused to walk away. Hudnut was everything Goldsmith wasn't—a people person who even dressed up as a leprechaun for the St. Patrick's Day parade. While Hudnut seemed to gain sustenance from sitting in a cafeteria and talking with everyday people, Goldsmith preferred to work long days administrating behind the scenes. And he hated campaigning.

"Steve would knock on 200 doors a day, but it led to a lot of shaking hands and looking at his watch," says Mike Wells, president of REI Investments and Goldsmith's campaign manager in the 1978 election. "A lot of people don't like that, especially in Indiana. They want someone to sit and have coffee with them for 45 minutes. In Goldsmith's world, that 45 minutes doesn't exist."

As Goldsmith waited in the wings for the city's top office, a feud played out publicly between him and Hudnut, with the two exchanging barbs in the press. (They had "buried the hatchet," observed *The Indianapolis News* about the relationship between the two men, "in each other's backs.") When Hudnut finally announced in 1991 that he would retire as mayor, Goldsmith couldn't step up fast enough. Despite his shortcomings as a campaigner, he sailed to victory in a city that had been pulling the Republican lever for 24 years. And he wasted no time in running Hudnut out of town. "Goldsmith can be vindictive," says Sheila Kennedy, an IUPUI professor of law and public policy who wrote a book on his administration titled *To Market, To Market*. "When Hudnut was named head of the Economic Development Council, Goldsmith called and told them if they wanted city money, they would reconsider."

Once mayor, though, Goldsmith launched an agenda that may be looked back on as the most successful in Indianapolis history. In keeping with his theory that a city couldn't develop around a decaying core, he transformed the Mile Square into a model for mid-market cities. He negotiated the deals to build Conseco Fieldhouse and Victory Field, keeping the Pacers and Indians in Indy. He courted the NCAA and provided tax incentives to spur the local expansions of Emmis Communications (owner of *Indianapolis Monthly*), Lilly, and WellPoint. He initiated the Fall Creek Place and Canal redevelopments, moves even his detractors praise. To finish Circle Centre mall, no more than a stalled project and a hole in the ground when he took office, he made personal visits to department-store CEOs and leaned on them to come to Indy. One of the pioneers of privatization, he put city services such as sanitation up for bid. Goldsmith, a notorious micromanager, even redrew the city flow chart so that every line looped back to him. He was known to call unsuspecting IPD officers directly to ask questions about conditions on the street.

Political historians still argue whether those successes were built on innovations or debt, but he became famous nationally for them. *The New York Times* and other papers came to town to herald the improvements. "Goldsmith has won a national reputation for putting city services out to bid," praised a 1994 *Times* article. A *Christian Science Monitor* piece on Goldsmith later in his term raved: "This Corn Belt capital is emerging from Midwest anonymity into a vibrant, marquee metropolis." Mayors from around the country, including Rudolph Giuliani of New York, visited to learn from his example. Like most things, though, Goldsmith didn't leave any of that to chance. Those closest to him recall him hiring a PR firm in Langley, Virginia, to publicize his success.

"He took plenty of criticism because he had a lot of new ideas, and he basically ramrodded them through," Wells says. "But if you look at the number of major projects he got done in eight years, no other mayor we've had compares. Steve stepped on the gas and made it happen."

At the heart of New York City Hall, a squat 198-year-old building surrounded by the towers of the Financial District, Steve Goldsmith sits in his cubicle munching on a lunch of carrot sticks. Except for a few marble busts along the wall, the large white room bustling with 50 mayoral staff members could be a call center. Behind Goldsmith—so close that he hits it when he leans back—sits the cubicle of Mayor Michael Bloomberg. Both men's office spaces possess all the grandeur of intern stations.

This is The Bullpen. When Bloomberg arrived in 2002, the billionaire abandoned a showy office in favor of an open room where his staff would have easy access to him. Goldsmith calls it "the democratization of information." Typically, the two executives banter back and forth about policy or their latest iPad app discovery. (Bloomberg

recently introduced Goldsmith to one that uses GPS to tell him not only where he is in the city, but the neighborhood's history.) On this day, though, Bloomberg is down the hall at a press conference, fielding questions about his controversial position on the mosque near Ground Zero. Unlike 61 percent of New Yorkers, he favors its right to exist—an issue that Goldsmith, who is Jewish, dodges every time he is asked.

Instead the trim deputy mayor nibbles on his downsized lunch at his downsized desk and researches ways to save the city money. "I have a personality defect that I developed in Indianapolis," he says. "I only know how to work. I exercise at 5:15 A.M., get here about 6:30 A.M., have meetings stacked on top of each other until 8 P.M., and get home about 10 to answer e-mails. Then I start again. No normal person would endorse this lifestyle."

For Goldsmith, who now lives with his wife in an apartment on the Columbia University campus, taking this job was one of the few things he never meticulously planned. After leaving the Indy mayor's office in 2000, he began teaching at Harvard. His 2009 book *The Power of Social Innovation* focused in part on innovations in Bloomberg's New York, and when the mayor came to meet Goldsmith and offered to write a foreword, Bloomberg was actually interviewing him—unbeknownst to the professor. When former deputy mayor of operations Ed Skyler stepped down to work in the private sector in March, Bloomberg offered the position (and its $213,000 salary) to Goldsmith by phone.

"The whole idea of hiring a former mayor to be your chief operating officer is a little odd, don't you think?" Goldsmith says as Bloomberg whizzes by the door. "I joke that it took me 10 years to get demoted from mayor to deputy mayor. But he's the perfect boss so far. He takes risks, and he's totally unafraid to say whatever he thinks is the right thing."

When Bloomberg introduced Goldsmith at a press conference in April, the mayor touted him as the man to untangle the Big Apple's enormous administrative thicket while running the agencies protecting its citizens. "Lots of people talk about reinventing government," the mayor said. "Steve Goldsmith has actually done it."

A car bomb turned up in Times Square one day later—lighting up the nation's television screens with a grainy image of a smoking SUV. Although Goldsmith dismisses the impact of that scare, the realities of his job must have been immediately clear. Updates from agency heads he hadn't even met came streaming into his phone every half-hour. For the next three days, until Faisal Shahzad was arrested for the crime, the entire world's attention turned to New York. The deputy mayor says he mostly let the police and fire departments handle the emergency. According to him, they already do that very well. But the crisis served as a nerve-jangling "Welcome to New York."

On less dramatic days, Goldsmith sees his role more as a consultant than as a director. Carving away at that $3 billion deficit consumes most of his time. In May, he discovered 10,000 empty city desks occupying leased space around town, the elimination of which, along with other cuts, will save New York $500 million a year. He is looking hard at the city's 80 data centers, a number he says he would like to reduce to "between 0 and 2." And more difficult decisions loom on the horizon. Closing some firehouses, a move that even a decade after 9/11 would be extremely unpopular, may now be on the table.

Doing the popular thing, though, has rarely concerned Goldsmith. A model of an emerging breed of Republicans—what *New York Times* columnist David Brooks recently called the "austerity caucus"—he joins members of his party such as Mitch Daniels and Chris Christie, governor of New Jersey, who shun grandstanding in favor of number-crunching. For the first time in his public career, he doesn't have to go out and mine votes. A man who has never lived in New York somehow finds himself totally in his element. He analyzes. He cuts. He makes the trains run on time. To the extent that Goldsmith enjoys anything, one gets the feeling he loves it.

For all his success, Goldsmith never got the three jobs he wanted most. When Dan Quayle became vice president in 1989, Goldsmith talked passionately with his staff about the steps he was taking to ensure that Governor Robert Orr named him to the vacated Senate seat. Some say they never saw that kind of enthusiasm from him before or since. But the job ultimately went to Dan Coats.

The second shortfall came in the governor's race of 1996. After several promising years as mayor of Indianapolis, Goldsmith should have made a formidable opponent for lieutenant governor Frank O'Bannon. But an ill-timed police brawl, in which drunken cops beat several African Americans downtown, cast a pall on his candidacy. And the grandfatherly O'Bannon, known to greet every person at campaign events, possessed a charm that Goldsmith found hard to muster. "We had a saying in the newsroom," says political observer Brian Howey, then a reporter for the *Fort Wayne Journal-Gazette.* "Every person that Frank O'Bannon met was a vote for O'Bannon. And every person that Steve Goldsmith met was a vote for O'Bannon."

Upon losing the governor's race and finishing his time as mayor, Goldsmith had a third opportunity at the national stage when President George W. Bush seemed to be courting him for his Cabinet. An early advocate of faith-based initiatives, he advised Bush, even spending the night at his Austin campaign headquarters the night of the disorderly 2000 election. But the Cabinet position never materialized, a disappointment Goldsmith rarely discusses. One explanation concerns his wife, who has suffered from lupus since age 22 and was undergoing chemotherapy at the time; he may not have been in a position to take the job. Others have speculated that Goldsmith's unilateral executive tendencies troubled Bush. A president who referred to himself as "the decider" might not have meshed well with another authoritarian.

Whatever the case, Goldsmith joined the faculty of Harvard's Kennedy School of Government later that year, and it appeared that his political career was behind him. Plenty of former mayors make a brief stop at Harvard after leaving office, but Goldsmith found a home there, fitting right in among the intellectuals. From the late '90s to 2010, he wrote five books on government. The most prominent, *The Twenty-First Century City,* landed him on *Charlie Rose* for a 20-minute interview. In op-ed pieces for the likes of *The New York Times,* he sang the praises of privatization. Founding a blog called "Better, Faster, Cheaper" about urban government, he also participated in the New Mayors Program at Harvard for rookie executives such as Greg Ballard.

And behind the scenes, Goldsmith still advises Ballard to this day. Ballard declined to comment, but Goldsmith says the two talk fairly often by phone. Many see the current mayor's recent push to privatize the city's parking meters as influenced by the elder statesman. Wells, Goldsmith's 1978 campaign manager, goes so far as to call the mayor "a disciple" of the man. Governor Mitch Daniels, too, has pursued an agenda with shades of Goldsmith—most notably leasing the Indiana Toll Road and creating efficiencies at the BMV. Kennedy, who wrote the book on the former mayor's administration, refers to Daniels as "Goldsmith with personality." So even if his shortcomings prevented him from scaling the heights for which he was otherwise bound, the brainy ideologue's presence remains in the political culture here. In some ways, he never left.

Ask the bartenders, shop owners, museum docents, Off-Broadway actors, and cab drivers of New York who Steve Goldsmith is, and most of them will answer with a blank stare. The position of deputy mayor for operations may carry enormous power, but it is of the clandestine variety. Which doesn't bother Goldsmith at all. "I don't care if the average New Yorker knows my name," he says. "Although the cab drivers probably will soon. We're going to be changing things for them—new designs for the cabs, cleanliness standards, the ability to tweet about the quality of the driver."

When Goldsmith talks, he tends to speak in outlines. Every answer has three or four components. In sharp contrast to Bloomberg, you won't find him wandering around City Hall, popping his head in offices and telling jokes. He understands his austere role: to manage the metropolis. For the first time in decades, Goldsmith, who rarely minced words in Indy, must watch what he says in public. His proximity to the mayor's chair in The Bullpen is such that any slip-up could be, in Goldsmith's words, "painful."

During his tour of the FDNY headquarters, the deputy mayor mostly observes. He asks a few questions about the logarithms that determine when an ambulance is sent with a fire truck and the costs involved, but the Central Tracking Center—a new room of perhaps 50 computer screens tracking every engine in the city—seems to satisfy the efficiency expert in him. Goldsmith and the fire commissioner trade jokes about which Manning brother is better, and then a handler politely pulls the deputy mayor to his next meeting.

As Goldsmith and a small group of staffers exit the building and cross the street for a tour of one of the data centers he hopes to privatize, several of the center's executives stand inside, looking warily through a window. They're familiar with the deputy mayor's reputation. They know why he is here. They will greet him warmly and try to sell the place as essential to the business of the city. Only one question remains: Which one is Goldsmith?

Critical Thinking

1. Of what major city was Steven Goldsmith mayor in the late 20th century and in what even larger city did he later become deputy major for operations?

2. As mayor, for what noteworthy changes and accomplishments was he responsible?

3. What does "privatization" mean, and what actions related to privatization did Mayor Goldsmith take while mayor?

4. Who appointed Goldsmith to his position as deputy mayor?

5. What did Goldsmith do between serving as mayor of one city and becoming deputy mayor in another?

From *Indianapolis Monthly Magazine*, December 2010, pp. 74–79. Copyright © 2010 by Indianapolis Monthly Magazine. Reprinted by permission.

Counter Cultures

Success in government demands a different set of skills than making it big in business.

MARTY LINSKY

My third tour in government was as chief secretary to then Republican Governor Bill Weld in Massachusetts in the early 1990s. My portfolio was politics and personnel—aka "patronage."

It was the early days of the merger and acquisition craze. As a consequence, there were a slew of men and women with highly successful track records in business whose jobs had ended on someone else's schedule. With impressive resumés, paid-up college tuitions behind them, and enough money squirreled away to get by on a public secular salary, they "wanted to give something back" by serving in an important position in state government. Status was still important. For example, if you had been the president of a successful local bank that had been swallowed up, you might well be addicted to a certain level of authority.

We recruited lots of those folks into the Weld administration. Anecdotally, it seemed as if they either blew out pretty quickly or they made the transition well and made significant contributions to the public good, at least as we defined it. Almost no one was just so-so.

I remember noticing the pattern at the time. It got me to thinking about the difference between exercising leadership successfully in business and doing so in government and politics, and why it was so difficult for many in business to match their private sector success in the public arena.

What are the cultural and value differentiators between these two worlds?

While my academic colleagues might be eager to attack that question with an elaborate research design, I'm too much of a journalist—and politician—to resist taking a stab at naming the most important of these many differentiators.

So based on what I have experienced and observed, here are four key differences I see between succeeding in the world of business and politics.

No. 1: Data Versus Anecdotes

For business, systematic data are powerful. In politics, anecdotal evidence is not an oxymoron.

People in government and politics—for our purposes here, let's use "politics" or "political environment" to cover both elected and appointed officials in the public sector—have different ideas about the utility of systematic data versus anecdotes in decision making. At one end of the spectrum, academics and scientists use many, many cases to come up with a general theory, which is then applied to a particular situation. Legislators, on the other hand, are forced by the nature of their work to use individual cases to make general rules. To a scientist, systematic analysis trumps intuition or any individual case. To a politician, intuition is a resource, and individual cases are legitimate pathways to general laws. Business people fall somewhere in between.

No. 2: Politics Is Not the Problem

To be successful in a political environment, you've got to acknowledge, respect and engage in the politics of policymaking, not disdain it. In business, the politics is just as present, but being explicit about the politics is, well, politically incorrect.

You've got to acknowledge, respect and engage in the politics of policymaking, not disdain it.

I was a three-term member of the Massachusetts House of Representatives. It was the most honest environment in which I have ever worked, including, among others, law firms, academic institutions, consulting firms and newspapers. It was honest because politics, which pervades everything from families to corporations, was upfront and explicit.

In most organizations outside of government, politics is very much present but below the radar. When I first joined the faculty at the Harvard Kennedy School nearly 30 years ago, a trusted colleague and I were having a candid conversation about my career when he suddenly stopped and said, "You know, I will have this conversation with you any time you want, but we can never have it with anyone else in the room."

The message was clear: Normal, human ambition and strategizing about it were not appropriate subjects for public conversation. The Kennedy School was founded to train people to speak truth to power on the assumption that the world would be a better place if we could only take the politics out of policymaking.

Many of our unsuccessful appointees from the private sector had the same idea. They thought their job was to eliminate the politics, instead of engaging in it because it was so real and relevant to making progress.

The central difference between functioning well in politics and functioning well in business is not whether the politics exists, but whether politics is accepted as an appropriate and public factor in decision making.

No. 3: Everything Is Connected

Once you accept the legitimacy of politics, certain other differentiators result. The most important of these is No. 3: In politics, there are no discrete issues. Everything is connected to everything else.

People who are successful in politics think systemically. If I am coming to a meeting with you, I want to know what else you care about besides what is on the agenda, who your friends and your enemies are, what other pressures you are facing, and whether I have done anything for you lately, or vice versa. People in business tend to want to hold on to the fiction that they can solve a value-laden problem in one place without ramifications everywhere else. Unexpected consequences are the result of lack of good political or systemic diagnoses.

One of the reasons that people in business can ignore the politics is they tend to work in more or less homogeneous worlds, with clear lines of authority and a shared objective, namely the bottom line. Working in a political environment, you are thrown together every day with people who have very different values, priorities and preferred outcomes.

Personal power derives as much from relationships—and the informal authority that comes from those relationships—as from formal authority. And people are where they are because of their differences, be they policy preferences, issue advocacy or geographical constituencies.

No. 4: A World of Ambiguity

In business, you can enjoy the comfort of being on a team and agreeing on your role and scope of authority. But to be successful in politics, you have to revel in being in an environment of ambiguous authority, and relish confronting the "other."

To be successful in politics, you have to revel in being in an environment of ambiguous authority.

In this space I can only touch on some of the most important cultural, value and structural differences between government and business, and how the willingness and capacity to overcome those differences affect the success of business people in government and politics. This is a mother lode of a subject, and I have only scratched the surface here.

But ironically, in the turbulent times in which we live, some of those distinctions will blur.

With huge challenges and diminished resources, government bureaucrats and politicians will to have to look more to rigorous analysis on which to make—and justify—hard choices.

On the other side, with such rapid change and future uncertainties, people in business must increase their tolerance for ambiguity and less clear lines of authority, collaborate with people who hold very different values and perspectives, and make more intuitive decisions based on insufficient data.

Critical Thinking

1. How are the worlds of business and politics distinguished by "data versus anecdotes"?

2. How are the worlds of business and politics distinguished by whether "politics" itself is accepted as an appropriate and public factor in decision making?

3. Does the notion that "everything is connected" apply better to the world of business or the world of politics? Why?

4. In which world—business or politics—does ambiguity fit more comfortably?

MARTY LINSKY is co-founder and principal of Cambridge Leadership Associates, a global leadership development consulting practice. He also is a longtime faculty member at Harvard's Kennedy School and a former three-term Republican representative in the Massachusetts House, where he served as assistant minority leader.

Rise of the Generals

With a Democrat in the White House, conservative state attorneys general are mobilizing against federal power.

JOSH GOODMAN

When state attorneys general agreed on a landmark settlement with tobacco companies in 1997, all they needed to finish the deal was approval from Congress. But Washington, D.C.'s powerbrokers balked at taking orders from the states' chief legal officers. "Who do these people think they are?" Sen. John McCain wondered.

Over the last 13 years, it's become quite clear who state AGs think they are. The tobacco settlement, finalized in 1998 with tens of billions of dollars in payments to states, was just the beginning. State AGs continued asserting themselves on a national level as the scourges of corporate bad guys and the guardians of consumer interests. In 1997, the national influence of state AGs seemed novel. Today it doesn't.

Yet many Democrats in Washington now are asking the same question as McCain: "Who do these people think they are?" That's because the powerful people state AGs are confronting aren't just in corporate boardrooms—they're in the White House and the U.S. Capitol. In the last few months, conservative AGs have become some of the nation's most prominent opponents of federal power in general and the Obama administration specifically. They're trying to block provisions of the federal health-care reform law in court, and they're working to limit the federal government's power to regulate guns and greenhouse gas emissions.

On the surface, these actions look like another reimagining of the state AGs' role. The tobacco settlement created a model for activism for a liberal Democratic AG. Perhaps then, conservative Republican AGs, with their states' rights stands, are developing their own model as to how to affect the nation's most important policy decisions.

But it's probably more accurate to say that the Republicans are developing a new twist on older models. After all, AGs of both parties long have fought to protect state prerogatives. Nor are today's Republican AGs the first to engage in a politically charged battle with a president of the opposite party. Democrats did the same thing to George W. Bush over environmental regulation.

New model or not, one thing is clear: Almost overnight, some of the country's most important, controversial politicians are Republican AGs. They can attribute their new clout to the presence of a Democrat in the White House.

After the tobacco settlement, AGs became stars—well, some of them anyway. Connecticut's Richard Blumenthal made a name for himself as a scourge of health maintenance organizations, insurance companies and power plants. California's Bill Lockyer sued car companies for auto emissions. Most famously, New York's Eliot Spitzer cracked down on the excesses of Wall Street.

Blumenthal, Lockyer and Spitzer are all Democrats. It took two years for the first Republican AG to join Democrats in their suits against tobacco. Most of the AGs who engaged in a major anti-trust case against Microsoft in the late 1990s also were Democrats.

It's not as though Republicans completely stayed on the sidelines. Most Republican AGs eventually participated in tobacco suits. And Republicans generally have been as happy as the Democrats to become involved in consumer protection cases. But with business groups complaining that the Democratic activists were bullies who overstepped their roles as state officials, Republican AGs never quite embraced the model that Spitzer and others refined. Conservatives didn't want to be anti-business or favor excessive regulation.

In fact, some conservative AGs, led by Alabama's Bill Pryor, actively rebelled against this model. But Pryor and his ideological compatriots largely were defined by what they weren't: activists in the Spitzer mold. Most Republican AGs weren't having a national impact in the way that some of their Democratic counterparts were. They didn't seem to have a coherent, common national purpose.

In that context, it's surprising how easily Rob McKenna, Washington state's Republican AG, articulates just such a purpose. "The role of the attorney general," McKenna says, "is to be a guardian of federalism and to protect state prerogatives."

For Republican AGs, protecting state prerogatives has meant battling the Obama administration and Democrats in Congress. In doing so, they've enjoyed instant influence.

When the Senate passed a version of health-care reform that included special Medicaid payments to Nebraska—the so-called "Cornhusker Kickback"—13 Republican AGs wrote to Congress threatening to sue, claiming their states weren't being treated equitably. Congress dropped the provision. Later, Democratic leaders in the House of Representatives considered using a procedure know as "deem-and-pass" to allow the House to give approval to the unpopular Senate version of health-care reform without a direct vote on the matter. Republican AGs threatened to sue again, arguing deem-and-pass was unconstitutional. The House dropped the strategy.

Those concessions, of course, didn't stop AGs from suing when Obama finally signed the health-care bill into law in March. The AGs argue that requiring everyone to buy health insurance is unconstitutional and that the law places an unfair burden on the states. So far, around 20 states are supporting legal action to block the law, and all but one of the participating AGs are Republicans.

Health-care reform is the most obvious example of the Republican activism, but it's not the only one. A group of Republican AGs and a few Democrats from energy-producing states also teamed up to try to prevent the federal Environmental Protection Agency (EPA) from regulating greenhouse gas emissions. Eight AGs—five Republicans and three Democrats—from conservative states are arguing in court that federal gun regulations shouldn't apply to firearms made and sold within their borders. "There is a sense now among conservative attorneys general that this position could be used creatively and aggressively to pursue conservative ends," says James Tierney, a former Maine AG who directs Columbia Law School's National State Attorneys General Program.

Among the Republican AGs, none has proven himself to be more aggressive—or more conservative—than Virginia's Ken Cuccinelli. Cuccinelli, a global warming skeptic, took the lead challenging the EPA over greenhouse gas regulations and now is challenging the EPA over new automobile fuel economy standards. Mere minutes after Obama signed the health-care reform bill, Cuccinelli filed a challenge to it that was separate from other states, arguing that a Virginia law prohibiting a health insurance mandate should supersede the federal law.

Cuccinelli also has created controversy back home. He wrote a letter to public colleges and universities telling them they couldn't bar discrimination on the basis of sexual orientation. He's demanding documents from the University of Virginia on a former faculty member's research, saying they might reveal the scientist's work on climate change to be fraudulent.

The end result is that Cuccinelli is a darling of the right and a villain to the left. He is perhaps as famous as Spitzer in his heyday. He's clearly just as polarizing. The remarkable thing: Cuccinelli took office just five months ago.

Other Republican AGs who also have been quite active, such as South Carolina's Henry McMaster and Texas' Greg Abbott, haven't become as famous. But even if they're not household names, what they're doing is national news. Democratic AGs now are the ones on the defensive. In conservative states such as Oklahoma, Arkansas and Georgia, Democrats have faced—and resisted—pressure to join the health-care suit.

While Cuccinelli is the person most closely linked to the states' rights revival, the state with the most enthusiasm for it is Utah. There, Republican Attorney General Mark Shurtleff has been an eager participant, though he hasn't completely had a choice in the matter: The Utah Legislature has demanded that he take on the federal government.

The legislature approved a resolution asserting the state's sovereignty under the Constitution's 10th Amendment. It passed a bill to opt out of federal gun regulations, setting up Shurtleff's participation in that issue. It even approved legislation directing Shurtleff to try to use eminent domain on federal lands to claim them for development.

The situation in Utah highlights one reason conservative AGs are becoming so prominent. Conservative legislators and governors are engaged in their own rebellion against the Obama administration. As states' legal officers, AGs logically are becoming some of the faces of this movement.

So is Shurtleff celebrating his brand-new sense of purpose? Well, no. "This isn't new for me," he says.

Shurtleff notes that Utah long has had a fondness for fighting the federal government. He points out that early in his term, he was battling with the George W. Bush administration over federal land issues. "I said, 'I don't want to sue my new Republican president, but it's states' rights,'" Shurtleff says.

Utah isn't unique. Western states have battled Washington over federal lands for years. AGs have been the forefront of these battles—and other ones with the feds. "States and their lawyers have long been suspicious of federal power," Tierney says. "That's why we have federalism. It would be unnatural for states not to protect themselves within the federal system."

Most of these fights are bipartisan. Almost every AG supported New York as it worked to preserve states' right to enforce their own lending laws. In 2009, the Supreme Court sided with the states.

Almost every AG teamed up again to ask the Obama administration to support ending federal pre-emption of state banking regulation in this year's financial reform legislation. The White House agreed. Tom Miller, Iowa's longtime Democratic attorney general, says financial reform shows the real story. It isn't that AGs are battling the White House more; they're actually battling it less.

"My view," he says, "is that the litigation against the federal government is the exception. Overall, the attorneys general have the best relationship with the Department of Justice in decades. That includes Democrats and Republicans."

But if health-care reform is an exception, it's an awfully big one. Obama has won approval of the most far-reaching domestic legislation under any Democratic president since Lyndon Johnson. The last people standing in the way from it becoming a reality aren't in Washington, D.C.; they're attorneys general in the states.

In principle, AGs may agree on defending states against federal power, but in this case they're divided. A group of Democratic AGs plan to submit their own brief defending the constitutionality of the health-care law.

The question is whether this divide is a sign of things to come. Sure, people such as Shurtleff have been fighting the feds for a long time, but the prominence of conservative AGs in the healthcare debate wasn't quite like anything that's happened previously. Over the long term, will conservative AGs become more aggressive in trying to check the grandest ambitions of the federal government?

Michael Greve, a federalism expert at the conservative American Enterprise Institute, has an interesting answer to that question: They shouldn't want to.

Greve's point is that limited government and reduced regulation—key conservative goals—aren't served by devolving power to the states. "It is a conceit and mistake on the part of Republicans to think that decentralization translates into smaller government," he says. "If you really wanted to form an effective coalition in favor of a deregulatory agenda, you'd have to oppose states that are on the pro-regulatory side."

If you look back at the role that Democratic AGs played during the Bush administration, you can see what Greve means. Liberal AGs fought for states to be allowed to set tougher auto emissions standards than the federal government. During the Bush years, more state power would have meant more stringent environmental regulation. That probably will be true again during the next Republican presidency. If conservative AGs were to fight for more state power regardless of who is in the White House, they'd end up doing so at the expense of conservative policy objectives.

But at least with regard to environmental rules, conservative AGs weren't fighting federal power under Bush. Instead, liberal AGs were. They didn't just ask to set their own emissions rules. They sued to force the Bush EPA to treat greenhouse gases as pollutants—and won before the Supreme Court.

On the policy question—whether there should be more or less environmental regulation—the two sets of AGs have been completely consistent over the last two presidencies. But on the federalism question—how much power the federal government

should have to design whatever environmental policies it wants—they've flipped. Democratic AGs wanted to constrict federal power under Bush. Republican AGs want to do it now.

That's why Tierney gives a pithy answer to the question of whether conservative AGs are doing something new by fighting Obama. "It's only new," he says, "because conservatives are doing what liberals did before." Maybe Republican AGs now are so committed to fighting the feds that they'll become prominent foes of the next Republican president too, but if so, *that* would be something truly new.

If, instead, the precedent set in the last two presidencies continues, then the influence of Republican AGs over national policy is likely to wane the next time a Republican is elected president. With a Republican in the White House, it will be Democrats' turn to battle the federal government—and to become the new political stars.

Critical Thinking

1. What landmark legal settlement in the late 1990s established state attorneys general as powerful and important players on the national scene?

2. Liberal Democratic state attorneys general were leaders in the tobacco settlement of the late 1990s. What group of state attorneys general is leading legal actions aimed at blocking implementation of the national health care reform law of 2010 and limiting other national government initiatives on gun regulation and greenhouse gas emissions?

3. To what extent do party affiliations of state attorneys general play a role in how active attorneys general are in doing battle with the national government?

Watching the Bench

Justice by Numbers

Mandatory sentencing drove me from the bench.

LOIS G. FORER

Michael S. would have been one of the more than 600,000 incarcerated persons in the United States. He would have been a statistic, yet another addition to a clogged criminal justice system. But he's not—in part because to me Michael was a human being: a slight 24-year-old with a young wife and small daughter. Not that I freed him; I tried him and found him guilty. He is free now only because he is a fugitive. I have not seen him since the day of his sentencing in 1984, yet since that day our lives have been inextricably connected. Because of his case I retired from the bench.

Michael's case appeared routine. He was a typical offender: young, black, and male, a high-school dropout without a job. The charge was an insignificant holdup that occasioned no comment in the press. And the trial itself was, in the busy life of a judge, a run-of-the-mill event.

The year before, Michael, brandishing a toy gun, held up a taxi and took $50 from the driver and the passenger, harming neither. This was Michael's first offense. Although he had dropped out of school to marry his pregnant girlfriend, Michael later obtained a high school equivalency diploma. He had been steadily employed, earning enough to send his daughter to parochial school—a considerable sacrifice for him and his wife. Shortly before the holdup, Michael had lost his job. Despondent because he could not support his family, he went out on a Saturday night, had more than a few drinks, and then robbed the taxi.

There was no doubt that Michael was guilty. But the penalty posed problems. To me, a robbery in a taxi is not an intrinsically graver offense than a robbery in an alley, but to the Pennsylvania legislature, it is. Because the holdup occurred on public transportation, it fell within the ambit of the state's mandatory sentencing law—which required a minimum sentence of five years in the state penitentiary. In Pennsylvania, a prosecutor may decide not to demand imposition of that law, but Michael's prosecuting attorney wanted the five-year sentence.

One might argue that a five-year sentence for a $50 robbery is excessive or even immoral, but to a judge, those arguments are necessarily irrelevant. He or she has agreed to enforce the law, no matter how ill-advised, unless the law is unconstitutional.

I believed the mandatory sentencing law was, and like many of my colleagues I had held it unconstitutional in several other cases for several reasons. We agreed that it violates the constitutional principle of separation of powers because it can be invoked by the prosecutor, and not by the judge. In addition, the act is arbitrary and capricious in its application. Robbery, which is often a simple purse snatching, is covered, but not child molestation or incest, two of society's most damaging offenses. Nor can a defendant's previous record or mental state be considered. A hardened repeat offender receives the same sentence as a retarded man who steals out of hunger. Those facts violate the fundamental Anglo-American legal principles of individualized sentencing and proportionality of the penalty to the crime.

Thus in Michael's case, I again held the statute to be unconstitutional and turned to the sentencing guidelines—a state statute designed to give uniform sentences to offenders who commit similar crimes. The minimum sentence prescribed by the guidelines was 24 months.

A judge can deviate from the prescribed sentence if he or she writes an opinion explaining the reasons for the deviation. While this sounds reasonable in theory, "downwardly departing" from the guidelines is extremely difficult. The mitigating circumstances that influence most judges are not included in the limited list of factors on which "presumptive" sentence is based—that an offender is a caretaker of small children; that the offender is mentally retarded; or that the offender, like Michael, is emotionally distraught.

So I decided to deviate from the guidelines, sentencing Michael to 11-and-a-half months in the county jail and permitting him to work outside the prison during the day to support his family. I also imposed a sentence of two years' probation following his imprisonment conditioned upon repayment of the $50. My rationale for the lesser penalty, outlined in my lengthy opinion, was that this was a first offense, no one was harmed, Michael acted under the pressures of unemployment and need, and he seemed truly contrite. He had never committed a violent act and posed no danger to the public. A sentence of close to a year seemed adequate to convince Michael of the seriousness of his crime. Nevertheless, the prosecutor appealed.

Michael returned to his family, obtained steady employment, and repaid the victims of his crime. I thought no more about Michael until 1986, when the state supreme court upheld the appeal and ordered me to resentence him to a minimum of five years in the state penitentiary. By this time Michael had successfully completed his term of imprisonment and probation, including payment of restitution. I checked Michael's record. He had not been rearrested.

I was faced with a legal and moral dilemma. As a judge I had sworn to uphold the law, and I could find no legal grounds for violating an order of the supreme court. Yet five years' imprisonment was grossly disproportionate to the offense. The usual grounds for imprisonment are retribution, deterrence, and rehabilitation. Michael had paid his retribution by a short term of imprisonment and by making restitution to the victims. He had been effectively deterred from committing future crimes. And by any measurable standard he had been rehabilitated. There was no social or criminological justification for sending him back to prison. Given the choice between defying a court order or my conscience, I decided to leave the bench where I had sat for 16 years.

That didn't help Michael, of course; he was resentenced by another judge to serve the balance of the five years: four years and 15 days. Faced with this prospect, he disappeared. A bench warrant was issued, but given the hundreds of fugitives—including dangerous ones—loose in Philadelphia, I doubt that anyone is seriously looking for him.

But any day he may be stopped for a routine traffic violation; he may apply for a job or a license; he may even be the victim of a crime—and if so, the ubiquitous computer will be alerted and he will be returned to prison to serve the balance of his sentence, plus additional time for being a fugitive. It is not a happy prospect for him and his family—nor for America, which is saddled with a punishment system that operates like a computer—crime in, points tallied, sentence out—utterly disregarding the differences among the human beings involved.

The mandatory sentencing laws and guidelines that exist today in every state were designed to smooth out the inequities in the American judiciary, and were couched in terms of fairness to criminals—they would stop the racist judge from sentencing black robbers to be hanged, or the crusading judge from imprisoning pot smokers for life. Guidelines make sense, for that very reason. But they have had an ugly and unintended result—an increase in the number of American prisoners and an increase in the length of the sentences they serve. Meanwhile, the laws have effectively neutralized judges who prefer sentencing the nonviolent to alternative programs or attempt to keep mothers with young children out of jail.

Have the laws made justice fairer—the central objective of the law? I say no, and a recent report by the Federal Sentencing Commission concurs. It found that, even under mandatory sentencing laws, black males served 83.4 months to white males' 53.7 months for the same offenses. (Prosecutors are more likely to demand imposition of the mandatory laws for blacks than for whites.)

Most important, however, as mandatory sentencing packs our prisons and busts our budgets, it doesn't prevent crime very

effectively. For certain kinds of criminals, alternative sentencing is the most effective type of punishment. That, by the way, is a cold, hard statistic—rather like Michael will be when they find him.

Sentenced to Death

In the past two decades, all 50 state legislatures have enacted mandatory sentencing laws, sentencing guideline statutes, or both. The result: In 1975 there were 263,291 inmates in federal and state prisons. Today there are over 600,000—more than in any other nation—the bill for which comes to $20.3 billion a year. Yet incarceration has not reduced the crime rate or made our streets and communities safer. The number of known crimes committed in the U.S. has increased 10 percent in the last five years.

How did we get into this no-win situation? Like most legislative reforms, it started with good intentions. In 1970, after the turmoil of the sixties, legislators were bombarded with pleas for "law and order." A young, eager, newly appointed federal judge, Marvin Frankel, had an idea.

Before his appointment, Frankel had experienced little personal contact with the criminal justice system. Yet his slim book, *Fair and Certain Punishment,* offered a system of guidelines to determine the length of various sentences. Each crime was given a certain number of points. The offender was also given a number of points depending upon his or her prior record, use of a weapon, and a few other variables. The judge merely needed to add up the points to calculate the length of imprisonment.

The book was widely read and lauded for two main reasons. First, it got tough on criminals and made justice "certain." A potential offender would know in advance the penalty he would face and thus be deterred. (Of course, a large proportion of street crimes are not premeditated, but that fact was ignored.) And second, it got tough on the "bleeding heart" judges. All offenders similarly situated would be treated the same.

The plan sounded so fair and politically promising that many states rushed to implement it in the seventies. In Pennsylvania, members of the legislature admonished judges not to oppose the guidelines because the alternative would be even worse: mandatory sentences. In fact, within a few years almost every jurisdiction had both sentencing guidelines and mandatory sentencing laws. Since then, Congress has enacted some 60 mandatory sentencing laws on the federal level.

As for unfairnesses in sentencing—for instance, the fact that the robber with his finger in his jacket gets the same sentence as the guy with a semiautomatic—these could have been rectified by giving appellate courts jurisdiction to review sentences, as is the law in Canada. This was not done on either the state or federal level. Thus what influential criminologist James Q. Wilson had argued during the height of the battle had become the law of the land: The legal system should "most definitely stop pretending that the judges know any better than the rest of us how to provide 'individualized justice.'"

Hardening Time

I'm not sure I knew better than the rest of you, but I knew a few things about Michael and the correctional system I would be throwing him into. At the time of Michael's sentencing, both the city of Philadelphia and the commonwealth of Pennsylvania were, like many cities and states, in such poor fiscal shape that they did not have money for schools and health care, let alone new prisons, and the ones they did have were overflowing. The city was under a federal order to reduce the prison population; untried persons accused of dangerous crimes were being released, as were offenders who had not completed their sentences.

As for Michael, his problems and those of his family were very real to me. Unlike appellate judges who never see the individuals whose lives and property they dispose of, a trial judge sees living men and women. I had seen Michael and his wife and daughter. I had heard him express remorse. I had favorable reports about him from the prison and his parole officer. Moreover, Michael, like many offenders who appeared before me, had written to me several times. I felt I knew him.

Of course, I could have been wrong. As Wilson says, judges are not infallible—and most of them know that. But they have heard the evidence, seen the offender, and been furnished with presentence reports and psychiatric evaluations. They are in a better position to evaluate the individual and devise an appropriate sentence than anyone else in the criminal justice system.

Yet under mandatory sentencing laws, the complexities of each crime and criminal are ignored. And seldom do we ask what was once a legitimate question in criminal justice: What are the benefits of incarceration? The offenders are off the streets for the period of the sentence, but once released, most will soon be rearrested. (Many crimes are committed in prison, including murder, rape, robbery, and drug dealing.) They have not been "incapacitated," another of the theoretical justifications for imprisonment. More likely, they have simply been hardened.

Sentence Structure

Is there another way to sentence criminals without endangering the public? I believe there is. During my tenure on the bench, I treated imprisonment as the penalty of last resort, not the penalty of choice. And my examination of 16 years' worth of cases suggests my inclination was well founded. While a recent Justice Department study found that two thirds of all prisoners are arrested for other offenses within three years of release, more than two thirds of the 1,000-plus offenders I sentenced to probation conditioned upon payment of reparations to victims successfully completed their sentences and were not rearrested. I am not a statistician, so I had my records analyzed and verified by Elmer Weitekamp, then a doctoral candidate in criminology at the Wharton School of the University of Pennsylvania. He confirmed my findings.

The offenders who appeared before me were mostly poor people, poor enough to qualify for representation by a public defender. I did not see any Ivan Boeskys or Leona Helmsleys, and although there was a powerful mafia in Philadelphia, I did not see any dons, either. Approximately three fourths of these defendants were nonwhite. Almost 80 percent were high school dropouts. Many were functionally illiterate. Almost a third had some history of mental problems, were retarded, or had been in special schools. One dreary day my court reporter said plaintively, "Judge, why can't we get a better class of criminal?"

Not all of these offenders were sentenced to probation, obviously. But I had my own criteria or guidelines—very different from those established by most states and the federal government—for deciding on a punishment. My primary concern was public safety. The most important question I asked myself was whether the offender could be deterred from committing other crimes. No one can predict with certainty who will or will not commit a crime, but there are indicators most sensible people recognize as danger signals.

First, was this an irrational crime? If an arsonist sets a fire to collect insurance, that is a crime but also a rational act. Such a person can be deterred by being made to pay for the harm done and the costs to the fire department. However, if the arsonist sets fires just because he likes to see them, it is highly unlikely that he can be stopped from setting others, no matter how high the fine. Imprisonment is advisable even though it may be a first offense.

Second, was there wanton cruelty? If a robber maims or slashes the victim, there is little likelihood that he can safely be left in the community. If a robber simply displays a gun but does not fire it or harm the victim, then one should consider his life history, provocation, and other circumstances in deciding whether probation is appropriate.

Third, is this a hostile person? Was his crime one of hatred, and does he show any genuine remorse? Most rapes are acts of hostility, and the vast majority of rapists have a record of numerous sexual assaults. I remember one man who raped his mother. I gave him the maximum sentence under the law—20 years—but with good behavior, he got out fairly quickly. He immediately raped another elderly woman. Clearly, few rapists can safely be left in the community, and in my tenure, I incarcerated every one.

Yet gang rape, although a brutal and horrifying crime, is more complicated. The leader is clearly hostile and should be punished severely. Yet the followers can't be so neatly categorized. Some may act largely out of cowardice and peer pressure.

Fourth, is this a person who knows he is doing wrong but cannot control himself? Typical of such offenders are pedophiles. One child abuser who appeared before me had already been convicted of abusing his first wife's child. I got him on the second wife's child and sentenced him to the maximum. Still, he'll get out with good behavior, and I shudder to think about the children around him when he does. This is one case in which justice is not tough enough.

By contrast, some people who have committed homicide present very little danger of further violence—although many more do. Once a young man came before me because he had taken aim at a person half a block away and then shot him in the back, killing him. Why did he do it? "I wanted to get me a body." He should never get out. But the mandatory codes don't make great distinctions between him and another murderer who came before me, a woman who shot and killed a boy after he and his friends brutally gang-raped her teenage daughter.

I found this woman guilty of first-degree murder, but I found no reason to incarcerate her. She had four young children to support who would have become wards of the welfare department and probably would have spent their childhoods in a series of foster homes. I placed her on probation—a decision few judges now have the discretion to impose. She had not been arrested before. She has not been arrested since.

Of course, the vast majority of men, women, and children in custody in the United States are not killers, rapists, or arsonists. They're in prison for some type of theft—a purse snatching, burglary, or embezzlement. Many of these criminals can be punished without incarceration. If you force a first-time white-collar criminal to pay heavily for his crimes—perhaps three times the value of the money or property taken—he'll get the message that crime does not pay. As for poor people, stealing is not always a sign that the individual is an unreasonable risk to the community. It's often a sign that they want something—a car, Air Jordans—that they are too poor to buy themselves. Many of them, if they are not violent, can also be made to make some restitution and learn that crime doesn't pay.

Of course, to most of us, the idea of a nonprison sentence is tantamount to exoneration; a criminal sentenced to probation has effectively "gotten off." And there's a reason for that impression: Unless the probationer is required by the sentencing judge to perform specific tasks, probation is a charade. The probationer meets with the probation officer, briefly, perhaps once a month—making the procedure a waste of time for both. The officer duly records the meeting and the two go their separate ways until the probationer is arrested for another offense.

When I made the decision not to send a criminal to prison, I wanted to make sure that the probation system I sent them into had teeth. So I set firm conditions. If the offender was functionally illiterate, he was unemployable and would probably steal or engage in some other illegal activity once released. Thus in my sentencing, I sent him to school and ordered the probation officer to see that he went. (I use the masculine pronoun deliberately for I have never seen an illiterate female offender under the age of 60). I ordered school dropouts to get their high school equivalency certificates and find jobs. All offenders were ordered to pay restitution or reparations within their means or earning capacity to their victims. Sometimes it was as little as $5 a week. Offenders simply could not return to their old, feckless lifestyles without paying some financial penalty for their wrongdoing.

Monitoring probation wasn't easy for me, or the probation officers with whom I worked. Every day I'd come into my office, look at my calendar, and notice that, say, 30 days had passed since Elliott was let out. So I'd call the probation office. Has Elliott made his payment? Is he going to his GED class? And so on. If the answer was no, I'd hold a violation hearing with the threat of incarceration if the conditions were not met within 30 days. After I returned a few people to jail for noncompliance, both my offenders and their probation officers knew I meant business. (Few probation officers protested my demands; their jobs were more meaningful and satisfying, they said.)

Of course, probation that required education and work and payment plans meant real work for criminals, too. But there was a payoff both the probation officers and I could see: As offenders worked and learned and made restitution, their attitudes often changed dramatically.

Time and Punishment

My rules of sentencing don't make judgeship easier; relying on mandatory sentencing is a far better way to guarantee a leisurely, controversy-free career on the bench. But my rules are, I believe, both effective and transferable: an application of common sense that any reasonable person could follow to similar ends. What prevents Americans from adopting practical measures like these is a atavistic belief in the sanctity of punishment. Even persons who have never heard of Immanuel Kant or the categorical imperative to punish believe that violation of law must be followed by the infliction of pain.

If we Americans treated crime more practically—as socially unacceptable behavior that should be curbed for the good of the community—we might begin to take a rational approach to the development of alternatives to prison. We might start thinking in terms not of punishment but of public safety, deterrence, and rehabilitation. Penalties like fines, work, and payment of restitution protect the public better and more cheaply than imprisonment in many cases.

Mind you, sentencing guidelines are not inherently evil. Intelligent guidelines would keep some judges from returning repeat offenders to the streets and others from putting the occasional cocaine user away for 10 years. Yet those guidelines must allow more latitude for the judge and the person who comes before him. While some states' sentencing laws include provisions that allow judges to override the mandatory sentences in some cases, the laws are for the most part inflexible—they deny judges the freedom to discriminate between the hardened criminal and the Michael. Richard H. Girgenti, the criminal justice director of New York state, has long proposed that the legislature give judges more discretion to impose shorter sentences for nonviolent and noncoercive felonies. This common-sense proposal has not been acted on in New York or any other state with mandatory sentencing laws.

Current laws are predicated on the belief that there must be punishment for every offense in terms of prison time rather than alternative sentences. But when it comes to determining the fate of a human being, there must be room for judgment. To make that room, we must stop acting as if mathematic calculations are superior to human thought. We must abolish mandatory sentencing laws and change the criteria on which sentencing guidelines are based.

Why not permit judges more freedom in making their decisions, provided that they give legitimate reasons? (If a judge doesn't have a good reason for deviating—if he's a reactionary or a fool—his sentencing decision will be overturned.) And why not revise the guidelines to consider dangerousness rather than the nomenclature of the offense? If we made simple reforms like these, thousands of non-threatening, nonhabitual offenders would be allowed to recompense their victims and society in a far less expensive and far more productive way.

You may be wondering, after all this, if I have a Willie Horton in my closet—a criminal whose actions after release privately haunt me. I do. I sentenced him to 10 to 20 years in prison—the maximum the law allowed—for forcible rape. He was released after eight years and promptly raped another woman. I could foresee what would happen but was powerless to impose a longer sentence.

And then there are the other cases that keep me up nights: those of men and women I might have let out, but didn't. And those of people like Michael, for whom justice shouldn't have been a mathematical equation.

Critical Thinking

1. What is mandatory sentencing?
2. What led Judge Lois Forer to resign from her judicial post in Philadelphia?
3. Why, according to Lois Forer, was the book *Fair and Certain Punishment* so influential in fostering mandatory sentencing laws?
4. To what four main indicators did Judge Forer pay attention when deciding on an appropriate punishment for someone convicted of a crime?
5. What steps did Judge Forer take to monitor probation for those convicted in her court?

LOIS G. FORER, a former judge of the Court of Common Pleas of Philadelphia, is the author, most recently, of *Unequal Protection: Women, Children, and the Elderly in Court*.

From *Washington Monthly*, April 1992, pp. 12–14, 16–18. Copyright © 1992 by Washington Monthly. Reprinted by permission.

Kids, Not Cases

Judges make better decisions when children and their families—with adequate legal representation—participate in child welfare proceedings.

SUSAN ROBISON

I never went to court. I have been in and out of foster care since I was a baby, and I really resent that I never got the chance to speak on my behalf or even be present when my future was being discussed." This South Dakota foster youth's experience is all too common. In addition to being excluded from the courts that make life-altering decisions, many children in foster care do not receive the legal representation that the rest of us expect as a fundamental, democratic right.

In Colorado, during 12 years in foster care, 19-year-old Andrew has been in 42 placements. And not once was he present for the numerous court hearings about his case. Despite state statutes requiring that all children with dependency cases have an appointed advocate, an "attorney guardian ad litem" who acts in the child's best interest, Andrew has met with his only a couple of times, and they have never had what he considers a meaningful, private conversation.

Access to court and legal representation for children who have been abused or neglected can vary from case to case and even from proceeding to proceeding. Both the decision-making process and the results for children can stray far from legislative intent, often without legislators even knowing it. The courts, the ultimate decision makers in these cases, are far removed from legislative scrutiny.

Instead of playing the blame game that seems to dominate child welfare discussions, a growing number of legislators are determined to forge a new, more informed and productive dialogue with the courts. And that includes shining a light on court performance.

Kids in Court

Although executive branch child welfare agencies are more often in the public and legislative limelight, the courts have a powerful role in the lives of children who have been abused or neglected.

"Once you are in the system, your life is in their hands, not yours," says a former foster child from California. Courts decide whether children are removed from their homes and families, how long they remain in the system, and what education and health care services they receive. Only the courts sanction foster care, terminate parental rights and grant adoptions.

Historically, children have been barred from the courtroom because of the belief that it was inappropriate and unhealthy for the young to hear bad things about their parents. Many young people in foster care see it differently. They want a choice. These youths report that by the time they enter foster care, they've already experienced trauma. Court participation helps them gain a realistic view of their family and a sense of control—both important for getting on with their lives.

In a 2006 California survey, youths in foster care who attended court reported real benefits. Some were able to take an active role in decisions about their lives, while others found it helpful to simply be present and see how the decisions were made. Young people and their legal advocates believe that better decisions result when the judge can interact with children face-to-face instead of only reading a case file. The judge can observe the child's appearance and interaction with others, hear firsthand the child's hopes and opinions, and see that the child is getting older and needs a permanent family. One lonely child in foster care was unable to convince her case worker, foster parents or guardian ad litem that she desperately needed to see her sister at least once a week—despite busy schedules and conflicting demands on the adults' time. When she presented her case directly to the judge, a visitation arrangement that met her needs was accomplished.

A Kinder, Gentler Court

In some states, legislators have required courts to notify young people about hearings and to consider whether their presence is appropriate. Minnesota and California lawmakers make participation in court proceedings a right. Recent federal legislation supports this approach. It makes court and agency consultation with children a requirement for states to receive Title IV-E foster care funding.

At the same time, foster youths and their advocates are not saying that it should be business as usual in the courtroom. Los Angeles County, home to 36,000 children in foster care, allows all children over 4 years of age to attend court. According to Leslie Heimov of the Children's Law Center of Los Angeles, children need support from a caring adult before, during and after the proceeding. They also need special kid-friendly waiting areas, opportunity for private discussions with the judges, and plain talk instead of legal jargon.

Many lawmakers are surprised when they learn that vulnerable children in their state do not receive adequate legal representation and are not given the opportunity to speak directly to judges. After all, every state has enacted statutes requiring appointment of an advocate to obtain firsthand understanding of the child's situation and to make recommendations to the court. Thirty-five states require an attorney to represent the child. But rarely do either statutes or court rules define the attorney's role, specify duties and responsibilities, or describe the necessary training. And there are few mechanisms for legislators to monitor the workings of the judicial and legal aspects of the child welfare system.

Lawyers and Courts

All too often, capable lawyers find little incentive to represent abused and neglected children or their parents. Attorneys object that they are not appointed in time to prepare a case or allocated the necessary time, resources and compensation to perform even the most basic legal services. In New York City, poor compensation accompanied by higher caseloads and court backlogs led to an exodus of attorneys. In turn, families were disrupted, and children remained longer in foster care.

In addition to numerous caseloads and low pay, lack of specialized training and performance standards for both attorneys and judges plague the judicial process. Not only are procedures for handling dependency cases unique, but they require skilled professionals who understand the complex dynamics of troubled families and the maze of resources and rules for responding to them. Only half of the 2,000 judges participating in a 2004 survey had received child welfare training before hearing child abuse and neglect cases.

Legislative Oversight

Ensuring that children's voices are heard in court is but one example of the need for greater oversight over courts and the critical decisions they make. Federal and state statutes make courts responsible for overseeing the actions of child welfare agencies in individual cases, but who oversees the courts? Although legislation and investment in the judicial system are necessary, some legislators are beginning to think they are not enough. With the public's eyes and ears on state government, legislators feel a responsibility to monitor court performance and its impact on children and parents.

This summer, NCSL took the unusual step of convening a group of lawmakers, judicial leaders and child welfare agency executives to examine how legislators can help strengthen the courts on behalf of vulnerable children. These leaders quickly cut to the heart of their dilemma: the risk that vulnerable children are caught in the middle of the constitutional separation of powers among the three branches of government.

To ensure an independent judiciary, courts traditionally resist legislative oversight. A Minnesota judge worried that legislators would attempt to manage the judiciary. Privately, judges admit their fear that legislators will try to influence the cases of individual constituents.

"We hold the public purse strings and are responsible for some oversight of how it's spent," says Washington Representative Ruth Kagi, chair of the House Early Learning and Children's Services Committee and member of the Appropriations Committee. Fellow Washington Representative and Human Services Committee Chair Mary Lou Dickerson agrees: "The Legislature funds state agencies and expects them to be accountable. The courts need to be accountable for taxpayers' money, too."

Sitting Down Together

Consensus among legislators was that it's up to them to improve communication and understanding as well as accountability. According to Fernando Macias, a former New Mexico legislator who now serves as a district Children's Court judge, "It isn't one branch of government ignoring another, but there is no transition." Texas Representative Harold Dutton, chair of the House Juvenile Justice and Family Issues Committee, agrees: "Judges don't feel included in the development of legislation, but legislators don't hear from judges upfront."

To receive new federal Court Improvement Grants authorized in 2005, state courts have developed multidisciplinary commissions, and they are ready-made vehicles for legislators to hear the judicial perspective. In some states, legislators themselves have created court commissions or other workgroups, and they serve on these bodies in Arkansas, California, New York, North Dakota, Utah, Vermont and Washington.

"It's a continuing process of court-legislative education— not just during session," says Arkansas Judge Joyce Williams Warren.

Lives Behind the Numbers

Legislators now have better tools for monitoring court performance. National judicial and legal organizations have joined together to develop performance standards for courts that handle child dependency cases. State courts are taking advantage of federal court improvement grants to ramp up data collection and analysis, so more courts are able to provide statistics about the cases they hear, how they are handled, and how they progress.

But legislators worry that courts will game their numbers, and Judge Macias, the former New Mexico legislator, says that caution is justified. "Everybody—the court, child welfare agencies, even the legislature—paints the most positive picture possible," he says. Instead of disregarding data, judicial expert Mark Hardin of the National Child Welfare Resource Center on Legal and Judicial Issues warns legislators, "Be careful when using statistics in connection with requests for funding or for the expansion or termination of programs." Hardin advises policymakers to ask impartial resource people to help them interpret court numbers.

New Mexico Representative Jim Trujillo speaks for other legislators who want to see beyond the numbers to ensure that individual children and families are getting fair treatment, "I'm worried about the quality, not just numbers." Experts suggest a method called quality service reviews to scrutinize performance of the child welfare system—agencies and courts alike. Independent reviewers randomly select a few cases to examine in depth, dig beyond case files to interview key parties (children, parents, teachers or others who know the family, case workers, attorneys, foster parents, court appointed special advocates and others), and carefully analyze actions. Findings can help identify and correct problems that affect both individuals' lives and child welfare system performance.

Holding Courts Accountable

Some legislatures have gone beyond shining a public light on the courts to make them more accountable. The Oregon legislature has directly imposed court performance measures and requires the judiciary to report on them. In both Idaho and Oregon, the legislature refuses to approve the judicial budget unless courts meet statutory guidelines.

Judge Nancy Sidote Salyers retired from the Cook County, Ill., bench where she was presiding judge of the Child Protection Division. At a time when foster care caseloads were growing unchecked, she worked with the state child welfare agency to reduce the court's dependency caseload from more than 58,000 to 19,000 and to quadruple the number of permanent homes secured for children.

She says the key to better performance for kids is getting beyond separation of power. "Incentives and outcome-based legislation can be tied to a shared vision when the powers come together."

Judge Salyers invokes the words of Andy Warhol—words that many youth in foster would no doubt find true: "They say that time changes things, but you actually have to change them yourself."

Representing Parents

Parents also face serious court obstacles that ultimately delay safe and permanent homes for their children—barriers that lawmakers often assume legislation has eliminated. Although 39 states require counsel for parents at some point during a child abuse and neglect case, representation is often too little and too late.

One parent described an experience that is not unusual: "When I arrived at court that morning, I was told this is my lawyer. My lawyer sat down with me for five minutes, asked me a couple of things, and told me to admit to drug addiction. I wasn't told the procedure of court. I didn't have any idea what was happening, and I was very much afraid, because the most important thing in my life had just been lost."

Many parents—especially absent fathers—aren't engaged until parental rights are being terminated. Parents' absence robs the court of the opportunity to correct case information that is all too often inaccurate, to give instructions and explain orders, and to have a direct impact on parents' behavior. In Washington, a cost study requested by the Legislature showed that family reunification rates improved after appropriations for legal representation of parents increased.

Critical Thinking

1. Historically, what belief has led to children being barred from courtroom proceedings that will help determine their custodial arrangements?

2. What sorts of decisions do courts make with respect to children who come before them?

3. How many states do not require that a child be represented by an attorney in court proceedings on custodial arrangements and other similar matters? How many states do not require that parents be legally represented?

4. What can (and, according to Susan Robinson, should) state legislatures do to reform and improve court proceedings involving children's welfare

---

SUSAN ROBISON is a national consultant on child and family policies. A former NCSL staffer, she lives in Durango, Colo.

UNIT 5

Cities and Suburbs, Counties and Towns

Unit Selections

Learning Outcomes

- Examine the ability of local governments in metropolitan areas to cope with contemporary urban problems.

- Assess whether major metropolitan areas would be better served if they had only one metropolitan-wide local government instead of a fairly large number of smaller local governments, as they typically do under current arrangements.

- Examine the role(s) that annexation and de-annexation can play at the local government level in the United States.

- Identify policy innovations that a big city government such as the City of New York can introduce and which can then be copied by other government jurisdictions.

- Discuss some applications of modern technology that a city government can use to improve its effectiveness and, in turn, citizens' quality of life.

- Question how zoning regulations can be consistent with the private property rights of owners and justify zoning by city governments.

- Determine the sorts of services that the governments of big cities provide to their citizens.

- Describe the function and the functioning of a New England town meeting.

- Evaluate how desirable a component of local government a New England town meeting is.

Student Website

www.mhhe.com/cls

Internet References

Alliance for Innovation
www.transformgov.org

International City/County Management Association (ICMA)
www.icma.org

National Association of Counties (NACo)
www.naco.org

National Association of Towns and Townships (NATaT)
www.natat.org

National League of Cities (NLC)
www.nlc.org

More than three-quarters of Americans live in cities or in surrounding suburban areas. In these densely populated settings, local governments face great challenges and opportunities. One challenge is to provide services such as policing, schooling, sanitation, water, roads, and public transportation at a satisfactory level and at a cost that taxpayers can and will bear. An accompanying opportunity is the possibility of helping to create a local setting that improves the lives of residents in meaningful ways. The challenges and opportunities arise amid a formidable array of urban and suburban problems: crime, violence, drugs, deterioration of public schools, racial tension, financial stringencies, pollution, congestion, aging populations, decaying physical plants, breakdown of family life, and so forth.

Cities are the local government jurisdictions that generally govern areas with relatively high population density. Major metropolitan areas usually have a large city at their center and a surrounding network of suburbs under a number of smaller local government jurisdictions. In smaller metropolitan areas, a single county can encompass both the center city and its surrounding suburbs. Smaller cities may be part of suburban rings around larger cities, or they may exist independently of major metropolitan areas, with their own smaller network of surrounding suburbs.

Cities of all sizes generally provide more services to their residents than other kinds of local government jurisdictions do. Thus, residents of cities expect their city governments to provide water, a sewerage system, professional police and firefighting forces, public museums, parks and other such recreational facilities, and sometimes various other services such as public transportation that are associated with city life. By contrast, local governments in rural areas are not expected to provide such services. Local governments in suburban areas typically provide some but not all of them. With the greater range of services provided in cities come higher taxes and more government regulatory activities.

Like urban areas, suburbs come in various shapes and sizes. Some are called bedroom or commuter suburbs because people live there with their families and commute to and from the central city to work. Others have a more independent economic base. Local governments in suburbs have often emphasized quality education (i.e., good schools), zoning plans to preserve the residential character of the locale, and keeping property taxes within tolerable limits. Generally speaking, suburbs have a greater proportion of whites and upper- and middle-class people than cities do.

One problem facing suburban governments today stems from aging populations. Older people need and demand different services than the young families that used to occupy suburbs in greater proportions. It is not always easy to shift policy priorities from, for example, public schooling to public transportation and recreational programs for the elderly. A second problem is structural in nature and relates to the overlapping and usually noncontiguous local government jurisdictions in suburban

© Patrick Batchelder/Alamy

areas—school districts, sanitation districts, townships, counties, villages, boroughs, and so forth. The maze of jurisdictions often confuses citizens, and sometimes makes coordinated and effective government difficult.

The goals of small suburban local governments, one or more counties, and the central city government in a single metropolitan area often come into conflict in policy areas such as public transportation, school integration, air pollution, highway systems, and so forth. Sometimes common aims can be pursued through county government, through cooperative ventures between suburban and city governments, or through creation of metropolitan-wide special districts. Sometimes, through annexation or consolidation, a larger unit of general-purpose local government is formed in an attempt to cope with metropolitan-wide issues more easily.

The New England town meeting is a remarkable institution that dates back to the earliest local governments in what are now the six New England states. Today town meetings seem feasible only outside major cities. In many rural, semi-rural, and suburban areas of New England, local government centered on annual town meetings remains the norm. In such traditional New England towns, policymaking or legislative authority is vested in an annual meeting in which every registered voter in the town is entitled to participate. The contrast between this traditional form of participatory local government and, for example, the government of the City of New York and its eight million citizens helps illustrates the diversity of local government structures in the United States.

Selections in this unit mostly focus on problems and opportunities facing metropolitan areas and urban governments. But suburban jurisdictions and New England town meetings are also addressed.

How to Save Our Shrinking Cities

Witold Rybzynski and Peter D. Linneman

The first half of the twentieth century saw the widespread emergence of large cities in the United States. In 1900, there were only six cities with more than half a million inhabitants; only 50 years later, there were 17 such cities. Much of this urban growth was stimulated by two world wars and the government-supported expansion of war-related industries, most located in big Northeastern and Midwestern cities. The largest cities also benefited from the fact that for more than a decade after the Second World War the United States was the only country in the world with its manufacturing facilities intact.

It was inevitable that eventually things would change. Europe and Japan rebuilt themselves and challenged the dominance of U.S. urban manufacturing. The previous rapid growth of large cities began to level out, and new urbanization patterns emerged. One of these patterns was a change in the kind of cities Americans chose to live in. We differentiate between small cities (100,000 to 500,000 inhabitants) and large cities (more than 500,000 inhabitants). In 1900, eight million Americans lived in large cities as compared to less than five million in small cities.

Over the next 50 years, the total population of the large cities increased at a faster rate than that of the small cities, and, by 1950, the large cities were home to more than 26 million people, compared to about 13 million for the small cities. However, after 1950, this pattern began to reverse, and the total population of small cities grew more quickly. By 1990, for the first time in the twentieth century, more Americans lived in small cities than in large ones. This situation is likely to continue for some time. For example, between 1980 and 1990, the total population of the small cities increased by a remarkable 17.3 percent, compared to 6 percent for large cities, and 9.7 percent for the nation as a whole.

Forces of Change

What drove this reversal? The growth of small cities and the decline of large cities in the postwar period resembled the contemporary restructuring of the steel industry, where new small plants replaced old large mills. Technological advances made the old steel plants obsolete and took their toll on large cities. The confluence of river and barge commerce, railroads, and the telegraph fueled urban centralization throughout the nineteenth century. In the early 1900s, these forces were reinforced by the efficiencies of scale in urban infrastructure technology, such as water supply, sewage treatment, and streetcars. However, the post–World War II period witnessed the predominance of car and truck commerce, the expansion of air travel, the evolution of modern telecommunications, and massively improved efficiencies in the provision of sewer- and water-treatment facilities. All of these changes facilitated urban decentralization. Air conditioning opened up large parts of the country to year-round occupancy, just as heating technologies had done centuries before. Entertainment and communication technologies, including television, the VCR, and the personal computer, greatly reduced the sense of cultural inferiority and isolation that historically characterized life in small cities. Now, a small city with an airport and access to an interstate highway became just as good a place from which to conduct business as the downtown of a large city. Land economics allowed residents of small cities to enjoy larger (and newer) homes while still being able to see their favorite sports team, watch first-run movies, and enjoy concerts on cable TV.

These technological changes were fueled by the evolution of increasingly efficient capital markets. Capital markets actively sought out, and provided capital to, the best businesses, even if they were not in the biggest cities. Examples include: The Limited (Columbus, Ohio), WalMart (Bentonville, Arkansas), Microsoft (Seattle), and Turner Broadcasting (Atlanta). In addition, the municipal bond market increasingly provided equal access to capital (for public infrastructure) to cities and communities that had previously been too small to tap this source.

In older cities, an aging infrastructure imposed increasingly high capital and operating costs. In contrast, smaller cities had recently installed new infrastructure with low maintenance and operating costs. Older cities flourished when they were the newest, cheapest, and most modern. The mantel has now passed to a new set of cities and suburbs.

However, not all large cities were equally affected by these trends. Of the 77 cities with current (1990) population in excess of half a million, 51 actually grew by an average of 539 percent between 1950 and 1990. The nine largest of these (Los Angeles, Houston, San Diego, Dallas, Phoenix, San Antonio, San Jose, Jacksonville, and Columbus) grew from 1950 to 1970, and continued to grow during the next two decades. Nevertheless, 26 of the 77 cities shrank (by an average of 24 percent) between 1950 and 1990. Moreover, these shrinking cities include some of the largest in the country. Seven of the largest cities that declined (New York, Chicago, Philadelphia, Detroit, Baltimore, Washington, D.C., and Boston) have been doing so steadily since 1950. Indianapolis, Milwaukee, and Memphis declined in population between 1970 and 1990, although they grew between 1950 and 1970. Only one major city, San Francisco, reversed its 1950–70 decline during the following two decades.

Two facts stand out about the decline of the largest cities. First, the population losses have been significant. Chicago, New York, and Detroit have each lost about half a million people each since 1970 while Philadelphia has lost more than 350,000 over this period. Second, this decline is neither merely recent nor episodic. The cities that are shrinking have been doing so steadily for the last half of this century, and, according to the recent U.S. Census figures, the decline continues to the present day.

Some of the population increases in the growing cities have been the result of the aggressive annexation of surrounding cities and towns. Since 1950, the fastest growing seven major cities (Phoenix, San Jose, San Diego, Jacksonville, Houston, Dallas, and San Antonio) have each at least doubled their areas through annexation. In the case of Phoenix and Jacksonville, the increase in area has been more than twentyfold. Some of the urban growth, especially in California, Texas, and Florida, has been due to immigration. In fact, were it not for the steady flow of immigrants, cities like New York, Chicago, and Washington, D.C., would have experienced massive population losses.

Against this backdrop of the decline of the largest cities and the growth of our smaller cities, it is imperative to remember that every metro area has experienced population growth since 1950. Thus, although the cities of St. Louis, Cleveland, and Detroit lost about half their populations between 1950 and 1990, their metro areas each notably expanded. Similarly, while the city of Philadelphia lost about half a million people during this period, Philadelphia's metro area grew by more than a million. This means that the cities that shrank did so not because they were part of dying regional economies but, rather, in spite of strong regional growth.

Vertical Cities and Horizontal Cities

The cities that have declined can be called vertical cities while the growing ones are best thought of as horizontal cities. These two prototypes differ radically with respect to infrastructure, amenities, and housing stock. The vertical city, which evolved during the industrial era, has highway, mass transportation, and rail systems designed to link the suburbs to city center. Its population density is high, typically more than 10,000 persons per square mile. Its amenities include large public parks. And it is known for downtown offices, manufacturing, and shopping and cultural activities. Typically, about half of its housing stock was built before 1939. It is comprised primarily of rowhouses, walk-up flats, and apartment buildings that were located to permit walking (or riding mass transit) to work and play.

In contrast, the horizontal city evolved after World War II and is designed for rapid car and truck movement, not merely from suburb to city but also from suburb to suburb. There is very little mass transit or rail infrastructure. Instead, massive transportation expenditures have focused almost exclusively on facilitating auto travel. The density is low (typically less than 3,000 persons per square mile), and urban amenities are more private than public. Equally important is the fact that the housing stock is much newer, typically offering single-family houses with large backyards (and large garages to "house" cars). The horizontal prototype is not simply a newer or updated version of the vertical prototype—it is a different kind of city.

Much of the current interest in the historic preservation of old buildings and efforts to recreate the "old time" urban fabric romanticize cities of the past. The stark reality is that, for the majority of working people, the vertical city offered cramped and noisy housing, little privacy, and relatively crude public amenities. One only need stroll through Chinatown in New York on a hot summer day to get a sense of what everyday life was like for the common New Yorker 50 years ago. The vertical city was built to house immigrants who had little money and who could not afford cars. The horizontal city has been built for a society with much greater disposable income (as a result of real income growth and two-earner families) and different quality-of-life expectations. It is a city that owns (indeed loves) cars. It is a crude generalization, and one that the proponents of traditional urbanism resist, but the horizontal city seems to have provided a kind of life that the overwhelming majority of Americans consciously chose—in spite of their romantic image of the old vertical city.

Is population loss always a bad thing for a city? We think not. Cities with more than a million inhabitants were rare before the twentieth century. There is no reason to assume that a smaller city is worse than a large one. In fact, an argument can be made that when a city is smaller it is also more human in scale, more livable, less anonymous, with a more manageable and responsive government. The problem with the decline of U.S. cities is not a question of size but, rather, a question of who is leaving and who is staying.

The people moving out of our cities are predominantly middle-income families of all races while those remaining—and entering—are predominantly poor minorities. If the 77 largest American cities are evaluated in terms of a diverse set of social barometers, such as poverty and unemployment rates, the number of families on public assistance, infant mortality rates, and average household incomes, a clear pattern emerges. Comparing the cumulative average rates for the 26 cities that have shrunk since 1950, with the cumulative average rates for the 51 cities that have grown, the shrinking cities as a group are currently worse with respect to all of these social welfare indicators. Only crime levels appear to be comparable—and appallingly high—for both groups of cities, although even they are slightly higher in shrinking cities.

Cities with High Vacancy Rates

A city that has lost much of its population has—to borrow a real-estate phrase—a high vacancy rate. When a shopping mall has a high vacancy rate, the owner suffers not only because of the lost revenue on the empty space but also because the overall vitality and attractiveness of the center's shopping experience is diminished. This, in turn, makes other tenants more likely to vacate, depressing rents on leased space. So, too, for a city with a high vacancy rate: It suffers not only a loss to its tax base but, unless it is successfully repositioned, it becomes a less attractive place to live and work.

The owner of the mall with high vacancy rates has a limited number of options. To be more competitive he can lower rents or offer special lease terms in an attempt to attract and retain tenants. He can also offer special services to prospective (and current) tenants in order to raise occupancy. He can refurbish the mall to attract new tenants or "shrink" the mall so that its (now smaller) space is fully occupied. If this doesn't work, the costs associated with the operation of the mall may not be covered by its income, and, in the short run, the owner will have to absorb the losses. If, in the end, he cannot cover his costs, the owner will close the mall and seek an alternative, more profitable use.

Of course, you cannot close a city. Some cities have privatized parts of their urban services (such as garbage collection and education) in an attempt to reduce their operating costs. Like a troubled mall owner, a city with a high vacancy rate can try to refurbish itself by redeveloping its downtown. Examples of urban redevelopment projects include stadiums, aquariums, world trade centers, river-boat gambling, and convention centers. Unfortunately, these strategies generally yield a poor return on public funds.

Cities need to mimic the strategies of the shopping-center landlord by lowering taxes, reducing onerous regulations, increasing the levels of public services, and improving the quality of local infrastructure. But this requires an admission that excessive taxes, burdensome regulations, and inadequate services have contributed to the city's decline. Such admissions do not come easily to a generation of politicians who have lived on the uphill slope of the Laffer Curve, raising taxes and regularly bemoaning the levels of support received from Washington and state governments. Unfortunately, as documented by Robert Inman of the Wharton School, cities that have "high vacancy rate" problems have already reached the point where further increases in local taxes produce declining tax revenues and an even greater decline in urban occupancy. Upon reflection, this is not surprising—imagine the fate of a troubled shopping center if the owner continuously raised rents as vacancy rose.

What happens when a city loses population? The fiscal difficulties associated with a reduced tax base are obvious. But, like a shopping mall that loses tenants, a city that loses population experiences additional problems. First, although people have left, the cost of maintaining the old infrastructure designed for the larger population—the roads, sewers, and transit systems—remains. In the case of the cities that expanded during the early 1900s, this infrastructure is in need of extensive repair and replacement. Just like the mall owners, cities must decide which services to curtail. Most city managers (like most shopping-center owners) invariably choose to defer infrastructure maintenance.

A second effect of population shrinkage is a reduction in population density. In theory, this should increase the quality of life. However, density is usually reduced by the creation of irregular gaps in the urban density pattern. Although the densities in vertical cities are still three or four times greater than in the horizontal cities, the vertical city was designed to function most efficiently with relatively continuous concentrations of people. As depopulation occurs, not only does the provision of normal municipal services become more expensive (unplanned vacant space is expensive to secure and maintain) but there may no longer be a sufficient population base to support neighborhood social and retail activities in many areas. This results in services being further reduced, inducing those who can to move away. Similarly, depopulation in vertical cities creates a lack of social energy and dynamism, as well as a reduced sense of safety. In short, shrinkage undermines the strategic operating engine of a vertical city.

Perhaps even more importantly, a vertical city with population gaps no longer possesses a continuous urban fabric. Instead, it becomes a series of disjointed areas separated by unplanned abandoned and vacant areas. Servicing a discontinuous city is very expensive. At the very time that vertical cities need to find more efficient servicing techniques to offset their declining tax bases, they are faced with an increasingly inefficient and expensive population pattern.

Finally, shrinkage lowers the quality of urban life. Buildings remain vacant, most in various stages of total decay. Lots become empty as buildings are burned and collapse. These lots become dumps, strewn with garbage of all types. While vacant space in the countryside can be aesthetically pleasing, and horizontal cities frequently include massive tracts of vacant space, population gaps are disastrous for vertical cities. Vacant buildings become vulnerable to further vandalism. They also become havens for illegal activities—a breeding ground for diseases and unsafe playgrounds for children. Streets lined with empty lots and deserted buildings become indefensible spaces, veritable "wild zones." That urban dereliction is a cancer is an apt cliché. Population gaps are not merely symptoms, they are primary causes of the continued disintegration of urban life in vertical cities.

The Regional Government Solution

What is to be done? The most common political response has been to counteract the social costs associated with a shrinking (and increasingly poor) population by raising taxes. This is a self-destructive response that makes the city an even less attractive place to live and work. Mayors, planners, and city-government officials must learn to accept the fact that the older, shrunken vertical cities will never grow back to their earlier size and prosperity. The goal must be, instead, to make their cities more livable, more attractive, and, probably, even smaller. They must reconfigure their cities to be competitively viable in modern times.

An examination of the 1992 population figures for cities shows that, although a few cities like Oakland, Louisville, Akron, and Rochester, New York have managed to reverse their earlier decline and are growing (very modestly), most shrinking cities continue to shrink. True, the rates of population decline have generally slowed, perhaps suggesting that a sustainable city may be evolving. But Philadelphia, Boston, Washington, D.C., St. Louis, Detroit, and Baltimore, which shrank even more rapidly during the 1980s than during the previous decade, continue to lose population in the 1990s. Such cities must reinvent themselves, becoming better cities as they grow even smaller than they are today.

One solution commonly proposed for shrinking cities is regional government. Since metropolitan areas as a whole are expanding, linking (poor) shrinking cities to (relatively rich) growing suburbs appears to provide the former with access to the financial resources of the latter. This argument has been advanced recently by David Rusk in *Cities Without Suburbs*. He presents convincing evidence that new growing cities (e.g., Houston, Phoenix, and San Diego) that have annexed suburban counties have many advantages over older cities whose boundaries remained largely unchanged.

There are, however, practical difficulties with the regional government proposal. Regional government is constitutionally difficult in most states; only Portland, Oregon is part of a directly elected regional government. It is true that several cities, such as Houston, Miami, Jacksonville, Charlottesville, Indianapolis, Nashville, and Minneapolis, have a system of cost sharing. However, with the exception of Minneapolis and Indianapolis, these are all growing cities. Troubled shrinking cities have little to offer suburban counties. As a result, suburbanites—most of whom consciously fled the city to leave its problems behind—can be expected to oppose any attempts at regionalization. The central cities themselves will resist, especially those with large numbers of ethnic minorities, who would lose their hard won political clout if they were incorporated into a larger, wealthier regional electorate.

In any case, regional government has its drawbacks. While size may generate some modest economies of scale with respect to infrastructure and finance, it also greatly increases inefficiencies of scale for the delivery of many services. Regional government would be more remote from—hence less responsible to—the voters, resulting in more corruption and inefficiency. Regional government, while it may solve the problems of servicing poor areas, will not address issues like an old and noncompetitive housing stock and the population gaps already prevalent in vertical cities.

Smaller Is Better

The clock cannot be turned back. The industrial cities that grew rapidly during the first half of the twentieth century (and shrank almost as rapidly during the second half) will never recover their primacy. History teaches that cities grow and decline. The most dramatic example is probably ancient Rome, which shrank from about a million at its imperial zenith to less than 100,000 by the Middle Ages. The population of Venice peaked in the seventeenth century at 180,000, but, as its mercantile empire collapsed, the city shrank, reaching a low point of 132,000 in 1880. The population in Venice today is only about 137,000. The populations of the great industrial cities of northern Britain—Glasgow, Liverpool, and Manchester—peaked in 1900 and have been declining since. The population of Vienna peaked in the decade before the First World War and, today, is about 20 percent smaller than at its zenith.

The critical lesson of Vienna, Venice, and even Glasgow (which has recently experienced a modest revival) is that a smaller city can be made a good place to live. Using these cities as role models, the question for shrinking cities is not, "How can we grow big again?" but rather, "How can we prosper and have a wonderful, smaller city?"

A fundamental change in mind set is required once we accept that smaller can be better. A city that has irretrievably lost large amounts of its population needs to examine ways to redesign itself to become more compact, perhaps even smaller in area. This will not be easy. City planners have traditionally favored growth and expansion. It is now time for planners to look for ways to shrink our cities. Just as physicians should allow gracious and healthy decline as people age, so too must our planners manage older cities. However, just as aging is not merely adolescence in reverse, urban planning for shrinkage is fundamentally different than planning for growth.

Historically, vertical cities expanded from the center by developing land at the periphery, by building on flood plains and near urban disamenities (e.g.; railroads), and by extending their urban infrastructure. But a shrinking city cannot merely retract its perimeter. Population losses have not been experienced equally across all parts of the city. Outlying parts of the city are generally quite strong, as are some city centers. Between these areas lies a complex web of decrepit housing stock and abandoned industry but also strong neighborhoods.

Are there alternative uses for the empty tracts? One could imagine formally planned versions of what has occurred in an unfunded and unplanned way in Detroit and East St. Louis, where vast empty lots are reverting to a sort of urban wilderness. In some cases, empty land might be turned into parks and recreation sites. This requires funds to undertake the expensive process of rehabilitation, soil replacement, and landscaping. The City of New York currently owns 20,000 vacant lots and has proposed asking private corporations to pay for converting empty land into parks and playgrounds. In return, the city would allow the companies to use the space for their own advertising. Corporate sponsorship is expected to provide on-going maintenance, which was lacking with earlier efforts, such as the Lindsay administration's "vest pocket parks." There are also commercial outdoor recreation possibilities. A developer has recently built a 30-acre golf course on vacant land in downtown Chicago, near the convention center. Large tracts could be consolidated and sold to the U.S. Department of the Interior for the creation of environmental zones, belated versions of the urban green belts that were a staple of Garden City planning in the early 1900s.

Another option would be to take advantage of the availability of empty land to begin to transform the vertical city into something that more closely resembles the horizontal postwar prototype. The three- and four-story rowhouses that characterize cities like Baltimore and Philadelphia were built at now commercially unacceptable densities of 30 to 40 dwellings per acre. Down-zoning of residential areas would allow two-story, semidetached houses at lower densities of about 20 dwellings per acre, or detached cottages of 5 to 10 dwellings per acre. However, such densities are only affordable if cities greatly reduce their development costs and regulations. In reducing these burdens they need to strive to become competitive with the most competitive suburb. If old cities cannot annex surrounding suburbs, they can, at least, begin slowly to transform part of their housing stock and begin to provide the kind of housing that today's households desire—single-family homes with space for backyards and off-street parking—rather than continuing to offer them a housing stock designed for their grandparents. The combination of much lower density housing with easy access to high-density downtown amenities may be the starting point for a new, post-industrial, urban prototype.

A Radical Proposal

Cities should also consider even more drastic alternatives. For example, they could de-annex parts of their territory to private developers. If large tracts, in excess of 100 acres, say, were sold as de-annexed, unincorporated areas with associated suburban cost structures, it is possible that developers would find this an attractive opportunity to create new "suburban" municipalities in the central areas of the city. Prototypes include such communities as River Oaks in Houston and Highland Park and University Park in Dallas. These "suburban" communities have been developed within the fabric of the city boundaries. New municipalities would be legally independent of the city. They would control their own governments, schools, and regulations. Like most suburbs, we suspect they would preserve a high degree of autonomy and probably a degree of exclusiveness. In fact, these new municipalities would probably need to alter traffic flows through the surrounding city into the community in order to provide the type of housing sought by today's buyers. Given the pattern of new planned communities in the United States, some form of common interest housing development governed by homeowner associations is likely to result.

The sale by the city of such property would create a more viable smaller city. How? First, the sale of the land would generate much needed funds, which would be used to offset years of deferred maintenance of urban infrastructure. Given the differential cost of operation and development in an unincorporated suburban municipality versus the city, the value derived from selling such land could be substantial. The city would also no longer be responsible for the maintenance and security of the land once it becomes a legally independent community. Third, and perhaps most importantly, although the city itself would shrink, the city's urban fabric would be enhanced as the new municipality developed. Many of the population gaps in the urban fabric could be filled in. There can be little doubt that these vacant parcels would develop more rapidly and successfully as independent suburban communities rather than as part of the city. In short, the city would be smaller, richer, and less vacant. At the same time, the population cavities would start to disappear.

Critical impediments to altering the current state of vacant urban tracts include irrational environmental standards. Too often these regulatory standards and procedures ask the irrelevant question, "Is it perfectly clean?" rather than the more pragmatic question, "Is it cleaner than it would have otherwise been?" The imposition of 1990s environmental sensibilities on areas that provided the factory jobs for previous generations means that massive tracts in urban areas are forever doomed to be economically undeveloped. As a result, the soil remains contaminated, the chemicals continue to seep into the groundwater, children continue to play in these abandoned lots, and the urban fabric continues to deteriorate. Environmental regulators, like city politicians, must realize that these areas will not be developed (and hence no environmental improvement will occur) unless dramatic compromises are made. These compromises may involve using federal funds to clean up these properties. Alternatively, development could be allowed if it significantly improves the environmental quality of the property, even though such clean-up may fall considerably short of current standards.

Future City

In our view, consolidation and de-annexation are not a "desirable" option for a city; however, for many shrinking cities, we see no other viable alternative. When population loss has passed a certain point, urban revival is likely to require drastic measures. Rehabilitation has usually worked only in downtown areas. Enterprise zones and empowerment zones have proved to be only marginally effective—where they have succeeded at all. Besides, they depend on the infusion of federal or state funds, which are not always available.

In any case, the obstacles to dealing effectively with urban shrinkage are massive, even possibly insurmountable. But to solve a problem, reality must be faced. In this case, the reality is that many cities will continue to shrink. Municipal politicians whose electoral bases will be eroded by consolidation or de-annexation can be expected to resist the idea of downsizing. Since the inhabitants of many of these affected areas will be minorities, the politics of consolidation and shrinkage will be opposed by these groups. Neighborhood activists, whose careers have been spent trying to promote local economic development from within will view shrinkage policies as defeatist, not the least because they will lose their own political power bases. Moreover, if selected urban areas are allowed to become autonomous suburban municipalities, the city as a whole will have to be protected from complete disintegration.

Shrinkage will also be seen by many as weakening the mechanism that has traditionally been used to elicit federal urban aid. Historic preservationists will undoubtedly object to wholesale demolition, since even decrepit areas contain buildings of architectural merit, and some of the worst areas are the locations of so-called industrial landmarks. Obviously, much will depend on how successfully consolidation deals with issues of dislocation, new housing, and new community services. But the challenge is clear: Our cities must be radically redesigned to be both better and smaller.

Critical Thinking

1. What growth pattern occurred in American cities during the first half of the twentieth century? The second half?

2. Why did small cities grow faster than large cities in the post-World War II era?

3. What distinguishes "horizontal" from "vertical" cities and what growth patterns did each have in the twentieth century?

4. What are some of the problems that accompany a city's loss of population?

5. What are the limitations of the regional government approach as a solution to the problems of shrinking cities?

6. What is the "radical proposal" that the authors of this article suggest as the best response to the shrinking of a major city?

WITOLD RYBZYNSKI is Martin and Margy Meyerson Professor of Urbanism at the University of Pennsylvania. His *A Clearing in the Distance* is published by Simon & Schuster. **PETER D. LINNEMAN** is the Albert Sussman Professor of Real Estate, Finance and Public Policy at the University of Pennsylvania and serves as senior managing director of Equity International Properties.

An earlier version of this article appeared in the *Warton Real Estate Review*, Fall 1997.

The Big Apple: Urban Incubator

Under Mayor Michael Bloomberg, New York City is becoming the "new California," where policy innovations are born.

ALAN GREENBLATT

Michael Bloomberg wants you to cut down on your salt. The mayor of New York City doesn't really plan to control how much salt you shake onto your fries; instead, his National Salt Reduction Initiative targets packaged and restaurant foods that account for nearly 80 percent of the average American's sodium intake. It may seem like overreaching for a municipal leader to try to dictate terms to giant food companies, but since Bloomberg's health officials launched the initiative early this year, he has enlisted the support of two dozen other local and state health departments. The group has won commitments from 16 companies to cut back on the salt in selected products, but the goal is clearly to push the Food and Drug Administration to set industry-wide standards. "Obviously, it has to be done nationally if it's to be done at all," says Linda Gibbs, New York City's deputy mayor for health and human services.

No one in the food industry discounts Bloomberg's chances of getting that done. Former members of his team are sprinkled throughout the Obama administration, including in the major health agencies, and the Big Apple has already demonstrated that it can change the national terms of debate when it comes to public health.

A comprehensive smoking ban enacted there in 2003 has spread to jurisdictions all over the country. After a dozen cities and states, encompassing about 20 percent of the U.S. population, essentially copied New York's legislation banning transfat, some restaurant chains replaced their old recipes with healthier ones. Likewise, after New York City began requiring restaurants to post calorie counts for their menu items, many other cities embraced variations of the concept. The National Restaurant Association—whose New York state branch sued twice, unsuccessfully, to block Bloomberg's law—eventually endorsed similar national requirements to avoid confronting a patchwork of regulations in different parts of the country. Congress included them in the health care overhaul legislation that it enacted in March.

"New York City has been extraordinary in the public health world," says Michael Jacobson, the executive director of the Center for Science in the Public Interest, a nutrition advocacy

Thinking Big

- From education and the environment to housing, public safety, and health, Mayor Michael Bloomberg has made his city a testing ground for policy innovation.
- "New York City is just the world's largest laboratory."
- Critics say that Bloomberg hasn't addressed problems such as poverty, inequality, inadequate revenues, and Wall Street's decline.

group. "On those issues, numerous other cities and states have followed New York's lead."

The city has made its mark in many other policy matters as well. From education and the environment to housing, public safety, and poverty programs, it has arguably emerged as the "new California"—where policy innovations are born and then widely copied by many other jurisdictions, including the federal government.

"New York City is just the world's largest laboratory," Memphis Mayor AC Wharton Jr. says.

Wall Street may not be as robust as it was a few years ago, and some of Bloomberg's economic development programs have yet to pay major dividends in the recession's wake. But at a time when innovation in governance seems to be happening in cities such as Youngstown, Ohio, and Detroit—places that are "in the process of managing decline," as Patrick Phillips, the CEO of the Urban Land Institute, puts it—the Bloomberg administration is thinking about how New York can enhance its reputation as the nation's most vibrant city.

A Whole System of Change

Bloomberg's formal blueprint for the city of 2030 is New York's first long-term planning document in 40 years. No one can yet say if the plan will succeed in nurturing the city's growth and livability, but Philadelphia, San Francisco, and other cities are already closely imitating Bloomberg's vision. What's more, his core notion of linking what have traditionally been considered separate, if not conflicting, issues in a mayoral portfolio—economic growth, environmental sustainability, and quality of life—is having a broad impact. "In some ways, mayors are just starting to realize the whole set of things going on in New York," says Carol Coletta, the president of CEOs for Cities, a Chicago-based nonprofit. "You can pick up one idea, but it's the whole system of changes in New York that makes it so exciting."

The Bloomberg administration, which won election in 2001 and is now in its third term, seeks what Phillips calls an "integrated perspective": Instead of thinking about individual projects, City Hall is developing policies that address large, underlying problems. The city has to deal with the costs of obesity and chronic diseases, so it has targeted such root causes as smoking and salt. Where the city needs more housing, rather than seeking a one-off deal to foster an apartment block, it looks for a way to reshape an entire area through job creation and transit and all of the other elements of a thriving neighborhood. "It's difficult to get mayors to focus less on brick-and-mortar projects and more on the kinds of decisions you have to make to attract that investment," Phillips says, but "that influence is now percolating across the country in small cities and big cities."

It's also showing up in the Obama administration. Bloomberg's former housing commissioner, Shaun Donovan, is putting these ideas into play as President Obama's Housing and Urban Development secretary. Donovan has been perhaps the lead convener in formulating Obama's nascent urban policy, working with the Environmental Protection Agency, the Transportation and Energy departments, and other agencies to wed programs together at the local level. The idea is to plan with a "place-based" focus, which means considering how programs such as worker training, housing, and environmental cleanup can operate symbiotically within a locale. The programs that address multiple priorities ought to be the ones that move forward, replacing the old paradigm of isolated projects funded by separate agencies.

Many disparate players have influenced the programs that Donovan and the White House Office of Urban Affairs are pursuing. The Brookings Institution's Metropolitan Policy Program holds a lot of sway among local officials and the administration; and other mayors, including Chicago's Richard M. Daley and Denver's John Hickenlooper, can claim considerable credit for the new approach.

Clearly, though, Bloomberg has had an impact. "Donovan comes from Bloomberg," says MarySue Barrett, president of Chicago's Metropolitan Planning Council. "It's not like these federal officials dreamed this up in a vacuum. It's actually what metropolitan places have come to on our own."

Bike Lanes and Budgets

People tend to hold their mayors to task for trash pickup, public safety, and fiscal stability rather than for their ability to persuade other cities—or even Cabinet secretaries—to imitate

their initiatives. Bloomberg, moreover, hasn't had an unerring Midas touch as mayor. He has chased his share of urban get-rich-quick schemes, such as a failed stadium deal and a hapless Olympics bid. The state rejected one of his signature ideas, a congestion pricing fee for people who drive their cars into Manhattan during peak traffic hours. "I don't think he's solved the basic problems of New York City, which are job creation and income inequality," says Joel Kotkin, an author and scholar in urban futures at Chapman University in California.

Bloomberg's large and highly engaged public-relations and political teams have unquestionably hyped many of his success stories. And critics say that some of his celebrated ideas, such as turning Times Square into a pedestrian plaza and opening up miles of bike lanes, don't count for much in a city that is facing a $5 billion deficit. "The health innovations, I basically support, but are they essential to the city's future? Not remotely," says Fred Siegel, a senior fellow at the Manhattan Institute. "Much of what he's doing is creating a platform for himself, presenting himself as a national and international figure."

Even Bloomberg's critics concede, however, that the city's look and feel have improved on his watch. Putting aside congestion pricing, his administration has succeeded in "calming" and improving transportation throughout the city. It has "upzoned" abandoned brownfields and unlocked long-abandoned stretches of property for development. The city has encouraged high-density housing around subway stations and added 500 acres of parkland—notably along the Manhattan Waterfront Greenway.

This spring, Coney Island opened its first amusement park in 50 years. "New York hadn't been thought of as a waterfront city since Marlon Brando," says Kathryn Wylde, president of the Partnership for New York City, the local chamber of commerce. "That was a long time ago and a different sort of waterfront."

Given its size and prominence, New York has always been a center of urban innovation. Central Park was the first landscaped public park in the country. Thomas Brophy, a city fire marshal in the early 20th century, practically invented the science of arson investigation. During the Depression, Mayor Fiorello La Guardia pursued a policy of slum clearance and construction of low-cost public housing that would serve as a national model until Robert Moses, the city's "master builder" of the 1960s, took it to extremes.

Mayor Rudy Giuliani lowered the city's crime rates during his two terms from 1994 to 2001, largely through aggressive precinct-by-precinct statistical analysis that other cities have widely imitated. In certain ways, Bloomberg has continued Giuliani's attack on crime, but the two mayors' managerial approaches are starkly different. Giuliani was a notorious micromanager and attention-grabber. When his police commissioner, William Bratton, began getting attention for the crime reduction—he made the cover of *Time* in 1996—Giuliani fired him rather than share the spotlight.

Bloomberg, by contrast, has given his police commissioner, Ray Kelly, plenty of latitude. The mayor generally delegates authority freely and has allowed other city officials to emerge as the public faces of prominent initiatives such as the transfat ban or the push to promote charter schools. He has been widely

Making a Difference

Not every policy idea that Michael Bloomberg has promoted as mayor has worked to perfection, and not all the ideas he's tried were his own. Bloomberg has borrowed freely from other U.S. cities and from London, Sao Paulo, Brazil, and Tokyo.

It is fair to say, however, that many of the ideas conceived, or at least tested, in New York have spread to other cities. Bloomberg's administration has left some mark on just about every issue of concern to urban officials, particularly transportation, housing, and public health.

Poverty

Bloomberg, "someone who could, frankly, be totally aloof from poverty, has such an intimate grasp of poverty and its effects," says Memphis Mayor AC Wharton Jr. Wharton, like other mayors, has consulted with Bloomberg on poverty issues. A delegation from San Antonio recently visited Manhattan to study New York's methods for helping poor households and communities gain better access to banking.

One anti-poverty idea that Bloomberg borrowed from overseas didn't work out so well. In March, the city announced that it would discontinue its conditional cash-transfer program, called Opportunity NYC, which gave poor families money for taking steps such as getting vaccinations and health checkups for children, and making sure they attend school. The program was begun as a pilot project supported by private funds (including money from Bloomberg's own foundation), but it showed few results. That same month, however, the U.S. Commerce Department adopted a method that New York City had developed for measuring poverty—examining expenses such as taxes, child care, and housing, as well as government assistance, rather than using the standard method of comparing income with only the cost of food.

Public Safety

It is fair to say that, aside from his performance after the terrorist attacks of September 11, 2001, the greatest legacy of Bloomberg's predecessor, Rudy Giuliani, was making New Yorkers feel secure again. It became the safest big city in the country, according to the FBI. Smarter community policing, better use of statistics, and low tolerance for minor infractions—along with a drop in the drug trade—helped bring down New York's crime rate by 57 percent.

Bloomberg has successfully followed the same path. Overall crime in 2009 was down by 35 percent from 2001, Giuliani's last year in office, and the murder rate was the lowest it's been since the city began compiling comparable statistics in the 1960s. Bloomberg has also given the NYPD important new responsibilities—1,000 officers, including a dozen stationed in trouble spots around the world, devote their time to intelligence and counterterrorism.

His pet initiative, Mayors Against Illegal Guns, which he guides in tandem with Boston Mayor Thomas Menino, has had difficulty gaining traction in an era that favors gun owners' rights. Their campaign suffered a big setback on June 28 when the Supreme Court ruled that localities cannot ban handguns. But New York has made a splash by running undercover investigations at out-of-state gun shows.

Environment

Over the past five years, many cities have tried to outdo one another with promises to combat climate change by reducing their carbon footprint. Many of their pledges have proved to be more symbolic than effective. New York, however, has been widely credited with taking some important steps.

Bloomberg's proposed $8 congestion pricing charge for cars entering Manhattan went nowhere in Albany. And he can't match Chicago Mayor Richard M. Daley's record in promoting green roofs. But New York is outpacing other cities when it comes to keeping its promise to plant 1 million trees. Aside from his emphasis on open space and the city's expansion of parkland, Bloomberg has set in place one of the strictest "green building" codes in the nation.

In December, the City Council approved legislation requiring New York's biggest buildings to reduce their energy consumption and to pay for energy audits and better lighting. Two months later, a panel of experts convened by the city released a list of 100 recommendations to make the city's building code even more rigorous on energy use. "We are the first major city to enact a green building code providing real incentives and ultimately mandates for retrofitting," says Kathryn Wylde, president of the Partnership for New York City. Bloomberg has been pushing regulations and incentives to convert the city's taxi fleet to hybrid vehicles.

In May, the New York Academy of Sciences issued a report praising the Bloomberg administration's attention to climate change, but its long list of recommendations suggested that the city still has a lot of work to do.

Education

Mayoral control of schools is something that Bloomberg's predecessors sought for decades. Since the state Legislature granted school control to Bloomberg in 2002, he and his chancellor, Joel Klein, have aggressively tried numerous strategies for improvement. "It would be hard to think of any big policy issues in education where Klein hasn't played an important role," says Michael Petrilli, vice president for national programs and policy at the Fordham Institute, a conservative education think tank.

Klein has had a "multiplier effect by getting people excited about reform," Petrilli says, because when his employees move to other places, they take the ideas with them. Baltimore's schools chief, Andres Alonso, for instance, had served as Klein's chief of staff and deputy chancellor. Klein's ideas—and the NYPD's ideas as well—have also traveled to many other cities.

New York has been at the forefront in promoting many fashionable education policies, including making schools smaller; incorporating formerly spurned charter schools as part of the district's overall strategy; and recruiting teachers who don't come from a traditional education-school background. New York's method of grading schools and using the grades in closure decisions has become a common approach for states in their applications for federal Race to the Top grants. Its "mutual consent" teacher-hiring provision morphed into a highly touted tenure evaluation law that Colorado enacted in April, as well as a closely watched new contract that Washington, D.C., teachers ratified on June 2.

"Joel Klein has given a lot of cover for changes that have happened elsewhere," says Andrew Rotherham, a prominent education consultant. "The aggressiveness with which they're doing things would be notable in any case, but the fact that it's New York, which is so large and is such a cultural touchstone, gives it additional resonance."

Like a lot of other big-city superintendents, Klein has tried out many ideas and has clearly improved school performance. The question is, how much? Sol Stern, a senior fellow at the Manhattan Institute, says that New York

City's results on state test scores "are completely inflated." Results of the National Assessment of Educational Progress tests came out in May. They showed that New York's fourth-graders are reading better than they were when Bloomberg and Klein took control, but eighth-graders show little improvement. "No doubt, New York City did better than Detroit and Chicago," Stern says, "but to me, that doesn't show fantastic achievement."

Julia Vitullo-Martin, a scholar of New York issues and a former city official, says that the proof of Klein's success lies in growing enrollments. "The big problem in New York—and this is something nobody could have predicted 20 years ago—is the tremendous increase in the demand for public schools."

—A.G.

praised for hiring talented people from outside his inner circle and from outside government altogether.

Bloomberg's financial information-and-media company landed him at No. 8 on *Forbes* magazine's list of the richest Americans last year. Many people speculate that his ability to finance his own campaigns means that he has not racked up political obligations to reward supporters with plum jobs. "He hires people more for their professional credentials than their loyalties to him," says Thomas Wright, the executive director of the Regional Plan Association, an independent research group covering the New York City metropolitan area, "and then he has them working on reforms and institutionalizing them."

Bloomberg's commissioners and deputy mayors are pretty much required not only to manage existing programs but also to contribute innovative ideas, Wright says. The mayor has fostered a sense of healthy competition at City Hall and among the agencies that they need to create the next new thing to improve life in the city. "He's been a huge supporter of ideas, many of which were called political suicide when they came up," Deputy Mayor Gibbs says. "As a commissioner, you really value that the important thing is to try, even if that means you have failures. If you don't fail, you're not trying."

That may sound like so much buttering up of the boss, but it is a strikingly unusual sentiment in the generally risk-averse culture of local government. Bloomberg often makes the same point. He retains the contrarian instincts that served him well as an entrepreneur, and he keeps looking for ways to learn not just from failures but also from apparent success.

Even after what is still probably viewed as his most heroic moment—his performance in informing and calming the city during the 2003 blackout—Bloomberg immediately sought input from inside and outside city government about what had gone wrong. He took the findings about breakdowns in communication and transportation and announced them himself to reporters, earning some rotten headlines but learning a lot in the bargain.

Not surprisingly for a man who amassed one of the world's great fortunes by moving information around rapidly, he is obsessed with data. He came into a City Hall where paper

notebooks abounded and BlackBerrys were practically unknown—a picture he quickly changed. Today, "there is a data-driven culture in New York that has been adapted to various degrees elsewhere in the best-run cities," says the Urban Land Institute's Phillips. "Not only has it changed local government decision-making, but anybody who does business with local government has to be able to defend their position using metrics, to defend the impact of their project."

When Bloomberg's subordinates develop an idea, they must show the mayor that they've done their homework—the specific ways the initiative will save money or otherwise improve the city. Turning Times Square into a pedestrian plaza "was not just a decision to do something because it would be cool," says Jeff Kay, director of operations for the mayor's office. The controversial move grew out of extensive research about transportation speeds and the potential impact of the change on small business.

In a city that has been challenged by declining revenue throughout much of Bloomberg's administration—despite his willingness to impose hefty tax increases—the mayor's team has consistently looked for ways to make government more efficient. New York was not the first city to set up a 311 citizen complaint hotline, but it has used the data drawn from the calls to identify the gaps in government performance. An uptick in complaints about graffiti led to the realization that six agencies shared responsibility for cleanup. Bloomberg reduced that number to two. "The measurement of things that matter to citizens and the transparency of those measurements all combine to make this administration in New York very special indeed," says Coletta of CEOs for Cities.

It's the Money

The most common complaint about Bloomberg is that he has been able to buy off critics because of his wealth and his willingness to use it. He has also spent public money freely to appease doubters. He used a 43 percent pay increase, for example, to sweeten an education contract that included changes in hiring practices and other policies that the teachers union wasn't crazy about.

From the Hudson to the Potomac

Along with such prominent New Yorkers as Secretary of State Hillary Rodham Clinton and Treasury Secretary Timothy Geithner, the Obama administration is heavily populated with former officials who have served under Mayor Michael Bloomberg.

The connections between the two administrations extend beyond the folks who have held formal offices in each of them. Steven Rattner, President Obama's first auto-industry czar, was a co-founder of the Quadrangle Group, a private equity firm that managed Bloomberg's blind trust (and later came under legal investigation in a pension-fund scandal). Rebecca M. Blank was an adviser to the Bloomberg task force that crafted poverty measures; she used the same template for a new federal formula she implemented this spring as an undersecretary at the Commerce Department.

Shaun Donovan

Obama administration: Housing and Urban Development secretary.

Bloomberg administration: Housing commissioner.

Background: Donovan once wanted to design cars, but he has spent his entire career in housing, working for a lender and a nonprofit community group before joining Bloomberg's government in 2004. He took a leave of absence to work on Obama's presidential campaign and never looked back.

Thomas Frieden

Obama administration: Director, Centers for Disease Control and Prevention.

Bloomberg administration: Health Commissioner.

Background: In his New York City office, the physician kept a bowl of condoms handy for visitors. Before Frieden took over, the city's health department devoted most of its attention to communicable diseases. When he arrived and found that 70 percent of the city's deaths resulted from other causes, he refocused its efforts on issues such as smoking and transfat.

Jarrod Bernstein

Obama administration: Director of local affairs, Homeland Security Department.

Bloomberg administration: Deputy director, Community Assistance Unit.

Background: Not to be confused with Jared Bernstein, Vice President Biden's chief economist, Jarrod Bernstein began his career as a press secretary for the city's office of emergency management before moving into community affairs. In 2007, he married Hildy Kuryk, a senior fundraiser for the Obama campaign in New York.

Rima Cohen

Obama administration: Health policy counselor to Health and Human Services Secretary Kathleen Sebelius.

Bloomberg administration: Director, Health and Social Services.

Background: Cohen served for a decade as chief health aide to then-Sen. Tom Daschle, D-S.D. At the beginning of the Obama administration, she was rumored to be in line to run the Centers for Medicare and Medicaid Services. Before joining Bloomberg, she worked for the Greater New York Hospital Association.

Robert Gordon

Obama administration: Associate director, Office of Management and Budget.

Bloomberg administration: Senior adviser to schools chancellor.

Background: Gordon oversaw many of the budgetary changes in the New York City school system; he gave principals more control over their school's money; and he divvied up about a third of the overall budget to track the movement of students between schools. He clerked for Supreme Court Justice Ruth Bader Ginsburg and once represented abused children for the Legal Aid Society in New York City.

Jessica Leighton

Obama administration: Senior science adviser, Food and Drug Administration.

Bloomberg administration: Deputy health commissioner.

Background: Leighton's long career in New York City predated Bloomberg's tenure. As deputy commissioner for environmental health, she dealt with matters as routine as beach and pool inspections, as serious as childhood lead poisoning, and as quintessentially New York as rat control.

—A.G.

Both Bloomberg's personal foundation and the Mayor's Fund to Advance New York City have helped pay for items on his official agenda. In his first term, Bloomberg spent $7 million of his money backing an unsuccessful ballot initiative to institute nonpartisan local elections. "Traditionally, interest groups buy mayors," says Siegel, the Manhattan Institute fellow and a historian at Cooper Union. "He's reversed the flow. He's bought the interest groups."

With a huge budget deficit to deal with and the prospect of worse to come, money is uppermost on the minds of Bloomberg's officials. In place of bold new initiatives, agencies are talking about ways to save money by sharing such services as fleet management and information technology.

But City Hall also hopes to extend the ethos of customer service that has made it easy for residents to call 311 when they have a problem. In effect, officials want to provide businesses a similar one-stop-shopping way of interacting with city government. As a headquarters city, New York has long been dominated by corporate priorities, but the Bloomberg administration is focusing increasing attention on the 80 percent of the city's businesses that are not behemoths. Officials recognize that they need to nurture these essential small businesses if New York is to move beyond its long-standing reliance on Wall Street as its main cash cow.

Bloomberg has established a Small Business Services Department and has changed tax laws to reduce costs for independent contractors and freelancers. His economic development team is setting up business incubators in a variety of fields—the biosciences, the arts, media, fashion, and food production—linking entrepreneurs with universities, and even making deals with landlords who are willing to rent surplus space at discounted rates. The city has put up money for seed grants, and some of the initiatives are starting to attract venture funding.

There's a saying in New York that government skims the cream off of Wall Street while Wall Street skims the cream off the rest of the country. That model looks to be broken, or at least in need of serious repair. If Wall Street doesn't generate the kind of profits that it has in recent years, the city will have to develop a economy in which people can get things done at a reasonable cost. So far, Bloomberg has not been able to bring the cost of doing business in New York down to reasonable levels, and that is perhaps the mayor's greatest ongoing challenge.

"Bloomberg still has the problem, like all New York mayors, of fiscal issues," says Vincent Cannato, a historian at the University of Massachusetts and the author of a biography of former New York City Mayor John Lindsay. "It's becoming even more than in the past what Bloomberg called a luxury city, of the very wealthy, of immigrants, and the poor. It's a city that middle-class people are still leaving."

Critical Thinking

1. What health-related policy innovations have occurred in New York City under Mayor Bloomberg's leadership?

2. How did the management style of Bloomberg predecessor Mayor Rudy Giuliani differ from that of Mayor Bloomberg in policing and crime-related policy?

3. What are Bloomberg's dispositions toward innovation and data?

4. How has Mayor Bloomberg's huge personal fortune affected, according to some observers, his hiring of top-level advisors and managers in New York City government and his dealing with interest groups?

5. How has New York City under Mayor Bloomberg used a 311 hotline to improve government performance?

The author, a freelance writer, covered state and local government issues at *Governing* magazine for nine years.

Unscrambling the City

Archaic zoning laws lock cities into growth patterns that hardly anybody wants. Changing the rules can help set them free.

CHRISTOPHER SWOPE

Take a walk through Chicago's historic Lakeview neighborhood, and the new houses will jump right out at you. That's because they're jarringly incompatible with the old ones. On one quiet tree-lined street, you'll find a row of old two-story colonials with pitched roofs. Then you walk a little farther and it seems as though a giant rectangular box has fallen out of the sky. The new condominium building is twice as high as its older neighbors and literally casts shadows over their neat flower gardens and tiny front yards. Angry Lakeview residents have seen so many new buildings like this lately that they have come up with a sneering name for them. They call them "three-flats on steroids."

Listening to the complaints in Lakeview, you might wonder whether home builders are breaking the law and getting away with it, or at least bending the rules quite a bit. But that's not the case. If you take some time and study Chicago's zoning law, you'll find that these giant condos are technically by the book. It's not the new buildings that are the problem. The problem is Chicago's zoning ordinance. The code is nearly half a century old, and it is an outdated mishmash of vague and conflicting rules. Over the years, it has been amended repeatedly, to the point of nonsense. Above all, it's totally unpredictable. In Lakeview, zoning can yield anything from tasteful two-flats to garish McMansions, with no consideration at all for how they fit into the neighborhood.

Chicago's zoning problem lay dormant for decades while the city's economy sagged and population declined. Back in the 1970s and '80s, not much building was going on. But then the 1990s brought an economic boom and 112,000 new residents. While almost everyone is happy that the construction machine has been turned back on, so many Chicagoans are appalled by the way the new construction looks that Mayor Richard M. Daley decided it was time to rewrite the city's entire zoning code. Everything about Chicago land use is on the table: not just residential development but commercial and industrial as well. It is the largest overhaul of its kind in any U.S. city in 40 years.

But while few communities are going as far as Chicago, many are coming to a similar conclusion: The zoning laws on their books—most of them written in the 1950s and '60s—are all scrambled up. They are at once too vague and too complicated to produce the urban character most residents say they want.

The zoning problem afflicts both cities and suburbs and manifests itself in countless ways. It takes the form of over-sized homes and farmland covered in cookie-cutter housing developments. It shows up as a sterile new strip mall opening up down the street from one that is dying. It becomes an obstacle when cities discover how hard it is to revive pedestrian life in their downtowns and neighborhood shopping districts. And it becomes a headache for city councils that spend half their time interpreting clumsy rules, issuing variances and haggling with developers.

What urban planners disagree about is whether the current system can be salvaged, or whether it should be scrapped altogether. Most cities are not ready to take the ultimate step. Chicago isn't going that far. Neither did Boston, Milwaukee, San Diego and San Jose. All of them retained the basic zoning conventions, even as they slogged through the process of streamlining the codes and rewriting them for the 21st century. According to researcher Stuart Meck, of the American Planning Association, there's a cyclical nature to all this. He points out that it's common for cities to update their laws after the sort of building boom many have enjoyed recently. "Cities are in growth mode again," Meck says, "but they're getting development based on standards that are 20, 30 or 40 years old."

Myriad Categories

For much of the past century, if you wanted to find out the latest thinking about zoning, Chicago was a good place to go. In 1923, it became one of the first cities, after New York, to adopt a zoning law. The motivation then was mostly health and

Picture-Book Zoning

While Chicago and a few other large cities struggle to update old zoning laws for the new century, some places are going in a new direction. They are experimenting with zoning concepts percolating out of the New Urbanist movement, writing codes that bear a closer resemblance to picture books than to laws. Conventional zoning, they have decided, is based on an abstract language that leaves too much to chance. They would rather start with a question—what does the community want to look like—and then work back from there. "It's not enough to change the zoning," says New Urbanist author Peter Katz. "Cities have to move to a new system. They should look at the streets they like and the public spaces they like and then write the rules to get more of what they like and less of what they don't. Conventional zoning doesn't do that. It just gives a use and a density and then you hope for the best."

On jurisdiction currently buying in to this new idea is Arlington, Virginia, a suburb of 190,000 people just across the river from Washington D.C. A few months ago, Arlington's county board adopted a "form-based" zoning code for a 3.5-mile corridor known as Columbia Pike, making it one of the largest experiments yet with this new idea.

Columbia Pike is a typical traffic-choked suburban drag, lines mostly with strip malls, drive-throughs and apartment complexes ringed by parking lots. Developers have ignored the area for years. County planners want to convert it into a place that more closely resembles a classic American Main Street. They want a walkable commercial thoroughfare, featuring ground-floor retail blended together with offices and apartments above. But the old zoning code made this nearly impossible.

Rather than starting with a clear vision of what Arlington wants Columbia Pike to look like, the old code starts with a letter and a number: "C-2." The "C" stands for commercial uses only, and the "2" means that development should be of a medium density. C-2 is so vague that it could yield any number of building types. But the code's ambiguities don't end there. Building size is regulated by "floor area ratio," a calculation that again says nothing about whether the building should be suitable for a Main Street or an interstate highway exit. Finally, the code doesn't say where on the lot the building should go—just that it shouldn't sit near the roadway. Mostly, developers have used this recipe to build strip malls. "The code is really absolute on things that don't matter to us at all," says Arlington board member Chris Zimmerman. "The tools are all wrong for the job we're trying to do."

The new code for Columbia Pike abandons these old tools. It begins with a picture: What does a Main Street look like? Rather than abstract language, the new code uses visuals to show the form that the buildings should take. Buildings are three to six stories tall. And they sit on the sidewalk, with ground-floor windows and front doors, not 50 feet back from the street.

Compared with traditional zoning, a form-based code doesn't focus on specific uses. It specifies physical patterns. Whether the buildings are occupied by coffee shops, law offices or upstairs renters makes little difference. "Traditionally," says Peter Katz, "zoning stipulates a density and a use and it's anyone's guess whether you'll get what the planners' renderings look like. Form-based codes give a way to achieve what you see in the picture with precision."

One of the most prominent New Urbanists, Miami architect Andres Duany, advocates taking the form-based idea even further. In Duany's view, it's not only buildings along a road like Columbia Pike that should be coded according to physical form rather than use: entire metropolitan regions should be thought of this way. Duany is pushing an alternative he calls "Smart Code."

The Smart Code is based on the concept of the "transect." The idea is that there is a range of forms that the built environment can take. At one end is downtown, the urban core. At the other end is wilderness. In between are villages, suburbs and more dense urban neighborhoods. As Duany sees it, conventional zoning has failed to maintain the important distinctions between these types of places. Instead, it has made each of them resemble suburbia. When suburban building forms encroach on wilderness, the result is sprawl. When they encroach on urban areas, the result is lifeless downtowns.

Nashville-Davidson County, Tennessee, is one of the first places to begin incorporating these concepts into its planning process. The transect isn't a substitute for a zoning code, says planning director Rick Bernhardt. But it helps planners think about how one part of the city fits into the region, and how to zone accordingly. "It's really understanding what the purpose is of the part of the community you're designing," Bernhardt says, "and then making sure that the streetscape, the intensity and the mix of land use are all consistent with that."

—C.S.

---

safety. Smoke-spewing factories were encroaching on residential neighborhoods, and the city's first ordinance sought to keep them out. By the 1950s, when more people drove cars, Chicago was a pioneer in rewriting the code to separate the places people live in from where they work and where they shop.

The 1957 zoning law was largely the creation of real estate developer Harry Chaddick, who proclaimed that the city was "being slowly strangled" by mixed uses of property. It classified every available parcel of land into myriad categories based on density. Residential neighborhoods, for example, were laid out in a range from "R1" (single family homes) to "R8" (high-rises). Land use rules were so strict as to dictate where ice cream shops, coin stores and haberdasheries could go. Chaddick's code was hailed in its time as a national model.

But over the years, one patch after another in the 1957 law made it almost impossible to use. Some parts contradicted other parts. Two attorneys could read it and come away with completely opposite views of what the code allowed. Finally, in 2000, the mayor tapped Ed Kus, a longtime city zoning attorney, to take charge of a full-scale rewrite. Kus thinks the law in the works will be equally as historic as Chaddick's—and more durable. "I hope the ordinance we come up with will be good for the next 50 years," Kus says.

Besides its rigidity, the old code has been plagued by false assumptions about population growth. Back in the 1950s, Chicago was a city of 3.6 million people, and planners expected it to reach a population of 5 million. Of course, it didn't work out that way. Like every other major city, Chicago lost a huge proportion of its residents to the suburbs. By 1990, it was down to fewer than 2.8 million residents. But it was still zoned to accommodate 5 million.

That's essentially how Lakeview got its three-flats on steroids. Had the city's population grown as the code anticipated, it would have needed a supply of large new residential buildings to replace its traditional two-flats and bungalows. The law made it possible to build these in lots of neighborhoods, regardless of the existing architecture or character.

For decades, this made relatively little difference, because the declining population limited demand for new housing in most of the city. Once the '90s boom hit, however, developers took advantage. They bought up old homes and tore them down, replacing them with massive condo projects. They built tall, and sometimes they built wide and deep, eating up front yards and side yards and often paving over the back for parking. "Developers are building to the max," Kus says. "We have all these new housing types and the zoning ordinance doesn't govern them very well."

There are other glaring problems. Although many people think of the 1950s as the decade when America went suburban, most retail business in Chicago was still conducted in storefronts along trolley lines, both in the city and the older close-in suburbs. The code reflects that mid-century reality. Some 700 miles of Chicago's arterial streets are zoned for commercial use, much more than the current local retail market can bear. Worse, the old code is full of anachronistic restrictions on what kinds of transactions can be conducted where. A store that sells computers needs a zoning variance to set up shop next door to one that fixes them. "If you're in a 'B1' district"—a neighborhood business corridor—"you can hardly do any business," Kus says.

All of these archaic provisions are quietly being reconsidered and revised on the ninth floor of city hall, where Kus heads a small team that includes two planning department staffers and a consultant from the planning firm of Duncan Associates. Their work will go to the zoning reform commission, a panel whose 17 members were picked by the mayor to hold exhaustive public meetings and then vote on the plan. The commission includes aldermen, architects, planners, business representatives and a labor leader. Developers are conspicuously absent, which may come back to bite

the whole project later. But for now, the rewrite is moving remarkably fast. The city council is expected to pass the new code this fall. That will set the stage for an even more difficult task: drawing new maps to fit the changed rules.

In the past, Chicago's zoning reforms sought nothing less than to transform the face of the city. This time, however, there is more of a conservationist bent. What the reformers are trying to do is to lock in the qualities Chicagoans like about their oldest, most traditional neighborhoods. That's not to say they want to freeze the city in place. The building boom is quite popular. But it's also widely accepted that the character of Chicago's neighborhoods is the reason why the city is hot again, and that zoning should require new buildings to fit in. "Cities that will succeed in the future are the ones that maintain a unique character of place," says Alicia Mazur Berg, Chicago's planning commissioner. "People choose to live in many of our neighborhoods because they're attractive, they have front yards and buildings of the same scale."

Made for Walking

The new rules being drafted for residential areas are a good example of this thinking. Height limits will prevent new houses from towering over old ones. Neighborhoods such as Lakeview will likely be "downzoned" for less density. New homes will be required to have a green back yard, not a paved one, and builders will not be allowed to substitute a new creation known as a "patio pit" for a front yard. Garages will be expected to face an alley—not the street—and blank walls along the streetscape will be prohibited.

In the same spirit, the creators of the new zoning code are also proposing a new category, the Pedestrian Street, or "P-street." This is meant for a neighborhood shopping street that has survived in spite of the automobile and still thrives with pedestrian life. The new code aims to keep things that way. Zoning for P-streets will specifically outlaw strip malls, gas stations and drive-throughs, or any large curb cut that could interrupt the flow of pedestrians. It also will require new buildings to sit right on the sidewalk and have front doors and windows so that people walking by can see inside.

There are dozens of other ideas. The new code aims to liven up once-vibrant but now-dying neighborhood commercial streets by letting developers build housing there. For the first time ever, downtown Chicago will be treated as a distinct place, with its own special set of zoning rules. The code will largely ignore meaningless distinctions between businesses, such as whether they sell umbrellas or hats.

The new code also will recognize that the nature of manufacturing has changed. Light manufacturing will be allowed to mix with offices or nightclubs. But heavy industry will get zones of its own, not so much for the health reasons that were important in 1923 and 1957, but because the big manufacturers want it that way and Chicago doesn't want to lose them.

For all the changes, Chicago is still keeping most of the basic zoning conventions in place. It is also keeping much of the peculiar language of zoning—the designations such as "R2" and "C3" that sound more like droids from Star Wars than descriptions of places where people live, work and shop.

On the other hand, the new code will be different from the old code in one immediately identifiable way: It will be understandable. Pages of text are being slimmed down into charts and graphics, making the law easier to use for people without degrees in law or planning. An interactive version will go up on the city's website. "Predictability is important," says Ed Kus. "The average person should be able to pick up the zoning code and understand what can and can't be built in his neighborhood."

Critical Thinking

1. What motivations led New York and other major American cities to initiate zoning laws in the early twentieth century?

2. How have such factors as population density, land use, and architectural style figured into zoning codes in Chicago? And how *should* they?

3. In the context of zoning, what is a Smart Code and what is a transect?

4. What is the new category of "the Pedestrian Street" in the world of zoning?

5. How many overall zoning codes had the city of Chicago had before this article was published in 2003? In what years were they written? (Look up the fate of Chicago Mayor Richard Daley's effort to overhaul the city's zoning code in the early 21st century.)

From *Governing*, June 2003. Copyright © 2003 by Congressional Quarterly, Inc. Reprinted by permission.

The Sentient City

Cameras and sensors can make a city aware of everything happening on its streets, helping it do more for less.

Zach Patton

Call it City 2.0: a metropolis where officials instantly monitor all of the urban environment's constantly changing dynamics—the outside temperature; snow or rainfall; traffic; and perhaps most importantly, people moving through the streets, flowing from one neighborhood to the next. This system helps officials send resources to the street corner where gangs are converging, manage traffic before it becomes congested, and respond to emergencies seamlessly—automatically—before they're even reported.

It may sound like science fiction, but the idea of a living, sentient city—one in which managers use real-time data to respond to events as they occur—isn't the stuff of fantasy anymore. By creating intricately linked networks of cameras and sensors throughout an urban area, cities in the U.S. and elsewhere are already making great strides toward tracking weather conditions and traffic flow, to name a few, and then using that data to govern more effectively.

The ultimate City 2.0 vision is of a "highly networked, highly metered environment so that an administrator can oversee the inputs and the outputs," says Rob Enderle, a technology analyst with the Enderle Group. Tapping into all this real-time data, he says, means "you can run a city cheaper and have happier and safer citizens." The city, in short, becomes a more efficient place for people to live and work. It also means a government can do more with less.

The reality isn't that far away. Many of the building blocks are familiar, even mundane: sensors that monitor weather conditions and air pollution; smart-grid technology that helps deliver energy more efficiently; cameras that track the flow of pedestrians and automobile traffic; devices that measure and relay snowfall to the public works department; and access to Wi-Fi and cloud computing.

Alone, each of these blocks performs one discrete function for one purpose. But if a city fused all of those different data streams, it could create a place keenly aware of changes in the urban environment. With that awareness, a city could respond rapidly and efficiently where and when needed.

The sentient city is still an emerging idea, and managers will have to address many issues—technological and otherwise—before smart cities can flourish. But as more and more cities implement and refine the tools used to gather and assess all this data, the idea of City 2.0 is a vision that's quickly coming into focus.

The genesis of these ideas is decades old. Enderle likens the vision of sentient cities to the concept of "arcologies," the classic sci-fi notion of megalopolises made up of gargantuan, self-contained structures that house thousands of residents in an all-encapsulating environment. At the arcology dynamic's core is the idea that if you can contain all aspects of a city's life and needs, you can monitor and control what happens there.

While arcologies remain firmly ensconced in the pages of Utopian literature, cities have begun implementing technologies that approach somewhat similar ideals of monitoring the urbanscape as a whole. Traffic-light cameras, for example, are ubiquitous in many places. Some localities have gone further, installing video cameras throughout the city and creating a network of video streams. Chicago is the most prominent U.S. city to outfit itself with such a web of cameras. In 2004, the Windy City installed 250 surveillance cameras at sites thought to be at risk of a terror attack. Those devices were linked to 2,000 other cameras already spread throughout the city and networked into Chicago's emergency dispatch center. Mayor Richard Daley said his goal is to have a camera trained on every single intersection in the city.

Then there are gunshot location systems—a technology that uses audio sensors attached to rooftops and telephone poles to detect when a gun is fired and pinpoint the location. In 1995, Redwood City, Calif., was the first in the nation to test this system, which lets police respond to shots without receiving a 911 call. Today more than 30 U.S. cities, including Chicago, Los Angeles and Washington, D.C., rely on the same acoustic sensors.

Surveillance cameras and gunshot detection were the first steps toward a fully sensor-equipped city. In more recent years as sensor technology has improved, the focus has broadened from public safety and emergency response to include subtler changes in environment. Matt Welsh, an associate professor of computer science at Harvard University, has spent the past four years designing and building a system of sensors to constantly monitor conditions in Cambridge, Mass. Welsh and his team have worked with the city to disperse nearly 30 sensors around the relatively small town. "We wanted to capture the ephemeral changes in environment," he says. Using the sensor data, Welsh hopes to gain understanding of how the city works on a minute level. He's recently begun looking at air pollution levels in areas with high automobile traffic, for example, and how those levels shift during the course of a day. The information from monitoring those outputs continuously on a city block, he suggests, could be extremely useful in the city's future decision-making.

Meanwhile, other cities are experimenting with monitoring residents' energy use in real time. Pilot programs that let citizens view their individual energy consumption as it's being used are up and running in Houston; Boulder, Colo.; and Dubuque, Iowa.

While the technology for a sentient city is already available, what's missing is the ability to connect all the different data streams to form a comprehensive picture of a city's happenings. Wilmington, N.C., however, is trying. In February, the city and surrounding New Hanover County launched a pilot that could make it the nation's first true smart city. Using cameras and sensors, the city will analyze and respond to everything from traffic congestion and fuel consumption to water quality and sewage capacity.

For the most part, though, cities have yet to make the leap to fusing different kinds of sensor data. "The concept of City 2.0, is that all these things would be networked," Enderle says. "But I don't see anybody doing a great job of connecting all these things together."

As with so many IT projects, the obstacles toward a fully networked sentient city aren't really technological. The issues are much bigger than that, says Mark Cleverley, the director of strategy for IBM's Global Government Industry. "It's about how technology is changing," he says, "but it's also about how society is changing."

It's also about getting a city's agencies to work together to share and analyze sensor data. And that can be a challenge.

"The big problem is working through the political structure," Enderle says. "It can be very turf-oriented and very fragmented when it comes to this kind of stuff." And what works for one city may not work for another. Cleverley worked with Stockholm to build a congestion-pricing system that utilized radio-frequency ID tags to track citizens' automobiles throughout the city. Cleverley says there's been widespread acceptance of the program and a general agreement that it's had a dramatic effect on reducing traffic congestion. But when New York City Mayor Michael Bloomberg floated the idea of congestion pricing in 2008, it took his citizens a New York minute to rebuke the notion.

Unsurprisingly there are privacy concerns. While most citizens probably don't mind the idea of pole-mounted devices collecting data on rainfall or air pollution, they are likely to be less receptive to the notion of cameras or traffic sensors that follow their movements throughout a city. Those kinds of concerns are not insurmountable, but they must be dealt with, says Cleverley, who notes that Chicago adopted a policy with its vast network of cameras that individuals' faces are, by default, blurred out. Law enforcement officials must go through an approval process, akin to obtaining a warrant, if they want to look for a specific person.

In the end, the collection of sensor data isn't what's important—it's how a city uses that information. "You can deliver better outcomes for society if you think about a city as a system of systems," says Cleverley. "What these technologies do is make it easier to track these systems. What they don't do is guarantee success."

Critical Thinking

1. How can modern technology be used to help city government leaders respond to urban events as they occur?

2. What different "data streams" can modern technology enable a city government to monitor in "real time"?

3. What privacy concerns arise in connection with a "sentient city" and what can be done to lessen such concerns?

4. What should be the ultimate objective of collecting sensor data reporting on multiple dimensions of urban life?

From *Governing*, April 2010, pp. 27–30. Copyright © 2010 by e.Republic Inc. Reprinted by permission via Wright's Media. contract #77805.

267 Years and Counting

The Town Hall Meeting Is Alive and Well in Pelham, Mass

TOD NEWCOMBE

On a cool autumn evening, Kathleen Martell, town clerk for Pelham, Mass., unlocks the doors to the Town Hall, turns on the lights, starts a fire in the fireplace and helps arrange chairs in neat rows, enough to seat 115 townspeople. Soon she is joined by newly elected town moderator Daniel Robb and the Board of Selectmen: James Huber, William Martell and Edward Martin. By 7 P.M., town residents occupy most of the chairs, with the overflow sitting on simple wooden benches that line the meeting room's walls. A few minutes later, Robb calls the meeting to order, the noisy crowd quiets quickly and so begins a Pelham tradition dating back nearly three centuries.

Town meetings have been a fixture in New England since the first one was held in Dorchester, Mass., in 1633. But only Pelham can lay claim to having the oldest town hall in continuous use for town meetings. The wooden, two-story structure, which stands on a hill at the corner of Amherst Road and Daniel Shays Highway (named after the leader of a post-Revolutionary War rebellion of farmers who battled government soldiers on the Town Hall's grounds), was built in 1743. For 267 years, Pelham residents have annually walked, ridden horses, driven in wagons or carriages—and now, cars and trucks—to the simple clapboard hall to discuss and vote on vital town issues.

Upstairs, where the meetings were held for many years, the rear of the room is lined with narrow pews; the backs consist of a single pine plank more than two feet wide. Centuries of carving by bored or restless residents have scarred the pews with names, doodles and images—some so deep they've left holes in the thick planks. Two wood-burning stoves sit on the floor, ready to provide heat. The entire structure is devoid of decoration, save for a small amount of wood carving in the form of two scallops on the wall near where a pulpit once stood. (The hall also served as a church until 1833, when Massachusetts formerly separated church and state with an amendment to the state constitution.)

These days, the meetings have been moved downstairs to accommodate disabled residents who can't climb the stairs to the second floor. At this year's fall gathering on Oct. 20, Robb

starts by calling for a moment of silence for a sick town member, and then reads the five warrant articles the town will discuss and vote on. Technically the meeting that evening is a special one—it's not the annual meeting that takes place in the spring. Special town meetings are held to consider business that must be dealt with prior to the annual meeting, according to town historian Joseph Larson. And he's quick to admit that Pelham makes sure it annually holds a special meeting to maintain the designation of having the oldest town hall in continuous use.

Town meetings often are called the purest and most democratic form of government—direct democracy where the town's business is discussed, debated and voted on by members of the community. Yes, anyone can speak, but unlike the mock town meetings seen on TV and the Internet during the health-care debates, with their confrontational and hyperbolic politics, the meeting in Pelham is civil and the participants engaged. Moderator Robb quietly reminds the residents to introduce themselves and state where they live before speaking. In fact, the governance process that evening, regarding rules of order, is discussed with almost as much fervor as the articles.

It quickly becomes clear which topic will be the most contentious when Robb reads Article 2, calling for the town to vote to raise the salaries of Pelham's fire chief and its volunteer firefighters. The sums are modest—$9,230 for the part-time fire chief and $10,386 for the firefighters. It has been six years since the last salary increase was passed, but a number of residents raise questions about the article's timing and amount. The debate continues, and with the room full of volunteer firefighters (all wearing their uniforms), a motion is passed to vote on the article by secret ballot.

Before voting begins, Pelham Fire Chief Raymond Murphy makes an impassioned speech in favor of the raises. He points out that the dollar amount will raise the hourly rate for the firefighters from $7.45 to $10. "Some of you have the idea that the fire department is a social club, a place to hang out because there's no bowling in town," he says. "But we're a professional organization, run by dedicated firefighters, willing to risk our lives for the safety of the community."

The final comments before the vote come from Thomas P. Lederle, an elderly man in the front row who speaks eloquently in a clear voice about his recent medical emergency and how the town's firefighters arrived quickly and transported him to the hospital, "saving my life." He implores the town to pass the modest increase. When the voting is done and the ballots are counted, the salary increase passes by a large majority.

Except for the chirping of the occasional mobile phone (which draws admonishment from Robb), Pelham's town hall meeting hardly differs from those that took place decades, even centuries, before.

But the town meeting—once a fixture in New England—has been slowly buffeted by change. Urbanization and depopulation of the hill towns has reduced the practice—as well as participation. Starting in the 1960s, however, town meetings in New England underwent something of a revival, according to Frank Bryan, author of *Real Democracy: The New England Town Meeting and How It Works*. The notion of "small is beautiful," along with skepticism for large-scale solutions, began drawing people back to participate in this simple form of democratic government.

Today though, that revival is beginning to lose steam. In Vermont, for example, only 7.2 percent of the state population voted at the annual town meetings in 2009, according to its secretary of state. Other New England states have reported decreases in town meeting participation. Bryan attributes the more recent decline to "commuter-based lifestyles and other demographic and institutional dislocations."

But Larson is optimistic about town meeting democracy in Pelham. He points out that the town has seen its population dwindle to just a few hundred residents at the turn of the last century, only to have it slowly return to its current level of 1,440 (about the same level as in the early 19th century). "That increase has kept the attendance at meetings going well," he says. And Larson is sanguine about the long-term prospects for the Town Hall. At the October meeting, Article 4, which calls for appropriating $2,400 to hire a historic preservation consultant to evaluate the building's exterior, passes by a near-unanimous vote.

Critical Thinking

1. When was the first town meeting held in New England?
2. Why are town meetings often called the purest and most democratic form of democracy? What sorts of government decisions can and do town meetings make?
3. In what ways has the town meeting been "buffeted by change" in recent decades?
4. What percentage of Vermonters voted at annual town meetings in 2009?

From *Governing,* December 2010, pp. 33–37. Copyright © 2010 by e.Republic Inc. Reprinted by permission via Wright's Media. contract #77805.

UNIT 6

Fiscal Matters and Economic Development

Unit Selections

Learning Outcomes

- Determine whether people who live in rented apartments or houses are likely to avoid the financial burden of property taxes, which are levied on the owners of real estate and buildings.

- Assess the pros and cons of property taxes as a source of revenue for state and local governments.

- Identify a number of actions that state and local governments can take to foster economic development within their jurisdictions.

- Assess the pros and cons of state government lotteries as a way to raise revenues. Include in your assessment a reaction to the notion that lotteries and casinos contribute to some people's tendencies to gamble excessively.

- Determine how the American Recovery and Reinvestment Act of 2009 (often called "the stimulus bill") has affected state and local government finances.

- Examine why the national government has assumed more and more of the burden for raising revenues for all three levels of government during the past century.

- Analyze the best mix of revenue raising measures for state and local governments from various alternatives: property taxes, income taxes, sales taxes, lotteries, user charges, and the like.

- Summarize the role that pension plans for state and local government employees have played in the fiscal problems facing many state and local governments today.

- Analyze the notion of a "creative class" and how the "creative class" fits into economic development efforts of states and localities.

Student Website

www.mhhe.com/cls

Internet References

U.S. Economic Development Administration
　www.eda.gov
Congressional Budget Office
　www.cbo.gov
National Association of Development Organizations (NADO)
　www.nado.org

All governments need financial resources to carry out their activities. State and local governments rely on a variety of revenue sources, including sales tax, income tax, and property tax; user charges (for example, motor vehicle registration fees and college tuition); lotteries and casinos; and grants of money from other levels of government. Despite this diversity of funding sources, the overall financial situation of state and local governments is often far from satisfactory, and the Great Recession of 2008–2009 significantly worsened their fiscal problems.

Conspicuous attempts to curb spending at all levels of government have been made in recent decades. An early and historically important success in this context was the passage of Proposition 13, an initiative that California voters approved in 1978. Proposition 13 imposed ceilings on local government property taxes and, in turn, curtailed the services and programs that California local governments could offer. The Proposition 13 tax revolt soon spread to other states. In the years after the passage of Proposition 13, measures designed to limit government spending were put into effect in states and localities across the country. At the national level, a constitutional amendment was proposed and legislation was enacted in attempts to make it more difficult to engage in deficit spending. But the clamor and controversy arising in the early years of the Obama administration about surging national government debt and the continuation of what seem to be unsustainable annual deficits reflect the ineffectiveness of those earlier measures.

Unlike the national government, state and local governments receive a sizable portion of their revenues from intergovernmental grants. The national government grants funding to state and local governments along with a variety of attached conditions. Money can be given with virtually no accompanying strings or with considerable limitations on how it can be spent. Similarly, states provide state aid to local governments with different sets of conditions. Governments providing financial grants, of course, exercise control over the amount of funds available and the conditions attached to such funds. This, in turn, can cause considerable uncertainty and numerous administrative burdens for governments receiving money from other levels of government. As should be apparent, intergovernmental relations and the financing of state and local governments overlap considerably.

The financial situation of state and local governments differs from that of the national government in other important respects. The national government can try to affect the national economy by manipulating the money supply and by running budgetary deficits or surpluses. By contrast, 49 state governments and most local governments are legally required to balance their budgets. For those few state and local governments not required to have balanced budgets, it is difficult to borrow money for large and persistent budget deficits. The fiscal crises

© Royalty-Free/CORBIS

of New York City and other local governments during the 1970s showed that lenders will go only so far in providing money for state and local governments whose expenditures are consistently greater than their revenues. The declaration of bankruptcy by Orange County, California, in 1994 reveals how tempting it is for local governments to pursue risky, although potentially very profitable, investment strategies, especially in financially difficult times. In 1997, several dozen school districts in Pennsylvania learned a similar lesson. Risky investment decisions made on their behalf by a reputed financial wizard resulted in the loss of millions of dollars and jeopardized the school districts' financial futures. But the bankruptcy or bankruptcy-like events just mentioned seem to pale into insignificance when contrasted with the number of state and local governments in fiscal strife in the aftermath of the Great Recession of 2008–2009. State governments have had to take over numerous local governments that have gone "broke," and many state governments find themselves in fiscal straits unrivalled since the Great Depression of the 1930s.

National, state, and local governments all try to promote economic development. New industries employ workers who pay taxes and, thus, increase government revenues for relevant government jurisdictions. What seems new in recent decades on the state and the local scene is the energy, persistence, and ingenuity with which states and localities compete with one another to attract new businesses to their jurisdictions.

Finances are a complicated but critical aspect of state and local government. This unit treats taxes, lotteries, and related revenue-raising matters, as well as economic development activities of state and local governments.

Two Cheers for the Property Tax

Everyone hates it, but the property tax has some good attributes that make it indispensable.

STEVEN GINSBERG

To most Americans, the property tax is about as revered as communism and as popular as a pro-lifer at a NOW rally. The reasons are not hard to understand. At first glance, the property tax system seems arbitrary, unreasonable, and just plain unfair. Every year property owners are hit with a large tax bill, demanding a nearly immediate lump-sum payment. In many jurisdictions, including our nation's capital, the government isn't even required to do you the courtesy of mailing that bill; if you miss the deadline, you must pay late fees whether you received your notice or not. Furthermore, as far as many homeowners are concerned, the manner by which both tax rates and individual property values are determined could not be more random if they were plucked out of a hat. In some cases this is because on-site assessments are only done infrequently—like every five or 10 years. This forces assessors to rely on unreliable estimation methods in the intervening years, such as setting the value of a property based on what neighboring real estate sold for that year, regardless of how the condition of those properties compares with that of the building being assessed. Thus a shack and a renovated loft in the same area can be valued at the same amount. In other communities, like those in California, property values are reassessed only when a building is sold. So a young family of four buying a home in San Francisco's pricey real estate market is slapped with an exorbitant tax bill, while the filthy-rich investment banker down the street is still paying the same amount in taxes as when he first purchased his home in 1979.

Property tax rates are just as varied. In each community, homeowners, businesses, and non-homestead residences (like apartment buildings) vie to lighten their portion of the tax load. Often, regardless of actual property values, whichever group happens to have the most lobbying clout gets a break, while the losing parties are left to shoulder more than their fair share of the burden. In Minnesota, for instance, between 1977 and 1990 homeowners were able to cut their share of property taxes from 45 to 36 percent, even as their share of real estate values rose from 51 to 56 percent. All of this financial finagling, of course, only strengthens taxpayers' conviction that the system is inherently unjust and highly politicized.

It's not surprising then that the property tax has earned such a bad rep among voters—and even less surprising that politicians have latched onto the issue. If you're looking to win votes, opposing the property tax is a no-brainer: It's like declaring that you're anti-drugs. Already, states as politically diverse as Oregon and New York have moved to defang the property tax.

But before we pop open the champagne to toast these developments, we need to take a close look at the upside of the property tax. (And, yes, there is a considerable one.) For although the list of the system's failures is long, people who advocate lowering or abolishing the tax outright are in many cases not considering the big picture.

For starters, contrary to popular belief, the property tax serves as a vital complement to other types of taxes. For instance, our income tax system may be geared to collect more from the affluent, but it also includes numerous loopholes that allow the rich to slip out of paying an amount of tax truly commensurate with their wealth. The property tax picks up where the income tax leaves off. Even if they manage to downplay their annual income, chances are, rich folks are going to buy property. They can't resist owning that summer home in Nantucket, that weekend home in the Hamptons, or that colonial mansion in Georgetown. After all, what's the point of having all that dough if you're not going to spend it? Thus the amount of property you own is as important an indicator of how well-off you are as the income you're officially pulling in each year.

Similarly, property taxes improve the accuracy with which the wealth of senior citizens—whose assets tend to dramatically outweigh their cash incomes—can be taxed. Without property taxes, many seniors would only be taxed on their fixed incomes—which often grossly underestimate how well-to-do they actually are. Now, we're not talking about the 70-year-old Brooklyn couple whose fixed income barely covers the taxes on the brownstone they bought 30 years ago. (An exemption can and should be made to ensure taxes don't force elderly people out of their homes.) But lots of seniors have invested in real estate other than their primary residences. Take the case of a retired speculator who bought property years ago and has watched gleefully as its value skyrocketed. He can enjoy the benefits of his good fortune long before he actually sells those investments. For instance, ownership of pricey real estate makes him eligible for large loans on which the interest is tax deductible. Furthermore, he can spend his fixed annual retirement income without a second thought—knowing that if he's ever low on funds, he can simply cash in his property. The property tax ensures that his tax bill reflects his good fortune. It's not surprising then, that the powerful AARP seniors lobby is pressuring states for an overhaul of the property tax system. And as baby boomers slide into their golden years, we can expect this branch of the anti-property tax lobby to grow even stronger.

Who Will Pick Up the Slack?

No doubt the rich and the elderly recognize that abolishing or lowering property taxes would deal a crushing blow to the schools in their communities—which is where the bulk of the tax's revenues go. But that's no skin off their noses: The rich can always send their kids to private school, and most old people's kids have already flown the nest. Of course, cash-strapped communities are unwilling to stand by as their schools are devastated and may raise other kinds of taxes—like sales taxes—to make up for lost revenue. But such taxes shift more of the burden onto the middle and lower classes, who must buy basic goods, even if they can't afford property.

If you have any doubts about the kind of fiscal havoc the elimination of the property tax can cause, you need only look at what's happened in the states that have "reformed" it. In Florida, the large and religiously anti-property tax seniors population has pushed lawmakers into reducing the property tax rates for some, and completely exempting others. The result is a maze of slimmed-down services and hidden "non-tax" fees that end up unfairly shackling the middle class. Worst of all, these alternative methods simply can't raise the same amount of revenue as the property taxes did. Consequently, notes Kurt Wenner, an economist with Florida TaxWatch, "the schools don't have much of a chance." Small wonder that Florida kids consistently place near the bottom in national reading and math tests, alongside much poorer states such as Louisiana.

In Texas, voters overwhelmingly approved Proposition 1, a ballot measure providing $1 billion in property tax "relief." The law's supporters in the legislature said they had to act "before there was a taxpayer revolt." Of course, almost immediately after the bill passed, school districts across the state announced that they would have to raise other taxes to make ends meet.

Taxpayers in Maine are looking to reduce their property tax bills by expanding the homestead exemption by $20,000, a measure that would rob the state of $200 million in funds. To compensate for the reduction in real estate taxes, Maine will be forced to extend its 6 percent sales tax to a wide range of everyday sources that directly hit middle-class wallets, including movie theaters, bowling alleys, beauticians, and barbers.

The situation is no different in New York; Governor Pataki, along with a slew of legislators, has vowed to cut property taxes. But as property taxes go down, local taxes, user fees, and college education prices continue to surge to make up the difference. The New York proposals are so unbalanced they prompted Patricia Woodworth, director of the budget for the State of New York, to complain to *Newsday* last April, "the benefits are going to go to those who have the greater monetary and financial interest in property holdings, which is not the average person. This plan is not truly tax relief."

But it is Oregon that gives us the most vivid example of what happens when property taxes are slashed. The northwestern state passed Measure 5 in 1990, putting a cap on all property tax increases. This, in turn, forced a massive transfer of state funds to support schools, which left the state with no choice but to cut spending on child welfare, prisons, and state police.

The bottom line: When property taxes are cut, other taxes must be raised to make up for lost revenues. And, as Chris Herbert, an economist at the Harvard-MIT Joint Center for Housing Studies, points out, the property tax is far more progressive than the alternatives. "Cutbacks in property tax have got to be made up and they're not going to be done by a more progressive tax," he says. "Localities can't get states to pick up the tab, so there's a big shift to user charges. You start getting taxes on trash collection and recreation facilities. With user fees things are becoming less progressive because you're paying as much as the next guy"—regardless of whether he happens to be a millionaire.

Mend It, Don't End It

But if we want to get the property tax off the political hit list, we need to address the legitimate problems with the current system. A handful of governments around the country have already started the ball rolling, instituting models that correct some of the more egregious flaws.

Washington state has perhaps the best system, having tackled the issue of favoritism head-on and passed a constitutional amendment declaring that statewide property tax rates must be uniform. For example, all real estate property is currently taxed at approximately 1.2 percent. In addition, all property tax revenues are split between the state and localities. This allows states to tap a deep vein of revenue and distribute it equitably. Under such a system, localities ultimately get to administer their portion of the pot, but the disparity between rich and poor districts is not so wide. "The real key is that the system is administered fairly," says Kriss Sjoblon, an economist at the Washington Research Council. "We have a good system of assessment that eliminates inequities, and the uniformity is vital. People should be treated fairly and folks shouldn't get deals."

Even jurisdictions with special needs can establish systems that are less arbitrary and that make sense to the average taxpayer. Pittsburgh, for instance, has initiated a "split-rate" system in an attempt to foster urban renewal. Property tax is really two separate taxes, one on land and one on building values; Pittsburgh simply separated these two values. The city then lowered the tax on buildings, giving property owners an incentive to maintain, build, and improve their properties, while at the same time increasing the levy on land values, thus discouraging land speculation and stemming urban sprawl. In Pittsburgh and other Pennsylvania cities where the "split-rate" is employed, 85 percent of homeowners pay less than they would with a flat rate, according to analysis by the *American Journal of Economics and Sociology.* The analysis also found that those who do pay more tend to be wealthier homeowners.

Most importantly, the system achieves its goal of encouraging economic growth in urban centers. A study conducted by University of Maryland economists Wallace Oates and Robert Schwab, comparing Pittsburgh to 14 other eastern cities during the decade before and the decade after Pittsburgh expanded its two-rate system, found that: "Pittsburgh had a 70.4 percent increase in the value of building permits, while the 14-city average decreased by 14.4 percent. These findings are especially remarkable when it is recalled that the city's basic industry—steel—was undergoing a severe crisis throughout the latter decade."

Aside from these more comprehensive systems, there are a number of basic steps localities could take to alter the perception of unfairness and ease the burden of property taxes:

- Use the property tax to pay for more than just schools. If seniors and the wealthy feel that the taxes support services they need, they will have reason to pause before directing their lobbying muscle against it.
- Raise the level of exemptions for people over 65. Property taxes do blindside some senior citizens, and there's no reason why they should have to move out of their lifelong homes because the market value of the house has gone up. A moderate raise in the exemption level would prevent poorer seniors from losing their homes, while still raising revenue from the wealthy.
- Stagger payments. A major reason property tax is so unpopular is that it's administered in huge chunks and people aren't allowed much time before hefty late fees

kick in. Distributing the burden over four or more payments a year, with more advanced notice, would take some of the sting out of the bill.
- Upgrade technology. Set it up so people can pay electronically. It's a small thing, but it will make a difference. Most cities allow offenders to pay parking tickets with credit cards, there's no reason they can't do the same with property tax.

Rooting out favoritism and slipshod assessment methods will help make the tax palatable to the majority of citizens. They will no longer see the property tax as a mindless ogre coming to swallow up their hard-earned money. Instead, they will see it as the soundest way to make sure that everyone, especially the wealthy, contributes his share to ensure a high level of public services. In short, they will see it for what it is.

Critical Thinking

1. Why, at first glance, does the property tax system seem "arbitrary, unreasonable, and . . . unfair"?
2. Despite the criticisms, what are the upsides of the property tax?
3. What inevitably happens when property taxes are cut?
4. What reforms would remedy many of the problems of local government property taxes as they currently operate?
5. What is the "split-rate" system of property taxing that Pittsburgh has used? What are the advantages of such a system?

STEVEN GINSBERG is an editorial aide at *The Washington Post*.

The Rise of the Creative Class

Why cities without gays and rock bands are losing the economic development race.

RICHARD FLORIDA

As I walked across the campus of Pittsburgh's Carnegie Mellon University one delightful spring day, I came upon a table filled with young people chatting and enjoying the spectacular weather. Several had identical blue T-shirts with "Trilogy@CMU" written across them—Trilogy being an Austin, Texas-based software company with a reputation for recruiting our top students. I walked over to the table. "Are you guys here to recruit?" I asked. "No, absolutely not," they replied adamantly. "We're not recruiters. We're just hangin' out, playing a little Frisbee with our friends." How interesting, I thought. They've come to campus on a workday, all the way from Austin, just to hang out with some new friends.

I noticed one member of the group sitting slouched over on the grass, dressed in a tank top. This young man had spiked multi-colored hair, full-body tattoos, and multiple piercings in his ears. An obvious slacker, I thought, probably in a band. "So what is your story?" I asked. "Hey man, I just signed on with these guys." In fact, as I would later learn, he was a gifted student who had inked the highest-paying deal of any graduating student in the history of his department, right at that table on the grass, with the recruiters who do not "recruit."

What a change from my own college days, just a little more than 20 years ago, when students would put on their dressiest clothes and carefully hide any counterculture tendencies to prove that they could fit in with the company. Today, apparently, it's the company trying to fit in with the students. In fact, Trilogy had wined and dined him over margarita parties in Pittsburgh and flown him to Austin for private parties in hip nightspots and aboard company boats. When I called the people who had recruited him to ask why, they answered, "That's easy. We wanted him because he's a rock star."

While I was interested in the change in corporate recruiting strategy, something even bigger struck me. Here was another example of a talented young person leaving Pittsburgh. Clearly, my adopted hometown has a huge number

The Creativity Index

The key to economic growth lies not just in the ability to attract the creative class, but to translate that underlying advantage into creative economic outcomes in the form of new ideas, new high-tech businesses and regional growth. To better gauge these capabilities, I developed a new measure called the Creativity Index (column 1). The Creativity Index is a mix of four equally weighted factors: the creative class share of the workforce (column 2 shows the percentage; column 3 ranks cities accordingly); high-tech industry, using the Milken Institute's widely accepted Tech Pole Index, which I refer to as the High-Tech Index (column 4); innovation, measured as patents per capita (column 5); and diversity, measured by the Gay Index, a reasonable proxy for an area's openness to different kinds of people and ideas (column 6). This composite indicator is a better measure of a region's underlying creative capabilities than the simple measure of the creative class, because it reflects the joint effects of its concentration and of innovative economic outcomes. The Creativity Index is thus my baseline indicator of a region's overall standing in the creative economy and I offer it as a barometer of a region's longer run economic potential. The following tables present my creativity index ranking for the top 10 and bottom 10 metropolitan areas, grouped into three size categories (large, medium-sized and small cities/regions).

—Richard Florida

of assets. Carnegie Mellon is one of the world's leading centers for research in information technology. The University of Pittsburgh, right down the street from our campus, has a world-class medical center. Pittsburgh attracts hundreds of millions of dollars per year in university research funding and is the sixth-largest center for college and university students on a per capita basis in the country. Moreover, this is hardly a cultural backwater. The city is home to three major sports franchises, renowned museums and cultural venues, a spectacular network of urban parks, fantastic industrial-age architecture, and great urban neighborhoods with an abundance of charming yet affordable housing. It is a friendly city, defined by strong communities and a strong sense of pride. In the 1986 Rand McNally survey, Pittsburgh was ranked "America's Most Livable City," and has continued to score high on such lists ever since.

Yet Pittsburgh's economy continues to putter along in a middling flat-line pattern. Both the core city and the surrounding metropolitan area lost population in the 2000 census. And those bright young university people keep leaving. Most of Carnegie Mellon's prominent alumni of recent years—like Vinod Khosla, perhaps the best known of Silicon Valley's venture capitalists, and Rick Rashid, head of research and development at Microsoft—went elsewhere to make their marks. Pitt's vaunted medical center, where Jonas Salk created his polio vaccine and the world's premier organ-transplant program was started, has inspired only a handful of entrepreneurs to build biotech companies in Pittsburgh.

Over the years, I have seen the community try just about everything possible to remake itself so as to attract and retain talented young people, and I was personally involved in many of these efforts. Pittsburgh has launched a multitude of programs to diversify the region's economy away from heavy industry into high technology. It has rebuilt its downtown virtually from scratch, invested in a new airport, and developed a massive new sports complex for the Pirates and the Steelers. But nothing, it seemed, could stem the tide of people and new companies leaving the region.

I asked the young man with the spiked hair why he was going to a smaller city in the middle of Texas, a place with a small airport and no professional sports teams, without a major symphony, ballet, opera, or art museum comparable to Pittsburgh's. The company is excellent, he told me. There are also terrific people and the work is challenging. But the clincher, he said, is that, "It's in Austin!" There are lots of young people, he went on to explain, and a tremendous amount to do: a thriving music scene, ethnic and cultural diversity, fabulous outdoor recreation, and great nightlife. Though he had several good job offers from Pittsburgh high-tech firms and knew the city well, he said he felt the city lacked the lifestyle options, cultural diversity, and tolerant attitude that would make it attractive to him. As he summed it up: "How would I fit in here?"

This young man and his lifestyle proclivities represent a profound new force in the economy and life of America. He is a member of what I call the creative class: a fast-growing, highly educated, and well-paid segment of the workforce on whose efforts corporate profits and economic growth increasingly depend. Members of the creative class do a wide variety of work in a wide variety of industries—from technology to entertainment, journalism to finance, high-end manufacturing to the arts. They do not consciously think of themselves as a class. Yet they share a common ethos that values creativity, individuality, difference, and merit.

More and more businesses understand that ethos and are making the adaptations necessary to attract and retain creative class employees—everything from relaxed dress codes, flexible schedules, and new work rules in the office to hiring recruiters who throw Frisbees. Most civic leaders, however, have failed to understand that what is true for corporations is also true for cities and regions: Places that succeed in attracting and retaining creative class people prosper; those that fail don't.

Stuck in old paradigms of economic development, cities like Buffalo, New Orleans, and Louisville struggled in the 1980s and 1990s to become the next "Silicon Somewhere" by building generic high-tech office parks or subsidizing professional sports teams. Yet they lost members of the creative class, and their economic dynamism, to places like Austin, Boston, Washington, D.C. and Seattle—places more tolerant, diverse, and open to creativity. Because of this migration of the creative class, a new social and economic geography is emerging in America, one that does not correspond to old categories like East Coast versus West Coast or Sunbelt versus Frostbelt. Rather, it is more like the class divisions that have increasingly separated Americans by income and neighborhood, extended into the realm of city and region.

The Creative Secretary

The distinguishing characteristic of the creative class is that its members engage in work whose function is to "create meaningful new forms." The super-creative core of this new class includes scientists and engineers, university professors, poets and novelists, artists, entertainers, actors, designers, and architects, as well as the "thought leadership" of modern society: nonfiction writers, editors, cultural figures, think-tank researchers, analysts, and other opinion-makers. Members of this super-creative core produce new forms or designs that are readily transferable and broadly useful—such as designing a product that can be widely made, sold and used; coming up with a theorem or strategy that can be applied in many cases; or composing music that can be performed again and again.

Beyond this core group, the creative class also includes "creative professionals" who work in a wide range of knowledge-intensive industries such as high-tech sectors, financial services, the legal and healthcare professions, and business management. These people engage in creative problem-solving, drawing on complex bodies of knowledge to solve specific problems. Doing so typically requires a high degree of formal education and thus a high level of human capital. People who do this kind of work may sometimes come up with methods or products that turn out to be widely useful, but it's not part of the basic job description. What they are

Large Cities Creativity Rankings

Rankings of 49 metro areas reporting populations over 1 million in the 2000 Census

The Top Ten Cities	Creativity Index	% Creative Workers	Creative Rank	High-Tech Rank	Innovation Rank	Diversity Rank
1. San Francisco	1057	34.8%	5	1	2	1
2. Austin	1028	36.4%	4	11	3	16
3. San Diego	1015	32.1%	15	12	7	3
3. Boston	1015	38.0%	3	2	6	22
5. Seattle	1008	32.7%	9	3	12	8
6. Raleigh–Durham–Chapel Hill	996	38.2%	2	14	4	28
7. Houston	980	32.5%	10	16	16	10
8. Washington–Baltimore	964	38.4%	1	5	30	12
9. New York	962	32.3%	12	13	24	14
10. Dallas	960	30.2%	23	6	17	9
10. Minneapolis	960	33.9%	7	21	5	29

The Bottom Ten Cities	Creativity Index	% Creative Workers	Creative Rank	High-Tech Rank	Innovation Rank	Diversity Rank
49. Memphis	530	24.8%	47	48	42	41
48. Norfolk–Virginia Beach, VA	555	28.4%	36	35	49	47
47. Las Vegas	561	18.5%	49	42	47	5
46. Buffalo	609	28.9%	33	40	27	49
45. Louisville	622	26.5%	46	46	39	36
44. Grand Rapids, MI	639	24.3%	48	43	23	38
43. Oklahoma City	668	29.4%	29	41	43	39
42. New Orleans	668	27.5%	42	45	48	13
41. Greensboro–Winston-Salem	697	27.3%	44	33	35	35
40. Providence, RI	698	27.6%	41	44	34	33

required to do regularly is think on their own. They apply or combine standard approaches in unique ways to fit the situation, exercise a great deal of judgment, perhaps try something radically new from time to time.

Much the same is true of the growing number of technicians and others who apply complex bodies of knowledge to working with physical materials. In fields such as medicine and scientific research, technicians are taking on increased responsibility to interpret their work and make decisions, blurring the old distinction between white-collar work (done by decisionmakers) and blue-collar work (done by those who follow orders). They acquire their own arcane bodies of knowledge and develop their own unique ways of doing the job. Another example is the secretary in today's pared-down offices. In many cases this person not only takes on a host of tasks once performed by a large secretarial staff, but becomes a true office manager—channeling flows of information, devising and setting up new systems, often making

key decisions on the fly. These people contribute more than intelligence or computer skills. They add creative value. Everywhere we look, creativity is increasingly valued. Firms and organizations value it for the results that it can produce and individuals value it as a route to self-expression and job satisfaction. Bottom line: As creativity becomes more valued, the creative class grows.

The creative class now includes some 38.3 million Americans, roughly 30 percent of the entire U.S. workforce—up from just 10 percent at the turn of the 20th century and less than 20 percent as recently as 1980. The creative class has considerable economic power. In 1999, the average salary for a member of the creative class was nearly $50,000 ($48,752), compared to roughly $28,000 for a working-class member and $22,000 for a service-class worker.

Not surprisingly, regions that have large numbers of creative class members are also some of the most affluent and growing.

Medium-Size Cities Creativity Rankings
Rankings of 32 metro areas reporting populations 500,000 to 1 million
in the 2000 Census

The Top Ten Cities	Creativity Index	% Creative Workers	Creative Rank	High-Tech Rank	Innovation Rank	Diversity Rank
1. Albuquerque, NM	965	32.2%	2	1	7	1
2. Albany, NY	932	33.7%	1	12	2	4
3. Tuscon, AZ	853	28.4%	17	2	6	5
4. Allentown–Bethlehem, PA	801	28.7%	16	13	3	14
5. Dayton, OH	766	30.1%	8	8	5	24
6. Colorado Springs, CO	756	29.9%	10	5	1	30
7. Harrisburg, PA	751	29.8%	11	6	13	20
8. Little Rock, AR	740	30.8%	4	10	21	11
9. Birmingham, AL	722	30.7%	6	7	26	10
10. Tulsa, OK	721	28.7%	15	9	15	18

The Bottom Ten Cities	Creativity Index	% Creative Workers	Creative Rank	High-Tech Rank	Innovation Rank	Diversity Rank
32. Youngstown, OH	253	23.8%	32	32	24	32
31. Scranton–Wilkes-Barre, PA	400	24.7%	28	23	23	31
30. McAllen, TX	451	27.8%	18	31	32	9
29. Stockton–Lodi, CA	459	24.1%	30	29	28	7
28. El Paso, TX	464	27.0%	23	27	31	17
27. Fresno, CA	516	25.1%	27	24	30	2
26. Bakersfield, CA	531	27.8%	18	22	27	19
25. Fort Wayne, IN	569	25.4%	26	17	8	26
24. Springfield, MA	577	29.7%	13	30	20	22
23. Honolulu, HI	580	27.2%	21	14	29	6

The New Geography of Class

Different classes of people have long sorted themselves into neighborhoods within a city or region. But now we find a large-scale re-sorting of people among cities and regions nationwide, with some regions becoming centers of the creative class while others are composed of larger shares of working-class or service-class people. To some extent this has always been true. For instance, there have always been artistic and cultural communities like Greenwich Village, college towns like Madison and Boulder, and manufacturing centers like Pittsburgh and Detroit. The news is that such sorting is becoming even more widespread and pronounced.

In the leading centers of this new class geography, the creative class makes up more than 35 percent of the workforce. This is already the case in the greater Washington, D.C. region, the Raleigh-Durham area, Boston, and Austin—all areas undergoing tremendous economic growth. Despite their considerable advantages, large regions have not cornered the market as creative class locations. In fact, a number of smaller regions have some of the highest creative-class concentrations in the nation—notably college towns like East Lansing, Mich. and Madison, Wisc. (See chart, "Small-size Cities Creativity Rankings.")

At the other end of the spectrum are regions that are being bypassed by the creative class. Among large regions, Las Vegas, Grand Rapids and Memphis harbor the smallest concentrations of the creative class. Members of this class have nearly abandoned a wide range of smaller regions in the outskirts of the South and Midwest. In small metropolitan areas like Victoria, Texas and Jackson, Tenn., the creative class comprises less than 15 percent of the workforce. The leading centers for the working class among large regions are Greensboro, N.C. and Memphis, Tenn., where the working class makes up more than 30 percent of the workforce. Several smaller regions in the South and Midwest are veritable working class enclaves with 40 to 50 percent or more of their workforce in the traditional industrial occupations.

Small-Size Cities Creativity Rankings
Rankings of 63 metro areas reporting populations 250,000 to 500,000 in the 2000 Census

The Top Ten Cities	Creativity Index	% Creative Workers	Creative Rank	High-Tech Rank	Innovation Rank	Diversity Rank
1. Madison, WI	925	32.8%	6	16	4	9
2. Des Moines, IA	862	32.1%	8	2	16	20
3. Santa Barbara, CA	856	28.3%	19	8	8	7
4. Melbourne, FL	855	35.5%	1	6	9	32
5. Boise City, ID	854	35.2%	3	1	1	46
6. Huntsville, AL	799	35.3%	2	5	18	40
7. Lansing–East Lansing, MI	739	34.3%	4	27	29	18
8. Binghamton, NY	731	30.8%	12	7	3	60
9. Lexington, KY	717	27.0%	28	24	10	12
10. New London, CT–Norwich, RI	715	28.1%	23	11	13	33
The Bottom Ten Cities	Creativity Index	% Creative Workers	Creative Rank	High-Tech Rank	Innovation Rank	Diversity Rank
63. Shreveport, LA	233	22.1%	55	32	59	57
62. Ocala, FL	263	16.4%	63	61	52	24
61. Visalia, CA	289	22.9%	52	63	60	11
60. Killeen, TX	302	24.6%	47	47	51	53
59. Fayetteville, NC	309	29.0%	16	62	62	49
58. York, PA	360	22.3%	54	54	26	52
57. Fayetteville, AR	366	21.1%	57	57	42	17
56. Beaumont, TX	372	27.8%	25	37	56	55
55. Lakeland–Winter Haven, FL	385	20.9%	59	56	53	5
54. Hickory, NC	393	19.4%	61	48	32	30

These places have some of the most minuscule concentrations of the creative class in the nation. They are symptomatic of a general lack of overlap between the major creative-class centers and those of the working class. Of the 26 large cities where the working class comprises more than one-quarter of the population, only one, Houston, ranks among the top 10 destinations for the creative class.

Chicago, a bastion of working-class people that still ranks among the top 20 large creative centers, is interesting because it shows how the creative class and the traditional working class can coexist. But Chicago has an advantage in that it is a big city, with more than a million members of the creative class. The University of Chicago sociologist Terry Clark likes to say Chicago developed an innovative political and cultural solution to this issue. Under the second Mayor Daley, the city integrated the members of the creative class into the city's culture and politics by treating them essentially as just another "ethnic group" that needed sufficient space to express its identity.

The plug-and-play community is one that somebody can move into and put together a life—or at least a facsimile of a life—in a week.

Las Vegas has the highest concentration of the service class among large cities, 58 percent, while West Palm Beach, Orlando, and Miami also have around half. These regions rank near the bottom of the list for the creative class. The service class makes up more than half the workforce in nearly 50 small and medium-size regions across the country. Few of them boast any significant concentrations of the creative class, save vacationers, and offer little prospect for upward mobility. They include resort towns like Honolulu and Cape Cod. But they also include places like Shreveport, Lou. and Pittsfield, Mass. For these places that are not tourist destinations, the economic and social future is troubling to contemplate.

Plug-and-Play Communities

Why do some places become destinations for the creative while others don't? Economists speak of the importance of industries having "low entry barriers," so that new firms can easily enter and keep the industry vital. Similarly, I think it's important for a place to have low entry barriers for people—that is, to be a place where newcomers are accepted quickly into all sorts of social and economic arrangements. All else being equal, they are likely to attract greater numbers of talented and creative people—the sort of people who power innovation and growth. Places that thrive in today's world tend to be plug-and-play communities where anyone can fit in quickly. These are places where people can find opportunity, build support structures, be themselves, and not get stuck in any one identity. The plug-and-play community is one that somebody can move into and put together a life—or at least a facsimile of a life—in a week.

Creative centers also tend to be places with thick labor markets that can fulfill the employment needs of members of the creative class, who, by and large, are not looking just for "a job" but for places that offer many employment opportunities.

Cities and regions that attract lots of creative talent are also those with greater diversity and higher levels of quality of place. That's because location choices of the creative class are based to a large degree on their lifestyle interests, and these go well beyond the standard "quality-of-life" amenities that most experts think are important.

The list of the country's high-tech hot spots looks an awful lot like the list of the places with highest concentrations of gay people.

For instance, in 1998, I met Gary Gates, then a doctoral student at Carnegie Mellon. While I had been studying the location choices of high-tech industries and talented people, Gates had been exploring the location patterns of gay people. My list of the country's high-tech hot spots looked an awful lot like his list of the places with highest concentrations of gay people. When we compared these two lists with more statistical rigor, his Gay Index turned out to correlate very strongly to my own measures of high-tech growth. Other measures I came up with, like the Bohemian Index—a measure of artists, writers, and performers—produced similar results.

Talented people seek an environment open to differences. Many highly creative people, regardless of ethnic background or sexual orientation, grew up feeling like outsiders, different in some way from most of their schoolmates. When they are sizing up a new company and community, acceptance of diversity and of gays in particular is a sign that reads "non-standard people welcome here."

The creative class people I study use the word "diversity" a lot, but not to press any political hot buttons. Diversity is simply something they value in all its manifestations. This is spoken of so often, and so matter-of-factly, that I take it to be a fundamental marker of creative class values. Creative-minded people enjoy a mix of influences. They want to hear different kinds of music and try different kinds of food. They want to meet and socialize with people unlike themselves, trade views and spar over issues.

As with employers, visible diversity serves as a signal that a community embraces the open meritocratic values of the creative age. The people I talked to also desired nightlife with a wide mix of options. The most highly valued options were experiential ones—interesting music venues, neighborhood art galleries, performance spaces, and theaters. A vibrant, varied nightlife was viewed by many as another signal that a city "gets it," even by those who infrequently partake in nightlife. More than anything, the creative class craves real experiences in the real world.

They favor active, participatory recreation over passive, institutionalized forms. They prefer indigenous street-level culture—a teeming blend of cafes, sidewalk musicians, and small galleries and bistros, where it is hard to draw the line between performers and spectators. They crave stimulation, not escape. They want to pack their time full of dense, high-quality, multidimensional experiences. Seldom has one of my subjects expressed a desire to get away from it all. They want to get into it all, and do it with eyes wide open.

Creative class people value active outdoor recreation very highly. They are drawn to places and communities where many outdoor activities are prevalent—both because they enjoy these activities and because their presence is seen as a signal that the place is amenable to the broader creative lifestyle. The creative-class people in my studies are into a variety of active sports, from traditional ones like bicycling, jogging, and kayaking to newer, more extreme ones, like trail running and snowboarding.

Places are also valued for authenticity and uniqueness. Authenticity comes from several aspects of a community—historic buildings, established neighborhoods, a unique music scene, or specific cultural attributes. It comes from the mix—from urban grit alongside renovated buildings, from the commingling of young and old, long-time neighborhood characters and yuppies, fashion models and "bag ladies." An authentic place also offers unique and original experiences. Thus a place full of chain stores, chain restaurants, and nightclubs is not authentic. You could have the same experience anywhere.

Today, it seems, leading creative centers provide a solid mix of high-tech industry, plentiful outdoor amenities, and an older urban center whose rebirth has been fueled in part by a combination of creativity and innovative technology, as well as lifestyle amenities. These include places like the greater Boston area, which has the Route 128 suburban complex, Harvard and MIT, and several charming inner-city Boston neighborhoods. Seattle has suburban Bellevue and Redmond (where Microsoft is located), beautiful mountains and country, and a series of revitalized urban neighborhoods. The San Francisco Bay area has everything from posh inner-city neighborhoods to ultra-hip districts like SoMa (South of Market) and lifestyle enclaves like Marin County as well as the Silicon Valley. Even Austin includes traditional high-tech developments to the north, lifestyle centers for cycling and outdoor activities, and a revitalizing university/downtown community centered on vibrant Sixth Street, the warehouse district and the music scene—a critical element of a thriving creative center.

Institutional Sclerosis

Even as places like Austin and Seattle are thriving, much of the country is failing to adapt to the demands of the creative age. It is not that struggling cities like Pittsburgh do not want to grow or encourage high-tech industries. In most cases, their leaders are doing everything they think they can to spur innovation and high-tech growth. But most of the time, they are either unwilling or unable to do the things required to create an environment or habitat attractive to the creative class. They pay lip service to the need to "attract talent," but continue to pour resources into recruiting call centers, underwriting big-box retailers, subsidizing downtown malls, and squandering precious taxpayer dollars on extravagant stadium complexes. Or they try to create facsimiles of neighborhoods or retail districts, replacing the old and authentic with the new and generic—and in doing so drive the creative class away.

It is a telling commentary on our age that at a time when political will seems difficult to muster for virtually anything, city after city can generate the political capital to underwrite hundreds of millions of dollars of investments in professional sports stadiums. And you know what? They don't matter to the creative class. Not once during any of my focus groups and interviews did the members of the creative class mention professional sports as playing a role of any sort in their choice of where to live and work. What makes most cities unable to even imagine devoting those kinds of resources or political will to do the things that people say really matter to them?

The answer is simple. These cities are trapped by their past. Despite the lip service they might pay, they are unwilling or unable to do what it takes to attract the creative class. The late economist Mancur Olson long ago noted that the decline of nations and regions is a product of an organizational and cultural hardening of the arteries he called "institutional sclerosis." Places that grow up and prosper in one era, Olson argued, find it difficult and often times impossible to adopt new organizational and cultural patterns, regardless of how beneficial they might be. Consequently, innovation and growth shift to new places, which can adapt to and harness these shifts for their benefit. This phenomenon, he contends,

is how England got trapped and how the U.S. became the world's great economic power. It also accounts for the shift in economic activity from the old industrial cities to newer cities in the South and West, according to Olson.

Olson's analysis presciently identifies why so many cities across the nation remain trapped in the culture and attitudes of the bygone organizational age, unable or unwilling to adapt to current trends. Cities like Detroit, Cleveland, and my current hometown of Pittsburgh were at the forefront of the organizational age. The cultural and attitudinal norms of that age became so powerfully ingrained in these places that they did not allow the new norms and attitudes associated with the creative age to grow up, diffuse and become generally accepted. This process, in turn, stamped out much of the creative impulse, causing talented and creative people to seek out new places where they could more readily plug in and make a go of it.

Most experts and scholars have not even begun to think in terms of a creative community. Instead, they tend to try to emulate the Silicon Valley model which author Joel Kotkin has dubbed the "nerdistan." But the nerdistan is a limited economic development model, which misunderstands the role played by creativity in generating innovation and economic growth. Nerdistans are bland, uninteresting places with acre upon acre of identical office complexes, row after row of asphalt parking lots, freeways clogged with cars, cookie-cutter housing developments, and strip-malls sprawling in every direction. Many of these places have fallen victim to the very kinds of problems they were supposed to avoid. The comfort and security of places like Silicon Valley have gradually given way to sprawl, pollution, and paralyzing traffic jams. As one technology executive told *The Wall Street Journal*, "I really didn't want to live in San Jose. Every time I went up there, the concrete jungle got me down." His company eventually settled on a more urban Southern California location in downtown Pasadena close to the CalTech campus.

Kotkin finds that the lack of lifestyle amenities is causing significant problems in attracting top creative people to places like the North Carolina Research Triangle. He quotes a major real estate developer as saying, "Ask anyone where downtown is and nobody can tell you. There's not much of a sense of place here. . . . The people I am selling space to are screaming about cultural issues." The Research Triangle lacks the hip urban lifestyle found in places like San Francisco, Seattle, New York, and Chicago, laments a University of North Carolina researcher: "In Raleigh-Durham, we can always visit the hog farms."

The Kids Are All Right

How do you build a truly creative community—one that can survive and prosper in this emerging age? The key can no longer be found in the usual strategies. Recruiting more companies won't do it; neither will trying to become the next Silicon Valley. While it certainly remains important to have a solid business climate, having an effective people climate is even more essential. By this I mean a general strategy aimed at attracting and retaining people—especially, but not limited to, creative people. This entails remaining open to diversity and actively working to cultivate it, and investing in the lifestyle amenities that people really want and use often, as opposed to using financial incentives to attract companies, build professional sports stadiums, or develop retail complexes.

The benefits of this kind of strategy are obvious. Whereas companies—or sports teams, for that matter—that get financial incentives can pull up and leave at virtually a moment's notice, investments in amenities like urban parks, for example, last for generations. Other amenities—like bike lanes or off-road trails for running, cycling, rollerblading, or just walking your dog—benefit a wide swath of the population.

There is no one-size-fits-all model for a successful people climate. The members of the creative class are diverse across the dimensions of age, ethnicity and race, marital status, and sexual preference. An effective people climate needs to emphasize openness and diversity, and to help reinforce low barriers to entry. Thus, it cannot be restrictive or monolithic.

Openness to immigration is particularly important for smaller cities and regions, while the ability to attract so-called bohemians is key for larger cities and regions. For cities and regions to attract these groups, they need to develop the kinds of people climates that appeal to them and meet their needs.

Yet if you ask most community leaders what kinds of people they'd most want to attract, they'd likely say successful married couples in their 30s and 40s—people with good middle-to-upper-income jobs and stable family lives. I certainly think it is important for cities and communities to be good for children and families. But less than a quarter of all American households consist of traditional nuclear families, and focusing solely on their needs has been a losing strategy, one that neglects a critical engine of economic growth: young people.

Young workers have typically been thought of as transients who contribute little to a city's bottom line. But in the creative age, they matter for two reasons. First, they are workhorses. They are able to work longer and harder, and are more prone to take risks, precisely because they are young and childless. In rapidly changing industries, it's often the most recent graduates who have the most up-to-date skills. Second, people are staying single longer. The average age of marriage for both men and women has risen some five years over the past generation. College-educated people postpone marriage longer than the national averages. Among this group, one of the fastest growing categories is the never-been-married. To prosper in the creative age, regions have to offer a people climate that satisfies this group's social interests and lifestyle needs, as well as address those of other groups.

Furthermore, a climate oriented to young people is also attractive to the creative class more broadly. Creative-class people do not lose their lifestyle preferences as they age. They don't stop bicycling or running, for instance, just because they have children. When they put their children in child seats or jogging strollers, amenities like traffic-free bike paths become more important than ever. They also continue to value diversity and tolerance. The middle-aged and older people I speak with may no longer hang around in nightspots until 4 A.M., but they enjoy stimulating, dynamic places with high levels of cultural interplay. And if they have children, that's the kind of environment in which they want them to grow up.

My adopted hometown of Pittsburgh has been slow to realize this. City leaders continue to promote Pittsburgh as a place that is good for families, seemingly unaware of the demographic changes that have made young people, singles, new immigrants, and gays critical to the emerging social fabric. People in focus groups I have conducted feel that Pittsburgh is not open to minority groups, new immigrants, or gays. Young women feel there are substantial barriers to their advancement. Talented members of racial and ethnic minorities, as well as professional women, express their desire to leave the city at a rate far greater than their white male counterparts. So do creative people from all walks of life.

Is there hope for Pittsburgh? Of course there is. First, although the region's economy is not dynamic, neither is it the basket case it could easily have become. Twenty years ago there were no significant venture capital firms in the area; now there are many, and thriving high-tech firms continue to form and make their mark. There are signs of life in the social and cultural milieu as well. The region's immigrant population has begun to tick upward, fed by students and professors at the universities and employees in the medical and technology sectors. Major suburbs to the east of the city now have Hindu temples and a growing Indian-American population. The area's gay community, while not large, has become more active and visible. Pittsburgh's increasing status in the gay world is reflected in the fact that it is the "location" for Showtime's "Queer as Folk" series.

Many of Pittsburgh's creative class have proven to be relentless cultural builders. The Andy Warhol Museum and the Mattress Factory, a museum/workspace devoted to large-scale installation art, have achieved worldwide recognition. Street-level culture has a growing foothold in Pittsburgh, too, as main street corridors in several older working-class districts have been transformed. Political leaders are in some cases open to new models of development. Pittsburgh mayor Tom Murphy has been an ardent promoter of biking and foot trails, among other things. The city's absolutely first-rate architecture and urban design community has become much more vocal about the need to preserve historic buildings, invest in neighborhoods, and institute tough design standards. It would be very hard today (dare I say nearly impossible) to knock down historic buildings and dismember vibrant urban neighborhoods as was done in the past. As these new groups and efforts reach critical mass, the norms and attitudes that have long prevailed in the city are being challenged.

For what it's worth, I'll put my money—and a lot of my effort—into Pittsburgh's making it. If Pittsburgh, with all of its assets and its emerging human creativity, somehow can't make it in the creative age, I fear the future does not bode well for other older industrial communities and established cities, and the lamentable new class segregation among cities will continue to worsen.

Critical Thinking

1. What is the "creative class" in the context of economic development?

2. What factors make up the so-called Creativity Index, which can be used to measure a region's overall standing in the "creative economy"?

3. What is meant by the "new geography of class"?

4. What is a "plug-and-play" community and how is that notion related to economic development in American cities today?

5. How does the notion of "institutional sclerosis" relate to economic development challenges facing American cities?

6. Why, in the age of the creative economy, are young workers more desirable than they were previously thought to be?

RICHARD FLORIDA is a professor of regional economic development at Carnegie Mellon University and a columnist for Information Week. This article was adapted from his forthcoming book, *The Rise of the Creative Class: and How It's Transforming Work, Leisure, Community and Everyday Life* (Basic Books)

Broke Town, U.S.A.

Everybody's suddenly petrified about municipal debt. But the fate of bondholders ought to be the least of our worries.

Roger Lowenstein

Vallejo, a city about 25 miles north of San Francisco, offers a sneak preview of what could be the latest version of economic disaster. When the foreclosure wave hit, local tax revenue evaporated. The city managers couldn't make their budget and eliminated financing for the local museum, the symphony and the senior center. The city begged the public-employee unions for pay cuts—all to no avail. In May 2008, Vallejo filed for bankruptcy. The filing drew little national attention; most people were too busy watching banks fail to worry about cities. But while the banks have largely recovered, Vallejo is still in bankruptcy. The police force has shrunk from 153 officers to 92. Calls for any but the most serious crimes go unanswered. Residents who complain about prostitutes or vandals are told to fill out a form. Three of the city's firehouses were closed. Last summer, a fire ravaged a house in one of the city's better neighborhoods; one of the firetrucks came from another town, 15 miles away. Is this America's future?

Cities across America are facing dire financial distress. Meredith Whitney, a banking analyst turned independent adviser who correctly predicted the banking meltdown, has issued an Armageddon-like prediction of mass municipal defaults. Others—notably Newt Gingrich—have suggested that state governments as well as cities should be allowed to file for bankruptcy. Congress held a hearing to examine the idea.

These forecasts of apocalypse have touched a nerve. Americans, still reeling from the devastating impact of the mortgage debacle, are fearful that the next economic disaster is only a matter of time. To anyone reading the headlines of budget deficits and staggering pension liabilities, it takes little imagination to conclude that the next big one will be government itself. The problems of cities are everywhere. The city council of Harrisburg, the capital of Pennsylvania, has enlisted a big New York law firm to explore bankruptcy as a means of restructuring a crushing debt. Central Falls, R.I., is in receivership. Hamtramck, Mich., a small city within Detroit's borders, says it could run out of money next month. Hamtramck has only 90 employees, yet it is saddled with the pensions and health care obligations of 252 retirees. Detroit itself is at risk. Large deficits will mean closing about half of the city's schools and will push high-school class sizes to 60 students.

These and other struggling locales do not begin to approach Whitney's forecast of hundreds of billions in municipal defaults this year. (It would take defaults by *40* cities with as much debt as Detroit to reach even $100 billion.) Some industry experts accuse Whitney of exaggerating the crisis and of worsening the cities' problems by frightening away investors. Whitney's theory is that states, whose finances are also in desperate shape, will cut off local aid to preserve their own budgets; cities that have been subsisting on government transfers would become fiscal orphans and, in a financial sense, unworkable. She has not elaborated on her thesis beyond a few well-chosen television appearances. (She declined to talk to me.) But in the two months following Whitney's warning, investors unloaded about $25 billion in shares of mutual funds that invest in municipal bonds. The selling spree sent the prices of these munis, typically among the most reliable investments, into a free fall.

If muni bonds were to default (causing investors permanent harm, as distinct from the temporary discomfort of price fluctuations), ordinary Americans would lose big. Munis are bonds issued by state and local governments, as well as agencies like hospitals, with the interest going to bondholders tax-free. Their relative safety, plus the tax break, has made them a favorite among individual investors, who own about two-thirds of the total, either directly or via mutual funds.

But what if the burden of municipal woes falls elsewhere than on bondholders? Yes, cities and states have creditors. They also have citizens who rely on their services and who pay the taxes, and they have public employees who are dependent on stable public-sector jobs and often-ample benefits. Whitney isn't wrong about a crisis in local government; the crisis is here. The question is, will it be articulated in terms of bond defaults or larger kindergarten classes—or no kindergarten classes at all? The efforts in Wisconsin and elsewhere to squash organized labor suggest that politicians are no longer so willing to protect public employees. Teachers and nurses are likely to suffer well in advance of investors.

The United States has nearly $3 trillion in municipal bonds outstanding. Though some are backed by specific projects like airports and toll roads, most are general-obligation bonds; local taxes are used to pay the interest on those bonds before other expenses. Unlike a corporation, whose revenue can disappear, cities do not go away—or at least, most of them don't. Detroit is in trouble because of its shrinking population, as are any number of towns in the former steel region of Western Pennsylvania. Many former industrial cities are burdened with governments that are out of proportion to their shrunken tax bases. Local budgets were stretched even before the recession; now, diminished tax receipts have threatened their ability to balance budgets. Bondholders in those municipalities have reason to sweat.

For areas with a stable economy, however, solvency is largely a matter of political will. Historically, far fewer than 1 percent of municipal bonds fail, and most that do tend to be issued for quasi public projects rather than cities. Typical is a monorail that links Las Vegas casinos—and that defaulted for lack of riders. In 2008, a record 166 issues defaulted, but the great majority were Florida land developments; essentially, builders used the tax code to finance sewers and water lines and then walked away when the mortgage bubble burst. The issues were small; defaults in 2008 totaled $8.5 billion. Last year, defaults fell to $2.8 billion.

Chastened by their failure to foresee the mortgage bust, the credit agencies have downgraded munis as the cities' troubles have accelerated. But the agencies that evaluate muni bonds are paid to worry about bondholders, not about kindergartners or local fire departments; consequently, they are not alarmed. Moody's says it expects defaults to rise in 2011. But the agencies do not predict a default epidemic. "Munis are not like subprime bonds," Eric Friedland, a managing director at Fitch Ratings, said.

Government entities do seem less exposed to the sort of chain-reaction panic that undid banks. Lehman Brothers needed financing every day; when confidence disappeared, Lehman disappeared, too. Cities are generally not dependent on short-term financing. (A sizable exception involves some $80 billion in variable credit lines expiring over the next six months—which could force some governments to scramble.)

Another factor that tilts against default is that states and cities carry much less debt relative to the size of their economies than do troubled national governments like those of Greece or Spain (or the United States, for that matter). And muni debts generally come due in a steady stream—not all at once. Robert Kurtter, a managing director at Moody's, says, "State and local governments really don't have a crushing *debt* problem."

Which is not to say they don't have a problem. For most of the past decade, local government was a growth business. Avid consumption and the real estate boom spurred an abundance of sales- and property-tax receipts; with dollars flowing in, governments got used to spending more and borrowing more. Then, in the recession, tax revenues dried up, while demands for services kept rising. For the last few years, both cities and states have faced severe, recurring budget gaps.

As part of the 2009 stimulus package, Washington gave the states $150 billion. The states became dependent on a higher level of federal aid—35 percent of their budgets, compared with about 25 percent before. But the stimulus is ending, and the states will have to cut.

Determining who will suffer from budget cuts is a political and a legal calculation. The cities' problem is that annual spending is greater than revenue; that imbalance does not entitle them to walk away from bond payments. Moreover, states and cities devote less than 10 percent of their revenue to annual debt service. In other words, they have ways of balancing budgets without defaulting. Lately, governments have been taking a chain saw to ordinary spending. The cuts sometimes reflect a retreat from what was once conceived as the essential mission of government. Education is being hit hard. Arizona is seeking a federal waiver to remove 280,000 adults from Medicaid rolls. Massachusetts is stripping out funds for homeless shelters. New Jersey has canceled a commuter-rail tunnel under the Hudson River. If the government doesn't build a rail tunnel, who will?

States are also cutting aid to cities—much as Whitney forecast—aggravating the loss of local tax revenues. Camden, N.J., which has one of the highest crime rates in the country, has dismissed nearly half its police force. Michigan cities have seen aid diminish by $4 billion. In San Diego, where the city has cut other spending to pay for spiraling pension costs, residents have formed 56 "maintenance assessment districts" to take care of parks and patch up sidewalks. When the city failed to pass a hospitality tax, local hotels banded together and agreed to charge a 2 percent visitors' fee. Scott Lewis, who writes about politics for the website Voice of San Diego, says, "I think the city is dissolving."

In Wisconsin, Scott Walker, the new governor, declared that the state was "broke." He does not mean that Madison intends to default on its obligations to debt holders; he means that public employees will have to increase contributions toward their benefits in an amount equal to 7 percent of their pay. For some employees, the cuts will mean real hardship. Public institutions like schools are also likely to suffer. Though elected officials prefer not to mention it, taxpayers will also have to ante up. Illinois sharply raised its income tax; Arizona voted for a sales-tax increase. Both of those states had markedly low tax rates to begin with, but Illinois's case should be troubling to bondholders. Even after raising taxes, the state is planning to borrow about $12 billion to cover pensions and past-due bills—pushing both benefit costs and current expenses into the future.

The deficit problems have, at times, seemed to blend with the issue of pensions into a single, giant mess. As E. J. McMahon of the Manhattan Institute observes, "This is a conflating of different things." States and cities have to put money aside to pay for future pensions, and the portion of that obligation that is "unfunded" represents a huge liability—from $1 trillion to $3.5 trillion, depending on your assumptions about future pension-fund investment returns. This underfunding won't be felt in a big bang but as a continuous burden for years to come.

Nonetheless, because governments are required to make catch-up payments to those funds, the pension problem is worsening the current budget squeeze. In some cities, the pressure is suffocating. In Miami, according to Fitch, the pension-fund obligation eats up 25 percent of the city budget. In Philadelphia, which has neglected to make payments, the pension fund could be exhausted as early as 2015, says Joshua Rauh of the

Kellogg School at Northwestern. Rob Dubow, the city's finance director, insists that "we'll make contributions to make sure that doesn't happen." The city has budgeted a huge $460 million contribution next year. "The real story" of the pension debacle, Dubow says, "is that it will leave less money for police and fire and sanitation."

For a long while, government budget-cutting obeyed a distinctive political calculus: pensions were considered untouchable, so jobs were eliminated instead. Now, governments are going after pensions. Many states have taken the easy step of reducing benefits for new employees. Benefits for existing workers were considered inviolable. But some, like New Mexico and Mississippi, are dunning employees for higher contributions, and Wisconsin may follow. Minnesota and Colorado have watered down pension cost-of-living increases; both have been sued.

Whether such efforts will significantly ease the states' burdens may depend on the courts. In Illinois, where the pension underfunding is among the most egregious, the state constitution says that "benefits shall not be diminished." This language has long been interpreted to mean that when a public employee is promised a pension that increases with each year of service, the rate of accrual can never be changed. Sidley Austin, a law firm in Chicago hired by a pro-business civic group, has circulated a memo arguing that the clause refers only to benefits already earned—not to the rate of accrual in the future. That interpretation, if acted on by the Legislature, would shatter previous notions of pension protections. Sidley also makes the even-more-explosive argument that if Illinois's pension funds dried up, the state could not be forced to contribute more. Let pensioners go hungry.

That is unlikely. Even in Illinois, pensions will be paid. Failure to do so would embroil the government in court for years. That may be the hope of ideologues, who envision that the courts—or possibly even a bankruptcy filing—could be used to alter employee contracts. In the 1930s, progressives persuaded Congress to let cities declare bankruptcy to escape the clutches of creditors. Now, conservatives want Congress to authorize states to file for bankruptcy. "Some people on the right see it as a chance to whack the public unions," says David Skeel, a law professor at the University of Pennsylvania who has written in favor of state bankruptcy. It's not hard to fathom why Gingrich, who as speaker of the House in the 1990s briefly shut down the U.S. government, would favor default by the states.

But the fantasy of using bankruptcy to suspend government runs up against a hard truth: even in bankruptcy, cities and states don't disappear—nor do their obligations. Orange County, Calif., which entered bankruptcy in the mid-1990s after its treasurer ran up massive losses in derivatives, ultimately paid every cent it owed. "Among the reasons so few [cities] choose to go this option is, it's not clear what they gain," Kurtter of Moody's says.

Another reason is that cities are creatures of their states, which fear a negative impact on their own credit. Connecticut prevented Bridgeport from declaring bankruptcy in the '90s, and Michigan is stopping Hamtramck now. In Pennsylvania, about 20 municipalities are operating under a program to nurse insolvent cities back to health. The program has helped Pittsburgh, despite its woefully underfunded pension plan, to slowly improve its credit.

Harrisburg is a different story. A former mayor wanted to create a destination city with a series of ambitious projects, including a Wild West museum. He also approved an expensive plan to refurbish an incinerator so that it could become a moneymaker—a project that has buried Harrisburg under a mountain of debt. There are other Harrisburgs, cities undone by foolhardy projects, but these cases are particular, not systemic.

Vallejo, which ran out of money when the economy imploded, is more representative. A blue-collar city of 110,000, it had been hurting since a naval base closed in the 1990s. In 2007, the Wal-Mart left town. Then, with the recession, property taxes crashed from $29 million to $20 million. Vallejo cut back on street repairs and vehicle maintenance and reduced its staff by a third. The city sought pay cuts from the police and fire unions, whose members' pay and benefits accounted for about 80 percent of the budget; the unions offered to defer pay raises. The council considered, but rejected, the idea of putting a tax increase to a referendum. Rob Stout, the outgoing finance director, who noted that the police chief is retiring on a $200,000 pension, says the general attitude was one of resistance to footing the bill.

Vallejo was a failure of political will. It is also an example of why bankruptcies for cities don't work. All the constituencies who might have hoped to avoid hardship are being walloped anyway. Labor costs are being cut (though not pensions) and holders of $54 million in city bonds will suffer losses—how much won't be known for years. Even Marc Levinson, a partner with Orrick, Herrington & Sutcliffe, which represents the city, calls the bankruptcy a waste of money and time. "It's better to cut a deal than go through the pain we have in Vallejo," he says. Pain is coming regardless. In some cities, bondholders will be burned. But America's failing governments may be one of those crises whose full impact is not registered in the muni market, or in any market. Until voters can agree on what government services they want and will pay for, it is possible that bondholders will bank the profits while taxpayers, employees and citizens share the losses.

Critical Thinking

1. What happened to Vallejo, California that reflects and illustrates a huge challenge to state and local governments today?

2. What are municipal bonds and what role do they play in city governments' contemporary fiscal woes?

3. What help did the 2009 stimulus package enacted in Washington bring to state and local governments? What problems did it cause for state and local governments two or so years after its passage?

4. What role do public employee pensions play in state and local governments' fiscal problems?

5. Why does bankruptcy not seem a viable or useful option for state and local governments?

Nothing Ventured

With venture capital firms scaling back, state governments are stepping in to fund early-state, high-risk startups.

RUSSELL NICHOLS

Driving around Youngstown, Ohio, can feel eerily like exploring a decimated city in a war-torn nation. Brick buildings downtown look like hollow, bombed-out shells. Houses abandoned by blue-collar workers sit empty. Bruce Springsteen's ode to the Rust Belt city sang of the steel mills that "built the tanks and bombs that won this country's wars." But those factories were shuttered long ago, their idle smokestacks looming over a crime-ridden town that for decades was better known as "Bomb City" and "Murdertown, USA."

But there's life emerging beneath these hardened scars. In the shadow of the iconic 1919 Home Savings and Loan Company building downtown, a managed cluster of high-tech start-ups is injecting new energy into the city. It's the Youngstown Business Incubator (YBI), a nonprofit corporation, and it's not only redefining the industry of this hardscrabble valley on the eastern edge of Ohio; it's changing the notion of what cities and states can do to spur innovation and investment. In the past decade, CEO Jim Cossler, who also refers to himself as "chief evangelist," has revamped the model of an incubator from a klatch of unrelated businesses to a targeted group of niche entrepreneurs—in this case, business-to-business software firms. Unlike traditional business incubators, Cossler doesn't "graduate" successful companies and send them packing. Instead, he keeps the portfolio companies on a single, mixed-use campus that promotes open source collaboration. He provides them with cheap or free rent, utilities and Wi-Fi to help them convert IT ideas into dollars and, in turn, jobs.

Bringing Silicon Valley into the Mahoning Valley was a hard sell at first, Cossler says. "When we announced to the world in 2001 that we were going to launch world-class software companies in the global market, the kindest thing that was said to us was, 'You're kidding, right?'" But in 2002, the Ohio Department of Development backed him up, pumping $375,000 per year into the incubator from the Ohio Third Frontier, a 10-year, $1.6 billion project designed to support innovation ecosystems around the state with early-stage equity investment capital. The gamble has been paying off. The YBI now boasts eight onsite companies with a total of 320 employees, many in highly skilled technical jobs. In 2010, Cossler says, the entire portfolio made about $65 million in global sales. One of the businesses,

Turning Technologies, which makes audience response systems, was ranked by *Inc.* magazine in 2007 as the nation's fastest growing software company.

The YBI is definitely a crown jewel in Ohio's push to cultivate small businesses, but it's only one piece of the state's venture capital efforts. Since 2002, the Third Frontier has created more than 60,000 jobs in Ohio. It has helped create, attract and capitalize more than 600 businesses and leveraged more than $5 billion in private investment. Last May, voters overwhelmingly approved a $700 million bond issue to extend the program for another four years. "It's helped create companies and careers that didn't exist in Ohio, or anywhere, just a few years ago," then-Gov. Ted Strickland said following the renewal. "They are inventing the cure for the Rust Belt."

The Youngstown Business Incubator is definitely a crown jewel in Ohio's push to cultivate small businesses, but it's only one piece of the state's venture capital efforts. Since 2002, the Third Frontier has created more than 60,000 jobs in Ohio.

Now more than ever, states are playing the part of venture capitalist—and despite the recession, it turns out they're uniquely suited for the role. As the recession froze private-sector investment, venture capital firms began avoiding early-stage deals, saving their money for less risky, later stages of development. That created a void. Governments began to realize they could fill the gap by providing seed money to new startups in all sorts of emerging industries, from biotech and health care to nanotechnology and solar power.

The idea isn't to supplant private-sector firms, but to plug a hole in the marketplace by funding new companies during the high-risk early stage frequently referred to as the "valley of death." It makes for riskier deals, but it also means that relatively small amounts of cash could bring a big payoff to governments that invest. "Many states are saying 'We see that valley of death, and we think we can fill it and create jobs for our residents,'" says Robert Atkinson, founder and president of the Information Technology and Innovation Foundation, a Washington, D.C.-based technology policy think tank. "It's something government knows how to do: They just write a check or give a tax break."

The idea of government as venture capitalist isn't exactly a new one. Around the globe, governments have been experimenting with that role for decades. Some efforts have produced positive results, while others serve as cautionary tales on how to blow billions of taxpayer dollars on a bad idea. Decades ago, Norway squandered some of its oil wealth on sketchy business ventures, and recently the Dubai government's investment in real estate projects led to massive deficits as the financial crisis hit. According to *The Economist,* Canada's venture capital experiment flopped because the Canadian Labor Fund Program had so much money that it scared off private venture capitalists. And in 2005, the Malaysian government opened its huge $150 million complex, called BioValley, prematurely, and it became mocked as the "Valley of the BioGhosts."

The United States, especially in recent years, is no stranger to tech incubation and venture capital efforts. As part of his State of the Union pledge to "win the future" by boosting innovation, President Obama in February launched a national campaign to provide mentorship and funding to help cultivate new businesses. Dubbed "Startup America," the program will eliminate the capital gains tax on some small business investments and speed up the patent process. The U.S. Small Business Administration will direct $2 billion over the next five years to match private-sector investment capital for under-the-radar startups and firms with high-growth potential.

The modern venture capital industry goes back to the 1970s. Private-sector capital firms set their sights on electronic, medical or data-processing technology, and began investing in the startups that soon would populate Silicon Valley. As the number of firms grew, leading venture capitalists formed the National Venture Capital Association and by 1978, the industry experienced its first major fundraising year, with venture capitalists raising about $750 million. At the same time, states were getting into the venture capital game. In the earliest approaches, state governments set up quasi-public corporations and made direct investments in companies, according to Dan Berglund, president and CEO of the State Science and Technology Institute (SSTI), a nonprofit organization that helps states build tech-based economies. "For more than 30 years, states have put money into programs to encourage access to capital," he says. "Over time, it's shifted. Now, more investment decisions are being made by private investors and states play a more passive role as a limited partner."

During the 1980s and '90s, the venture capital wave rose and fell and rose again, leading up to the boom in 2000, followed by the dot-com bust and a decade in recovery mode. Today, in the face of an unstable market, state governments, desperate for jobs, are aiming to capitalize on untapped potential with seed money, investment programs, partnerships and economic development funds to nurture new businesses and create innovation clusters. California and Massachusetts dominate the country in earlier-stage per capita growth and deals. But several states, including Colorado, Connecticut, Maryland, Ohio, New York and Washington, are boosting capital opportunities for early-stage entrepreneurs, according to the SSTI.

In New York state, for instance, Empire State Development joined forces with the University of Rochester Medical Center to help high-tech startups commercialize their ideas through a $2 million pilot seed fund project. In February, Maryland Gov. Martin O'Malley announced plans to spur job creation in cutting-edge industries by unlocking $100 million in venture capital through InvestMaryland. Various other states, from Oregon to Georgia to Connecticut, have been setting up similar programs to advance innovation in emerging fields. "We know these kinds of programs do work and make a difference," Berglund says. "In a down economy, now is the time when you really have to invest in the future. It's even more critical at this point."

While state-funded venture capital efforts promise payoffs around the country, they're particularly valued in the Rust Belt and Midwest, where the recession has exacerbated the existing hardships of the shift to a post-industrial economy. In addition to Youngstown, cities such as Ann Arbor, Mich.; Madison, Wis.; and Pittsburgh have powered forward with business acceleration strategies that have attracted up-and-coming entrepreneurs and generated millions from venture capital firms, not to mention the cash coming in from individuals who invest in startup businesses, known as angel investors. For example, Ann Arbor Spark, a nonprofit and business acceleration organization, serves as the administrator over the Michigan Pre-Seed Capital Fund. As of January, 52 startups had received investments from the fund, which have totaled more than $11.6 million.

While state-funded venture capital efforts promise payoffs around the country, they're particularly valued in the Rust Belt and Midwest, where the recession has exacerbated the existing hardships from shifting to a post-industrial economy.

"The West Coast and Boston and Texas, they don't need money the same way that the Midwest states do," says Jim Jaffe, president and CEO of the National Association of Seed and Venture Funds. "There is an emphasis in some of these areas and some money is starting to flow."

But the key for a successful state venture capital program, Jaffe says, comes down to how much money governments can afford to put on the table. Not all states can invest on the level of Ohio Third Frontier. And places that can't put up enough capital run the risk of handicapping all their venture capital efforts. "The states have to be willing to invest enough money in this process to make it worthwhile," Jaffe says. "If you're investing $500,000 or you've got $20 million over a few years, you can't make enough of a difference at that rate to create a lot of jobs."

That lack of sufficient investment is what usually undermines government efforts to spur innovation, says Harvard Business School professor Josh Lerner. In his book, *Boulevard of Broken Dreams,* Lerner examines the history of government venture capital activity. True, he says, government investments helped create success stories like Silicon Valley. "But for each effective government intervention," he writes, "there have been dozens, even hundreds, of failures, where substantial public expenditure bore no fruit."

In addition to underinvesting, Lerner says states that set up capital programs tend to rush to give away cash. "In their eagerness to jump-start entrepreneurial activity, governments frequently race to hand out capital," he writes. "This is equivalent to serving the main course before setting the table and unlikely to lead to a successful dinner party." Expecting quick results can torpedo a state's venture capital program.

That was part of the problem with a program in Florida designed to attract biotech firms to the state. In January 2010, news media made hay of a state report showing that Florida's hefty investment in biotech firms hadn't had much of an impact. According to the report from the Florida Legislature's Office of Program Policy Analysis and Government Accountability, titled *Biotechnology Clusters Developing Slowly; Startup Assistance May Encourage Growth,* the $1.5 billion in state and local taxpayer funds to turn the state into a biotech hub had so far only generated some 1,100 jobs. Lacking proper private-sector venture capital funds, the Legislature in 2007 set up the Florida Opportunity Fund to direct public money to biotech startups. But the massive investment of cash, according to last year's report, "has not yet resulted in the growth of technology clusters in the counties where program grantees have established facilities."

Some deals in Ohio haven't worked out as well as others, Third Frontier officials say, but the overall default rate is only one-tenth of 1 percent. The new voter-approved extension of the program shows the public's support for the job-creating potential of the program, says Norm Chagnon, executive director of the Third Frontier Commission. "Most people say they want to stay in Ohio and want to raise families, but they can't find the jobs," he says. "This signals our commitment."

Between 2004 and 2008, total venture capital investment in Ohio grew by 13.2 percent per year, from $243 million to $445.6 million, according to a 2008 report published by Michael Camp, academic director of the Center for Entrepreneurship at the Ohio State University's Fisher College of Business. That's more than double the annual growth rate of total U.S. venture capital investment during the same period. And the state continues to invest in startups through the Third Frontier, as well as its Technology Investment Tax Credit Program and the Ohio Venture Capital Authority. Gov. John Kasich, who took office in January, brought in longtime friend Mark Kvamme to run the Ohio Department of Development and analyze the state's capital investment programs. Kvamme, a Silicon Valley venture capitalist, took the interim development director job for $1, and by midyear he plans to complete the transition of the state agency into a new public-private partnership, JobsOhio. "We're evaluating programs to figure out where we want to double down," Kvamme says. "We want to fund entrepreneurs who have intestinal fortitude."

Back in Youngstown, Cossler says he truly believes technology has the power to change the local landscape. "We're not Palo Alto," he says. "We don't have indigenous tech companies here. But no one wants to know the origin of software."

In other words, unlike the massive steel factories of the past, a Web-based company can deliver products from anywhere with a computer and an Internet connection. Now Cossler's on a mission to bring home "the Youngstown diaspora" and grow the tech campus to support 5,000 jobs. The incubator currently occupies three buildings in downtown Youngstown, a mix of renovated historic structures and a modern glass addition. Cossler plans to expand into a fourth building soon, putting to use a long-dormant brick warehouse next door, where a weathered sign still reads, "Furnitureland of Youngstown."

"This is a city that essentially was dying," says the SSTI's Berglund. "And they've taken a really innovative approach with their incubator program."

While some may consider it a waste of taxpayer money to heap funds on luring high-tech firms to the Rust Belt, Cossler says Ohio's venture capital investment is critical. And, he says, it's not even all that different from the industry that built Youngstown in the first place. "If you reduce software to a common denominator, it's a steel company," he says. "You're taking raw materials and blending them together to create a value-added product. It's all manufacturing."

Critical Thinking

1. What is the Youngstown Business Incubator and what does it do?

2. What is the Ohio Third Frontier and what does it do?

3. What is "venture capital" and what happened in the U.S. economy late in the first decade of the twenty-first century that made private venture capital firms more cautious in their investment strategies?

4. When did the "modern venture capital industry" begin and when did state governments begin to operate as venture capitalists?

Lacklu$ter Lotterie$

STATE LEGISLATURES

In 1964, New Hampshire became the first state in recent history to create a lottery. Fast forward 44 years, and Arkansas becomes the latest state to adopt a lottery after voters approved a ballot question amending the state constitution in November 2008. State lotteries are now authorized in all but seven states.

Over the past two decades, policymakers have turned to lotteries to generate revenue without raising taxes, especially for popular programs such as college scholarship funds or environmental protection. As the effects from the recent recession continue to linger, however, reliance on state lotteries as a stable revenue source is no longer a sure bet.

Lottery revenues declined in FY 2009 in 25 states, the District of Columbia and Puerto Rico. That's more than 61 percent of all lottery states and territories. Revenues were flat in 10 states and increased in seven. Indiana saw the greatest drop in revenues at −18.1 percent, probably because racinos opened in 2008. North Carolina, where the lottery is relatively new and still expanding, saw the greatest increase, at 17.4 percent.

Critical Thinking

1. What state in what year became the first state in recent history to create a lottery?

2. In how many states are lotteries authorized today?

3. How have lottery revenues fared in recent years?

The Ups and Downs of Lottery Revenue

Declined	Changed Less than 1 Percent		Increased
	FY 2008 **($ millions)**	**FY 2009** **($ millions)**	**Percent** **Change**
Arizona	$145	$129	–10.7%
Arkansas	n/a	n/a	n/a
California	1,095	1,053	–3.8
Colorado	122	120	–2.2
Connecticut	283	283	0
Delaware	39	37	–5.3
Florida	1,283	1,285	0.1
Georgia	868	872	0.5
Idaho	35	35	0.7
Illinois	657	625	–4.9
Indiana	224	183	–18.1
Iowa	57	61	7.2
Kansas	70	67	–3.9
Kentucky	187	194	3.2
Louisiana	132	136	3.1
Maine	49	50	0.7
Maryland	529	493	–6.9
Massachusetts	935	844	–9.7
Michigan	753	700	–7
Minnesota	116	120	2.9
Missouri	265	259	–2.3
Montana	11	10	–8.1
Nebraska	31	30	–2.5
New Hampshire	75	68	–9.7
New Jersey	882	875	–0.8
New Mexico	41	41	0
New York	2,153	2,115	–1.8
North Carolina	350	411	17.4
North Dakota	6	6	7.8
Ohio	672	702	4.5
Oregon	703	596	–15.2
Pennysylvania	928	934	0.7
Rhode Island	60	59	–0.4
South Carolina	266	260	–2.1
South Dakota	123	118	–4.1
Tennessee	286	280	–2
Texas	1,046	1,032	–1.3
Vermont	23	21	–7.7
Virginia	455	431	–5.4
Washington	130	120	–7.6
West Virginia	41	41	–0.7
Wisconsin	141	130	–8.1
District of Columbia	0.7	0.7	–2
Puerto Rico	151	125	–17.4

Notes. The Arkansas lottery started in FY 2010. Video lottery revenues are excluded in Delaware, New York, Rhode Island and West Virginia. July–June revenue data are reported for Michigan, New York and Texas.

Source: Rockefeller Institute Fiscal Studies Report, September 2009, and NCSL survey of state lottery agencies, 2010.

UNIT 7

Policy Issues

Unit Selections

Learning Outcomes

- Enumerate as many services, programs, regulations, and the like provided by state and local governments as you can. Compare your list with a similar list of services, programs, regulations, and the like provided by the national government.

- Identify those items on your list of state and local government services, programs, regulations, etc. that have affected you in a typical day.

- Identify some services or policies provided by your state government or one of your local governments that you consider undesirable. Also identify some services or policies that are desirable.

- Assess the pros and cons of state and local governments contracting with private companies to produce goods and render services such as garbage collection, fire protection, school maintenance, incarceration of prisoners, and so forth.

- Summarize the current legality of same-sex marriage in the 50 states. Assess the different ways that same-sex marriage policy has been determined in different states.

- Assess the arguments for and against uniform national or state government standards for public schools. Also assess whether local control of public schooling through the nation's approximately 15,000 school districts is desirable.

- Identify what you think is the single most important service provided by state governments. Similarly, identify the single most important local government service.

- Summarize events that led California to change from being known as the "Golden State" in the 1960s to the troubled condition in which the state of California finds itself today.

- Identify the biggest policy challenge facing state governments today. Also identify the biggest policy challenge facing local governments today.

Student Website

www.mhhe.com/cls

Internet References

American Bar Association—Criminal Justice
www.americanbar.org/groups/criminal_justice.html

American Public Transportation Association
www.apta.com

Community Oriented Policing Services (COPS)
www.cops.usdoj.gov

In the Public Interest
www.inthepublicinterest.org

U.S. Charter Schools
www.uscharterschools.org

One only has to look through a daily newspaper to realize the multiple and diverse activities in which state and local governments engage. Indeed, it would be an unusual American who, in a typical day, does not have numerous encounters with state and local government programs, services, and regulations.

State and local governments are involved in providing roads, sidewalks, streetlights, fire and police protection, schools, colleges, daycare centers, health clinics, job training programs, public transportation, consumer protection agencies, museums, libraries, parks and swimming pools, sewage systems, and water. They regulate telephone services, gambling, sanitation in restaurants and supermarkets, land use, building standards, automobile emissions, noise levels, air pollution, hunting and fishing, and consumption of alcohol. They are involved in licensing or certifying morticians, teachers, electricians, social workers, childcare agencies, nurses, doctors, lawyers, pharmacists, and others. As these listings should make clear, state and local governments affect very many aspects of Americans' everyday lives.

Among the most prominent state and local government functions is schooling. For the most part, public elementary and secondary schools operate under the immediate authority of more than 15,000 local school districts. Typically headed by elected school boards, these districts are collectively responsible for spending more than $600 billion a year and have no direct counterparts in any other country in the world. State governments regulate and supervise numerous aspects of elementary and secondary schooling, and school districts must operate within the usually considerable constraints imposed by their state government. In addition, most states have fairly extensive systems of higher education. Tuition charges are higher at private colleges than at state institutions, and taxpayers make up the difference between what students pay and the actual costs of operating state colleges and universities. While the national government provides some aid to elementary, secondary, and higher education and also involves itself in some areas of education policies, state and local governments have been the dominant policymakers in public education for decades. That having been said, the controversial No Child Left Behind law, enacted early in the George W. Bush administration, has undoubtedly increased the national government's profile—and influence—in public elementary and secondary schooling.

Crime control and order maintenance constitute another primary function of state and local governments. Criminal statutes, police forces, prisons, traffic laws (including drunk driving laws and penalties), juvenile detention centers, and courts all relate to state and local government activities in the area of public safety.

Presidents and presidential candidates have sometimes talked about crime in the streets and what to do about it, but the reality is that state and local governments have traditionally had far more direct responsibility in this policy area than the national government has ever had. The September 11th terrorist attacks, however, have caused a reconsideration and readjustment of national, state, and local roles in protecting public safety.

Singling out education and public safety in the preceding two paragraphs is not intended to slight the many other important policy areas in which the state and local governments are involved: planning and zoning, roads and public transport, fire protection, provision of healthcare facilities, licensing and job training programs, and environmental protection, to mention just a few. Selections in this unit should provide greater familiarity with various activities of state and local governments.

Related to the provision of services by state and local governments is the distinction between the *provision* and *production* of goods and services. For example, a local government may be responsible for *providing* garbage collection for residents and might meet that responsibility by paying a private firm or a neighboring unit of local government to *produce* the service. Similarly, a state government may be responsible for providing penal institutions to house certain kinds of criminal offenders, but might meet that responsibility by paying a private concern or another state government to produce (plan, build, organize, and operate) a prison where inmates will be confined. In recent years, the concept of privatization has figured prominently in discussions about the best ways for state and local governments to deliver services.

This unit addresses issues facing state and local governments in various policy arenas—marriage laws, criminal justice, teenage driving privileges, public schooling, and the like. Policies and policymaking processes treated in this unit of the book can be viewed as the consequences of topics treated in earlier units. Intergovernmental relations, finances, elections, parties, interest groups, and governmental institutions all shape state and local government responses to policy issues. In turn, policies that are adopted interact with other components of state and local politics and modify them accordingly. Thus, the subject matter of Unit 7 is a particularly appropriate way to conclude this book.

Same Sex Redux

How did same sex marriage re-emerge as one of the most vexing social issues facing lawmakers?

CHRISTINE NELSON

When President Bill Clinton signed the Defense of Marriage Act in 1996, defining marriage as between one man and one woman, it seemed inconceivable that same sex couples would ever be allowed to marry.

In the 12 years following the federal act, more than 40 state legislatures enacted similar statutes. Fearing judicial intervention, 30 of the states went a step further and placed "one man, one woman" marriage laws in their state constitutions. In addition, no constitutional amendment placed on a ballot and put before voters has ever failed.

So, how is it that same sex marriage is quickly becoming one of the most challenging states' rights issues of our time?

The tug of war between judicial decisions, which in some cases have forced states to legalize same sex marriage, and public opinion, which has routinely disapproved of same sex marriage, has left legislators squarely in the middle of a divisive political hot potato.

"I've been spending a lot of time on this issue for 20 years," says New York Senator Ruben Diaz Sr., "and of course, it will continue."

> **"I've been spending a lot of time on this issue for 20 years and of course, it will continue."**
> —New York Senator Ruben Diaz Sr.

Plenty of Action

In the last seven years, both the judiciary and state legislatures have played key roles in the fight to recognize same sex marriage. Massachusetts and Connecticut began performing same sex marriages as the result of judicial decisions in 2003 and 2008, respectively. And just last year, the Iowa Supreme Court upheld a lower court decision that ruled denying same sex couples the right to marry was a violation of the equal protection clause in the state constitution.

In addition to Iowa, three other states—Vermont, Maine and New Hampshire—enacted same sex marriage in 2009 as a result of legislative action without a judicial mandate.

Money Talks in Massachusetts and New Jersey

In an era of tough budget decisions, some advocates of same sex marriage are finding success by sidestepping the moral questions surrounding the issue and talking money.

A 2008 study from The Williams Institute at UCLA estimated money spent on wedding-related expenses—travel, ceremonies, meals, parties, transportation, flowers and photographs—in Massachusetts by same sex couples from outside the state would be a $111 million boost to the state's economy over three years. This study helped legislators repeal a 1910 Massachusetts law prohibiting marriage if the couple did not intend to reside in the state. The law made it impossible for same sex, nonresidents to marry.

Today, gay and lesbian couples are encouraged to visit the state in order to marry, largely for the economic benefit. More than 9,000 gay marriages have been performed in Massachusetts so far, and that number is expected to rise dramatically in coming years.

A similar 2009 report estimated that extending marriage to same sex couples would boost the New Jersey economy by almost $200 million during the next three years, creating approximately 1,400 jobs and generating more than $15 million in revenues for the state budget. Nearly $14 million would come from estimated state and local tax revenues, and an additional $1.3 million would be generated from marriage license fees.

Maryland, New York and Rhode Island now recognize same sex marriages performed in other states and that could mean an even larger fiscal impact in New Jersey.

These estimates do not include spending by family members and friends on gifts or by those traveling within New Jersey to attend weddings. The estimate also does not include the standard multiplier for tourism spending: each $1 spent in the state generates more than $2 in additional spending. According to UCLA, if these factors are taken into account, the total gain for New Jersey could be close to half a billion dollars.

The Vermont legislature was the first of the three to pass same sex marriage, overriding the veto of Governor Jim Douglas. The District of Columbia Council passed same sex marriage and the measure took effect in March.

And lawmakers in New York and New Jersey recently passed legislation in one chamber to allow it, but failed to do so in the other.

As a result of these developments, an important secondary question has emerged: Are states without same sex marriage obligated to recognize same sex marriages performed in other states?

In New York, Rhode Island and Maryland, the answer is yes. New York Governor David Patterson issued an executive order in 2008 directing all state agencies to recognize same sex marriages from other states. Attorneys general in Maryland and Rhode Island have issued opinions on the matter, drawing parallels between the recognition of common law marriage, which can only be established in a handful of states, but is recognized as a legal marriage in all states. And, just prior to legalizing same sex marriage, the District of Columbia Council also passed a resolution to recognize same sex marriages performed elsewhere.

Coordinated Campaigns

It's not a coincidence that Northeastern states are a hotbed of activity. Six by Twelve is a coordinated campaign led by same sex marriage advocates to change the laws in six Northeastern states by 2012.

The campaign was started because the Northeast was seen as fertile ground for reform. Three states in the region had previously allowed civil unions, viewed by many as an intermediate step toward same sex marriage. Public opinion polling showed that a majority of New England residents favored some form of relationship recognition for same sex couples. Trinity College in Hartford, Conn., reported Northeastern residents as the least religious in the country, which is significant given that opposition to same sex marriage is often based on religious beliefs. Higher education levels in the region also correlate well to surveys showing those with college educations tend to favor same sex marriage.

Most important, however, is that Northeastern states for the most part do not have initiative and referendum processes that could allow voters to overturn legislative actions.

There are exceptions, however, one of which is Maine.

Battle for Public Opinion

Though used infrequently, the state of Maine does allow for a "People's Veto" of legislative referenda. Despite the success of the Six by Twelve campaign, Maine's voters rejected same sex marriage by ballot initiative in November 2009. Question 1 passed with 53 percent of voters agreeing to overturn the Act to Promote Marriage Equality and Affirm Religious Freedom, passed in May 2009. Because the ballot measure was certified before the law took effect, no same sex marriages were ever performed.

Public opinion has been a huge stumbling block for same sex marriage advocates. In addition to Maine, opponents have successfully led campaigns to restrict marriage and limit domestic partnerships in Arizona, California and Colorado. In the last 10 years, when voters have been asked to cast a vote expanding relationship recognition for same sex couples, the answer has always been a resounding "no."

Yet a recent survey by the Pew Forum on Religion and Public Life reports a clear majority favors allowing gay and lesbian couples to enter into legal agreements with each other that would give them many of the same rights as married couples: civil unions. When the survey was first conducted in 2003, only 45 percent of respondents favored civil unions; today, that number is 57 percent.

Although support for civil unions has grown, the majority of Americans continues to oppose same sex marriage by a margin of 53 percent to 39 percent, numbers that remain unchanged in the last year. Diving into these percentages, Pew reports 72 percent of liberal Democrats favor same sex marriage, while 81 percent of conservative Republicans oppose it. Whites and Hispanics are more supportive than African Americans, women are more supportive than men, and young people under the age of 29 are more supportive than any other age group. Most Southerners and Midwesterners oppose same sex marriage, 60 percent and 54 percent, respectively.

Representative Democracy?

For some state lawmakers, these survey numbers matter and reflect opinions they regularly hear from constituents. Their vote on same sex marriage is based largely on public opinion, and some believe that the issue should be squarely in front of voters.

"I firmly believe that my vote against the marriage equality legislation reflects the wishes of the vast majority of my constituents," says Senator Shirley Huntley of New York. "I also firmly believe that any decision on marriage equality should, ultimately, be made by the people of New York state, not the Legislature. I would fully support a referendum to allow the people to decide the issue."

> **"I believe any decision on marriage equality should be made by the people of New York State, not the Legislature. I would fully support a referendum to allow the people to decide the issue."**
>
> —New York Senator Shirley Huntley

For others, the issue of same sex marriage is simply ill-timed. Paul Koering, a gay man serving in the Minnesota Senate, voted against two marriage equality bills that were introduced in the Legislature last year. He argues same sex marriage distracts from other more pressing issues, such as people who have lost their jobs or their homes, and leaves the Legislature open to criticism.

"You have to understand how politics works. The electorate will say, 'My goodness, what's wrong with these people? Why are they talking about this issue now?'"

"You have to understand how politics works. The electorate will say, 'My goodness, what's wrong with these people? Why are they talking about this issue now?'"

—Minnesota Senator Paul Koering

Like Huntley, Koering believes that his constituents don't want him to support same sex marriage. Rather than legislative action, he urges advocates to work harder to "change the hearts and minds of people."

And for legislators, their vote on same sex marriage is intensely personal—and never easy.

Maine Representative Larry Sirois and New York's Diaz are both leaders in their hometown churches. Sirois is a deacon in Turner, Maine; Diaz is a Pentecostal minister in the Bronx. Both had to explain their positions on same sex marriage to their congregations.

Sirois told them that he was planning to support same sex marriage, despite knowing that "90 percent of them didn't agree with me."

He told them: "I am not trying to convince you of anything. . . . It is purely an issue of fairness. I don't agree with the gay lifestyle, but those people deserve the same rights."

By contrast, Diaz, who has two gay brothers, says: "I love them. But I don't believe in what they are doing. They are my brothers. They are my family. For me to accept this, I have to turn my whole value system upside down."

He went on to say people don't want same sex marriage. "They didn't want it in California; they didn't want it in Maine. And the people of upstate New York . . . they sent a message they don't want gay marriage. Forget about it. People don't want it."

Political Costs

While it is too early to tell whether lawmakers who voted in favor of same sex marriage last year are at greater risk of losing their seats in the next midterm election, there have been political consequences in the past.

Former Vermont Representative Karen Milne voted in favor of a civil union bill in 2000. Forced by the Vermont Supreme Court to create legislation on marriage equality, Vermont became the first state in the country to offer civil unions.

She—along with 17 other legislators who voted for the bill— lost their seats in the next election.

Backlash is unlikely this time around, according to Garrison Nelson, a political science professor at the University of Vermont, given that many other states have acted since 2000. Indeed, in addition to five states and the District of Columbia that allow same sex marriage, New Jersey allows civil unions. California, Nevada, Oregon and Washington allow domestic partnerships that include a full range of benefits for same sex couples. Hawaii, Maine and Wisconsin also offer domestic partnerships, but with a more limited set of benefits.

Although 2009 was a harbinger for same sex marriage surprises, expectations for 2010 are low. In an election year, both advocates and opponents agree that legislative activity needs to be minimal in order to avoid potential electoral backlash.

With the majority of state lawmakers seeking re-election this year, the level of legislative activity on same sex marriage, civil unions and domestic partnerships has dropped dramatically. Fewer than 10 states considered these issues in the early part of 2010, compared with more than 20 states a year ago.

Even without much legislative activity, same sex marriage will likely continue to dominate headlines. An opinion in the high profile federal case challenging Proposition 8 in California, where voters rejected the legalization of same sex marriage, could be released this year. In Massachusetts, a case challenging the Defense of Marriage Act was filed in federal court. Both cases could significantly shape the national landscape, and may end up before the U.S. Supreme Court in coming years.

Critical Thinking

1. When did President Bill Clinton sign the national government's Defense of Marriage Act?

2. Between 1996 and 2008, how many state legislatures passed laws reserving marriage for one man and one woman, and how many states amended their constitutions with a similar provision?

3. What has happened since 2008 to bring the issue of same sex marriage back into prominence?

4. What are "civil unions" and what proportion of Americans now support their legality? What proportion support same sex marriage?

CHRISTINE NELSON tracks same sex civil unions and marriage for NCSL.

One Size Doesn't Fit All

Rick Hess's big new school reform idea is that no big new school reform idea works everywhere.

STEVEN M. TELES

Since arriving at the American Enterprise Institute in 2002, Rick Hess has become the de facto education spokesman for respectable, reality-based conservatives. His new book, *The Same Thing Over and Over Again: How School Reformers Get Stuck in Yesterday's Ideas,* is as close as the feverishly productive Hess is ever likely to get to a genuine magnum opus. No one will be shocked that a scholar at AEI has a lot to say that will infuriate liberal defenders of the educational status quo. The book's real surprise is that he is perfectly willing to take on the sacred doctrines of conservative education reformers, arguing that some of them may actually be hampering the process of educational innovation.

Much of what we now accept as fundamental, almost definitional, aspects of schools—that a school must be a wholly geographically based institution, for example—was a "makeshift response to the exigencies of an earlier era," says Hess. Standard "chalk and talk" schooling made sense for a basically agrarian, small-town nation in which communications and transportation were slow and expensive and schools could rely on an army of talented, underpaid women who had few job opportunities outside of teaching, nursing, and secretarial work. The length of the school day is another relic of a time when relatively few women worked outside the house. Today it makes little sense that most schoolchildren are let loose at three P.M. when their parents often don't get home from work until the dinner hour. Our current model is increasingly obsolete in a society where demand for high-skilled labor has accelerated, the population has become urbanized, and young people are as comfortable communicating virtually with people around the world as they are with someone at the front of the class.

Almost all efforts at major education reform over the last few decades have been compromised by the failure to recognize this obsolescence. School districts have accepted (if sometimes reluctantly) demands for higher teacher preparation standards, additional Advanced Placement classes, and a greater focus on the "core" subjects of math, science, English, and history. But more radical changes—such as replacing teachers with technology, using a global labor pool, or hiring a lower-paid staff—face much fiercer opposition. This has led reformers, for all their good intentions, to simply add more rules and regulations over existing ones. The result is an accumulation of claims on institutional time and resources which makes for an increasingly resentful bureaucracy and schools that have become unmanageable.

It isn't just the school districts and teacher's unions that resist systemic change. Interests as varied as school construction firms, textbook publishers, summer camps, and amusement-park owners (whose survival depends in part on America's relatively long summer vacations) have a powerful stake in the maintenance of outdated educational practices.

All this because most of us have difficulty imagining schooling occurring outside of a single, physical place led by a full-time, salaried professional who teaches students organized by age-appropriate grades. Even more prosaic are the physical constraints of our existing schools, in which the practices of the past are often quite literally bolted in place. Challenging these deeply embedded practices would require the kind of institutional and physical creative destruction—comprehensive, systemic change from the inside out—for which even the most enthusiastic of reformers may lack the stomach.

As a result, advocates for better education have repeatedly latched on to a depressing litany of fads as the panacea for what ails American education. Believing that they have only a short window of opportunity for change, these reformers push for their ideas to be applied uniformly across the board. "New math," standardized testing, centralization, merit pay, small schools, community control, mayoral control, and dozens of other ideas have ripped through schools, often with disappointment and disillusion not far behind.

Many of these ideas actually did have some merit, says Hess, in the sense that they could help some specific students in some specific circumstances. For example, a rigorous focus on a narrow set of tested subjects may be reasonable for schools in chaotic, urban contexts where simply focusing on *anything* counts as success. But that treatment, like chemotherapy, has powerful side effects that should not be risked on the (relatively) healthy "patients" in more advantaged school districts.

The same can be said about the often-furious conflict over pedagogical practices. From the start, there should have been more discussion about what style of teaching or curriculum fits the needs of particular students, rather than the establishment of a one-size-fits-all model. Instead, we have seen wave after wave of disappointment, as some promising changes have been overapplied and not worked as advertised. Which, in turn, paves the way for the next overapplied fad, creating another cycle of failure and disillusionment.

Hess is a refreshing change from many other analysts who hold forth on the subject of education. He is unafraid to take on flaws even in policies he largely supports—such as merit pay, school choice, and greater competition, which, he says, were at once oversold and misunderstood.

But the most critical lesson from the book is Hess's powerful theory about what makes schools succeed or fail. That theory, simply put, is that the basic components of schooling—parents, children, school leaders, and teachers—are irreducibly diverse. Parents have different ideas about what a "well-educated" child is, and children differ quite significantly in temperament, aptitude, habits, and interests. School leaders vary as to how they think schools should be run, while teachers have different skill levels, enthusiasm for different tasks, and ideas about what children should learn and know.

Successful education requires alignment between these four groups. Educators will always be less effective if they are made to teach in a way that they believe is wrongheaded or that they haven't bought into. Students will have difficulty learning if they are forced to work at a pace that is too fast or too slow, or if they are taught in a manner that doesn't match their individual learning styles. Parents can be disengaged or hostile if the pedagogy, discipline, or school culture differ fundamentally from what they think is right for their child. And schools as a whole will be incoherent and disorganized if they cannot count on some baseline of agreement as to what—and who—the school is for.

The implications of this simple set of assumptions are profound. If you take them seriously, almost every aspect of schooling—how students are assigned to schools, who teaches and how they are trained, where and when teaching and learning occurs, who provides education and who regulates it, and, most radically, how disagreements are settled—must be called into question.

For almost the entire span of America's experiment with universal education, we have had two ways of dealing with the diversity and conflict that are inherent in public education. For those without substantial mobility or means, that approach has been democracy: parents and other interested community members argue about what schools should do, and then the majority determines what plans will be put into place. Parents and their children can either accept what they are given or organize through the political system for change.

Persons with means and mobility, however, have a different set of educational options: they can try to match their preferences and attributes to a public jurisdiction they think is appropriate; they can supplement public schools with other educational experiences in order to bring their children's education closer to their preferences; or they can opt out of public schools entirely and place their children in private schools. The preferences of the well-to-do thus are aggregated through the classically liberal mechanisms of choice and markets, while those without such means must content themselves with majoritarian, democratic mechanisms.

One takeaway of Hess's argument is that, where education is concerned, democracy is distinctly inferior to liberty. The basic issues we fight over in education, he suggests, are not susceptible to definitive settlement. We will never agree on the question of what it means to be truly educated, because this is a matter of principle and preference rather than science. We will never be able to come up with a single model of schooling that works for everyone, because the needs and habits of students differ so dramatically. The reforms most likely to creative vibrant, creative organizations are those that are most freely consented to—those in which students, parents, teachers, and school leaders are all on the same page, because they have agreed in advance on the fundamentals.

> **The basic issues we fight over in education are not susceptible to definitive settlement. We will never agree on the question of what it means to be truly educated, because this is a matter of principle and preference rather than science.**

Rather than aggressively imposing a single set of best practices on all schools, then, Hess argues for narrowing the scope of choices that are made by majorities, and increasing those made by smaller, self-chosen groups of common sentiment. Policy changes that insist on one way of compensating, training, and recruiting teachers, one way to use the school day or year, one way of organizing classrooms or defining what should go on in them—regardless of how they try to establish this uniformity—are steps in the wrong direction. "The frustrating truth," Hess tells us, "is that there are no permanent solutions in schooling, only solutions that make sense in a given time and place.

"Rather than education reform again being, as in the 1980s, a matter of prescriptive state policies on teacher ladders and additional course requirements, or as in the 2000s, a matter of accountability systems and mandated interventions in low-performing schools," he continues, "perhaps it is time for an agenda that creates room for problem solvers rather than prescribing solutions." Much the same thing could be said about other reform favorites, such as the adoption of Common Core State Standards (a set of standards now approved, as of this writing, by forty-three states and the District of Columbia), a greater use of standardized tests, and "value-added" metrics of teacher effectiveness and merit pay. These may be great ideas in particular places and with certain groups of students. But we cannot be presumptuous enough to assume that they will work in all the nation's schools.

The key to effective reform, Hess concludes, is ridding ourselves of the pipe dream that dramatically improved schools are just one silver bullet away. Instead of doubling down on a particular set of supposedly research-driven "best practices," we should hedge our bets by allowing radical new models of schooling and eccentric and unproven ideas to gain entry into the system—while resisting any force, be it public, private, or philanthropic, that would foist a new orthodoxy on a system which has already seen far too many of them.

Critical Thinking

1. What is Rick Hess's fundamental theory about "what makes schools succeed or fail"?

2. What, according to Hess, is needed for successful education?

3. What are the two ways that have been used to deal with the diversity and conflict related to education since the early days of public schools in the United States? Which, for Hess, is the better of the two ways?

4. What is, for Hess, the key to effective educational reform?

STEVEN M. TELES is associate professor of political science at the Johns Hopkins University and the author most recently of *The Rise of the Conservative Legal Movement*.

From *Washington Monthly*, March/April 2011, pp. 43–45. Copyright © 2011 by Washington Monthly Publishing, LLC, 1319 F St. NW, Suite 710, Washington DC 20004. (202)393-5155. Reprinted by permission. www.washingtonmonthly.com

Giving Teens a Brake

Stricter laws for teenage drivers have helped prevent injuries and save lives.

MELISSA SAVAGE

Colorado—A 17-year-old girl is charged with careless driving after crashing into a car pulled over with a flat tire and severely injuring the two teenage boys who were changing it. The boys, both on the high school wrestling team, lose their legs.

Utah—A 19-year-old driver's car veers off the road and hits a tree. The teen is pronounced dead at the hospital.

Florida—A teenage driver runs over and kills a fifth grader walking to school.

Missouri—A teen passenger is severely injured in a crash when the teen driver loses control of the car, swerves over the center line and hits another car head on.

Virginia—A teen driver is headed to court after killing one of his passengers in a crash resulting from driving at more than 100 mph.

South Carolina—Two toddlers and a 12-year-old are critically injured after riding in a SUV that the 15-year-old driver crashed into a tree.

Crashes like these are common on highways and streets across the country. Motor vehicle wrecks claim the lives of more teens than does any other accident or illness, more than cancer and more than drowning. This plague affecting teens is nothing new—it's been a problem for years. But stricter laws covering drivers in this age group have allowed for progress in cutting back the number of teen deaths and injuries.

Beginning in the mid-1990s state legislatures began passing driver's licensing laws aimed at teens. Under these laws young people acquire their licenses through a gradual process. The laws vary greatly. According to AAA, 43 states and the District of Columbia have three-stage graduated driver's licensing laws for teens. The automobile association says the other seven states lack either an intermediate licensing stage or a mandatory learner's permit.

States have concentrated on strengthening licensing procedures for teen drivers in the past few years, restricting passengers, nighttime driving and cell phone use. In addition, lawmakers have lengthened the minimum period to hold a learner's permit and extended the entire graduated driver's licensing program.

A Step Further

Illinois has taken teen licensing a step further. Although the Insurance Institute for Highway Safety has rated the Illinois graduated driver's licensing law as "good," it wasn't good enough for Jesse White, the Illinois secretary of state. Inspired by a series of articles by the Chicago Tribune focusing on the toll of deadly teen crashes, White formed the Illinois Teen Driver Safety Task Force. Made up of state legislators, judges, traffic safety advocates, law enforcement and

The Idea of Graduated Licenses

The idea of a graduated driver's license was born when a North Carolina study in the early 1970s found that young drivers, especially at night, were statistically more likely to be involved in fatal crashes.

From that research, graduated licenses were recommended in a model system developed by the National Highway Traffic Safety Administration in 1977. Although California and Maryland adopted a few of the model's concepts into their driver's licensing scheme, the first successful graduated licensing program was started in 1987 in New Zealand.

A graduated driver's license involves three stages in licensing teenage drivers. The first stage, the "learner stage" requires teenage drivers to be accompanied and supervised by an adult. The "intermediate stage," sometimes known as a "provisional" stage, allows unsupervised driving, subject to certain restrictions such the number of passengers or the time of day. The final stage is full licensure when all restrictions and provisions are lifted for the teen driver.

The Insurance Institute for Highway Safety has a rating system for states with graduated licensing laws. The institute assigns points to various components of the GDL law. The highest rating, "good," would earn six or more points. Regardless of the point totals, no state is given a rating above "marginal" if it grants an intermediate license to someone under 16 years of age or if it allows unrestricted driving before age 16 and a half.

—Anne Teigen, NCSL

educators, the group began meeting last summer and came up with recommendations to improve teen driver safety that were turned into legislation this session.

In March, the Senate Transportation Committee approved the bill, which increases the time teens must hold learner permits, adds nighttime driving restrictions, requires at least six hours of actual street driving in driver's education and makes teens wait a little longer before giving rides to their friends. Teenagers must also drive citation-free for 15 months before they can receive a full license.

Nine Recommendations from Illinois

1. Extend learner's permit phase from three months to nine months.
2. Change nighttime driving restriction from 11 P.M. to 10 P.M. on weekdays and from midnight to 11 P.M. on weekends. Extend restriction to cover 17-year-old drivers.
3. Restrict passengers for a year instead of six months.
4. Eliminate exemptions that allow student drivers to pass drivers' education programs with less than six hours of actual behind-the-wheel training with a certified drivers' education instructor.
5. Create an offense for a teenage passenger who violates the passenger restriction law.
6. Require a nine-month conviction-free driving period before a teen can move from permit phase (age 15) to initial licensing phase (ages 16 to 17) and another six-month conviction-free driving period before a teen can move from the initial licensing phase to full licensure (ages 18 to 20).
7. Suspend the driver's license of anyone under 21 who receives three traffic convictions in a two-year period.
8. Change law that now allows teen drivers charged with a traffic offense to appear before a judge without a parent or guardian. Require teens with traffic citations to attend traffic school and remain violation-free in order to get offenses erased from their record.
9. Establish strict penalties for teen drivers involved in street racing.

If the legislation passes, Illinois will have one of the toughest teen driver laws in the country. And that's exactly what Senator John Cullerton wants to happen. Cullerton, a member of the task force and the Senate sponsor for the legislation says the recommendations from the task force are essential to saving teen lives and preventing injuries. "The goal of the task force was to reduce the number of Illinois teens dying each year on our state highways," he says. "This legislation will help us reach that goal."

New Jersey lawmakers approved a new law this session, creating a special commission charged with studying teen driver safety. The commission will conduct research about the effectiveness of drivers' education and training programs geared toward teens, and study the leading factors contributing to teen crashes—distraction, aggressive driving and speed. Senator Ellen Karcher, the bill's sponsor, hopes that the special commission will, "hit the ground running, and make needed recommendations to the Legislature, law enforcement community, parents, and everyone concerned with safety on our roadways to protect our kids from tragic auto accidents."

Senator Karcher knows what it's like to worry about the safety of a child. "As a parent of a teen driver, I know personally how hard it was to hand over the keys to my son. Parents will always worry about the safety of our kids. Legislators need to take a comprehensive approach to examining teen driver safety, and begin pushing for safer standards and greater education for our young drivers."

Not everyone agrees. In late March, the Arkansas House rejected teen driving legislation by a vote of 27–63. It would have added nighttime driving restrictions and limited the number of teen passengers allowed in the car of a teenage driver. Representative Billy Gaskill says it's unfair to target teens this way and asked his colleagues to "leave these kids alone." Other legislators question the wisdom in having more cars on the road—a potential issue arising from limiting teens ability to carpool.

Positive Results

Research shows conclusively that graduated driver's licensing laws decrease fatality and injury rates for teens ages 15–19. In a recent study by the AAA Foundation for Traffic Safety, states with the most comprehensive laws show tremendous success in reducing teen fatalities and injuries. States with the most restrictions on teen drivers have had the greatest drop in fatalities and injuries for young drivers. The AAA Foundation commissioned the study from Johns Hopkins and says it should be a wake-up call for parents and legislators.

"States with five of seven common components of graduated driver licensing saw 40 percent reductions in injury crashes and 38 percent average drops in fatal crash involvement for 16-year olds," says Justin McNaull, state relations director for AAA. "States with fewer components had lesser results. Put bluntly, when states enact comprehensive graduated driver licensing, fewer teens die on our roads and we're all safer."

The study looked for teen driving regulations that require:

- A minimum age of 16 years for receiving a learner's permit.
- At least six months on the learner's permit before qualifying for a license that allows unsupervised driving.
- At least 30 hours of supervised practice during the learner's stage.
- An intermediate stage of licensing with a minimum entry age of 16 and a half years.
- Nighttime driving restrictions for intermediate license holders starting no later than 10 P.M.
- A restriction of no more than one passenger for intermediate license holders.
- A minimum age of 17 for full, unrestricted licensure.

"The research on teen licensure is clear: graduated driver licensing reduces crashes, injuries, and deaths for teens and everyone else who travels on our roads," says McNaull of AAA. "For legislators, a vote to improve teen licensure is a vote that will save lives."

Critical Thinking

1. What is the general idea of "graduated licenses" for young drivers?
2. What is an example of a graduated license system?
3. What does research show about the results of graduated licensing laws?

Fixing the Rotten Corporate Barrel

States grant corporate charters; they should start taking some of them away.

JOHN CAVANAGH AND JERRY MANDER

The global corporations of today stand as the dominant institutional force at the center of human activity. Through their market power, billions of dollars in campaign contributions, public relations and advertising, and the sheer scale of their operations, corporations create the visions and institutions we live by and exert enormous influence over most of the political processes that rule us.

It is certainly fair to say, as David Korten and others have, that "global corporate rule" has effectively been achieved. This leaves society in the daunting position of serving a hierarchy of primary corporate values—expanding profit, hypergrowth, environmental exploitation, self-interest, disconnection from communities and workers—that are diametrically opposed to the principles of equity, democracy, transparency and the common good, the core values that can bring social and environmental sustainability to the planet. It is a basic task of any democracy and justice movement to confront the powers of this new global royalty, just as previous generations set out to eliminate the control of monarchies.

The first step in the process is to recognize the systemic nature of the problem. We are used to hearing powers that be—when faced with an Enron or WorldCom scandal—explain them away as simple problems of greedy individuals; the proverbial few rotten apples in the barrel; the exception, not the rule. In reality, the nature of the corporate structure, and the rules by which corporations routinely operate, make socially and environmentally beneficial outcomes the exception, not the norm.

Public corporations today—and their top executives—live or die based on certain imperatives, notably whether they are able to continuously attract investment capital by demonstrating increasing short-term profits, exponential growth, expanded territories and markets, and successful control of the domestic and international regulatory, investment and political climates. Questions of community welfare, worker rights and environmental impacts are nowhere in the equation. Given such a setup, Enron's performance, like most other corporate behavior—especially among publicly held companies—was entirely predictable, indeed, almost inevitable. Enron executives were only doing what the system suggested they had to do. Corporations that can successfully defy these rules are the rare good apples in an otherwise rotting barrel.

That such structural imperatives should dominate the global economic system and the lives of billions of people is clearly a central problem of our time; any citizens' agenda for achieving sustainability must be rooted in plans for fundamental structural change and the reversal of corporate rule.

New Citizen Movement

Around the world, the spectrum of anticorporate activity is broad, with strategies ranging from reformist to transformational to abolitionist. Reformist strategies include attempts to force increased corporate responsibility, accountability and transparency, and to strengthen the role of social and environmental values in corporate decision-making. Such strategies implicitly accept global corporations as here to stay in their current form and as having the potential to function as responsible citizens.

A growing number of activists reject the idea that corporations have any intrinsic right to exist. They do not believe that corporations should be considered permanent fixtures in our society; if the structural rules that govern them cannot be fixed, then we should seek alternative modes for organizing economic activity, ones that suit sustainability. These activists seek the death penalty for corporations with a habitual record of criminal activity. They also demand comprehensive rethinking and redesign of the laws and rules by which corporations operate, to eliminate those characteristics that make publicly traded, limited-liability corporations a threat to the well-being of people and planet.

Possibly the most visible and growing arm of this anticorporate movement is the one that focuses on the corporate charter, the basic instrument that defines and creates corporations in the United States. Corporations in this country gain their existence via charters granted through state governments. As the landmark research of Richard Grossman and Frank Adams of the Program on Corporations, Law and Democracy (POCLAD) has revealed, most of these charters originally included stringent rules requiring a high degree of corporate accountability and service to the community. Over the centuries corporations have managed to water down charter rules. And even when they violate the few remaining restrictions, their permanent existence is rarely threatened. Governing bodies today, beholden to corporations for campaign finance support, are loath to enforce any sanctions except in cases of extreme political embarrassment, such as has occurred with Enron, Arthur Andersen and a few others. Even then, effective sanctions may be few and small.

At the same time, corporations have obtained many rights similar to those granted human beings. American courts have ruled that corporations are "fictitious persons," with the right to buy and sell property, to sue in court for injuries and to express "corporate speech." But they have not been required, for the most part, to abide by normal human responsibilities. They are strongly protected by limited liability rules, so shareholder-owners of a corporation cannot be prosecuted for acts of the institution. Nor, in any meaningful sense, is the corporation itself vulnerable to prosecution. Corporations are sometimes fined for their acts or ordered to alter their practices, but the life of the corporation, its virtual existence, is very rarely threatened, even for great crimes that, if carried out by people in many states of the United States, might invoke the death penalty.

Of course, it is a key problem that these "fictitious persons" we call corporations do not actually embody human characteristics such as altruism or, on the other hand, shame—leaving the corporate entity literally incapable of the social, environmental or community ideals that we keep hoping it will pursue. Its entire structural design is to advance only its own self-interest. While executives of corporations might occasionally wish to behave in a community-friendly manner, if profits are sacrificed, the executive might find that he or she is thrown off the wheel and replaced with someone who understands the rules.

State charter changes could alter this. State corporate charter rules could set any conditions that popular will might dictate—from who should be on the boards, to the values corporations must operate by, to whether they may buy up other enterprises, move to other cities and countries, or anything else that affects the public interest. In Pennsylvania, for example, citizen groups have initiated an amendment to the state's corporation code that calls for, among other things, corporate charters to be limited to thirty years. A charter could be renewed, but only after successful completion of a review process during which it would have to prove it is operating in the public interest. In California a coalition of citizen organizations (including the National Organization for Women, the Rainforest Action Network and the National Lawyers Guild) petitioned the attorney general to revoke Unocal's charter. Citing California's own corporate code, which authorizes revocation procedures, the coalition offered evidence documenting Unocal's responsibility for environmental devastation, exploitation of workers and gross violation of human rights. While this action has not yet succeeded, others are under way.

Revoking a charter—the corporate equivalent of a death sentence—begins to put some teeth into the idea of accountability.

Eliot Spitzer, Attorney General of New York, declared in 1998: "When a corporation is convicted of repeated felonies that harm or endanger the lives of human beings or destroy our environment, the corporation should be put to death, its corporate existence ended, and its assets taken and sold at public auction." Although Spitzer has not won a death sentence against a habitual corporate criminal, he has taken up battle with several giants, including General Electric.

Even if corporations were to be more tightly supervised, that would not be enough to change society. Such actions must be supported by parallel efforts to restore the integrity of democratic institutions and reclaim the resources that corporations have co-opted. But tough charters and tougher enforcement would be a start.

Alternatives

Names like Exxon, Ford, Honda, McDonald's, Microsoft and Citigroup are now so ubiquitous, and such an intimate part of everyday life, that it is difficult for many people in the industrial world to imagine how we might live without them. But there are hundreds of other forms of economic and business activity. And by whose logic do we need transnational corporations to run hamburger stands, produce clothing, grow food, publish books or provide the things that contribute to a satisfying existence?

Transition to more economically democratic forms becomes easier to visualize once we recognize that many human-scale, locally owned enterprises already exist. They include virtually all of the millions of local independent businesses now organized as sole proprietorships, partnerships, collectives and cooperatives of all types, and worker-owned businesses. They include family-owned businesses, small farms, artisanal producers, independent retail stores, small factories, farmers' markets, community banks and so on. In fact, though these kinds of businesses get very little government support, they are the primary source of livelihood for most of the world's people. And in many parts of the world—notably among agricultural and indigenous societies—they are built into the culture and effectively serve the common interest rather than the favored few. In the context of industrial society, the rechartering movement and the parallel efforts to eliminate "corporate personhood" and exemptions from investor liabilities are important steps in a similar direction, seeking to alleviate the dominance of institutions whose structural imperatives make it nearly impossible for them to place public interest over self-interest.

Critical Thinking

1. What, according to some political observers and activists, is the "dominant institutional force" at the center of contemporary human activity?

2. What is a corporate charter and who grants corporate charters?

3. What rights have courts granted to corporations, and what requirements or responsibilities have *not* been imposed?

4. What could state governments do to shape corporations' behavior more than they currently do?

JOHN CAVANAGH, director of the Institute for Policy Studies, and **JERRY MANDER**, president of the International Forum on Globalization, are authors, along with seventeen others from around the world, of *Alternatives to Economic Globalization: A Better World Is Possible* (Berrett-Koehler), from which this article is adapted.

California, There It Went
The Irreparable Tarnishing of the Golden State

Jennifer Rubin

More than 40 years later, I still remember the bright sun and the palm trees when we got off the plane. California in 1968 was a magical place, a magnet for those seeking new opportunities or to lose an old identity. The Golden State was allowing the rich to get richer and the middle class to live out the American dream in its pristine state. The public schools and expanding state-university system (two separate systems, in fact) were the envy of the nation. The corruption and Mob influence that had paralyzed many eastern and midwestern states and cities were largely absent.

When my parents announced they were uprooting the Glazer family from a cozy suburb of Philadelphia, as 5 million people did from eastern and midwestern towns between 1950 and 1980, the news was met with a mixture of awe ("California . . ." they would breathlessly whisper) and bewilderment ("But what is *there*?"). The very act of migrating by plane was itself somewhat grand. In the years before airline deregulation, one dressed up to fly, as if sailing on an ocean liner, and at prices not all that much lower than an ocean voyage's. And yet those we were leaving behind acted as though we were traveling by caravan, leaving civilization and going into the wilderness.

In a real sense, even in 1968, California *was* the wilderness. If the cost of air travel was prohibitive for a family of modest means, they usually drove, and from the flatness of the Midwest they found themselves left speechless by the vision of the Rocky Mountains, rugged coastlines, wide beaches, and empty space they knew only from the movies. Like emigrants leaving the old country in the 19th century, they often arrived friendless and unaccustomed to the habits of their new environment. Public transportation was in scarce supply; instead there were gleaming freeways with five lanes on each side. Tie and jacket? More and more restaurants didn't care. Informality pervaded dress and speech at a time when, back east, adults still commonly addressed acquaintances as Mister and Missus.

In Southern California, the aerospace industry was booming, and middle-class professionals from all over the country flocked to work in and around it. The movie studios had fallen into distress and decay due to the growing popularity of TV (before the blockbuster era of the 1970s drew audiences back out of their living rooms), but if you went to the Norton Simon Museum in Pasadena, you might spot the billionaire in a corduroy jacket whose name was above the door escorting Cary Grant around his collection. Every now and then you'd have a Fred Astaire or a James Stewart sighting.

In Northern California, Haight-Ashbury was still awash in the haze of the Summer of Love from the year before, the hippies and the gay community were moving in on the old Republican establishments of San Francisco and Berkeley, and San Jose was a sleepy town where a family of modest means could own a four-bedroom house near terrific schools for $27,000. Silicon Valley was farmland.

Forty-two years after I arrived in California, the very notion of an affordable, happy-go-lucky, optimistic, and "golden" state seems otherworldly. Its financial condition resembles Greece's. Self-dealing and political scandals involving public-sector unions have become commonplace not only in Sacramento but also in cities from Mexico to Oregon. Thirteen percent of the state's workforce is unemployed. Taxes (sometimes disguised as "fees" or "special assessments") are among the highest in the country, school days are being cut, and state universities have cut off financial aid as they squeeze out in-state residents in favor of higher-paying out-of-staters.

> **Forty-two years after I arrived in California, the very notion of an affordable, happy-go-lucky, optimistic, and "golden" state seems otherworldly.**

After a decade of energy brown-outs that shut down air conditioners in the sweltering summer, spending cuts that have increased the decrepitude of roads and public facilities, and mushrooming retirement obligations to state workers that have crowded out basic public services, California is only now teetering on the crest of a fiscal sinkhole from which it will be impossible to emerge.

But when we and a horde of other young families arrived, Los Angeles was frantically *expanding* to fit us. As was the case during the boom after World War II that produced the Levittowns of the East Coast, builders were racing to meet the needs of newcomers. Suburbs grew and multiplied with construction sites where new tracts of a hundred or more homes were being thrown together, three or four models repeated for blocks whose newly poured concrete sidewalks gleamed in the sun.

"Hidden Glenn—Worth discovering!" and other similar signage adored the entrances of the tracts. You could walk into any house, ignore the furnishings, and know the layout as soon as you assessed which model you were in. Before remodeling and landscaping differentiated the homes, there was an institutional sameness. "Neighborhood" seemed a quaint term, as if from a novel about a time long past. Just for fun, we'd drive (no other way to get around, of course) to nearby tracts, walk through partially completed homes, and guess which room would be which (look for the telltale signs—plumbing, size, proximity to kitchen).

There was a thriving apartment-rental business for families waiting for their homes to be completed. The builder promised October? Savvy mothers like mine knew that meant January and kept the Chanukah menorah in the boxes marked "apartment."

Part of the lure was the sheer newness of it all—new homes, new schools, new roads. The accumulated decay and grime of midwestern and eastern cities was nowhere to be seen. The claustrophobia of indoor schools and boxy malls was replaced by year-round temperate sunshine that allowed for outdoor strip shopping and schools with no indoor corridors. Parallel parking was an unnecessary skill—there were parking lots everywhere, free at malls and five or 10 dollars all day downtown. The Los Angeles Dodgers were rained out only once before 1976. "Snow days" disappeared from our vocabulary.

The residents were new as well. Most everyone was from somewhere else. Freed from the bonds of family and friends, you could remake your life anew. If you were raised a Catholic but wanted to be a Buddhist, no one cared. If your business flopped in Detroit and you wanted a clean break, no one would be the wiser.

It was not all paradise. The Manson murders and the Berkeley riots reminded the newcomers that California was not immune to the rest of the country's maladies. But in the age before cable news and the Internet, young children in the sparkling suburbs of Los Angeles breezed through it all, feeling blessedly far from the fires and destruction convulsing eastern cities in the wake of Martin Luther King's assassination.

Only in retrospect is it clear that there was a larger political and indeed cultural crisis in the making even then.

In their new book, *California Crack-up: How Reform Broke the Golden State and How We Can Fix It*, Joe Matthews and Mark Paul detail a history of dysfunctional government and fiscal disarray that seems to have been written into the state's DNA. Through the past century, layer upon layer of well-intentioned reforms have led to the promulgation and emendation of a gargantuan, unreadable state constitution now running into the tens of thousand of words. The result of these good-government repairs, as Matthews and Paul write, was that "it would become harder and harder for voters to know whom to hold responsible for problems."

Through the past century, layer upon layer of well-meaning reforms have led to a state constitution now running into the tens of thousands of pages.

The reform era that began after the turn of the last century, a reaction to the railroad-baron-dominated government of the 19th century, contributed a heavy dose of direct democracy—a system of referenda, initiatives, and recalls that allowed the public to bypass the state legislature but also to accelerate the influence of special-interest groups that learned to draft and promote measures ranging from budget protection for teachers' unions to bans on horse meat. The result was an unworkable governmental maze in which lobbyists and public-employee unions came to wield huge power.

Liberals finger the tax revolt of the 1970s and the successful passage of the Proposition 13 referendum in 1978 as the culprits for the state's fiscal woes. They are correct in part, but for reasons they would prefer to ignore and the reform's authors never imagined would result from it. In the 1970s, the influx of new residents and the frenzy for home-buying coincided with a nasty bout of inflation. Real-estate prices rose to astronomical levels. Middle-class families and the elderly faced crushing property-tax bills and the potential loss of their homes. California's boom was imperiled. When the legislature proved unresponsive, the citizenry organized and launched the anti-tax crusade that is a direct precursor to the Tea Party movement of today.

As promised, Prop 13 drastically reduced property taxes and permitted residential homes to be re-assessed only at the time of sale, fixes that relieved homeowners of the heavy tax burden that had fueled the revolt. But Prop 13 had other effects as well. Local governments lost nearly a quarter of their revenue, and the state, which was then flush with cash, stepped in to take over school and social-welfare funding. This centralized spending in Sacramento and made the state capital an unparalleled target of opportunity for special-interest groups, which became expert in navigating the unwieldy bureaucracy and convoluted budgeting apparatus.

Over time, even well-intentioned legislators found their hands tied by the exigencies of fiscal law and the legislature's political dynamics. Since the 1930s, a two-thirds majority of both state houses has been required to pass spending and budget bills. Prop 13 added a two-thirds vote requirement to pass tax hikes. While this reform was intended to compel fiscal discipline, it actually empowered small numbers of legislators to hold out for pork-barrel spending in their districts—effectively blackmailing the governor and more-responsible leaders, who felt compelled to pass timely budgets. An annual face-off would occur as the state edged closer to the budget deadline. California took to issuing IOUs while awaiting the passage of budgets. Crafty maneuverers, as Matthews and Paul explain, learned to reach budget compromises "through questionable borrowing and accounting gimmicks." Thus, "in many ways, Prop 13 represented a liberal dream come true."

California went on an unprecedented spending spree. Between 1990 and 2009, according to a 2009 Reason Foundation report, "state spending—including the General Fund, special funds, and bond funds—has increased 180.9 percent, or an average of 5.91 percent a year. . . . Since FY 1990-91, General Fund spending alone has increased 156.8 percent, or 5.37 percent a year." The number of state employees soared by almost 40 percent. Per capita spending increased 95.9 percent in the same time period.

Despite the common argument that Proposition 13 had starved the state of revenue, cash flowed steadily into Sacramento's coffers. "Since FY 1990-91," the Reason Foundation report revealed, "revenues have increased 166.9 percent, or 5.61 percent a year. . . . Based on these revenues, if California had simply limited its spending increases to the 4.38 percent average increase in the state's consumer price index and population growth each year since FY 1990-91, instead of a $42 billion deficit, the state would be sitting on a $15 billion surplus this year."

The *Wall Street Journal* editorial page explained that in 1999, then-Governor Gray Davis, in cahoots with the California State Employees Association, passed "the largest issuance of non-voter-approved debt in the state's history. The bill . . . granted billions of dollars in retroactive pension boosts to state employees, allowing retirements as young as age 50 with lifetime pensions of up to 90% of final year salaries." The California Public Employees' Retirement System (known as CalPERS) promised that no additional state contributions were needed and that the plans would be "fully funded." It was the ultimate something-for-nothing scheme: "They also claimed that enhanced pensions would not cost taxpayers 'a dime' because investment bets would cover the expense."

But CalPERS and Davis didn't tell the voters that the state would have to pick up the tab if the ludicrous investment predictions (for example, that the Dow would hit 25,000 by 2009) failed to pan out. The shortfall turned out to be hundreds of billions of dollars. Nor did voters learn that "CalPERS's own employees would benefit from the pension increases [or that] . . . members of CalPERS's board had received contributions from the public employee unions who would benefit from the legislation."

A sense of unreality still pervades. In August 2010, on the site of the Ambassador Hotel in Pasadena, a new high school named for Robert F. Kennedy (who was killed there on the night of the 1968 state primary) opened at a cost of $578 million, almost nine times that of an average new school in the state and the most ever spent on a high school. According to the Associated Press, it features "fine art murals and a marble memorial depicting the complex's namesake, a manicured public park, a state-of-the-art swimming pool and preservation of pieces of the original hotel." Meanwhile, "nearly 3,000 teachers have been laid off over the past two years [and] the academic year and programs have been slashed. The district also faces a $640 million shortfall and some schools persistently rank among the nation's lowest performing." A school-building advocate dryly observed, "Architects and builders love this stuff, but there's a little bit of a lack of discipline here."

That would aptly describe the state as a whole. This year, an official budget shortfall of $19 billion and record unemployment have Californians reeling. But even that understates the problem. The real extent of the state's debt, including unfunded liabilities, now runs into the hundreds of billions. New scandals break daily—bloated pensions, lavish state salaries, and threatened draconian cuts in services. If you make more than $60,000 a year, a relatively modest wage considering the cost of living, your top marginal state income tax rate is now over 9 percent—and given the severity of the cuts in basic services, you have little to show for the money taken from you.

The notion that growth would be endless, that debt could be piled on future generations, and that government could provide an ever-growing array of services with no impact on the state's ability to retain and attract wealth has reached its inevitable conclusion: full-fledged financial chaos. And while there are many responsible parties (Democratic-dominated legislatures, weak Republican governors, labor unions), at bottom Californians created their own morass. Much of the debt was piled on by popular referenda. Lawmakers were elected and re-elected. The people acted, and the people are now suffering the consequences.

The notion that government could provide an ever-growing array of services with no impact on the ability to retain and attract wealth has now met reality.

Even so, some of those consequences were entirely unintended. Property-tax reform led to the centralization of power, which allowed interest groups to become politically preeminent. Term limits were supposed to end the reign of professional politicians, but the policy simply shuffled politicians from one post to another and strengthened the grip of outside interests and more-experienced bureaucrats.

Gerrymandered districts—and the population division of the state between liberal, urban areas and rural, conservative ones—have protected state legislators of both parties from any real competition. The latest reform, a jungle primary system (candidates of all parties appear on a ballot, with the top two vote-getters facing off in the general election) meant to make races more competitive and drive politicians toward the center of the political spectrum, will face constitutional challenge and, if history is any guide, produce results not remotely anticipated by its draftsmen.

California today bears little resemblance to the land of opportunity whose promise of a better life in a perfect climate once lured so many. Schools, even in expensive residential areas, are substandard and getting worse. Public parks are unseemly and unsightly. Libraries are understaffed and understocked. Commutes have extended from 30 to 60 to 90 minutes or longer.

Because the 21st-century economy is global and portable, residents and businesses have other options. Employers and educated people can uproot themselves, and they have been, fleeing the congestion, the traffic, the crumbling infrastructure, and the deficient schools. Between 1990 and 2000, 2 million more left the state than arrived from other states.

The U.S. Census Bureau report noted that a number of states have benefited from California's woes: "199,000 of the 466,000 people who moved to Nevada during this time came from California. . . . Between 1995 and 2000, 644,000 people moved to Colorado from other states, led by 111,000 migrants from California."

California's unemployment rate at present hovers a few points above the national average, in part due to a state judiciary hostile to business and the proliferation of pro-plaintiff litigation rules that have made the state a toxic environment for employers. In recent years, Northrop Grumman, Fluor Corporation, Hilton Hotels, Computer Sciences Corporation, and defense contractor SAIC all moved their headquarters out of the state.

The optimism of the 1960s has been replaced by cynicism and resignation: *Did you hear that gubernatorial candidate Jerry Brown gets multiple pensions totaling $78,000 a year? Did you read about the little city of Bell's council members who pay themselves nearly 100 grand a year and paid the city administrator $1.5 mil a year?* Gallows humor, appropriate for a dying state, is de rigueur among the state's political class.

The optimism of the 1960s has been replaced by cynicism and resignation. Gallows humor is now de rigueur among the state's political class.

My own family has come full circle. My husband (whose family moved from Indiana to Northern California a year before mine moved from South Jersey) and I joined the out-migration in 2005, moving East with our two sons. It was our turn to amaze West Coast friends and family by leaving home. But unlike the trek four decades earlier, there was little confusion about the reasons for our departure. Instead, people seemed wistful, curious about whether they would learn from us that there might be a better life elsewhere, with workable schools, functioning state and local governments, and more modest taxes.

And in the years since our exodus, we have become acquainted, once again, as we had been in our youth, with normal public schools, pleasant neighborhood parks, well-stocked libraries, and state and local governments that live within their means, more or less.

Flying over Los Angeles on an annual summer visit, I peer through smog so thick that the coastline is hard to see. It is only three in the afternoon, but the cars are backed up for miles on the freeways, which remain largely in the same state of disrepair that greeted me last year. The state is literally deteriorating before my eyes. In an age when discount airfares are plentiful and one can wear shorts on American Airlines, California for me has become a nice place to visit. But who would want to live there?

Critical Thinking

1. How does our image of California in the 1960s differ from our image of California in the early 21st century?

2. What role did the passage of Proposition 13 in 1978 play in California's problems of today?

3. What dysfunctional government actions besides Proposition 13 have led to the current situation in which California finds itself?

4. What are some of the shortcomings and problems in California today?

JENNIFER RUBIN, *Commentary's* contributing editor, last wrote for the magazine about the Supreme Court decision on campaign-finance reform.

Prison Break

How Michigan managed to empty its penitentiaries while lowering its crime rate.

Luke Mogelson

Anyone involved with rehabilitating former prisoners learns to live with modest accomplishments. In its last study on recidivism, in 2002, the Department of Justice found that over two-thirds of former prisoners were rearrested within three years of being released. There's no reason to think those numbers have improved. The recidivism rate in California, for instance, has hovered at around 70 percent for the past twenty-five years. On such bleak terrain, gains are measured by a hairsbreadth.

That's why eyes are turned to Michigan. In 2003, the state launched the Michigan Prisoner Reentry Initiative (MPRI), which amounts to the most comprehensive program in the country for helping parolees transition from prison back into society. The premise of the MPRI is familiar: that it's both cheaper and safer to invest in preventing ex-cons from reoffending than it is to repeatedly incarcerate them. The methods, however, are new. And preliminary data from the Michigan Department of Corrections is promising: parolees who have been released through the MPRI are returning to prison 27 percent less frequently than similar offender types released without it. Other measures also point to progress. Last year saw the fewest parolees committing new crimes since 2005 and the smallest percentage of total paroles revoked since record keeping began more than twenty years ago.

During the past three years, the number of state inmates in Michigan has shrunk by 12 percent. The turnaround enabled Governor Jennifer Granholm to shut down ten prisons last year.

When parolees are less likely to reoffend, more prisoners can be let go without jeopardizing public safety. Going hand in hand with Michigan's improved recidivism rates, therefore, has been a correspondent increase in parole approvals. Over 3,000 more prisoners were paroled in 2009 than were paroled in 2006; approvals for violent offenders have gone up by more than half (from 35 to 55 percent), while approvals for sex offenders have

more than quadrupled (from 10 to 50 percent). As a result, during the past three years, the number of state inmates in Michigan has shrunk by 12 percent, reversing a sixteen-year trend of steady prison population growth. The turnaround enabled Governor Jennifer Granholm to shut down ten prisons last year, and an additional eight are slated to be closed by the end of 2010.

A few months ago, I sat in on an MPRI employment readiness seminar at the Oakland County parole office. The office is in Pontiac, the former hub of Automation Alley, where over half of the workforce is still employed by General Motors. Some twenty-five parolees—white, black, young, old—crowded into a small room, where they listened to Chaka McDonald, a sharply dressed case specialist, explain things like the difference between a laptop and a desktop.

"Who's surfed on Yahoo?" asked McDonald midway through the class.

Two men raised their hands.

"Who has e-mail?"

Four hands.

"Who's familiar with Facebook?"

One hand.

McDonald held aloft a black Dell notebook. "How could it benefit you, knowing what kind of computer this is, if you're meeting with an employer?"

"The job might be ran on them," answered a young man in his twenties.

McDonald nodded and moved on to explain how a wireless USB internet adaptor worked. "How could this benefit me, if I go see an employer and I'm not shocked looking at this thing protruding out of this computer?"

A man with a shaved head, who'd been running a comb through his long black goatee, raised his hand. "It shows you have a working knowledge of the technology."

"There you go. Because at some point we know we gonna have to address the felony. So if I know at some point I'm addressing the felony, if I can let this employer know I'm still computer literate, won't that diminish that felony a little bit?"

After the class, a reentry coordinator named Sherry Carter pulled the man with the goatee and shaved head into her office. The man's name was David, and he'd recently been released after doing ten years for having had sex with a thirteen-year-old girl. (David had been seventeen at the time.) He was hoping to get a job at the Silverdome, but he knew his prison tattoos would disqualify him. "SCORPIO" was inked on one side of his neck, "BETTY" on the other, and "D-A-R-K-N-E-S-S" across his knuckles.

"Are you interested in having your tattoos removed?" Carter asked him.

The Pontiac parole office has an agreement with American Pride, a local parlor that performs laser removals. In David's case, the procedure would likely take two sessions, each costing $100, but the Michigan Department of Corrections, with MPRI funds, was willing to pay for it.

Later, David told me that when he was released from prison the MPRI set him up with an apartment, provided him with bus passes, gave him vouchers for clothes, and helped him create a resume and apply for jobs. MPRI officials also got him enrolled in Oakland Community College, where he will be pursuing a degree in automotive technology.

This sort of assistance is a big change. Prior to the MPRI, Michigan parolees received a little bit of cash and two weeks of transitional housing. After that, one former parole agent says, "They were out on their ass, either sleeping on a park bench or in the shelter."

Under such circumstances, David told me, he probably wouldn't have made it. "A guy like me, I did ten years in the joint. You get out and you got nothing. I had one outfit when I got out. That's the only thing I had in my entire possession. If it wasn't for the MPRI program, I'd be on the street right now."

Between 1970 and 2005 the number of incarcerated Americans grew by 700 percent, accounting for one-fourth of the world's prisoners. A 2008 study by the Pew Center on the States found that more than 1 in 100 adults were behind bars. This isn't just grim in humanitarian terms; it's also extremely expensive, costing over $60 billion a year. If states are to cut back on the vast sums spent on prisons, they will need to focus on keeping parolees from reoffending. No state has taken the lead on this more than Michigan. More important, what Michigan's example suggests, at least for now, is that there's a way to accelerate releases—and to do it safely. Despite releasing more than 6,000 convicted felons onto its streets, Michigan has seen per capita violent crime decline by over 10 percent since 2005.

Michigan has set an important example. Despite releasing more than 6,000 convicted felons onto its streets, the state has seen per capita violent crime decline by over 10 percent since 2005.

Understanding Michigan's transition from building prisons to closing them requires looking at how incarceration became such a large part of the state's budget in the first place. In 1973, Michigan had a prison population of 7,874 inmates, and $38 million, less than 2 percent

of the state's general fund, went to corrections. Crime was rising, however, and prison capacity was insufficient. Like many other state legislatures across the country, Michigan lawmakers attributed their worsening crime rates to what they viewed as overly lenient sentencing guidelines, so they enacted tougher policies and built more prisons. By the end of 1984, Michigan's inmate population had nearly doubled, reaching 14,658. Five years later, it had more than doubled again, to 31,834.

The increase in incarceration alarmed some state officials, but events conspired to keep the prison population climbing steadily upward. In 1992, a parolee named Leslie Allen Williams confessed to kidnapping and murdering four teenage girls, burying their bodies in shallow graves northwest of Detroit. Williams was a repeat offender who'd been released after serving a minimum sentence for assault. Public outrage was immediate and fierce. "The parole board represents the bureaucratic interests of emptying beds and not one of them represents the public safety interest," one Michigan prosecutor told The New York Times. At the time, Michigan's parole board was composed of civil service employees such as criminal justice experts and law enforcement officials. After Williams, however, the legislature granted the governor new powers to appoint and remove board members at will. Republican John Engler soon overhauled the board and encouraged its new members to get tough. In the decade that followed, the parole approval rate dropped by 20 percentage points, and the number of parolees annually returned to prison for technical violations doubled.

By 2003, when Jennifer Granholm became governor, Michigan's prison population had increased to 50,591, and corrections expenditures had reached $1.6 billion, almost a fifth of the state's general fund. It was becoming unsustainable. "If something wasn't done, we'd be building more prisons, and that simply was not in the cards," remembers Beth Arnovits, executive director of the Michigan Council on Crime and Delinquency.

Factors such as police per capita correlate far more closely with crime rates than do prison sentences, and longer lengths of stay do nothing to increase the likelihood of success on parole.

With the state hitting hard times (Michigan's recession predates the economic downturn by a decade), Granholm and other officials were finally ready, if warily so, to listen to new ideas. What they heard from prison reformers was that Michigan's sentencing policies, along with the rest of the country's, were based on two flawed assumptions: one, that heavier sentences meaningfully deter crime; and two, that fewer grants of parole decrease recidivism. In fact, reformers had long argued, research shows that factors such as police per capita correlate far more closely with crime rates than do prison sentences, and longer lengths of stay do nothing to increase the likelihood of success on parole. A study of 76,000 Michigan convicts, for example, found that prisoners who were paroled later reoffended at the same rate—and, in some categories of offender type, at a *higher* rate—as those paroled earlier.

As a first step toward reforming the state's correctional system, Granholm appointed Dennis Schrantz as her deputy director for corrections. Schrantz is a North Carolinian who came to Michigan in 1990 to head the state's Community Corrections Office, a new agency created to bring down prison admissions by improving probation options. Schrantz's efforts had reduced the overall commitment rate for convicted felons (that is, the proportion of felons actually being sent to prison) from 32 to 22 percent, the lowest in the country. (The national average is 35 percent.)

Now Schrantz's attention would be shifted from the front end of the system to the back end: finding safe—and politically feasible—ways to reduce the length of stay for inmates, most of whom were serving more time for their offenses than prisoners in neighboring states. (About sixteen months more, on average.) Schrantz knew this would require a focus on parole. Like thirty-three other states, Michigan uses a form of indeterminate sentencing in which each inmate gets a minimum (determined by a judge) and a maximum (established by the legislature). Often, the gap between the two can be vast—a sentence of three to twenty years, for instance. After serving his minimum, the inmate becomes eligible for parole; if he is never granted parole he eventually "maxes out" and goes free. While indeterminate sentencing has its drawbacks (parole decisions can seem arbitrary), it offered an important opportunity to Schrantz and other prison reformers: they could reduce lengths of stay without seeking authorization from the legislature, where partisan grandstanding has consistently prevented lawmakers from voting for sentencing guidelines that might be portrayed as soft on crime. As long as Schrantz could persuade the board to raise the rate of parole, prison crowding could be brought down.

In order to win over the board, Schrantz first had to make more resources available for released inmates. This didn't take long. He'd learned from his experience working with probationers that effective programs seldom need to be created; they already exist in the community. "We gave the locals a lot of authority and control, and that proved to be the ticket," Schrantz says. "The state did what I think the state should do, which is create the policy framework and provide the funding and let the people that are closest to it do the work." (Nongovernmental partnerships have remained a hallmark of the MPRI. Today, in Detroit alone, the Department of Corrections contracts with more than sixteen nonprofit organizations to work with parolees, offering services that include substance abuse counseling, classes on domestic violence prevention, family reunification, mentoring, and housing and employment assistance.)

Schrantz also opened up communication between parole board members and DOC leadership, something he says had never happened. "States don't do a very good job of making certain the parole board is part of their process," he says. "It's as if the parole board is off on their own, and in many cases they are physically off on their own." When Schrantz had asked his predecessor's chief of staff to describe the relationship between the board and the outgoing corrections director, the

chief of staff told him that he wouldn't know a parole board member if she walked into the room.

Schrantz's strategy for persuading the board to release more inmates from prison on parole was so straightforward it seems incredible that it hadn't been tried before. "I asked them, 'What do you need? Under what conditions would you consider paroling these individuals?'" Schrantz recounts. Members of the board say they were thrilled to be asked this simple question. They first brought up the problem of the mentally ill, who make up roughly a sixth of Michigan's total prison population (7,100 out of 44,500). Mentally ill parolees reoffend at a much higher rate than other parolees, and the board told Schrantz they rarely felt comfortable releasing them because they knew that the parolees would receive nothing more than sixty days of medication. Schrantz and his team responded by creating the MPRI Mental Health Initiative, which put in place contracts with community providers to offer paroled inmates sustained mental health services and guidance on obtaining other state and federal entitlements. Today, when mentally ill prisoners appear before the board, they bring packets detailing individually tailored, long-term master care plans. Parole approvals have spiked, and now only 28 percent of mentally ill parolees return to prison, compared with 50 percent prior to the initiative.

Today, mentally ill parolees get individually tailored, long-term master care plans. Only 28 percent of them return to prison, compared with 50 percent prior to the new reforms.

For regular prisoners, Schrantz worked to equip those going up for parole hearings with plausible plans for what to do once they were released. "What the parole board in Michigan saw was prisoners coming to them for the first time better prepared," says Le'Ann Duran, director of the Justice Department's National Reentry Resource Center. "Couple that preparedness with the huge investment that Michigan made in the community-based resources which never before existed, and that's very attractive to the board."

Schrantz also introduced into the decision-making processes new academic research to which board members and corrections officials had never been exposed. "It was a whole new language," says Patricia Caruso, Michigan's director of corrections and a former prison warden. Often, the research had produced remarkably counterintuitive findings, calling into question long-held assumptions. Caruso recalls one especially memorable example of this. "Very early on [Schrantz] said to me that there is not a correlation between misconduct in prison and success on parole," she says. "When Dennis first said this to me, I was absolutely aghast." But Caruso says she eventually accepted the logic when Schrantz explained how, for women, unruliness in prison can actually be tied to *success* on parole. "So many women come to prison because they don't have a voice. They're often victims of men abusively guiding their actions," says Caruso. "So getting a voice, and being able to tell the correction officer to go F himself, may not be the preferred way of conducting yourself in prison. But it does mean that when you get out you're going to stand on your own two feet.... Those types of things—within the first year, I really got it. I really embraced it."

Meanwhile, Granholm and Caruso gradually replaced every member of the Engler parole board save one. In 2007, after winning reelection and implementing the MPRI statewide, Granholm appointed a former corrections officer named Barbara Sampson as chair of the parole board. "When Barb took over, everything changed," Schrantz says. Sampson, who previously worked at a nonprofit for battered women, believed strongly in the MPRI and welcomed the new criminal justice research that Schrantz was recommending. When we met in her office in Lansing, her desk was cluttered with folders, books, and binders containing various academic literature on incarceration and recidivism. "We know what we think we know intuitively and with our gut," Sampson said. "But what does the evidence really say?"

Perhaps the most striking example of how instinct and evidence can diverge concerns sex offenders. Historically, sex offenders have been denied parole far more often than other types of inmates. When Sampson became chairperson, the approval rate for sex offenders was a mere 10 percent. Last year, however, the board approved 50 percent of the sex offenders it considered for release. "For years, the board lumped all sex offenders into one category—evil predators," Sampson explains. "[But] within the broad category of sex offenders, there are groups. And what we had to do as a board was educate ourselves about the different characteristics of the different groups. For instance, individuals who commit incest, when you look at the data, the re-offense rate is very low." While the spike in paroled sex offenders has been a particularly hard sell, even with the governor ("She's no big fan of releasing sex offenders," Schrantz says. "She had her way, we'd castrate them"), the approach has so far been allowed to continue, without any obviously adverse effects to public safety. Since 2005, reported rapes in Michigan are down 13 percent.

Despite the success of the MPRI, there are, unsurprisingly, many opponents of Michigan's new parole practices. In January, the Prosecuting Attorneys Association of Michigan held a series of coordinated press conferences across the state, enlisting victims and their families to warn against the danger of paroling violent offenders. One attorney likened the spike in paroles to "a fire sale." Another called it "death for dollars." Mike Cox, a Republican and former marine who succeeded Granholm as attorney general in 2003 and now hopes to succeed her as governor in November, recently established a Parole Objection Project in his office. "These felons should not see the light of day, and I will do everything I can to ensure they won't," Cox promised.

The press has reinforced such sentiments. *The New York Times* has characterized the Michigan parole surge as a compromise of public safety brought on by the state's deficit ("Safety Is Issue as Budget Cuts Free Prisoners" was the headline of a front-page story last March), largely glossing over the belief of reformers that the MPRI is an attempt to improve correctional outcomes. Local outlets have often gone much farther in stoking public fears. When I met with Larry Payne, an MPRI community coordinator in Saginaw, he'd just spent the week managing the fallout from recent television coverage of a Bay City house the MPRI had contracted to accommodate sex offender parolees. "They're scaring the hell out of everybody," Payne said of the local news station. People in Bay City "were totally under the impression that we were putting pedophiles on the bus stop to snatch their kids."

While resistance to Michigan's new parole policy brings out an inevitable quotient of opportunism—no candidate ever lost a political race for being tough on crime—there is no doubt that many of its opponents are informed and sincere. One of these is Mike Thomas, Michigan's director of the National District Attorneys Association, whom I met at the Saginaw County Courthouse. Every year since 2003, the FBI has ranked Saginaw the most violent city in the nation in per capita crime, and not coincidentally its populace is rapidly fleeing (more than 10 percent have moved elsewhere in the past few years). For Thomas, who grew up in Saginaw and has been its elected prosecutor for more than two decades, Michigan's crime rate is a deeply personal concern. His views are shaped by victims he considers neighbors and crimes he remembers daily in all their gruesome specificity. And he worries that his city will lose even more residents and businesses if more prisoners hit the streets.

"Just because somebody is in prison for safe cracking doesn't mean that they can't commit a violent crime," Thomas told me when I questioned the effectiveness of longer lengths of stay in prison. "Why do I say that? Because Keith Wood murdered his fifteen-year-old cousin when he got out of prison on his third parole release for the nonviolent offense of safe cracking and burglary. I tried the case a couple years back. He killed her because she had the audacity to have a young black boyfriend from Heritage High School in Saginaw Township. Now, after he was convicted of first-degree murder—'cause he got caught with her nude body in the back of his trunk as he was driving without any lights in the middle of a snowstorm—January comes to mind—then he got religion in jail and told the chaplain there that he'd done a lot of other things. He confessed to another murder that he'd done in our county while he was out on parole for nonviolent safe cracking—a black night manager at a Burger King out in Shields, Thomas Township here—and two or three other murders in Michigan and other states. He also confessed to literally hundreds of other arsons, robberies, burglaries."

Such stories of parolees who return to crime—and there will always be a proportion of parolees (as well as ordinary ex-prisoners) who return to crime—pose an immense challenge to the MPRI. One incident was horrific enough that it threatened to derail the program altogether. In 2006, a Michigan parolee named Patrick Selepak brutally tortured and murdered three people in New Baltimore. Two of the victims were a young husband and wife. The husband was intravenously injected with bleach while the wife, who was pregnant, was strangled.

"The board was distraught," says Patricia Caruso. "When you see someone you paroled go out and kill innocent people, you question every decision you make." For a while, the board cut down dramatically on parole approvals, and Michigan's prison population subsequently increased by more than 2,000.

By the end of 2007, however, the parole board had resumed its earlier pace of approvals. "You had Dennis [Schrantz] and you had the director and everybody doing all of this evidence-based, data-driven work," Sampson remembers. "And steadily dangling that work, saying, 'Board, take a look at this information. This is a study that came out of Kansas. Look at the Pew report.'" Caruso, who still has all the *Detroit News* and *Free Press* clippings about Selepak in her office, says she was determined not to let "one bad crime become the namesake for everything. It has not stopped us from what we're doing. It does stop other people. But it has not stopped us."

Schrantz is adamant about the merit of statistics and the danger of focusing on case studies. When I mentioned some of the stories Mike Thomas had told me, he said, "What these people do is they're gonna want to talk about cases. They should be forced to talk about trends and large numbers of people. That's how you run systems. Don't judge us one case at a time. Judge us by the system." And trends do bolster Schrantz's case. Since crime in Michigan is decreasing, it is reasonable to assume that the current allocation of resources for crime control are, despite what can sometimes be terrible failures, making the state safer than it was under the old system.

Ultimately, aside from concerns over reoffending parolees, a different problem may pose the greatest threat to the MPRI: Michigan's severe recession. In reporting across the state, I spent time with numerous MPRI parolees, many of whom had done remarkably well: a former gang member who now works at Habitat for Humanity, a former sex offender who now is a line cook, a former crack addict who now balances two jobs while she attends college, and a former murderer who now takes care of the crocuses and petunias outside his parole office. But what most of them had in common was employment. Absent that, a critical anchor is missing. Michigan's unemployment rate has reached almost 13 percent, 3 points above the national average. As Mario Dewberry, Wayne County's reentry coordinator, says, "An individual who's only been locked up for the last three years, they're coming out to a completely different world. There's been so many instances of: The aunt I used to stay with, whether they were renting or paying a mortgage, the house is no longer there. My uncle who had a lawn care business or worked for GM? Gone." Ironically, the same dire economic straits that spurred Michigan to reduce its prison population in the first place might also endanger the MPRI's long-term success.

Still, Schrantz and his colleagues in Lansing are optimistic. Perhaps more encouraging, so are many of the parolees I met with. While prison reform advocates complain that opponents and the press focus on frightening anecdotes rather than statistics, I found myself impressed less by Schrantz's data than by the individual stories of successful parolees.

In Kalamazoo, Michael Brown, a Korean War veteran with a graying flattop, grayer mustache, and several missing teeth, told me he had been in and out of prison six times. Five of those times it was the same parole agent who sent him back on technical violations. This December, he was released through the MPRI. Now Brown has a new parole agent who couldn't be more different, and Brown has changed, too. "Anything I do, if I'm the slightest bit worried about getting in trouble, I talk to him first," Brown told me. "In the past, you didn't have that. They were there to monitor you and they didn't really care about you. They didn't care if you had problems. They didn't care if you wanted to reconcile with your family. The best you could get out of a parole officer was, 'See you next month.'"

I asked what things might have been like if he'd had the MPRI during any of his previous paroles. Brown shook his head. "I probably would've never come back. I think things would've been a lot different. I'd probably still be married to the same woman and been able to raise my kids instead of not being there for her or them. It's a world of difference."

Critical Thinking

1. What is the Michigan Prison Reentry Initiative (MPRI)?

2. What is the premise of the MPRI?

3. How and why did incarceration become so big and expensive a part of Michigan's state budget?

4. How do "instinct" and "evidence" diverge on many questions relating to incarceration, recidivism, and parole?

LUKE MOGELSON is a freelance writer living in Brooklyn.

From *Washington Monthly*, November/December 2010, pp. 38–43. Copyright © 2010 by Washington Monthly Publishing, LLC, 1319 F St. NW, Suite 710, Washington DC 20004. (202)393-5155. Reprinted by permission. www.washingtonmonthly.com

Test-Your-Knowledge Form

We encourage you to photocopy and use this page as a tool to assess how the articles in *Annual Editions* expand on the information in your textbook. By reflecting on the articles you will gain enhanced text information. You can also access this useful form on a product's book support website at www.mhhe.com/cls.

NAME: DATE:

_____

TITLE AND NUMBER OF ARTICLE:

_____

BRIEFLY STATE THE MAIN IDEA OF THIS ARTICLE:

_____

LIST THREE IMPORTANT FACTS THAT THE AUTHOR USES TO SUPPORT THE MAIN IDEA:

_____

WHAT INFORMATION OR IDEAS DISCUSSED IN THIS ARTICLE ARE ALSO DISCUSSED IN YOUR TEXTBOOK OR OTHER READINGS THAT YOU HAVE DONE? LIST THE TEXTBOOK CHAPTERS AND PAGE NUMBERS:

_____

LIST ANY EXAMPLES OF BIAS OR FAULTY REASONING THAT YOU FOUND IN THE ARTICLE:

_____

LIST ANY NEW TERMS/CONCEPTS THAT WERE DISCUSSED IN THE ARTICLE, AND WRITE A SHORT DEFINITION:

We Want Your Advice

ANNUAL EDITIONS revisions depend on two major opinion sources: one is our Advisory Board, listed in the front of this volume, which works with us in scanning the thousands of articles published in the public press each year; the other is you—the person actually using the book. Please help us and the users of the next edition by completing the prepaid article rating form on this page and returning it to us. Thank you for your help!

ANNUAL EDITIONS: State and Local Government 15/e

ARTICLE RATING FORM

Here is an opportunity for you to have direct input into the next revision of this volume.
We would like you to rate each of the articles listed below, using the following scale:

1. **Excellent: should definitely be retained**
2. **Above average: should probably be retained**
3. **Below average: should probably be deleted**
4. **Poor: should definitely be deleted**

Your ratings will play a vital part in the next revision.
Please mail this prepaid form to us as soon as possible.
Thanks for your help!

RATING	ARTICLE
	1. Federalist, No. 17
	2. Federalist, No. 45
	3. Nature of the American State
	4. The American System of Townships . . .
	5. Local Government: Observations
	6. Demographics and Destiny
	7. Taking Stock
	8. Eminent Domain—For the Greater Good?
	9. Devolution's Double Standard
	10. On the Oregon Trail
	11. Caperton's Coal: The Battle Over an Appalachian Mine Exposes a Nasty Vein in Bench Politics
	12. The No-Tax Pledge
	13. California, Here We Come
	14. Taking the Initiative
	15. Public Meetings and the Democratic Process
	16. Reloading at the Statehouse
	17. Bloggers Press for Power
	18. Cities without Newspapers
	19. Cross Examination
	20. A Shift of Substance
	21. The Legislature as Sausage Factory: It's about Time We Examine This Metaphor
	22. Termed Out
	23. What Legislatures Need Now
	24. Are City Councils a Relic of the Past?
	25. First, Kill All the School Boards

RATING	ARTICLE
	26. The Private Life of E-mail
	27. When I Run Out of Fights to Have, I'll Stop Fighting
	28. The Badgered State: Wisconsin Governor Scott Walker Is the Left's Public Enemy No. 1
	29. If He Can Make It There . . .
	30. Counter Cultures
	31. Rise of the Generals
	32. Justice by Numbers
	33. Kids, Not Cases
	34. How to Save Our Shrinking Cities
	35. The Big Apple: Urban Incubator
	36. Unscrambling the City
	37. The Sentient City
	38. 267 Years and Counting: The Town Hall Meeting Is Alive and Well in Pelham, Mass
	39. Two Cheers for the Property Tax
	40. The Rise of the Creative Class
	41. Broke Town, U.S.A.
	42. Nothing Ventured
	43. Lacklu$ter Lotterie$
	44. Same Sex Redux
	45. One Size Doesn't Fit All
	46. Giving Teens a Brake
	47. Fixing the Rotten Corporate Barrel
	48. California, There It Went: The Irreparable Tarnishing of the Golden State
	49. Prison Break

BUSINESS REPLY MAIL
FIRST CLASS MAIL PERMIT NO. 551 DUBUQUE IA

POSTAGE WILL BE PAID BY ADDRESSEE

McGraw-Hill Contemporary Learning Series
501 BELL STREET
DUBUQUE, IA 52001

ABOUT YOU

Name   Date

_____

Are you a teacher? ❑ A student? ❑
Your school's name _____

_____

Department

_____

Address   City   State   Zip

_____

School telephone #

_____

YOUR COMMENTS ARE IMPORTANT TO US!

Please fill in the following information:
For which course did you use this book?

_____

Did you use a text with this ANNUAL EDITION? ❑ yes ❑ no
What was the title of the text?

_____

What are your general reactions to the Annual Editions concept?

_____

Have you read any pertinent articles recently that you think should be included in the next edition? Explain.

_____

Are there any articles that you feel should be replaced in the next edition? Why?

_____

Are there any World Wide Websites that you feel should be included in the next edition? Please annotate.

_____

May we contact you for editorial input? ❑ yes ❑ no
May we quote your comments? ❑ yes ❑ no